A SHARED CINEMA

A SHARED CINEMA

Michel Ciment

Conversations with N.T. Binh

Foreword by
Adrian Martin

Sticking Place Books
New York

Le cinéma en partage: Entretiens avec N.T. Binh
© Editions Payot & Rivages, 2014

Translation by Paul Cronin © Sticking Place Books, 2024
Foreword © Adrian Martin, 2024
Cover photograph © Gilles Ciment, 2022
Designed by Goran Tovilovic

www.stickingplacebooks.com

All rights reserved.

No part of this book may be reproduced, stored in or introduced into a retrieval system, or transmitted, in any form or by any means (electronic, mechanical, photocopying, recording or otherwise) without the written permission of the publishers, except in the case of brief quotations embodied in critical articles or reviews.

ISBN: 978-1-942782-37-7

CONTENTS

A note from the translator	vii
Michel Ciment: The Heart of Cinema by Adrian Martin	ix
Introduction by N.T. Binh	1
Childhood, Adolescence, Schooling	3
From Cinephilia to Criticism	25
The Pleasure of Teaching	67
On Air: The Radio Experience	77
The Books and their Origins	93
Documentarian	149
The Festival Scout	159
Reflections and Clarifications	187
Grand Cinematic Planet	261
The Seven Cardinal Virtues of the Critic	295
Quel spectateur êtes-vous? Didier Péron, *Libération*, 29 September 2012	305
Bibliography	309
Index	311

A NOTE FROM THE TRANSLATOR

Interview books are, generally, a distinctly *un*-literary medium. *A Shared Cinema*, a series of conversations with film scholar and critic Michel Ciment, is unashamedly informal in tone. Given that this book – created by N.T. Binh, who writes for *Positif* under the name Yann Tobin (and has been doing so since 1979, when he was a medical student in Paris) – was first published a decade ago, some of what follows is inevitably out of date. But much of Ciment's historical account, his opinionated explanations and descriptions, will be forever relevant.

Film and book titles appear sometimes in French, sometimes in English, depending, most usually, on which is more immediately recognisable to English speakers. Selective, brief footnotes have been added. The bibliography has been revised and English language titles added.

My thanks to N.T. Binh, Evelyn Ciment, Gilles Ciment, Adrian Martin, Gary Crowdus, Marie-Martine Serrano and especially the dogged Stacey Knecht, who has corrected so many of my mistakes these past few years.

This English edition is dedicated, of course, to Michel. The group dynamic and collective management of *Positif*, the practical mix of teaching and criticism that he practiced for so long, his traditional bent, the lack of an impervious ideology or critical method – it's all madly appealing, and close to my heart: *une génération disparue*.

I spent some time with Michel over the years, in Paris (his apartment, followed by metro rides to the Cinémathèque française at Bercy, a building I first visited as the short-lived American Center in 1994) and New York (Upper East Side eateries), and began interviewing him. When this book – *Le cinéma en partage* – came along, in 2014, we continued talking, but our focus became preparing an English-language version of this text, which I knew couldn't be improved on. I'm sorry it took this long, and that Michel is not around to grasp it.

Paul Cronin
New York
November 2023

MICHEL CIMENT:
THE HEART OF CINEMA
BY ADRIAN MARTIN

Michel Ciment (1938-2023) is among the towering, legendary figures of international film criticism. His profile differs, however, from the saintly halo ascribed to André Bazin or Roger Ebert, the ornery eccentricity of a Manny Farber, or the unrepentantly subjective taste-and-opinion-machine known as Pauline Kael.

    The book you are about to read gives a vivid picture of Ciment, and especially his cultural passions and involvements. From his beginnings as a critic in the early 1960s, he hardly ever slowed down: from one film festival to another, one book to the next, teaching, serving on selection committees, intervening in public debates, writing and editing. And on top of that we must overlay the many thousands of films he watched (and, usually, evaluated), the books he read, the art he witnessed. We might form the mental image of an extraordinarily well-organised, systematic, devoted worker – yet Ciment, in these pages, also makes no secret of the fact that he also proudly acted on the basis of his temperament, walking away from professional situations when they exasperated or bored him. He must have many times arrived at the conclusion, like the poet Rimbaud, that *real life is elsewhere* – and that the heart of cinema, too, was to be found elsewhere, not in the sclerotic atmosphere of reigning trends, fashions and institutions.

Ciment says it loud and clear: *discovery* should be among the principal impulses that drives a film lover and critic. To appreciate the already canonised classics, to uphold worthy traditions, to keep the achievements of the past in constant circulation – all of that is crucially important, but cinephilia cannot stop there. Inspired by the lifelong work of his globetrotting friend and colleague Pierre Rissient (1936-2018), Ciment placed a high value on cultivating openness to the first works, whether short or feature length, of emerging filmmakers. It's what he regarded as true *insight* – an uncanny but well-founded ability to see into the future of the cinema medium. Like Rissient, Ciment often found himself in the opportune position to make recommendations to festival directors, film distributors, and programmers of all stripes. A case of insider trading? For Ciment it was, rather, a way of making a personal contribution to the entire ecological system of film culture, and helping to maintain its health by promoting the infusion of new blood from all over the world.

Ciment was certainly, himself, a citizen of that world, constantly in the public eye (in print, on radio and TV, at festivals and conferences). Even his willingness to give book-length interviews about the vocation of criticism is a rare and precious case of professional and personal transparency. It's also (let's say it) a very French trait, culturally speaking: Jean Douchet and Raymond Bellour have given themselves over to similarly autobiographical interview-book projects, but can we imagine Jim Hoberman in USA or Mark Kermode in UK boldly walking the same plank?

Rather than pushing the barrow of his own individual sensibility, however, Ciment very much saw himself as the prime representative of a more-or-less collective perspective: that of the French film publication *Positif*, for which he first wrote (at age 25) in 1963, and on which he served for many years, right up to his death, as chief editor. Indeed, his close comrades Philippe Rouyer and Yann Tobin (aka N.T. Binh) go so far as to describe Ciment, in the editorial of their January 2024 issue, as the very "incarnation of the magazine."

Intriguingly, from the 1980s onward, Ciment wrote precious few critiques or essays for *Positif*. But his presence was announced, above all, in the in-depth interviews that he tirelessly conducted, and in his often incendiary editorials.

As Marcos Uzal, the current editor of *Cahiers du cinéma*, sympathetically remarked, if the war between *Positif* and *Cahiers* still registers in the cinephilic mind, it's because Ciment single-mindedly did his level best to keep those polemics going – and usually for good reasons.

In the 1980s, he mocked those faddish critics who, to his mind, overpraised a postmodern flash-in-the-pan such as Leos Carax, rather than attending to the mature works of Akira Kurosawa or Marco Bellocchio. In the '90s, he led a one-man campaign against what he dubbed the Bermuda Triangle, i.e., the proliferation of critics of the *Cahiers* persuasion into key newspapers and periodicals. In the 2000s, he railed against the interpretive delirium of Cinémathèque française or Centre Pompidou programmers who proposed (for instance) that Hitchcock's *Psycho* or Antonioni's *L'Avventura* are best read as symptomatic, unconscious reflections on the Holocaust (because a central character in them goes missing). These were not arguments just for the sake of arguing; in every case, Ciment sought to defend the achievements and values that he felt were in danger of being lost within film culture at large.

Beyond firing off provocative *Positif* editorials, Ciment's speciality was the in-depth interview – and not only with directors, but also actors, screenwriters, cinematographers... Virtually alone among critics, he managed to develop and sustain friendly relations over many decades with a bunch of filmmakers – including Elia Kazan, Francesco Rosi, John Boorman, Stanley Kubrick and Jane Campion – and was then able to string those interviews from across time into deeply revealing books, backed up by solid contextualisation and analysis.

There was a classical side to Ciment's profound cinephilia. He respected the *craft* of filmmaking as much as its art, and so was always ready to praise a solidly scripted, well-acted, professionally photographed piece. As he argues, a director must achieve *mastery* of all the elements – a word that seems dreadfully old-fashioned or even politically suspect to some these days, but we neglect it at our collective peril. To return to the historic *Cahiers/Positif contretemps* for a moment, I am reminded of what Michel Chion once wrote in a disapproving *Cahiers* review of Ciment's book on Boorman in 1985: he compared Ciment's evident taste for "talent, rhythm, vitality" and "meaning, content, eloquence" to his own magazine's preference for the "creation as rupture, excess, risk, disequilibrium, error, dynamism." But guess what? For quite some years now, Chion has found the steady-as-she-goes *Positif* to be a more congenial home for his own inspired musings than the constantly regime-changing *Cahiers*!

At the same time, Ciment recognised and prized what was novel and modern in the "new cinema" of any given period. Unkind polemics that tend to cast him as a stern gatekeeper of cinematic quality overlook that fact that, from early on, he championed the works of Glauber Rocha and Ruy Guerra from Brazil (look at his chapters on them in the 1970 book published by UK's *Movie* magazine, *Second Wave*), or that he was among the first to interview Barbara Loden at length about her extraordinary and singular manifesto of women's cinema, *Wanda* (1970). Or, more generally, that those authors he revered, like Luis Buñuel or Joseph Losey, constituted, in his opinion, the ideal combination of classical and modern.

I would like to comment, especially, on Ciment's practice as a critical writer. This book concludes with a delightful proposition concerning the "seven cardinal virtues of the critic." Most of the virtues he proposes are beyond argument, although it is always good to be reminded of them: possessing solid background information; attending to how films are made, technically and formally; exhibiting passion and curiosity. He nominates a critic who, in his opinion, embodied the ideal fusion of all the virtues: his friend and mentor Roger Tailleur (1927-1985), superb commentator on everything from Hollywood musicals and war films to Michelangelo Antonioni and Agnès Varda. Tailleur (who gave up film criticism at the close of the 1960s) is sadly very little known beyond mainly "old school" devotees in France but he, too, represents an invaluable combination of classical and modern.

However, I am not entirely in accord with everything on Ciment's triumphant list, and I wish to respectfully make clear why. Surely Ciment, if he were still alive, would welcome the debate, as he always did!

Although Ciment stands up for the role of *analysis*, I believe he was not such an adept when it came to matters of *interpretation*. What do I mean by this distinction? Ciment clearly disliked – even in some articles published by his beloved *Positif* – the type of bold hermeneutic speculation that seemed, to him, far removed from the intentions of the makers, and the sources of their inspiration. Indeed, much of what Ciment considers the cardinal virtues of criticism amounts to being able to intuit, research and intelligently discuss what he would consider the *correct*, most *appropriate* reference points from history and culture.

Consider, as an example, one of Ciment's finest essays, readily available in a good English translation: "Terrence

Malick's Garden," written on the French release of *Days of Heaven* in 1979 (a year after its initial US appearance). The piece begins by identifying and delving into the archival photos seen during the opening credits, which leads to an important preliminary point: "The cinema is not a mere extension of photography... It is the child of the magic lantern." Like Kubrick or Boorman, Malick is grasped as an artist who "chose to return to cinema all of its visual and auditory powers." Next, the film's emphasis on ravishing visual beauty and colour is yoked to "the purest romantic tradition." Ciment's strengths as an historian and particularly an Americanist gradually move to the fore as he traces Malick's evocation of influences including the writings of Mark Twain and the films of Kazan, and probes the "death of the pastoral" in American culture. Theoretical reference-points are not absent: Ciment wields the schema of "triangular desire" devised by René Girard, and even nods to a teacher he encountered in his youthful trip to the US: Leo Marx and his 1964 book *The Machine in the Garden*. Ciment's conclusion stakes a large claim: "The word 'culture' in every sense seems particularly appropriate to define a work that aims at nothing less than the original purpose of the cinema, which is to become a synthesis of all the arts that preceded it." Once you have read *A Shared Cinema*, you will readily see how many of Ciment's lifelong preoccupations and convictions are condensed in this action-packed review of *Days of Heaven*.

Nonetheless, Ciment keeps within strict limits of reasonable conjecture here; he works from a sense of what Malick himself has actually or probably seen and read, and the national traditions to which he no doubt belongs. This general attitude to criticism on Ciment's part helps explain his impatience, for instance, with the briefly faddish theory that films with missing persons in them are automatically part of "Holocaust cinema." Yet do we really want to discredit that theory – and many others of its ilk – so quickly? To remain healthy and vibrant, criticism must, I believe, be willing, at least sometimes, to risk *transversal* leaps, to make unexpected connections across films and film-types in place and time, to forge wild speculations about deep (or superficial) cultural contexts. Ciment looks down upon the critic "writing about a different film, the one he wanted to see or make." The point is well taken, but criticism sometimes makes great strides by daring to be creative, by going beyond the reasonable, rational limits. Manny Farber, rather than Tailleur, would be our historic guide in that.

For some opponents, Ciment's approach to interpretation plays it too safe, does not take the necessary risks.

I have often heard, along the gossip routes of international film culture, the complaint that Ciment's view of cinema was shrouded in a woolly type of grand, universal, centre-left humanism, and that he was not predisposed, intellectually, to immerse himself in the nitty-gritty of political debate about the complexity of cinematic representations.

The French-born, US-based Bérénice Reynaud, an equally brilliant critic-teacher-programmer who also died in 2023, once told me the story – while her eyes rolled uncontrollably in disdain – of a festival panel discussion she shared with Michel. She and other speakers addressed the problems and possibilities of using character stereotypes (of race, class, sexual identity) in film. When time came for Michel to say his piece, he played the schoolteacher: "Excuse me, you are all speaking of cultural *stereotypes*... when it would be altogether more useful to speak of *archetypes*." That statement reflected his investment in global mythology and Jungian psychology – an investment he (by the way) shared with some of his favourite filmmakers. But for Bérénice, in that specific public situation, his declaration served only to close down, rather than open up, further discussion.

Likewise, I am not so certain about Ciment's grand bet on a "hierarchy of judgement" – the sure ability to proclaim that a Kubrick film is, at all times and in all levels, superior to a Jesús Franco movie. In recent years, Ciment often expressed impatience with the rising tide of "cult film" appreciation, reflected as much in a trend of Cinémathèque programming devoted to *cinéma bis* (pornography included) as in the specialist DVD/Blu-ray market worldwide. What a perverse overturning of established values!

But such revolts in the palace of taste are, to my mind, an integral and necessary part of the annals of film criticism. To set absolute store on the cinema's creative "greats" and its hallowed "masterpieces" – words that, yet again, make people very nervous nowadays! – is to miss so much of what Ciment's friend Bertrand Tavernier (1941-2021) once rightly hailed as "the texture, the richness and life of cinema [in] all those 'imperfect' films which are more meaningful and alive than frozen, dated 'classics.'" The fleeting, ephemeral joys of a single, inventive scene in an otherwise unremarkable B movie – or, conversely, the strange, revealing slips and excesses occurring in even the most "mastered" classic by Orson Welles or F.W. Murnau – are as much part of the adventure of cinema as its certified slices of perfection. Ciment's own well-cultivated taste for surrealism should have alerted him to this! But, on this point at any rate, his fighting temperament led him away from the most expansive possibilities of filmic appreciation.

To end on a wholly positive note, however, let's re-enter Ciment's list from another door. The cardinal virtue I find most charming and appealing in his system is *style* – referring not to attentiveness to a film's style, but the critic's own style as a writer. It's what he admires in *Positif* stars including Tailleur, Gérard Legrand and Petr Král – and what he finds lacking in the stodgy, "film historian" prose of a Georges Sadoul or Jean Mitry, or indeed much academic work today. "Criticism is a literary activity," Ciment asserts – and he's right. This is a facet of critical work too often overlooked altogether, but he makes it primary, which is refreshing. Writing on film must absorb the reader, entertain, tell a story, and somehow mimetically capture the form and qualities of the work under discussion. Critical writing as talent, rhythm, vitality… meaning, content and eloquence. And perhaps also at least a little bit of rupture, excess, risk, disequilibrium, error and dynamism!

Michel Ciment's work, poised between the certainties of tradition and the challenge of innovation, etches an essential chapter in the ongoing history of film criticism.

To the memory of my father,
and also to Robert Benayoun and Roger Tailleur,
two great film critics who invited me to join *Positif*
and so set me on the path.

If a man should ascend alone into heaven
and behold clearly the structure of the universe
and the beauty of the stars,
there would be no pleasure for him
in the awe-inspiring sight,
which would have filled him with delight
if he had had someone to whom he could describe
what he had seen.

Cicero, *De Amicitia*

INTRODUCTION
BY N.T. BINH

Michel Ciment is both well-known to the world and, at the same time, thoroughly discreet. As a critic, he is accustomed to keeping himself to himself, and refracting his ideas through the work of others. He never wrote an autobiography, but if he had done, the result would no doubt have been less the story of his life than a book similar to François Nourissier's *À défaut de génie*, a volume dedicated to his encounters with the creators – including filmmakers – whom he has admired, rubbed shoulders with, accompanied, supported and encouraged for more than fifty years.* That said, to write such a book he would have had to set certain things aside, momentarily abandon a watch on the world around him, and re-focus attention on himself. In short, to put his hyperactivity, his thirst for discovery, his avowed impatience, and his engagement with contemporary cinema, all on temporary hold. Despite all that, Ciment felt the urge to share his experiences and take stock of the extent of the journey travelled.

The initial trigger was his participation in Simone Lainé's 2010 documentary about him (which bears the same title as this book) in which numerous filmmakers testify to the role that Ciment has played in recognising their talent. Among

---
* François Nourissier (1927–2011). French journalist and writer.

other friends and colleagues, I myself was featured in the documentary. I was still a student when Michel welcomed me to the editorial staff of *Positif*, a mark of confidence that changed my life. Lainé filmed us together interviewing the director Nuri Bilge Ceylan, then visiting the bookshop in the Cinémathèque française. It was during moments like these that the idea of creating a memoir through a series of interviews began to take shape, not unlike the interviews Michel himself has conducted with filmmakers he admires, from Francesco Rosi to Jane Campion.

The project came to fruition thanks to the enthusiasm of a long-time accomplice in cinephilia, François Guérif[*] of Éditions Payot & Rivages. It was quickly decided that the interviews would be conducted in early August, a slow season for film releases, and that the various activities Michel has pursued, often in parallel, would be evoked "in order of appearance": the press, teaching, radio, books, documentaries, film festivals. This is followed by more general reflections on cinema, criticism, history, painting, politics and philosophy, and a gallery of portraits of filmmakers. We felt it fitting to conclude the book with a statement of the seven cardinal virtues of the critic, as Michel sees them.

The pages that follow are the result of extensive conversations with Michel Ciment in the summer of 2013, at his home in Vileneuve-de-Berg, in the Ardèche, and were revised and completed a year later. Professional experience alternates constantly with critical reflection. More than a memoir, it is an evocation of a journey spanning more than half a century, guided by a passion for cinema and the need to share it.

---

[*] François Guérif (b.1944). French publisher.

CHILDHOOD, ADOLESCENCE, SCHOOLING

From the war to the world of cinema

Let's begin at the beginning: your childhood, the environment in which you were brought up, your first memories of film.

My family are artisans. My father, Alexander, or Sandor in Hungarian, was a Hungarian Jew who came to France as a young man in the early 1920s and worked making handmade pleats for high-end fashion designers. My mother, Helen, from the age of fourteen or so, was in the same business, and ended up working for my father. They got married and had a daughter, Helen, who worked in the hotel business. My mother already had one child, my half-brother Marcel, who became director of a loans company. I wasn't brought up with my sister and brother because we were ten years apart, so in a way I was an only child. It was my mother who got me interested in the performing arts, cinema in particular. She was a secondary school graduate, knew how to spell, and was always very curious. An avid reader of novels, she especially liked plays, including works by Jean Anouilh, Henry Bernstein, Marcel Achard and Jean Giraudoux. In the 1930s, she saw Gaby Morlay, Pierre Fresnay, Pierre Richard-Willm – all those great actors of stage and screen. When I was fifteen, I went to see Julien Green's play *Sud* [1953], in which Anouk Aimée made her stage début with Pierre Vaneck. Theatre interested me, but I found film more exciting, and it quickly became more important to me. I was really no different from any other child my age.

Do you remember the war?

I do. My father was forced to flee Paris because of the Germans, and only just managed to escape the Vél' d'Hiv Roundup in July 1942. I was told that young French soldiers came to warn my mother, saying, "Your father had better not be here tonight." There were lots of real bastards about, but there were others who, deep down, had some sense of morality. My father hid at my mother's sister's place, or with one of his friends, which was risky because they would have all been deported with him. Eventually he managed to escape. It was getting more and more dangerous, so he decided to go to Normandy, to Berd'huis, a small village near Mans, where they rented a house among the locals. My father and I were in hiding there while my mother went back and forth to Paris to work. During the bombings we took shelter underground.

How old were you?

I was born in 1938, so I was about five. It was around 1943. Later I saw the Americans arriving. My nanny Teresa took care of me, and I remember writing on a card about a film that we both liked: "Love for Teresa and fighting for me." After that, between 1945 and 1947, there was a big surge of adventure films, war films and detective films which really caught my eye. We were back in Paris, living in Montholon Square in the 9th arrondissement, where my father had his workshop. For most of my life I have lived in the 9th, the Grands Boulevards neighbourhood, where there are lots of cinemas. In *Je me souviens*, Georges Perec refers to "Balzac Helder Scala Vivienne." The Helder and the Vivienne were in the 9th, and so were the Buffault, which later became the Action-Lafayette, the Dauphin and the Roxy, which was on Rue Rochechouart. There was also the Marivaux, the Max Linder and the Grand Rex, with its magical water fountains. I mainly went to see French and American films, the ones with big stars. My strongest memories, immediately after the war, were of Cecil B. DeMille's *The Story of Dr. Wassell* with Gary Cooper, Errol Flynn films which hadn't been released during the Occupation, like *The Sea Hawk*, and anything with Robert Mitchum. As for French films, it was Gérard Philipe and Jean Gabin.

The first films you see mark you for life. I feel a little sorry for anyone who discovered cinema in a university class, watching things like Duras, Godard and Straub. Of course, you can come to appreciate those kinds of films later, but I think it's better to begin with more popular entertainment, which is the backbone, the roots, of cinema – like Louis Feuillade serials and early Fritz Lang, which I loved watching until I was about fifteen. I didn't subscribe to *Ciné Revue* and *Cinémonde* but would always be sure to skim them.

A high school cinephile

Did you go to the cinema with friends?

Absolutely. When I was about fourteen, I went to school at Condorcet, where I met Claude Novarezzio and Pierre Peroni, who unfortunately died young, when he was only nineteen. We went diving one time in Corfu and he never came back up. Much later one of my oldest friends,

Michel Sineux,* who was at the Lycée Carnot, joined me at *Positif*. Back then there were first run cinemas, second run cinemas and neigbourhood cinemas. Films had a longer life, sometimes two or three months, and you would hear about them through the grapevine. When I was little, I would go alone or with my mother, but when I was in high school we would go as a group. That was the next phase of my cinephilia. We went to all the independent cinemas – Cardinet, Agriculteurs, Studio Parnasse, Studio 26, Studio Bertrand – and discussed what we had seen. I kept a kind of log of what I was reading and watching, which was sort of my first step in criticism.

Did you make lists of directors?

Around 1953 or 1954, I discovered the idea of the writer-director. I was already a student of literature, but films, with rare exceptions, were more about the genre and the actors. When I was eight or nine, for example, I knew who Walt Disney was – even though he didn't actually direct films himself – and a little later became familiar with DeMille, Hitchcock and Chaplin. That's probably about it. On the other hand, I started to discover the big names in literature and read all the classics, including Benjamin Constant, Conrad, Dostoyevsky, Balzac, Tolstoy, Dickens and plays by Molière, Racine and Corneille.

This was when you were in high school?

Yes. My teachers played a big part. I remember an English instructor, Mr. Billot, who was extremely well read but a nervous wreck. When the class was noisy, he would go outside and walk in the courtyard for fifteen minutes, then come back in and sit down and wait for us to calm down. For our essays, he would take a short story, by Marcel Aymé for example, and ask us to continue it, or add an ending instead. I remember there was one which ended with "For once, the two sisters weren't fighting." On the last day of class, he told us, "Next year you're going to lose your individuality. You're going to be trained to write analytically about other people's work instead of expressing yourselves." It was about using our imagination, which isn't the best spur to becoming a critic.

---

* Michel Sineux (1938-2022). Director of the Médiathèque musicale de Paris and head of the Scientific Service of Paris municipal libraries from 1995 to 2000.

The following year we had a great teacher named Paul Bénichou,* who really knew how to get us excited about reading. He was a North African Jew who had lost his job during the war because of antisemitic laws and escaped to Argentina, where he met Roger Caillois,† also an exile. Bénichou had translated Borges for Gallimard in the Forties, and in 1948 published *Morales du Grand Siècle*, a study of eighteenth-century literature. He really was one of a kind. He worked fifteen hours a week as an adjunct teacher at Condorcet. He was never given a university job because he hadn't written a thesis, even though his book had been read by every teacher and was considered a standard reference book which was cited everywhere and much plagiarised. The Americans, who were less strict about such things, invited him to teach at Harvard, so he went and taught in the United States for a semester, which was much better paid than in France. He also wrote books for José Corti, then Gallimard. While I was studying English, I did my master's thesis on D.H. Lawrence. One day at the Sorbonne library I saw Bénichou, who was taking notes and working like a madman. Thanks to the Americans who supported him so he could write for the rest of the year, Bénichou became one of the greatest writers on French literature.

The religious paradox

Did religion make an impact?

My father was Jewish, but I discovered, much later on, a few years before she died, at the age of ninety-five, that my mother was actually also Jewish, which makes me one hundred percent Jewish. I was astounded when my mother told me that her mother's name was Lévy and that she and her grandmother were both buried in the Jewish cemetery at Pantin. Jérôme Clément wrote something similar about his own family – the discovery of his mother being Jewish. I was extremely surprised, given that my mother wasn't easily accepted into my father's family because she was a goy. If she knew she was Jewish, why didn't she tell my father? She suppressed her Judaism, which is what saved her life during the war, because she put it completely out of mind. Her entire family would have been killed.

Her family tree was rather complex. She had a half-sister, Roberte Marna, who after the war was songwriter

---

* Paul Bénichou (1909-2001). Algerian-born French literary historian.
† Roger Caillois (1913-1978). French literary critic.

Vincent Scotto's favourite singer. My mother had me baptised, and my first three years of secondary school were at the Lycée Rocroy-Saint-Léon, rue du Faubourg-Poissonnière, which was a Catholic school. I was even in the choir at Saint-Vincent-de-Paul and Notre-Dame-de-Lorette, which wasn't uninteresting, but I quickly had my fill of it. Around the same time, I broke with all things religious. I always thought that the Church, especially back then, was coercive, reactionary and repressive. I felt closer to Protestants, who seemed more open.

I actually have a theory that all totalitarian regimes in Europe have developed in Catholic or orthodox countries. This holds true for Russia's priests and the Colonels in Greece, both Orthodox countries. Nazism was born in Vienna, which has a huge Catholic population. Hitler, who was Austrian, ended up in Bavaria, which is also a Catholic region. Berlin was the city that resisted Nazism most strongly, before it was engulfed by the rest of Germany. Think of Mussolini's Italy, Franco's Spain and Salazar's Portugal. It's really only in Protestant countries like Sweden, Norway, Finland, The Netherlands, England, Canada and America where throughout the last century democracy held strong as totalitarianism flourished.

I sensed this without being able to fully comprehend it when I was thirteen, so I stopped going to church, confession and mass. I rejected this kind of domination, the forced deference to the pope, which included seeing only those films sanctioned by the Catholic church. When I was very young and began reading the great Surrealist writers, I was attracted to their anti-religious ideas but also their metaphysical obsessions, which was something Sartre, the most influential thinker of the time, didn't touch. I liked Breton's taste for mystery and the unknown, but I was never into his most esoteric ideas. It meant I was absolutely overwhelmed by Carl Dreyer's *Ordet*, which otherwise wouldn't have had any effect on me. This became something of a problem when I began at *Positif* because I had to deal with people who were so deeply antireligious that even the hint of spirituality in a film meant it was rejected out of hand. In general, Romanticism was seen as some kind of a return to religion, which never really made much sense to me. I was interested in other people's ways of thinking, and the mystery of existence – the holy – made an impression on me. I liked Brecht and Claudel. I had a school friend, François Regnault, who later became an influential figure in the theatre world, for whom Brecht and Claudel, even though they were each other's opposites, were the two greatest playwrights of the twentieth century. Actually, maybe they weren't so different, since one was under the lash of the Communist party and the other was under yoke of the church. What they both did was transcend their respective beliefs. If you read Brecht's *Life of Galileo*, you can't help but see an equivalence between Galileo being condemned by the Pope with what was happening in the Soviet Union, where, in the same sort of way, great thinkers were forced to deny their work if it contravened the tenets of dialectical materialism.

Writers, including Surrealists, who rejected religion often had a reason for doing so, perhaps as a reaction to their education.

Absolutely. And Catholics are some of the most rebellious writers there are. In most cases, Catholicism can foster tremendous submission and conformism, and at the same time people like Mauriac and Bernanos carried themselves really quite magnificently. Throughout his life – except in his later years – Aragon* was an apologist for Stalin, while Bernanos,† who was a supporter of Action française‡ and an anti-Semite in the early Thirties, condemns the priests during the Spanish Civil War in *Les Grands Cimetières sous la Lune*. He was exiled in Brazil before the war and united with General de Gaulle in 1940. Mauriac was in the resistance during the war, then opposed the Algerian War. There has always been a streak of rebelliousness in Catholics, like Léon Bloy.§ Compared with the significant number of leftists who have endorsed totalitarianism with no questions asked, Catholic intellectuals have shown great consistency in their political lucidity.

Phases of a young film cinephile

Did you read literary journals before you discovered film magazines?

Yes. I read two very carefully, which initially meant I became more interested in – if I may say so – content and style, or society and art, in any case. On the one hand was *Les Temps*

---

* Louis Aragon (1897-1982). French Surrealist poet.
† Georges Bernanos (1888-1948). French novelist.
‡ French far-right monarchist political movement.
§ Léon Bloy (1846-1917). French novelist.

modernes, a very political journal. I was interested in politics and history. On the other, for style, was *La Nouvelle Revue française*, which was banned after the war because of accusations of collaboration. I began reading it when it reappeared in 1953 and discovered the work of many writers, like Cioran, Georges Perros, Marcel Arland, Jean Paulhan, Jean Grosjean and some remarkable literary critics. When it came to literature, I was instantly aware of the writer's personal universe. It wasn't like that right away with film, but luckily, I had the opportunity to live through a time which saw the rise of more and more great filmmakers. That was my second phase as a filmgoer.

Can you give examples?

When I was about fifteen, I saw some films and realised there was something new happening. Not necessarily better, but different from *She Wore a Yellow Ribbon*, *Colorado Territory*, *The Maltese Falcon* and *The Big Sleep*. You had *Les Vacances de Monsieur Hulot*, for example, in 1953, or *Lola Montès* in 1955, and Fellini's first films that we saw in France: *La Strada*, *Il bidone*, *Nights of Cabiria*. A bit later, in 1956, Ingmar Bergman and Bresson appeared. *A Man Escaped* was a real eye-opener for me, in the same way that Antonioni's *Il Grido* was. All at the same time, an entire wave of great filmmakers was expressing their version of modernity. At the Cinémathèque française I entered the third phase of my cinephilia.

When was that?

In 1956, when I began going regularly to the cinema on rue d'Ulm. I was accepted into preparatory classes at Louis-le-Grand which were designed to send students to the École normale supérieure, a hundred metres from the Cinémathèque. That's where I discovered silent cinema. After the great genre films and all those modern directors, I took a step backwards and began exploring silent cinema. Another eye-opener for me. I discovered the power and importance of the image. It was a completely new language for me because apart from Chaplin I hadn't seen a single silent film. I went to all the retrospectives Henri Langlois[*] organised, like Buster Keaton and Erich von Stroheim, and even saw the last screening of a film that later burnt up in a fire, the second part of von Stroheim's *The Wedding March*.

---

[*] Henri Langlois (1914-1977). French film archivist, co-founder of the Cinémathèque française.

It was the only copy in existence. Nobody else saw it after 1956. And then there were the great silent films by Fritz Lang, Murnau, Dreyer and von Sternberg, the Swedes, lots of Russian films, especially Dovzhenko's *The Earth*, *Ivan* and *Aerograd*, Eisenstein and Pudovkin.

In 1957, when I was nineteen, I met André Malraux at Cardinet. He was with his two children, who shortly afterwards both died in a car accident. I was walking out of the cinema after just having seen Rossellini's *Paisan* and ran into him. Since I loved his books, as well as *Les Voix du Silence* and *La Métamorphose des dieux*, his essays on aesthetics, I told him I wanted to ask him some questions about cinema. In 1940 he had published an interesting text called *Esquisse d'une psychologie du cinéma*, the last line of which is "Par ailleurs, le cinéma est une industrie" ["Besides, cinema is an industry"]. He told me to write to him, which I did, asking him ten questions. He responded with a one-page letter which unfortunately I have since lost, which is all the more annoying since his daughter Florence told me he didn't often write letters.

Travel and art

Did your love for art begin at this time?

Painting has always been connected with my experiences of travel. I took two holidays to Italy with my class from Condorcet. One was in the south, from Rome to Naples, the other was in the north: Florence and Venice. It was in all those museums we explored that I truly discovered painting. I had been to the Louvre, of course, but it was in Italy where I found myself so moved by all those bursts of colour and form. Painting really became something of an obsession, and today I collect art books and catalogues, and go to as many exhibitions as possible. I'll gladly travel to Amsterdam, London or Brussels to look at art. I'm less of a music lover because I don't like listening to music while I'm doing something... and I'm usually doing something. Actually, I'm remembering something else now, which is that I studied German as a second language and went on an exchange trip to Seekirchen, very close to Salzburg, where I lived with an Austrian family. I listened to broadcasts of the Salzburg festival, most memorably Furtwängler conducting Beethoven's Seventh. I had never heard it before and was profoundly moved. Music wasn't much of a big deal at home.

Was your discovery of art accompanied by an exploration of critical writing on the subject?

I have always liked criticism, whether it's about books, films or paintings. I read Baudelaire's *Les Curiosités esthétiques*, Fromentin's *Les Maîtres d'autrefois*, and in 1955, starting with its very first issue, began reading *L'Œil* magazine. Back then, there were very few exhibitions and much less coverage of painting, except what was going on in private galleries. Museums were the primary focus. *L'Œil* was a fancy magazine printed in Switzerland, each issue with eight colour pages – a rarity back then – and for me was an important introduction to contemporary art. I read articles on Nicolas de Staël, Germaine Richier and Jean Bazaine. The magazine featured writings from the generation of future leading experts on seventeenth-century French painting, which until then had been largely overlooked, aside from four or five names: Poussin, Lorrain, Le Nain, La Tour. A generation of young curators and scholars, including Pierre Rosenberg, Michel Laclotte, and Jacques Thuillier, made important contributions to *L'Œil*, which was a hybrid academic journal and popular magazine. Back then it wasn't like it is today, where every art magazine covers the same things and does a Hopper special issue when there happens to be a Hopper exhibition opening. *L'Œil* published articles that had nothing to do with contemporary art. They would visit an artist in his workshop, for example, a bit like Alain Resnais with his first short films. Old painters, about whom we knew nothing – there were no books or exhibitions – were rediscovered. For me, *L'Œil* was a guide, a reference point. Perhaps because of its influence, in *Positif* I place a strong emphasis on the simultaneous exploration of old and new.

Readings and discussions

When did your thoughts on cinema start to become more serious?

It was because of the journals I was reading. I bought at least two: *Cahiers du cinéma* and *Positif*, which I read religiously, but without adhering to the edicts of either. I loved Huston and Hitchcock, but I wasn't beholden to anyone or anything. I bought every book on cinema in French, which filled two shelves. There were also some monographs, like Jean Mitry on Chaplin and John Ford, or others by Marie

Seton on Eisenstein or Emilio Sales Gomes on Vigo. There were also essays by Henri Agel.

And Georges Sadoul?*

Yes, but I never really read film history books the way I read *L'Histoire de l'art* by Élie Faure, which I devoured cover to cover. I used them as reference books. From the point of view of style and sensibility, I preferred Bardèche† and Brasillach.‡ They were fascists, it's true, but I found their *Histoire du cinéma* more readable. Sadoul knew a lot and was well-travelled, but he lacked style, and for me the quality of writing was always important. I often went browsing in bookshops, especially La Fontaine, across the street from the Jardins du Luxembourg, and the Minotaure on rue des Beaux Arts, run by Roger Cornaille and his associate, who from time to time would publish beautiful books on art. It was an Aladdin's cave. They had all the journals and magazines, even foreign ones. Pierre Prévert went there, Jean Boullet and Jean-Claude Romer too, who later started *Midi-Minuit Fantastique*.§ I probably bumped into Jacques Lourcelles¶ and Bertrand Tavernier. On Saturday mornings we would meet up and talk about films.

The film club culture was an important way of teaching people about cinema after the war.

That's true. At Jean-Louis Cheray's Studio Parnasse, they would show a double feature, and after the screenings there were discussions with writers from *Cahiers* and *Positif*, along with a notebook at the exit for us to share our complaints. People like Jacques Rivette and Roger Tailleur** showed up. It was bit like the Cinémathèque, where Langlois would sometimes hold debates, except that at Parnasse it was never-ending. I was an occasional member of three or four film clubs. There was the Nickelodéon, where Bertrand Tavernier, Bernard Martinand†† and the poet Yves Martin

---
* Georges Sadoul (1904-1967). French film critic and author. Author of the six-volume *Histoire générale du cinema*.
† Maurice Bardèche (1907-1998). French art critic. Co-author, with Robert Brasillach, of *Histoire du cinéma*.
‡ Robert Brasillach (1909-1945). French author, executed for wartime collaboration.
§ French film magazine, focused on horror and science fiction, which ran for a decade starting in 1962.
¶ Jacques Lourcelles (b.1940). French film historian and screenwriter.
** Roger Tailleur (1927-1985). French film critic, contributor to *Positif*.
†† Bernard Martinand (b.1939). French historian and archivist.

would lobby on behalf of specific film directors. And there was the Ciné Qua Non that Bernard Cohn created. He invited people from *Positif* like Kyrou* or Benayoun.† There was also the Sorbonne film club, where Max Tessier‡ was an active member.

Influences and trends

Did you study film at school?

Not really. At Louis-le-Grand I had an English teacher, Albert Laffay, who before 1950 had published theoretical essays in the *Revue de filmologie*, though after that wrote nothing more about cinema. He's actually the person who inspired me to study English. I was supposed to be a historian because I got an honourable mention in the history entrance exam, but I had a teacher who taught by drawing battle plans on the blackboard, which was enough to turn me off the subject. This fellow, Mr. Monnier, later became a school inspector. All those poor teachers who were inspected during class! So I decided to take English instead. Laffay had published a magnificent book of his translations of Keats, one of my favourite poets, with a 150-page introduction. I couldn't see myself getting a teaching certification in history, but I wanted to improve my English, so I changed subjects and was accepted, which was no easy feat. I had a good chance of getting into the École Normale, but by that point I was sick of cramming for exams, so I changed directions again and went straight for an English diploma at the Sorbonne, which is how I encountered Gilles Deleuze, who for a single year was teaching at Lycée Louis-le-Grand. Before that he was in Orléans, and eventually ended up at the Sorbonne.

You certainly landed on your feet!

I was in class with him for nine hours a week. The theme was "Qu'est-ce que fonder?" ["What does it mean to create?"] Unfortunately, he never published on the subject, and I can't find my class notes. Maybe along with my classmates we could have collectively pieced together his ideas on the foundations of philosophy. He was charismatic but somewhat underappreciated because he didn't make us study very

---

* Ado Kyrou (1923-1985). Greek-born French film critic, contributor to *Positif*.
† Robert Benayoun (1926-1996). Moroccan-born French film critic.
‡ Max Tessier (b.1944). French film critic.

hard, which meant he didn't really prepare us for exams. He practiced maieutics, like Socrates, and spoke with an incredibly captivating voice, encouraging us to think and interact. Deleuze was a very important person to me, especially – and this I have come to appreciate even more strongly today – because he distrusted systems. I liked that approach because about two years before, in 1954, I had been interested in Mendès France.* I was suspicious of Marxism and communism, and obviously also of right-wing politics. Engaging in dialogue and debate was more my kind of thing. And also – I'm not ashamed to name it – social democracy, the Scandinavian model, what Germany and France aspired to, the Mendès France model. Liberty. I've always thought that there's nothing more destructive than fanatical convictions and the utopian ideal of a perfect life and society. The twentieth century stands as proof of this awful truth. The road to utopia leads to mass death and bloodshed. So even back then I put my weight behind something perhaps less noble and less idealistic, but which took human nature into account.

But still with a leftist point of view?

Absolutely.

Where did that belief come from? Your family? The books you read?

I think it's indisputably connected with family, from the fact that I saw my father pursued and that his parents were murdered in Hungary. Fortunately, his closest relatives – his brothers and sisters – survived. At the same time, I wept when Soviet troops entered Budapest in 1956. When I was fifteen, in 1953, I heard about the repression in Poland. Totalitarianism certainly had its effect on me. I've always been suspicious of monism – the idea, held by some people, that there is only one way of seeing things. Throughout human history, which spans thousands of years, man is happiest under social democracy. It gives us the freedom to think and write, to create systems of healthcare and education. It has been a haven amidst centuries of enslavement, intolerance and war.

Would that be your definition of democracy?

---

* Pierre Mendès France (1907-1982). French prime minister for eight months from 1954 to 1955.

Yes. The critic can only truly exist in a society where all points of view can be expressed. Being a critic isn't about restraints and dictums. It's about not being concerned with being arrested one morning. As Churchill put it, "In a Democracy, when someone rings your door at six in the morning, it's the milkman, not the police." Unless you're practicing hara-kiri, the critic can't be in favour of dictatorship, which is why I think that people like Brasillach or Sadoul, the fascist and the communist, were able to express their ideas in France, because they lived in the country where freedom of expression is valued. It's true that Brasillach thought that Pétain's France wasn't exactly the country of his dreams, that it wasn't radical enough. But if they were honest, Sadoul – like Brasillach – should have admitted, as Beaumarchais' Figaro did, that "Sans la liberté de blâmer, il n'est point d'éloge flatteur" ["Without the freedom to criticise, there is no true praise"]. I consider this idea to be inseparable from the profession of a critic. It's like being a teacher. And I think that throughout my life I've had this chance to be truly free. I was free in high school and took the classes I wanted. I had even more freedom at university because there wasn't even an established programme, so I created one myself. I'm free at *Positif* because we decide together what to publish. At the radio station where I work, I'm free to invite anyone I want onto my programme. I have the freedom to say what I want. And what a joy it is... I can't even say I deserved such treatment, because it just happened. I've been able to pursue my career with complete freedom.

The lessons of Deleuze

What were the most important things you learned from Deleuze?

I found him fascinating – what he said, his passion. After reading his books, I realised he was anti-Hegelian, anti-Marxist. He was anti-system. He was also against any grand theory which claims the truth, and sided more with Bergson, Nietzsche and Hume, one of the founders of Anglo-Saxon imperialism about whom he wrote his first book. In a way, in his maeiutic fashion, he gave me a taste for the clash of ideas. That's why sometimes I read publications which I don't necessarily agree with, with which I'm not on the same wavelength, because often our opponents stimulate us. They point out our faults and allow us to see things from different angles. Maurice Pialat always told me that he learned more from people who rubbished his films than those who praised them. Reading opinions diametrically opposed to your own isn't a particularly strange idea. I'm not saying I agree with Robespierre's Reign of Terror, which would be the opposite to what I'm talking about, but nevertheless the revolution of 1789 seems to me an indisputable historical moment when it comes to human rights and freedom. I find it fascinating to read Burke and Joseph de Maistre, great conservative thinkers, who wrote against the French Revolution during the nineteenth century. It's the kind of thing that can help identify the dead ends and weaknesses in our own ideas. I like Philippe Muray,* whose views on many subjects are the complete opposite to mine and who I read long before he was trendy. He's a reactionary, very much pushing against the times. I'm not at all against my times, even if I have mixed feelings about them. I can see the good and the bad. And so in this sense, Deleuze taught me a great deal. He gave me a philosophy award that I'm very proud of.

Deleuze was passionate about film.

At the time he was a real cinephile. We would go to Balzar, the restaurant on rue des Écoles, next to Louis-le-Grand. He read *Positif* and liked Benayoun's articles. He loved W.C. Fields, Buster Keaton and Jerry Lewis, which wasn't very common in 1956. He probably must have gone to the Cinémathèque to see Stroheim's *Foolish Wives* and *Greed*, which he also loved. Then, for the next fifteen years, he forgot about film. He didn't have time to see anything because he wrote, almost every year, one massive, important book after another, from *Logique du sens* to *Différence et Répétition*. Later he jumped back into film and published two books, *L'image-mouvement* et *L'image-temps*. That's when I started seeing him more frequently. He lived on the rue de Bizerte and we would meet at the Wepler on Place de Clichy. I brought him issues of *Positif*. He liked to read articles by Michael Wilson, Alain Masson, Gérard Legrand, Robert Benayoun and you. He was out of touch because it had been so long since he had gone to the cinema, so he was sort of catching up by reading the issues I gave him – *Cahiers* as well as *Positif*.

Did he contribute anything theoretically which helped you as a critic?

---
* Philippe Muray (1945-2006). French essayist and novelist.

Not really, although because of him I became more open-minded and learned to be more sceptical of systems. In the 1950s, French intellectual life was dominated by great spiritual leaders and philosophers like Sartre. There were the Existentialists, arm in arm with the Marxists, like Althusser and Balibar. The Communist Party had a strong influence on the intellectual crowd. Not only did a quarter of the population vote PCF,* it was also a strong presence on campuses. We read the *Les Lettres françaises* and *La Nouvelle Critique*, any number of journals and newspapers. Allied to Sartre's followers were the Christians, who followed Mounier† and read the journal *Esprit*. On the other side was the right wing and the remnants of the collaborationists, and also the Hussards,‡ *La Table ronde*,§ Blondin¶ and Nimier,** which attracted people like Truffaut and Rohmer. I certainly didn't share the hatred for Camus which, deep down, all these people felt, starting with the communists. The Christians took him with a pinch of salt and the right-wingers made fun of his humanism. I liked him. I wouldn't say he was my favourite writer, but I have read his books and never understood why the Surrealists were so down on *The Rebel*.

The two faces of Surrealism

You were already drawn to Surrealism?

Yes. The Surrealists, André Breton in particular, had a strong impact on me in the late 1950s when I began reading their books and buying their journals, including *Medium*. I spent time at Éric Losfeld's Le Terrain vague bookshop, which, along with Jean-Jacques Pauvert, was their most important publisher. I felt a real fascination for Breton because he combined so much of what I had been reading, even if he had nothing to do with the *NRF*†† or *Temps modernes*, which he was actually quite antagonistic towards, despite his sympathy for Paulhan.‡‡ For me, Surrealism brought together two things I was interested in. First, there was political commitment. The Surrealists had

---

* Parti communiste français.
† Emmanuel Mounier (1905-1950). French philosopher and theologian.
‡ A French literary movement in the 1950s, in opposition to Sartre's Existentialism.
§ French publishing house, in opposition to Sartre's *Les Temps modernes*.
¶ Antoine Blondin (1922-1991). French novelist.
** Roger Nimier (1925-1962). French novelist.
†† *Nouvelle Revue française*, French literary journal, founded 1909.
‡‡ Jean Paulhan (1884-1968). French literary critic and publisher, longtime editor of NRF.

never given support to any brutal regimes and had criticised Communism as much as Nazism. They were anti-Hitler and anti-Stalin. Breton hadn't been in the Resistance but instead went to America, where he worked for the Free French radio. The Surrealists were unique in protesting the Colonial Exhibition of 1931 because everyone else considered it quite normal to see black people sporting fezzes and serving coffee. They were against the Algerian War, which I had protested when I was a member of UNEF.* And then, at the same time, they were poets who revered style and were also interested in film, jazz, naïve art, comic books and popular literature. In a way, Breton brought together everything I liked about life. On the other hand, I found Sartre to be quite sordid. When he wrote about Baudelaire it wasn't the beauty of his work that interested him, only the social and psychological issues. Later it was the same with Flaubert. What I liked about Breton was the aesthetic dimension connected to an indignation, an anger, against the state of the world.

To America

Between your love for literature, cinema and Anglo-Saxon culture, everything seems to be falling into place for you.

The unusual thing is that it all happened six thousand kilometres away. In the middle of my bachelor's degree, after my first two certificates in English, I applied for a Fulbright scholarship, which enabled me to travel to the United States on a paid trip. That was very useful as I had no money. I signed a contract with the IPES† which gave me a salary during my four years of study at the Sorbonne. In exchange, I signed a contract to be a teacher for ten years. My salary – minimum wage – was enough to cover my needs, especially as in the beginning I lived with my parents.

What did this scholarship entail?

I taught six to eight hours of French at an American university, and at the same time took English classes. As I already spoke pretty good English, since I had been on holiday several times to stay with a family in England, I was admitted into a very good college, Amherst, in Massachusetts. Emily Dickinson was from Amherst. There were resident writers, like the

---
* Union nationale des étudiants de France.
† Instituts de préparation à l'enseignement secondaire.

great poet Robert Frost, who we would see walking around campus. My time there really changed my life.

I had already been a film fanatic in Paris, and at Amherst I created a film society. Film wasn't being taught anywhere in America, with the exception of some classes at UCLA. Amherst, as opposed to the University of Massachusetts, which was located in the same town, was a private university, but it was well equipped and had a thousand students – 250 in each year plus 150 faculty. It was the cream of the crop. Leo Marx was there. He wrote *The Machine in the Garden*, a study of the relationship between industrialisation and agriculture, the conflict between technology and the "pastoral." Terrence Malick must have read it. C.L. Barber, the great Shakespeare scholar, was there, as was Henry Steele Commager, an expert on international law, and Karl Loewenstein, a German Jew who escaped Nazism and taught international diplomacy. One day my idol Pierre Mendès France visited. He showed up with Stanley Hoffmann, a Harvard professor. I spent an evening with him in a small group because I was one of the two French people at the college. Amherst was revolutionary to me because I was coming from the Sorbonne, where there were five hundred students in the lecture hall and we had little direct contact with professors. It was just awful. We would wait in line to get handouts and wait two months to get our work back. Over in Amherst, I would sit with a group of students in Leo Marx's garden, in a kind of seminary, talking about American myths, and his wife would serve cookies and tea. It was the same with every professor. An absolutely unique experience.

You must have felt you were living in a dream.

The library, open from nine in the morning until midnight, had a complete run of *NRF*, going back to 1909. They subscribed to every one of the world's important journals. They had books we could take from the shelves, unlike at the Sorbonne, where we could borrow only three books and had to wait an hour to get them. I created a film club and ordered films. I was attacked by The Daughters of the American Revolution and extreme right organisations after screening Eisenstein's *Alexander Nevsky*, who they insisted was a red. I showed Orson Welles' *Macbeth*, *Rules of the Game*, *A Man Escaped* and other classics and more recent films, which the Americans had never heard of. I wrote my first articles in the daily school newspaper. There was a radio station and a small journal where we published essays. I wrote a paper in English on the relationship between Albert Camus and Herman

Melville. It was my intellectual emancipation. I understood what it meant to get to work. I was part of a fraternity – Alpha Theta Xo – that would meet up in the evening. Some prominent people came to the film club, like the son of the Taiwanese ambassador, a student who later won the Nobel Prize in physics, and another whose father was the head of a New York railway company and who invited me to spend a fortnight on his Long Island estate. That was America for me back then – a real openness of mind. My views of the place have changed, but what I experienced was a real eye-opener. I certainly knew I was privileged.

Importantly, over the past ten years a new kind of aesthetic criticism had developed in America, while back in France we were mainly concerned with ideological or purely biographical analysis. Over there, I was dealing with people who seriously studied the language of a book or poem, its form and structure. It was genuinely exciting. I discovered subjects I had never studied before. I had never read Freud, for example, at high school or university. We studied great thinkers like Marx, Darwin and Weber. In France we could study Freud only if we took German. If not, we were never given the chance. It was all a vital part of my education.

One Easter, I went to Florida with two German friends and an American. Rich Americans would go on holiday there and pay students a small amount to drive their cars down. We slept in sleeping bags under the moonlight. As the four of us got along really well, one summer we decided to go cross country and went all the way to San Francisco. We saw the Grand Tetons, Mount Rushmore, Arizona, the Grand Canyon. We made a lot of detours down south before going further west. We also went to the cinema quite a few times. I saw *Vertigo* in New Orleans and John Ford's *The Horse Soldiers* at a drive-in. Our trip lasted almost a month. We didn't have much money and ate mostly hamburgers. It was a road movie before its time. I discovered America in all its complexities.

Interlude with Buñuel

How did your tour of the United States end?

My schoolmates left me in San Francisco, and I hitchhiked to Los Angeles. I didn't know America that well and asked the driver to drop me off in the centre of town. He didn't quite know where to take me because, of course, there is no centre to Los Angeles. In the end he dropped me off at UCLA, where I found a place to sleep. Then I took a bus to Mexico, where the director of the Alliance Française kindly offered me his spare room. I spent a week in Mexico and saw Buñuel's *Nazarin*, which had just been screened at Cannes. I decided to look up Buñuel in the phone book and, with the audacity of a 21-year-old, called him. "Mr. Buñuel, I'm a young French student," I said to him. "I just saw *Nazarin*. I don't understand Spanish, but I love your films. I've seen them all." He invited me over and I ended up spending an entire day with him. He started by showing me his house. Clearly, he was nostalgic for his time in Paris because I remember a giant map of the Paris metro behind his bar. We spoke about film. Later on, at *Positif*, Ado Kyrou was shocked when I told him that Buñuel spoke highly of Bresson's *Angels of Sin* because the foot-washing scenes had turned him on. He was clearly a true fetishist. After that, he drove me to the Churubusco studios, where we sat in on a film shoot. That's where he filmed all his Mexican films. I can't remember in detail exactly what we said to each other, but it was a real conversation, very long, lasting five or six hours. Then he took me back to the Alliance Française and I eventually caught a bus to the border before hitchhiking back to New York.

It's funny to talk about it now because years later, at the 1973 Cannes film festival, American critics didn't like Jerry Schatzberg's *Scarecrow*, particularly one of the bigshots, Andrew Sarris. "You like this film? Of course you do. You don't really understand America. You don't know the country, so you can't really judge it." He even dared say to me, "You miss the nuances of the English language." "In that case," I said to him, "how is that you're the American specialist on the French New Wave? You don't even speak French. I, at least, speak English fluently. And you live in a beautiful building on Park Avenue. I probably know more about the American heartland of *Scarecrow* than you do. Have you ever slept at the Salvation Army in Nebraska to save a few dollars? Have you ever waited five hours for a Greyhound bus? Have you ever stayed in a seedy Faulknereque hotel overnight, scared out of your wits, because you can't lock the door? I have lived all that, and understand Max and Leo's lives better than you ever will."

Return to France

How was life in France once you returned home?

Immediately after getting home, I got my first professional job as a journalist. I had come by boat and was met by my parents at Le Havre. They rented a couple of rooms at a hotel in Normandy so I could rest for a week before going back to university. There was a great reporter staying there named Éric Rouleau, a political commentator who specialised in the Middle East. I spoke regularly with him throughout that week at the hotel, about politics and other things, at which point he said to me, "Would you be interested in doing an internship at *Le Monde*?" I accepted his offer and found myself working at the newspaper, in the international department, for a month. Back then it was headed by André Fontaine, who later became the paper's senior editor. Rouleau was one of his correspondents. Mitterrand eventually appointed him the Turkish ambassador. For a month I read all the dispatches and summaries from the news agencies. An intern obviously couldn't be trusted to write articles about foreign policy, but it was a wonderful experience. I saw what a newsroom was all about, what it meant to work in a group, and practiced what they call in America "text reduction." A text comes in and you have to cut it down to two pages, then twenty lines.

After that you went back to school?

Yes. My dissertation advisor, Jean-Jacques Mayoux, was a renowned literary critic, the only English professor at the Sorbonne I admired. I can't remember any of the others, except Robert Ellrodt, a specialist on English Romantic poets. Apart from everything else, they all spoke terrible English, even if they were senior English professors. One of them used the word "magnetophone" because he didn't know the word "tape recorder." But Mayoux – who wrote for *Les Lettres modernes*, edited by Maurice Nadeau, another critic who played a major role in my discovery of literature and who asked me to write for his *Quinzaine littéraire* – published *Vivants Piliers*, a series of studies on great writers. I consider it one of the most beautiful books on Anglo-Saxon literature. I suggested to Mayoux that I do my dissertation on D.H. Lawrence, who at the time was out of favour. James Joyce, Virginia Woolf and T.S. Eliot were the preferred writers of the moment. Influenced by my stay on the other side of the Atlantic and by contemporary American criticism, I chose as my subject "From Sensations to Images in the novels of D.H. Lawrence." It was clearly the visual side that interested me, exploring how, in Lawrence's work, sensations – fire, ice – stimulated the imagination and created images and feelings. Mayoux wasn't too keen on Lawrence, but he agreed to be my thesis advisor, and at the end of the year told me I had reignited his interest in Lawrence. I really liked Mayoux. After he signed the Manifesto of the 121,[*] his apartment was blown up by the OAS.[†] With friends from college, in pairs and in eight-hour shifts, I took turns because his door had been kicked in, keeping watch in front of his place.

---

[*] An open letter signed by 121 intellectuals, published on 6 September 1960, denouncing the war in Algeria.
[†] Organisation armée secrète, a far-right dissident paramilitary organisation that sought to prevent Algerian independence.

FROM CINEPHILIA
TO CRITICISM

First critical weapons

How did you come to publish your first writings on cinema?

When I came back from America I couldn't wait to get writing. I knew Bernard Cohn through the Ciné Qua Non film club. A modest journal had been founded, *Cinéma-Textes*, mimeographed in five hundred copies under the aegis of the Sorbonne, directed by François Porcile, later a great specialist of film music and collaborator of Truffaut. He also authored numerous books, including one on Maurice Jaubert. Porcile brought together a group, people like Bernard Cohn and me, who had never written anything, along with more experienced people like Claude Gauteur and Claude Beylie, who were already writing in the holy of holies – *Cahiers du cinéma* – but still had time for what was essentially a student journal. Michel Nuridsany, who became a great journalist at *Le Figaro* and wrote, among others, a book on Warhol, was also there. This was at the end of 1962 and the beginning of 1963. I remember writing about three Italian films in particular: Rosi's *Salvatore Giuliano*, De Seta's *Bandits a Orgosolo* and Olmi's *Il posto*. I wrote a piece from London about two films I had seen but which hadn't yet been released in France: Minnelli's *Two Weeks in Another Town*, which I didn't like as much as *The Bad and the Beautiful*, and Arthur Penn's *The Miracle Worker*.

I often went to London to see films, mostly at the National Film Theatre, their Cinémathèque, which was run by the British Film Institute. Among the journals I read starting in the mid-1950s, there was one that Minotaure carried, *Sight and Sound*, an excellent quarterly published by the BFI. It was wide-ranging, not at all partisan like *Cahiers* or *Positif*, not so focused on controversies and innovation. I went to their offices to meet them, and the difference between the climate in Paris and London was striking. We French filmgoers would all find ourselves impatiently at 2pm on the Champs-Elysées to see the latest Hitchcock or Hawks or Minnelli or Kazan or Cukor or Ford or Preminger as soon as it was released. In London, on the other hand, I arrived in the offices and asked, "Have you seen *Splendor in the Grass*?" The response would be: "No" – even though it had been out for three weeks. "I should go see it…" Or "Have you seen *Advise and Consent*?" "No, but it looks interesting. Someone is reviewing the film for us." There was a lack of passion that seemed to explain the difference between the two countries.

Sight and Sound did a good job of dealing with film history, but there was no real excitement behind any of it. Compare that to *Sequence*, the journal that Lindsay Anderson and Karel Reisz founded in the early 1950s, which is closer to *Cahiers* or *Positif*. *Sight and Sound* was the "institutional" review of the British Film Institute. At the National Film Theatre you could see rare films, like Kubrick's *Paths of Glory*, which hadn't yet been released in France.

You went to visit the offices of Cahiers du cinéma.

Yes, I was a reader of *Cahiers du cinéma* and *Positif* primarily, along with other journals. I started reading *Cahiers* around issue number 50, and *Positif*, which was published irregularly, around number 16. In 1958 I went to the *Cahiers* offices on the Champs-Elysées to buy some old issues. Truffaut was there. I knew him by sight because he used to come to Studio Parnasse and the film clubs. I don't think he had made a film yet – maybe *Les Mistons*. I told Truffaut that I liked reading the journal, but there was someone whose writing I really didn't understand because, in my opinion, it had little to do with the films he was discussing. An example was his recent review of *Bitter Victory* in which he wrote about everything except Nicholas Ray's film. Truffaut told me I was wrong, and that actually he was the most gifted of everyone at *Cahiers*. The person we were talking about, of course, was Godard. And in fact, when you read his review of *Bitter Victory* after watching *Breathless*, you see that he's talking about pinball games on the Champs-Elysées and young women. It's Jean Seberg selling the *Herald Tribune*. These very subjective articles were pre-narratives of cinema. They were his own obsessions rather than critiques of films, which Truffaut and Rohmer's reviews were.

Beginning at *Positif*

Why did you choose to write for Positif?

At Le Terrain Vague bookstore one day I met André S. Labarthe,* who was walking in with his friend Jacques Siclier.† "You should write for *Cahiers*," Labarthe told me. I liked *Cahiers* but felt closer to *Positif* politically because it was a left-wing journal, which *Cahiers* – before its Maoist turn, it took somewhat right-wing, self-indulgent positions

---

* André Labarthe (1931-2018). French filmmaker.
† Jacques Siclier (1927-2013). French journalist and historian.

– was not. And *Positif* was interested in the other arts too. *Cahiers* had undeniable literary taste, but painting, music, politics weren't in its field of interest. I had the feeling that at *Positif* there was more of a mix of culture, as well as an attachment to Surrealism – Gérard Legrand,* Ado Kyrou and Robert Benayoun wrote for it. At the time all meetings were held in Benayoun's extraordinary apartment on rue de la Pompe. It was a gigantic dream-like room, full of books and paintings. He had accumulated so many treasures: paintings by Brauner and Toyen, manuscripts, letters from Breton. That's where I sent a text for the first time, after writing something in *Cinéma-Textes*, which vanished a couple of years later, I think after fourteen or fifteen issues.

Bernard Cohn and I both frequented the library at the Sorbonne, where I was preparing for the civil service entrance exam, and as I was going to his film club and writing for *Cinéma-Textes*, one day he said to me, "Why don't you try writing something for *Positif*? They took something I wrote and are always looking for new contributors." With this suggestion in mind, I did what I often do, which is challenge the prevailing consensus. Orson Welles' *The Trial* had been vilified by most reviewers in France, and wasn't any better received in America. They said it was pompous and pretentious, a betrayal of Kafka. If I saw it again, I probably wouldn't say it was Welles' greatest film – and I didn't think so at the time – but it seemed superior to so many films that were being released. And so Wellesian, too. As I had also read practically all of Kafka, as well as Marthe Robert† and other commentators, I had a good understanding of his work. Having also seen every Welles film, I was ready to write about the connections between Welles and Kafka, and argue that Welles hadn't, in fact, betrayed him. In any case, I defended the film, suggesting it was one possible interpretation of Kafka, and posted my article to *Positif*. I then bought the latest issue of *Positif*, number 50-51-52, and what do I find but a sixteen-page round table on *The Trial* with all the leading lights of *Positif* brilliantly discussing Welles' film, two-thirds of whom liked the film. It was the most important thing about *The Trial* that had been published in the French press. I figured that there was no chance of my article appearing now. And then, ten days later, Benayoun called me and said, "We read your text. It will appear in number 53." *Positif* was published every three or four months, which meant the article appeared long after the film's release. It was 1963, and they asked me

---

* Gérard Legrand (1927-1999). French film critic, Surrealist poet, contributor to *Positif*.
† Marthe Robert (1914-1996). French essayist and translator, Kafka specialist.

to continue to send in articles. I really was a bit provocative, because one of my first submissions after *The Trial* was about Jacques Demy's *La Baie des Anges*. Paul-Louis Thirard* had given *Lola* a good review, and Tailleur adored Demy, but there was still an anti-Demy clique. *Positif* was never completely cohesive, and there were disagreements. Everyone was very friendly, but there was a more modern, more open-minded stream, as represented by Benayoun and Tailleur, and a more ideological one, which was Kyrou and Seguin,† who didn't like Demy at all, especially *Lola*. And then a newcomer shows up, a novice, who writes a eulogy of *La Baie des Anges*...

A bystander in Venice

Were you still studying at that time?

Yes, and for sixteen months I did military service. As I was already the father of a son – Gilles, born in 1962 – I was exempted from conscription in Algeria. The war was ending anyway but I might have been sent there for a few months. I did four months of classes near Paris. I passed my HGV license and drove a truck – and I haven't driven since! Because I was an "intellectual," I was sent to Paris and became the secretary to an intelligence officer. The amazing thing is that a few months ago I had lunch with someone I hadn't seen for fifty years who was in the same office as me during our service. "Weren't you surprised back in 1963," he asked me, "when you were stationed in the intelligence services, they came to your office at two in the afternoon and, without warning, told you to go to the Dupleix barracks and report to the commander in charge of transportation?" It's true that I had never understood why that had happened... My initial posting was quite interesting, because on the one hand we were in charge of stamping all these files, for example papers relating to the American landing in Cuba. Everything had to be classified top secret, including Christopher Columbus' discovery back in 1492. It was all completely meaningless. And on the other hand, every evening I had to take down masses of useless documents and have them shredded so the "enemy" would never see them, except that the chap in charge of the shredder didn't put them into the machine because they were carbon copies which clogged up the mechanism, so we put them in rubbish bags instead and dumped them out on

---

* Paul-Louis Thirard (1932-2019). French film critic, contributor to *Positif*.
† Louis Seguin (1929-2008). French film critic, contributor to *Positif*.

the street, where the Soviets, if they had wanted to, could have picked through everything.

I was eventually removed from that position, and fifty years after the fact discovered that the army had actually investigated me and found out that my father had been born in Hungary and that he might still have family there. Anyone with family in Eastern bloc countries wasn't given important army work to do because the enemy could blackmail them. They were worried about possible connections behind the Iron Curtain. I found myself secretary to the commander of the Dupleix barracks who was in charge of transport. Eddy Mitchell, who had the job before me, warned me that my work would essentially consist of going to the Montparnasse station to buy local newspapers from the entire western region of France because the commander was into horse racing and wanted the race results. Other than that, I did absolutely nothing.

A real cushy job.

That's right. And while I was doing my military service, Benayoun told me that he had to go on an assignment for *France Observateur*, where he published regularly. "Listen," he said to me. "I'm going to Los Angeles" – that's when he published his great travelogues, including stories of his meetings with Tex Avery – "and I can't go to the festival in Venice. Would you go in my place?" This was 1964. It was the final two months of my military service, when I was basically free of all duties but still officially in the military. I went to Venice and filed a report under my name, which was completely forbidden, because I wasn't allowed to leave France during military service. And moreover, I was writing for an anti-Gaullist newspaper! But I was proud to have something published in *France Observateur*. I wrote about Losey's *King and Country*, Antonioni's *Red Desert* and Godard's *A Married Woman*. This precipitated a second crisis, when Kyrou took me for a mole!

The editorial board

Did it take a while for you to become part of the editorial board?

I didn't officially join until 1966, but fairly quickly, maybe six months after my first article, I was attending editorial meetings with Benayoun. It was quite chaotic. There were lots of people coming in and out, like the filmmaker Ruy

Guerra, who was a friend of Michèle Firk.* *Positif* appeared only four or five times a year, which was more than in the 1950s, but not at all like today. Articles were assigned, but it's not as if we covered everything. The articles were read aloud in front of everyone on the committee, followed by jeering, depending on who was reading.

Who was Michèle Firk?

She was the only woman on the editorial board, a former IDHEC† student, a classmate of Annie Tresgot, with whom I later made two of my documentaries. Michèle was an activist. She was in the Communist Party, like Gérard Gozlan,‡ but she was a dissident and always pushed back. Like Paul-Louis Thirard,§ she carried suitcases for the FLN.¶ Before I got to *Positif*, many people who wrote for it had signed the Manifesto of the 121. Firk was close with Guerra, a radical political filmmaker from Mozambique who was living in Brazil. Eventually she left for Guatemala, where she died. When she was surrounded by the Guatemalan army, rather than being tortured and risk giving up her friends, she shot herself in the mouth. Michèle was very important to the landscape of *Positif* at the time.

Which critics were an influence on you?

Aside from *Positif*, I was impressed by Truffaut's articles. I didn't always agree with him, but the quality of his analysis, the way he talked about films, his breakdown of the storytelling – it was always wonderfully vivid. Jacques Rivette didn't write much, but his pieces on Fritz Lang and Preminger were wonderful. At *Positif* I had great respect for real writers, like the extremely structured, philosophical, conceptual thought of Louis Seguin, even if he was otherwise completely rigid in terms of taste. I also liked Kyrou's outbursts, including his books, which

---

* Michèle Firk (1937-1968). French film critic, contributor to *Positif*.
† Institut des hautes études cinématographiques, France's national film school, today called La Fémis (École Nationale Supérieure des Métiers de l'Image et du Son).
‡ Gérard Gozlan (1935-2017). Algerian-born French filmmaker, contributor to *Positif*.
§ Paul-Louis Thirard (1932-2017). French film critic, contributor to *Positif*.
¶ The Réseau Jeanson (Jeanson network), a group of French left-wing militants who helped Algerian National Liberation Front (FLN) agents operating in France during the Algerian War by carrying documents and money, were called "les porteurs de valises" ("suitcase carriers").

were steeped in Surrealism, like *Amour-Érotisme et Cinéma*. I found that kind of writing, which wasn't in the least scientific or historical, very stylish. I also liked the seriousness and attention to detail of Jacques Demeure,* who would read us these extraordinary texts, sometimes forty pages long, before disappearing into thin air with his manuscripts. We did our best to grab his notes before he left but he always insisted they weren't finished. Demeure, who had exceptional knowledge of Eastern European cinema, remains a mystery to me. He contributed some important articles to *Positif* but clearly had psychological problems. An unbelievable perfectionist, he was unable to actually finish anything. Paul-Louis Thirard had – and still has – a wonderful sense of humour, and I adore what he wrote about an invented imaginary country, Dubrovnie, and the imaginary filmmaker Maurice Burnan, as part of a questionnaire to which "serious" people like Boris Vian or Georges Sadoul responded. But the two personalities that fascinated me the most were undoubtedly Roger Tailleur and Robert Benayoun.

Tailleur and Benayoun

They didn't think alike.

They were definitely at odds, but still admired and respected each other. In the end they were the ones I felt closest to, but for different reasons. Benayoun had a sparkling, colourful style, full of metaphors. He was truly a master, as comfortable analysing Antonioni as he was writing about Resnais, Huston or Jerry Lewis, who he practically made famous in America. While Benayoun had good general knowledge, Roger Tailleur was unbeatable. He placed a lot of importance on Hollywood history, which he knew inside out and could discuss with real brilliance. While *Cahiers* writers were interested primarily in directors, Tailleur was somewhat unique because he focused on screenwriters. He could make connections between two Westerns made by different directors because they shared the same screenwriter. He could talk about musicals in relation to the choreographers or analyse the different studio cultures and explain the differences between RKO and MGM, and he had vast knowledge of literary and visual culture. His parents were farmers, and he was from an extremely modest

---

* Jacques Demeure (1929-2008). French film critic, contributor to *Positif*.

family. He had only a high school diploma and worked as a clerk at the Ministry of Higher Education. He had been a leftist his entire life but was shaken by May '68, by young bourgeois radicals who insisted that Jean Vilar* was a fascist, that everything had to be destroyed, this "let's wipe the slate clean" sensibility. He had gone to primary school, raised himself up, had read all the books and passed all the exams to get where he was, wrote for *Positif*, published magnificent works on Kazan and Antonioni, and was recognised by Truffaut, who regularly asked him to collaborate in *Arts*.† I think 1968 completely demoralised him – a bit like Pasolini at the time, who was also shocked and even took a provocative position by defending the CRS,‡ who were the sons of workers, against the demonstrators, who were the children of the bourgeoisie. Tailleur didn't go that far, but he was still quite shaken up. I remained good friends with him but after 1968 he shifted to painting and more or less stopped writing about cinema. He took buses – because he didn't drive – to find a particular fresco in a church in a small village in Umbria or Tuscany. He would go to the Louvre and summon a museum curator to tell him that the attribution of such and such a painting was wrong, and became an expert in the Sienese School. Frédéric Vitoux wrote a beautiful book about him in 1986, *Il me semble désormais que Roger est en Italie*, in which he writes about all this.

Auteur policy or auteur theory?

The New Wave had already passed when you began writing criticism, but there was still something new in the air.

In 2012, for the sixtieth anniversary of *Positif*, we played a little game. Each writer was asked to say what had impressed them about the films made the year he or she joined. I said that for me, in 1963, there was a kind of retreat from the central axis of New Wave Cinema – Truffaut, Godard, etc. Personally, I really liked *Breathless* – unlike *Positif* – and *The 400 Blows*. I don't think there was a Truffaut film in 1963. Chabrol released *Ophélia* and *Bluebeard* that year, and Godard came out with *Les Carabiniers* and, in December, *Le*

---

* Jean Vilar (1912–1971). French actor and theatre director, attacked in 1968 for being too "bourgeois."
† Weekly magazine that promoted the French New Wave filmmakers.
‡ Compagnies républicaines de sécurité, the riot control branch of the French National Police.

Mépris. But for me, the year wasn't marked by these films. What did strike me, however, was Italian cinema. The line is that the New Wave changed everything in the early '60s, but for me Francesco Rosi, with his film *Salvatore Giuliano*, which was eventually released in France, then *Hands Over the City*, made much more of an impact than the French New Wave ever did. There was also Fellini's *8½* and Visconti's *The Leopard*, Risi's *The Easy Life* and Marco Ferreri's *The Conjugal Bed*, Olmi's *Il posto* and Zurlini's *Family Diary*. Those films are among the most beautiful of the decade. On the other hand, without denying the importance of the New Wave, I very much appreciated its "left bank" tendency – the filmmakers who weren't considered the hard core and were nicknamed because they were more left-wing and frequented the Left Bank, while the *Cahiers* offices were on the Champs-Élysées and were more right-wing. As far as "young French cinema" went, around the same time we got Resnais' *Muriel*, *Les Abysses* by Nikos Papatakis, Rozier's *Adieu Philippine* and Marker's *Le Joli Mai*, Varda's *Cléo from 5 to 7* and Demy's *La Baie des Anges*, *Le Feu follet* by Louis Malle, *The Suitor* by Pierre Etaix, and Michel Deville's *À cause, à cause d'une femme*.

Did the auteur theory of Cahiers du cinéma influence all contemporary criticism, including Positif?

That's just the same old rehashed falsehood, which stems from Godard's audacious, self-promotional outbursts, things like, "*Cahiers du cinéma* ont imposé l'auteur, qui avant nous n'était pas considéré." ["*Cahiers du cinéma* introduced the concept of the auteur, which didn't previously exist"]. In fact, the auteur was acknowledged as far back as the 1920s.

The director as author of a film?

Between 1921, with Louis Delluc's creation of *Cinéa*, through to 1928, with Jean-Georges Auriol's *La Revue du cinéma*, the precursors of journals from the 1950s, what were people reading? Portraits, interviews, statements, studies of DeMille, Stroheim, Lubitsch, Sternberg and Chaplin. There's even an issue of *La Revue du cinéma* from 1930 on King Vidor and *Hallelujah!* with texts by André Gide, Darius Milhaud and Michel Leiris – all major intellectuals of the time. European directors – Dreyer, Sjöström, Stiller, Eisenstein, Dovzhenko, Pudovkin, Lang, Murnau, Pabst, René Clair, Gance, Epstein – were all discussed. The framework was right there in front of us. *Positif* was a continuation of this kind of criticism of the 1920s, and people like Ado Kyrou were its heirs. When Kyrou writes about Sternberg's personal universe, for example, he's referring to the texts of the Surrealists, like Artaud and Desnos. So the auteur theory dates from the 1920s. It asserts that in the best of examples – and this is what I believe myself – the director is the dominant creative force of a film. This is what cinema should aspire to, without overlooking everyone else who contributes to the making of a film. Right up to today, *Positif* has acknowledged the role played by production designers, composers, screenwriters, producers, editors, sound engineers, not to mention actors – all of whom are at the service of the director. Great technicians, like actors, know this. They acknowledge the director as the primary creator, the conductor of a film. The difference is that for *Cahiers* critics, it was more a political stance than anything else. And then, when Andrew Sarris brought the baggage of *Cahiers* to America, he made use of a curious semantic shift, in that he didn't talk about "the auteur policy" but "the auteur theory." From the moment that this deviated into the notion that an auteur is never wrong, and that an auteur's latest work is his or her best, then all bets are off. Jean Renoir's *Le Petit Théâtre* is more important than *Rules of the Game*? The worst film by an auteur, like Jacques Becker's *Ali Baba and the Forty Thieves*, will always be better than the best film by an "artisan" like *Knave of Hearts* by René Clément or *La Vérité sur Bébé Donge* by Henri Decoin? That just doesn't hold water. It was really a "policy," in the sense that the objective of political discourse is always there to sweeten the pill, to promise what can't be delivered. It was a power play. But we really have to stop with this idea that it wasn't until the 1950s that the director was recognised as the true auteur of a film.

Meeting a master

Fritz Lang was the first "veteran" you met for Positif, *someone who dates back to the silent era.*

I have a clear memory of that meeting, which included Louis Seguin, Roger Tailleur and Goffredo Fofi. It was in 1967, during one of my first trips to Venice, where several *Positif* critics were part of a round table on expressionism. Lang was sarcastic: "The table isn't round and there is no such thing as expressionism in cinema!" Like many artists, he didn't like being pigeonholed. With him was his old friend and future biographer Lotte Eisner, from the Cinémathèque française. She was a wonderful old Jewish lady who had emigrated to Paris in the early 1930s and later worked with Langlois and wrote important books on Murnau and Lang. Lang mocked Eisner, really quite cruelly, asking her to define expressionism. "I'm not asking you for a definition in relation to impressionism," he told her. "I'm just asking you what expressionism is." On leaving the Hotel Excelsior, still quite excited after having met Lang, who I considered to be a genius, I ran into Ulrich Gregor, one of the great left-wing historians of post-war Germany. He wrote a history of cinema with a Marxist bent, and later ran the Berlinale Forum. Overwhelmed, with the enthusiasm of a young man, I told him, "I just met Fritz Lang!" I was taken aback by Gregor's response: "You know how obnoxious he is to his housekeeper?" It's certainly important to treat our housekeepers well. As Sacha Guitry said, "nul n'est un héros pour son valet de chambre" ["No one is a hero to his valet"]. Reducing Lang – director of *Metropolis*, *M*, *The Big Heat* and *You Only Live Once* – to such nasty behaviour seemed a bit reductive, but from a Marxist point of view made good sense.

How did he behave to the young French cinephiles who so venerated him?

I met him several times afterwards, thanks to Pierre Rissient, who was kind of Lang's *cicerone*, notably at the San Sebastian festival. He was an affable man with a sense of humour, but you could tell he had a certain self-importance. He was certainly no longer the tyrannical Lang that Mankiewicz told me about later, who terrorised people on the set of *Fury*, where at 2.30 in the afternoon Spencer Tracy said to him, "I think we could take a lunch break" and Lang replied, "*I* decide when we break for lunch." Tracy immediately wiped off his makeup and shouted, "Lunch!" Lang was still working as if he was at UFA in the 1920s, with a whip, boots and monocle. This attitude didn't go down to well in the United States because there were unions and the way of doing things was more Anglo-Saxon than Germanic. In any case, Lang changed in his old age. It had been years since he had directed anything, and the French critics had rehabilitated his American films. He was very flattered by this kind of recognition because he no longer had any real standing in the United States.

Years later you wrote a monograph about him for the Découvertes Gallimard *series.*

No easy task that, because the number of scholarly works about him is overwhelming. My aim was to write a book which would explore, through its visuals, Lang's connections to expressionist painting and architecture, for example the Viennese architect Adolf Loos. The Découvertes collection made that underlying cultural backdrop possible.

A change in continuity

Lang is one of the great veterans who is claimed by both Cahiers *and* Positif. *But in the initial antagonism between the two journals, each had their preferred auteurs. I gather your arrival at* Positif *shook things up somewhat.*

It did, yes, which makes sense, because of my particular starting point, the fact that I read both *Cahiers* and *Positif*, and, as I mentioned, admired Hitchcock as much as Huston. There was also an overall evolution of criticism, which meant that the new *Positif* contributors didn't much care about those old feuds. We were a long way from 1954, when a ridiculous text appeared anonymously in *Positif* – probably by Raymond Borde, though there's no proof of this – which had been scribbled on a tabletop and given a green light: a list of overrated directors, including seven or eight of the greatest American filmmakers of that time. Subsequently in *Positif* there were dossiers on many directors who weren't widely appreciated when the journal began, like Jacques Tourneur, Hawks, Hitchcock and Preminger.

Among those new writers was Gérard Legrand.

A great friend of mine who arrived just before me, in 1962. He was ten years older than me and had written for *L'Âge du cinéma*, a small Surrealist journal edited by Benayoun and Kyrou which lasted only six issues between 1951 and 1952. It joined forces with *Positif*, which left Lyon and moved to Paris. After Bernard Chardère left to do his military service with his friends from Lyon, Kyrou and Seguin, among others, took over and *Positif* became Parisian. Legrand, meanwhile, had practically stopped writing. He was contributing poetry and prose to various Surrealist journals before later returning to film criticism, contributing to *Positif* and *Présence du cinéma*, another film journal of the period which emerged from the Mac-Mahon circle.* Along with Tailleur, he provided great support during certain disagreements within *Positif*. These weren't battles fought tooth and nail because ultimately decisions were made through voting. We later brought in writers from different backgrounds, like Frédéric Vitoux, who became very well known. *Positif* was evolving. People like Kyrou who loved American cinema had narrowed it to a small group of names like Welles, Huston and a few others because they were fixated on the constraints of the studio system and how it held people back. Perhaps the new writers overcorrected. It seems justified to rehabilitate Fritz Lang's American films and claim Blake Edwards as a great filmmaker, but are Hugo Fregonese and Edgar Ulmer really fully-fledged auteurs?

After May 1968, Cahiers went through a radical Maoist period.

They pretty much gave up on film criticism, and at one point weren't even mentioning the names of films. What's bizarre is that when they declared the death of the auteur, which they were supposed to have created, it was the names of the critics who were on the cover. There were still auteurs, but they were the authors of the articles…

Our May '68

Did that kind of extremism ever infect Positif?

No, we never changed so radically. I think it's fair to say that *Positif* has retained its leftist tendencies: anti-imperialist, anti-Stalinist, anti-fascist, totally in sync with the May '68 movement. It has accomplished what the Surrealist movement, in its own covert way, set out to create. In the 1950s, Breton – who died two years before May '68 – said that Surrealism had to be downplayed. He succeeded in that, and it took people like me to reawaken interest in the movement, which had vanished from the mainstream. No one mentioned it anymore. They were selling five hundred copies of their publications. Even Pauvert's quality journals, like *Le Surréalisme*, or *La Brèche* and Losfeld's *Médium*, didn't sell.

---

* The Mac-Mahon group of cinephiles, including Bertrand Tavernier and Pierre Rissient, was named in the 1950s after the cinema located on the Avenue des Champs-Élysées where they often met.

The libertarianism of the May '68 movement, the *amour fou* promoted by Kyrou, the humour, subversion and anarchism, the criticism of institutions, the popular culture and graffiti – *Positif* loved all that. The Communist Party put the brakes on the movement as much as possible because it wasn't in control, leading to the Matignon agreements,* which got people back to work. As for the Maoists, rather than slowing down they sped up, moving ever faster towards a kind of radicalisation. For me, someone like Cohn-Bendit† is perhaps the most coherent and lucid French politician of the last forty-five years because he's the only one who isn't after power, while most everyone else is, and are always so calculated in what they say. Cohn-Bendit is free to speak his mind.

There was always a rejection of dogma at *Positif*, of belief in a single interpretive framework: semiology, structuralism, Leninist Marxism, Lacanism, all these successive ways of reading the world. *Positif* never experienced this blind ideological approach. We have published authors who draw from psychoanalytic, political, sociological and aesthetic perspectives, depending on their personality and training, but there has never been a rallying cry to any exclusive method.

In April 1973, I went with Marc Ferro‡ to a conference organised by Oberlin College in Washington D.C. to represent the French university system. At the time, semiology, deconstruction, structuralism – in short, French theoretical philosophy – were all the rage in America. Just before leaving Paris, I bought Roland Barthes' *The Pleasure of the Text* which had just appeared and in which he made a 180-degree turn. After the "scientism" of semiology, this wondrous little book marked a return to subjectivity. I translated two or three pages into English so I could present it at the colloquium. I let the American specialists speak for a day and a half, then read them Barthes' eulogy to subjectivity. They were bewildered, and wondered if it wasn't a fake, some sort of trick I was playing on them.

At the end of the 1960s, you gained more influence at Positif. *At the same time, antagonisms between* Cahiers *and* Positif *shifted. As* Cahiers *became more isolated,* Positif *took the opportunity to assert itself.*

---

* Accords de Matignon (1936) gave workers a forty-hour week and two weeks of paid vacation.
† Daniel Cohn-Bendit (b.1945). Student leader in 1968, leader of Greens–European Free Alliance in the European Parliament.
‡ Marco Ferro (1923-2021). French historian.

Yes. What has worked in *Positif*'s favour, and what helped establish its reputation abroad – *Variety* called it "by far the best film magazine in Europe" – is that, despite its evolution, it always maintained a consistent position on things. In my opinion, what may have saved *Positif* was that its writers didn't become filmmakers, while *Cahiers* has been, if not a school, at least a stepping stone into directing. With each generation at *Cahiers*, a group left to make films, and each time fresh blood was needed. The result has been differences – ruptures and gaps from one generation to the next. There are very few connections between *Cahiers* Maoists and the *Cahiers* of Rohmer. As Truffaut once said in a documentary to Serge Toubiana, "You should have changed your name." On the other hand, I don't think – and Bernard Chardère, who founded *Positif*, is witness to this – that there is any noticeable shift between the editorial published in the very first issue of *Positif* and the one in number 660.

International *Positif*

Let's define your position more carefully.

I think it was first about creating an "international list." The first ten years of *Cahiers* were marked by the domination of American and French culture, while at *Positif* from the outset there was a genuine openness to all kinds of film culture, especially from Italy, which was expressed as an immediate interest in Visconti and Antonioni. The first dossier on Antonioni published anywhere, including Italy, was in *Positif* in 1958. The same goes for Poland – *Positif* published early pieces on Kawalerowicz, Wajda and Munk – and Latin America and England. There has always been a certain natural curiosity at *Positif*. The list of people we've published includes a lot of foreigners. Paulo Antônio Paranaguá, for example, a Brazilian exile in France who escaped the politics of his homeland, where he had been a member of the Surrealists, became a member of the editorial board. Thomas Elsaesser, Jan Aghed from Sweden, and Mark Le Fanu, an Englishman, were all frequent contributors. Before them were Lorenzo Codelli and Goffredo Fofi, who helped popularise Italian comedy and Westerns. Petr Král, who was involved with Czech Surrealism, wrote about silent slapstick cinema, Wim Wenders and Antonioni. This kind of open-mindedness and curiosity, these contributions from outsiders, reflect certain characteristics of *Positif*, which once again align with Surrealism – inherently an international movement.

Style matters

Is there a particular way of writing for Positif?

What characterises the writing is a rejection of jargon and inflexible theorising. There are some articles that touch on film theory, and these days we have a section entitled "Chantier de réflexion," which deals with issues of criticism, narration, images, new trends, various interdisciplinary movements – none of which are pure theory. Personally, I'm sceptical about the role of criticism in dictating what cinema should be. Film critics can't say that henceforth cinema *must* be atonal or melodic. From now on cinema *must* be deconstructed. From now on cinema *must* be optimistic. From now on cinema *must* be lyrical. No! Cinema *is*, and it will *become* whatever it wants to be. It isn't up to the critic to announce such things. He can reflect on the evolution of cinema and possibly deplore trends. The critic must, of course, express an opinion, but he's there to observe, analyse and possibly judge what's happening, not to impose guidelines, otherwise we end up with what happened at one point in painting, when critics decreed that painting could no longer be anything but abstract, that the figurative no longer existed, and as a result museums in France stopped buying Morandi, Bacon, Hopper and Balthus – all the painters who today we consider the equals of Manessier and Bissière, or perhaps even superior to the French school of abstraction which cluttered the picture rails because "that was painting" at the time, after the war. No! Hopper exists, and so does Pollock. You might prefer Pollock and be able to explain why, but that's different from an outright rejection of figurative painting. These dictates are extremely harmful because they lead to conformity and, among the young, the desire to imitate. How many imitators of Antonioni or Godard or Bresson have there been? That's the danger. *Positif* has never worked within a theoretical model of cinema. It has always tried to draw lessons from the films themselves. Let the artists issue manifestos – of Surrealism, Lettrism, Futurism. That isn't the job of critics.

Does Positif *deliberately avoid this inflexible theorising?*

No, I wouldn't say that there's some kind of masterplan behind this rejection of trends. *Positif* is appreciated and recognised by professionals, by filmmakers, by historians and critics, but it's never been exactly synchronous with the spirit of the times. It's never been the journal that everyone reads. It doesn't ride the waves of the zeitgeist. I think that's an important distinction. It's a group of individuals, which means there is no *Positif* "style." I remember that in *Time* and *Newsweek* at a certain point the articles had no bylines because they were all rewritten in the same style. At *Positif*, if there is a shared spiritual kinship, there are still diverse ways of writing and varied sensitivities. That's always been the case. Even the approaches of Legrand and Benayoun, both with a background in Surrealism, were totally different. We're back to the rejection of one-track thinking, to pluralism, and to what I call democracy.

At Positif, *would you say there's more of a "critic-writer" tendency rather than a "critic-director" one?*

You could say that. Frédéric Vitoux, who became a novelist and essayist and was elected to the Académie Française, proves that *Positif* can lead anyone anywhere, provided they break away. Emmanuel Carrière started at *Positif* at the age of nineteen and today is one of the best writers in France. Petr Král has written poetry for Flammarion, as well as travel books, and his essays on cinema are also literary essays. Legrand assisted Breton with *L'Art magique*. He might, in fact, have written a good part of it himself. He published many books of poetry and essays, including on Breton himself. Benayoun wrote plays, but like Kyrou he also made films, the first of which, *Paris n'existe pas*, made quite a splash. Jean-Philippe Domecq has written about twenty books plus political essays and even novels. More recently Noël Herpe, a former member of the editorial board, has published several memoirs and a biography of Rohmer. Adrien Gombeaud wrote a book on Tiananmen Square and another on photographer Ed Feingersh and his relationship with Marilyn Monroe. The array of writers who have contributed to *Positif* is partly explained by its multidisciplinary nature, which has always been linked to the other arts, in particular literature. There's a sense of emulation because, in fact, *Positif*'s critics are former readers. You don't get into *Positif* by sending the same message – like a throwing a bottle overboard – to ten different editors. Without our knowing it, new writers who are welcomed in have been reading us for three, five, ten years. That creates a conducive atmosphere. And if they read *Positif*, it isn't only for the opinions expressed but also for its spirit and distinctive style of its writers. A person who reads a journal like *Positif*, with its page after page of lengthy articles, is a person who enjoys reading. I get the feeling that these days some people buy *Cahiers* but don't actually read it. They pick it up out of habit because they think they have to have a copy at home. It's a must-have for cinephiles, a reference point. But the people who buy *Positif* really take an interest and actually read it, especially since we're rarely mentioned in the press, except occasionally in *Les Inrocks*. Our readers appreciate the quality of writing.

The interview as criticism

Interviewing began early for you, more or less at the same time you became a critic. There is a tradition at Positif *that interviews are conducted by more than one person.*

That's true, although I have done many on my own. My book *Une renaissance américaine* contains thirty of them, half of them done by me alone, the other half with people like Hubert Niogret, Michael Wilson and you. At *Positif*, for technical and practical reasons, we often do interviews together. The technical reasons are that it's always better to have two recorders because breakdowns sometimes happen. It's happened to you, and it's happened to me, as it has to almost everyone at least once, that you do an interview and then have to start over again. The second reason is that while you're answering a question, the other interviewer is listening and thinking about the next question, which allows for a more constructive, richer exchange. Two interviewers bring more ideas to the table than just one. That said, it's true that I have been very gung ho when it comes to doing interviews for *Positif*.

Were you inspired by the lengthy interviews published by Cahiers *during its yellow period?*

There's no doubt that *Cahiers* was doing it first – thanks to Rivette, Truffaut, Domarchi, Bitsch, Chabrol, Rohmer and others. The entire future New Wave did a lot of interviews, something made possible starting in the mid-1950s with the emergence of portable tape recorders, which replaced much bulkier machines. It's understandable because these writers wanted to be directors and were curious to find out how films were actually made. *Positif* occasionally published interviews, but it was only in the mid-1960s that we began to do more of it. It so happened that in the 1970s, when *Cahiers* went almost underground – swearing allegiance to *The Red Detachment of Women*, Straub, Godard and the Dziga Vertov group – they practically stopped interviewing. *Positif* developed a reputation among cinephiles for publishing detailed interviews, three or four in every issue, by people who knew the history of cinema and the industry, and who were able to ask intelligent questions.

Good and not-so-good interviewees

We talked about maieutics when discussing Deleuze's philosophy classes. Is there sometimes, among certain interviewees, an almost therapeutic need to express themselves?

Absolutely. You can see that kind of thing in many *Positif* interviews. Directors often like to be interviewed by us early on because it enables them to sharpen their ideas. They know that the questions we put to them will be focused, which can lead to elaborate answers, and they get to see early responses to their film, which prepares them for future interviews. It's undeniable that the kind of questions we ask the directors we interview push them to discover things about themselves. Cinema is an extremely complex art – artistically, technically, economically, as a forum for collaboration, and even more at the level of meaning. A critic can dig into a film and unearth much more than what the director might themselves have to say. Many filmmakers have no interest in analysing their own work. The Coen brothers, for example, are extremely reluctant to do so. Just as there are great theoretical painters – Delacroix, Kandinsky, Paul Klee all spoke admirably about their craft – there are many artists who prefer to keep quiet. Writers, because of their job, tend to be more analytical about their work. But they have only a pen and paper, or a computer, and a painter has a canvas. The way a film comes into existence can be such a complicated affair that, given what I've learned from all the reading and interviewing I've done over the years, I would never talk about cinema the same way I did back when I was eighteen and watching films at Les Agriculteurs. I'm much more precise about things today. For example, someone wrote that the best footage shot by Kubrick was the first ten minutes of *Spartacus*. But actually, Kubrick didn't shoot the first ten minutes – Anthony Mann did. Through interviews so much is uncovered: the ups and downs of production, the compromises made, the cuts that have been imposed, the contributions of the set designer, the actors, the cinematographer, the editor. A film is such a complicated undertaking that it bears no relation to other arts. Interviewing filmmakers is important because those kinds of conversations shed light on the work.

An interviewee who doesn't like to talk can be a handful.

Stephen Frears, for instance, has a knack for dodging questions. Having interviewed him many times and having known him for so many years, I'll say something that no one else would dare say: "Stephen, listen – I'm here to do an interview. Make an effort. Please try to answer my questions!" And at that moment he relents. The Coen brothers too. They're really quite uncooperative when it comes to interviews.

Surely some like to talk.

Peter Greenaway and David Cronenberg have a real talent for self-analysis. Greenaway has prepared speeches which he adapts to any questions asked of him. Like Nabokov, he ideally wants to be given the questions in advance so he can write out his responses. That's not something I'm willing to do. You see this contrast in literature, too. There are writers, and even painters, who analyse their own work wonderfully, and then there are others who don't keep their distance. Greenaway represents a baffling trend for the English, who usually prefer realism. British critics never quite figured out how to handle directors like Michael Powell, John Boorman, Peter Greenaway and Terry Gilliam, who is American by birth. They belong to an eccentric current that has always existed in English literature and which was somewhat suppressed by Victorian Puritanism. From Shakespeare to Swift, via William Blake, the Gothic novel, Lewis Carroll, Mervyn Peake – there's a strong esoteric, almost surreal English tradition. It's much less accepted in the cinema, except perhaps in comedy, like the Ealing classics. British criticism, on the other hand, places above all else the realist vein that began with the documentary school of the 1930s, continued by Free Cinema fiction and non-fiction, then by Ken Loach and others. Alongside this you have what they call "heritage films," usually literary or theatrical adaptations, which make someone like James Ivory appear English when he's actually American. On the other hand, those who the Americans call "mavericks" – the eccentrics who don't run with the herd, who roam the countryside on their own, who belong to no one – have always struggled to establish themselves. Greenaway had this problem, although he sort of brought it on himself by declaiming that everything other than his own filmmaking is worthless. Unless you're ready for a very meagre menu of exclusively Greenaway, if you had to choose between him and everything else, you would pick everything else. Stephen Frears made a documentary about British cinema to celebrate its hundredth birthday, and Greenaway wasn't included. I consider him an important artist nonetheless.

Dealing with disappointment

Is it possible to maintain impartiality when it comes to filmmakers you have been writing about for years?

Positif has stayed true to a guiding principle, to the point where some people have mistakenly thought that we are unconditionally devoted to certain filmmakers. It's not our fault if Kubrick's work is now almost universally accepted as a unified whole. We championed *The Shining* and *Full Metal Jacket* at a time when they were reviled by many critics. And if you look at Buñuel's career as a whole, there are very few missteps. At the same time, we didn't hold back by suggesting that his first Mexican films aren't as important as the others. When John Huston missed the mark with a film like *Escape to Victory*, we wrote about it. I remember an English journalist who was flown to Canada at the studio's expense to cover the shooting of Huston's *Phobia*, which was financed through a tax shelter. She asked Huston what his favourite film was. "It's hard to say," he said, "although I know that my least favourite is the one I'm shooting now." Artists can be insightful. Unfortunately, not all of them have Huston's sense of humour.

There are auteurs whose careers have been disappointing.

We've given up on some of them along the way. In recent years we've started to find Andrzej Wajda interesting again. *Tatarak* and *Katyn* seemed like a return to form, but for twenty years, when he was making films on commission and academic literary adaptations, we more or less ignored him. We liked Alain Tanner's *La Salamandre* and *Charles, Dead or Alive*, and even two or three other later films, but ended up leaving him behind. Glauber Rocha played table football with me at festivals. We often had dinner together and exchanged correspondence when he was in political exile, and I wrote the preface to *Terre em transe* when it was published in *L'Avant-scène*. But my feelings changed completely with *The Lion Has Seven Heads* and *Cutting Heads*. I was on the jury in Venice in 1980 with Suso Cecchi d'Amico, Margarethe von Trotta and Umberto Eco. Rocha's *The Age of the Earth* was in competition, but didn't win anything. Irvin Kershner came over from the Hotel Excelsior and said, "There's a rather rustic-looking guy, very tanned, standing on an armchair in the lobby of the Excelsior and insulting you, saying you're a CIA agent and that Suso Cecchi d'Amico is Visconti's whore and that Umberto Eco is all smoke and mirrors. Who is it?" I walk over there and find Glauber ranting at me and the others because he hadn't been given a prize. These things happen. *Positif* has stopped giving its support to certain directors who once mattered. In 1970, for example, Bertrand Tavernier – who was a critic then – and I did what is probably the longest interview that John Frankenheimer ever gave. In the 1960s, he was one of the best American directors, but then he fell apart before recovering towards the end of his life with *Path to War*. Carlos Saura was a great Spanish filmmaker who came after Buñuel and before Almodóvar. We backed him, we did seven or eight interviews, we put his films on the cover. But apart from his flamenco films – which are very well made – our interest waned. There are many other filmmakers I could mention, but it would be embarrassing for them.

Some might perceive that as a betrayal or abandonment.

One day I received an insult-laden letter from Gérard Blain, calling me all sorts of names. I hadn't liked his film *Pierre and Djemila*, though I had ardently defended him before and written articles praising his earlier films. He was unimaginably nasty. That kind of thing doesn't happen very often. He must have been extremely upset to write something like that.

I don't understand how anyone could accuse us of being unconditional in our praise, although some people find it strange that we love all of Sautet's films. But tell me: which of his films is bad? There are some less accomplished than others, but a bad Sautet film – I don't know of any. So why not stand up for him? Meanwhile there are Truffaut films that are duds. I admit that we can be wrong. We have made more than a few mistakes. But we must have enough intellectual honesty to be willing to tell someone we don't like their film, even if we know them very well. It's important to explain the reasons for our disappointment, which sometimes isn't easy. But that's *Positif*'s way of doing things.

Sometimes the disappointment is temporary and doesn't prevent Positif *writers from following up on a director.*

I had an experience with Wong Kar-wai that sheds light on the relationship critics should have with filmmakers, which is to say: complete freedom. The first films of his that I saw, I really liked: *Chungking Express* at Locarno, then in Venice the same year *Ashes of Time*, a martial arts film with a somewhat obscure narrative but astonishing craftsmanship. I did a long interview with him in Venice about his early career. The following year, I arranged an interview with him in Berlin, but then I saw his film *Fallen Angels*, which just wasn't as good as his previous films. We were supposed to meet at a bar in Berlin. "We need to talk," I told him. "I can't do the interview because I won't publish it. Your film was a disappointment. I'm looking forward to your next films." And I explained why. He still remembers that conversation, which wasn't pleasant for either of us, but I think it's important to say what needs to be said with absolute honesty. Then he made *Happy Together*, about a gay Chinese couple from Hong Kong who reunite in Argentina, which I thought was dazzling and which won the Best Director award at Cannes. And *In the Mood for Love*, of course, deserved more than just an acting award, but was successful around the world. I have followed him since, right up to *The Grandmaster* in 2013, a return to martial arts cinema with even greater scope and success than *Ashes of Time*.

Friendships with filmmakers

Can friendship with a director be compromising for a film critic?

I'm not afraid to burn bridges. I would write to Glauber Rocha telling him why I no longer liked his films, and before becoming completely paranoid towards the end of his life, he would respond with great dignity. His long letters, which I found and were published in Brazil in a volume of correspondence, were quite beautiful. It was a real dialogue we had, in which he explained himself. If he had made eight films like *Black God, White Devil* or *Terre em transe*, I would have written a book with Glauber Rocha. I might have also written a book about Frankenheimer if he had made other great films after the 1960s and 1970s. But it wasn't to be. I think I'm quite open-minded about all this, but it's true that perhaps we're more forgiving about someone's work when we know them personally. If it comes to that, you just have to make a decision. Either you never conduct interviews, you just sit in your ivory tower and don't meet anyone, you don't go to festivals, you don't have lunch with filmmakers, you refuse to see them, worried that you might establish a connection or find them too friendly when you no longer have the same views about them. Or you go out and meet people and do interviews and discuss things with them so you can get a better grip on how they make their films, even if it means at some point breaking things off. I've gone through a few breakups with people I used to see very often because I no longer like their films. It actually happens quite a lot. Some filmmakers continue to make remarkable films, but some hit a rough patch. But look, maybe I'm wrong and they're right. There are films by Tavernier that I like less than others, for example *Spoiled Children* and *Holy Lola*, even though I hold many of his films in very high regard.

It's certainly possible to maintain strong friendships. Kiarostami, for example, who I met in Locarno. I think I was the first person from Western Europe to interview him. He was showing a film, and we were on the jury together the following year. I took advantage of the fact that we got on. He was reluctant to do interviews, but it was one of his first trips to the west and we recorded a lengthy conversation. I ended up interviewing him quite frequently, sometimes with Stéphane Goudet, until I was disappointed by his Italian film, *Certified Copy*. There was no sense in that film of his exceptional sensitivity as a painter of Iranian landscapes. "Listen, Michel," he told me. "Maybe in ten years I'll tell you that you were right. Or maybe you'll tell me I was right." It was very classy of him, which is how it should be between a filmmaker and a critic. It's hard for a filmmaker to deal with a critic who has supported him from the start but who then disengages. You spend three years making a film that means a lot to you, and the critical judgements are handed down in a matter of hours. I can understand that. But as Billy Wilder used to say, if you care about whether the public or the critics liked one of your films, then you can hardly say they're wrong when they don't like another one. Do that and you're basically saying their opinions are worthless, which means their praise doesn't count for anything either.

When you see the latest film by a filmmaker you know, do you tell them if you didn't like it?

If they ask. I found Luis Bacalov's music for Rosi's *The Truce* quite pompous, for example, and told Rosi so. The same for Boorman. I saw an early cut of *Beyond Rangoon* without music. It's a good film, but not one of his best. The score by Hans Zimmer that was added really weighs it down. But films aren't always made under the same conditions, and filmmakers don't necessarily have the freedom they once had. Many filmmakers of the 1970s don't experience the same kind of drive and excitement, nor the same trust that producers used to put in them, that they had when they were young, which may explain why their films are less interesting. For Boorman, *Beyond Rangoon* and *In My Country*, about South Africa, or even – although it's a much more personal film – *The Tiger's Tail*, are undeniably not at the level of *Point Blank*, *Leo the Last*, *Deliverance* or *Excalibur*. The economic conditions of cinema have changed, especially in the west. When Altman made his television films *The Laundromat* and *Vincent and Theo* in Paris, he had neither the same freedom, nor the same budget, nor the same possibilities as when he made *The Long Goodbye* or *Nashville*.

Ties to films of the past

Another key Positif *characteristic is an interest in film history.*

Positif was born out of this idea. Very early on, our founder, Bernard Chardère, published a special issue on Jean Vigo, who had already been dead for twenty years. That kind of thing, that gesture of appreciation, was groundbreaking, with no equivalent anywhere. Nothing had been written about Vigo. It all boils down to the idea that all those young people brought with them from the provinces, a year after *Cahiers* was created, the idea that cinema should be considered an art. Just as with literature there is still a lot to be said about Baudelaire and Montaigne, not just contemporary authors, similarly with cinema we delve into the past. Alongside the exploration and explication of new filmmakers, which has always been one of *Positif*'s strengths, there is indeed considerable effort to rediscover the history of cinema. The present leads to a re-reading of the past. It isn't set in stone. In painting, for example, it was only after Cubism emerged that people started taking an interest in Piero della

Francesca, who had been overlooked for so long. Countless painters and writers are re-evaluated because they resonate with today's sensibilities. It's the same for cinema. Consider, for example, the rediscovery of Keaton in the 1950s long after he had been eclipsed by Chaplin. When *Positif* did an issue on Capra in the early 1970s, he was a somewhat forgotten filmmaker. The publication of his memoirs was an opportunity for rediscovery. This happens everywhere, all the time, of course. Very little is known about Italian cinema of the Mussolini era, for example – the melodramas of Poggioli, the comedies of Camerini. It's so important that we explore in all directions. No one ever says, "I read an old novel by Stendhal or an old poem by Baudelaire," but too often you hear, "I saw an old film on television." Cinema is looked upon as an art of the present, which is a mistake, because great cinema from the past is still very much alive. When we watch films from seventy or eighty years ago, it's sometimes surprising how modern and daring they are, even more so than much of what is produced today.

There's this idea of forging film culture as a literary or music critic might. In one of your first articles, on Minnelli's The Pirate, *you criticise the critics for not having taken Minnelli's previous films into account when writing about the film.*

Absolutely. Truffaut's famous phrase "Il faut s'habituer à l'idée qu'on sera jugé par des gens qui n'ont jamais vu *L'Aurore* de Murnau" ["Get used to being judged by people who have never seen Murnau's *Sunrise*"] would never apply to literature. It's unthinkable that a literary critic would never have read Balzac, Rabelais or Shakespeare. One of the reasons why *Positif* has been able to maintain some continuity is that future contributors, who are currently readers, are interested in classic cinema, which a good chunk of each issue – about a quarter to a third – is dedicated to. These future writers arrive with a solid foundation in film culture and a real desire to rediscover the past, which makes it easy for them to blend in. Don't forget that *Positif*'s sales have increased significantly – compared to forty or fifty years ago, the number of readers has tripled – because DVD, cable TV and now the internet have changed the way people read about cinema. It's a whole new game. When I began writing film criticism, I talked with young writers from *Cahiers* who were my age, like Jean-Louis Comolli or Jean Narboni. They came from Algiers, where the film club, run by Barthélemy Amengual, showed films that weren't easy to see. *The Rules of the Game*, for example, played once every two years at the Cinémathèque, and you absolutely had to be there, because if you missed it, there was no other way to see the film. I was lucky to have already seen it, but anyone who arrived late was out of luck. Nowadays, with all the available resources, film enthusiasts can get their hands on these films, though that doesn't necessarily mean there's any kind of burgeoning film culture today. In the Soviet Union, where everything was censored and finding books was difficult, there was still a substantial literary culture. Once it becomes like a supermarket, with thousands of films being offered to "consumers," the sheer volume can be overwhelming. But I think this phenomenon has significantly changed the way people read a journal like *Positif*. We can include articles on William Wellman or Vincente Minnelli, Jacques Becker or Chris Marker, Oshima or neorealism, because these days most of the films are accessible, so the articles are generally about films which readers have already seen.

A journal without an editor

To come back to the peculiarities of Positif, *it's a journal without an editor, but you are the "directeur de publication." ["head of publication"] What's the difference?*

"Directeur de publication" is a purely legal term. The law requires any periodical to appoint an editor-in-chief because in cases of defamation, bankruptcy or misconduct, he is held responsible. I don't want to show false modesty, but some *Positif* writers have been more active than others. When I started it was clear that Benayoun was one of the driving forces. The meetings took place at his house. He knew a lot of people and was always travelling everywhere. Nobody had any problems with this – it was just how things were. It's true that the fact of having written books, my experience, my connections, might make it easier for me to weigh in on certain things. But regardless, at no point in *Positif*'s history have decisions about its contents ever been made by a single person.

Can you explain how it works?

Usually with a film journal the editor goes to see a film before everyone else, on his own, sometimes when it's still a rough cut, and walks out saying it's going to be on the cover of the next issue. That kind of thing would never happen at

Positif. There are usually at least four or five of us who have seen a film before it's selected for the cover and a preview screening. For almost twenty years we've been doing monthly previews for our subscribers at the Forum des Images, where Laurence Herzberg is a trusted accomplice. So it's a collective decision. The same goes for the contents of each issue. One of the reasons for *Positif*'s longevity and credibility is the clarity of its contents. There isn't much advertising, so it's easy to spot. It's immediately clear from the cover what three or four films are being given special attention that month with a review and an interview, as well as the feature dossier, which takes up twenty pages and can focus on contemporary or classic themes. Then there are between three and seven films that are the highlighted reviews of the month, which we consider deserving of a closer look, and around thirty short capsule reviews, which can be of films we like but not enough such that we would publish anything of any length, and films that we consider less important. There are regular sections, like "Le cinéma retrouvé" ["Rediscovered Cinema"], which is less extensive than the dossier and includes two or three reviews of films re-released in the cinema that haven't been seen for a while. And then there are sections that have been created over the years which didn't exist in the early days of *Positif*, like "Voix off," which is non-newsworthy, previously unpublished text by someone who isn't a critic – a filmmaker, an actor, a writer, a musician, a producer. Then there's "Chantier de réflexion" ["Reflection Workshop"], which the late Françoise Audé came up with, consisting of an often cross-disciplinary article on an aesthetic, economic, sociological or thematic question related to cinema, not necessarily linked to current events. This allows us to create "le temps de la réflexion" ["time for reflection"], to borrow the title of a glorious journal that used to be published annually by Gallimard.

Director of collections, head of publications, coordinator... You like bringing people together, getting things going, leading teams.

Instead of being the boss, I prefer coordinating, talking things through, working as a team. I prefer that to doing things on my own. And let me say it again: I believe there can be more than one right answer to a question. Nothing is worse than clinging fanatically to a single idea. It's an important moment when you realise there are multiple solutions to a problem, that there are various ways of looking at things. The end result is open-mindedness and a sense of liberation. That's what we do at *Positif* every Sunday, where everyone can pitch their ideas. If a majority isn't excited by a suggestion, no one fights to impose their point of view. That's the kind of pluralism I appreciate when it comes to politics. Despite its flaws, I remain a staunch supporter of democracy. As Churchill said, all political systems are bad, but some are less bad than others. And as of now, parliamentary democracy – "bourgeois," as some contemptuously describe it – is still the best way doing things.

You call yourself a coordinator, but you don't limit yourself to logistics. You exercise a certain authority.

In any group dynamic there are people who participate more than others because of their experience or the extent of their previous contributions, and there are certainly a few of us who are more closely involved than most in running *Positif*. One of the main qualities of a politician – a position which might be compared with that of a critic – is to surround himself with the very best people. Some managers avoid hiring talented people who would otherwise bring a great deal to the operation because they're afraid of being overshadowed. I never thought that by surrounding myself with mediocre people, I would have more control over things. I know that in the end, the better *Positif* can be, the more satisfied I will be – not financially, but personally. Its strengths are reflected in the people who work on it. When you arrived thirty-five years ago, or when, much more recently, we welcome new team members, it's as if we're getting the cream of the crop in terms of ideas for articles. As you can see, I'm a huge fan of our *Positif*.

Volunteering and freedom

Writers at Positif *are volunteers, which implies they all have other jobs. Committee meetings take place on Sundays. Seen from the outside, this might appear a little strange.*

As with the absence of an editor, the fact that *Positif* relies on volunteers might seem odd. We're finally in the black, which hasn't always been the case. We've had times when we were running a small deficit, and our publishers held on as best they could, hoping, despite everything, to be able to continue publishing our prestigious journal. For financial reasons some couldn't hold on. Éric Losfeld of Le Terrain Vague was pushed out after legal restructuring, Éditions OPTA went bankrupt, and later on, Jean-Michel Place, followed by Scope Éditions, faced major difficulties. *Positif* has had about a dozen publishers over sixty years – which is a lot. They were usually publishers of literature, like Le Terrain Vague, which was the main publisher of Surrealism. The prominent Paul Otchakovsky-Laurens, who created Éditions P.O.L, published *Positif* for five years and did a lot for its sustainability, image and distribution. Since September 2011, there has been a collaboration between the Institut Lumière in Lyon and Actes Sud. It's the first time we've been associated with a film institution, something which is common enough abroad – like *Bianco e nero* in Italy, published by Centro Sperimentale, *Sight and Sound* in England, which is run by the British Film Institute, and *Film Comment* in New York, which comes out of Lincoln Center. But it's a first in France. For *Positif* to get the interest of the Institut Lumière – considering the magazine was born in Lyon – is like coming back home. And Actes Sud is another major literary publisher.

As for volunteering, we calculated that if *Positif* writers were paid at the minimum rate, it would cost nearly 60,000 Euros a year. That's the size of the financial hole it would create, since the magazine doesn't make a profit. I remember a quality magazine called *Écran* which originated out of a split within *Cinéma*, where some great writers worked, like Claude Beylie, Max Tessier and Pascal Mérigeau. At one point they were no longer able to meet their financial commitments, and when the editor, Henry Moret, suggested temporarily cutting wages, a majority of writers rejected this idea and the whole magazine fell apart. Volunteering brings with it certain advantages. It means people get noticed for their writing, which can open doors to book deals, teaching jobs or opportunities to work for other outlets, like newspapers. It also gets writers invitations from associations or institutions to debates and conferences, free press screenings and invites to festivals, and free books and DVDs for review. These might be secondary and modest benefits, but they're very real. Another advantage of volunteering is that no one struggles to write about something they aren't really interested in. The fact that writing for the *Positif* won't pay the bills means that the main motivation of our reviewers is a love not just of cinema but of writing about cinema. Contributors acquire a certain notoriety. Our photographer Nicolas Guérin, who started out fifteen years ago, is one of the most important portraiture photographers in the world today.

It means that it isn't a problem when writers with outside commitments have to step away. It's easy to make room for newcomers.

Exactly. Sometimes people are surprised because our era, where everything is monetised, is excessively materialistic. Some young people find it difficult to understand. There are two kinds of people who apply to write for *Positif*, and they have completely different reactions. The first kind starts by asking, "How much do you pay?" And when I tell them they won't be paid, the conversation usually ends right there. Others respond by saying they don't care. They figure even if they were paid the standard rate, one article a month wouldn't cover their rent anyway. It would actually amount to almost nothing. So either they have another job or they're still students. Plenty of teachers have written for *Positif*, also librarians, tax inspectors, journalists, producers. In this day and age, our approach can be strange, but if you look at the big art magazines, like *Esprit* and *La Révolution surréaliste*, no one was paid. Writers for *NRF* got a symbolic payment. The journals that made a mark on intellectual history all had very small print runs. Even in the early days of *Cahiers*, when Truffaut or Rohmer were contributing, they only printed five thousand copies. That was enough, as it was for *Positif*, to make an international impact. Surrealist magazines with two thousand copies are reprinted today, unlike newspapers that print six hundred thousand. It's well known that ours is a relatively limited audience, but they're people as passionate as us who want to deepen their knowledge of cinema. Neither *Positif* nor *Cahiers* have ever had a mass readership.

For whom we write

Would you say that Positif *is "elitist"?*

Absolutely not, as far as the language we use goes. We sell only ten thousand copies, but it's widely read in libraries and each issue is passed around. There are many more readers than buyers. We're talking about roughly forty thousand readers, which hardly makes us elitist, suggesting wildly obscure articles written in a coded language or just complete gibberish that only a few people could ever understand. It's a film journal, not a poetry journal. Unfortunately, poetry doesn't interest many people today. Even though there might have been some slip-ups, which we can never entirely avoid, we've always aimed at expressing ourselves as clearly as possible. Most of the great writers I like are very readable, thinkers like Montaigne, Nietzsche, Benjamin Constant, Cioran, Breton. That's not to say absolutely everyone would understand them, because a certain cultural background is required, but they're certainly all accessible writers, which is important to me.

However, it's also about avoiding the populist temptation that France shares with many countries today. In America, this populism is the language spoken by mass audiences, the language of "the majority." As Paramount producer Adolph Zukor put it in the title of his autobiography, "The public is never wrong." This is a notion to be avoided at all costs, because just like the critics, the public can certainly be wrong. *Everyone* can be wrong. On the other hand, the public can be right, just as the critics can. What sets critics apart from audiences isn't whether they're right or wrong. Populism is gaining ground, and it's infiltrating people's minds – the idea that if something doesn't do well at the box-office, it's automatically a failure. I think there's something very wrong with that.

I belong to a generation that would travel across Paris to see *Sawdust and Tinsel* at the Pagode or *Charles, Dead or Alive* or *Loves of a Blonde* at Saint-André-des-Arts. The fact that a film played in just one cinema wasn't a sign that it wasn't worth being shown on many more screens. It was a deliberate choice. These kinds of films pulled in big audiences of perhaps a couple of hundred thousand. The re-release of von Sternberg's *The Scarlet Empress* thirty years after its release drew an audience of two hundred thousand, and there were two-page articles about it in *Le Nouvel Observateur* and *Le Monde*. Today, there's a kind of stigma if a film is released in only a handful of cinemas. People think it must not be any good.

Well, the same goes for *Positif*, which has become more difficult to find these days. It's tucked away in street kiosks and you really have to search for it. These days, readers are impressed by tall stacks. Bestsellers are piled up on bookstore tables, but you have to search to find masterpieces that have been relegated to the shelves. It's the same for journals, which are stacked up, but people are wary if there are only a handful of copies of something.

What's the difference between a journal and a film magazine?

Without implying any negative implications, periodicals like *Studio* and *Première* are magazines. They don't have in-depth articles about films or long critical pieces and historical reports like we do. They're more about what's happening *now*, and with a few exceptions have a particular focus on French and Hollywood cinema. They're big on pictures, short critiques and gossip, and as a result can't really compete with the Internet – websites and blogs that are full of interviews with actors, opinion pieces, rating films on a scale of one to five stars instead of real critical thinking. At the same time, I think the decline or disappearance of these magazines hurts everyone because, even if it's a less specialised way of looking at cinema, they help educate a lot of youngsters who, at fourteen or fifteen, aren't going to go read *Positif* – which is completely understandable. For many of them, unless they have been really into film for years, *Positif* is probably a difficult read. On the other hand, they can switch to *Positif* after a few years. This isn't a value judgement, but I think there's a difference between a magazine and a journal. You would never think of saying that *NRF*, *Les Temps Modernes* or the *Revue des deux mondes* are magazines. They're journals, like *Positif*. Still, our journal isn't written in academic gibberish. It's accessible to all and always contains lots of photos.

A natural renewal

What has changed at Positif *since you started writing for it?*

The main thing is that there are more writers. For the first fifty issues, before I arrived, *Positif*'s editorial team was a tight-knit group of ten. If we take into account every writer, including those abroad, that figure has quadrupled. Today there are twenty members on the editorial board, plus around twenty regular contributors. Those contributors can't join the committee since they would need to attend meetings at least twice a month and screenings too. But we've got foreign correspondents who write a lot, like Floreal Peleato in Spain or Lorenzo Codelli in Italy. So that's about forty people altogether, which is a big change. We've also amped up news coverage. With more of us, we can discuss more films, although that can be a double-edged sword since before, we could content ourselves with writing about four or five films in a single issue, plus maybe including something like a seven-page article on *Belle de jour*. Today it's almost impossible to do that, for reasons of space. A current film gets three or four pages maximum. But we cover a lot more festivals than before, even if it's not our readers' favourite section because we write about films they aren't familiar with. It's essential for a journal to do this kind of groundwork and keep updated on global cinema. We go to San Sebastian, Rotterdam, Locarno and Karlovy Vary, and festivals that focus on film history like Bologna, Lyon and Pordenone. In this regard, *Positif* has grown considerably. We've created new sections, as I mentioned, and we run obituaries in every issue. So it has become much more diverse.

I think it's fair to say that what hasn't changed is the continual and natural turnover of writers. There are really only two monthly journals left in France that deal with contemporary cinema: *Cahiers du cinéma* and *Positif.* Globally speaking, I think that's quite a unique situation. In America, for instance, *Film Comment* comes out every two months, *Cineaste* and *Film Quarterly* every three months. There is no longer a monthly magazine in Italy. Having these two monthlies in France fosters stimulating competition and mutual inspiration.

I would like to clarify that despite our fundamental and even surface-level differences, my relations with successive generations who led *Cahiers* have often been cordial, whether it's Michel Delahaye and Jean Narboni in the 1960s, then Serge Toubiana and Serge Daney – I remember the breakfasts I had with the latter in Berlin, where we talked a lot about tennis, one of my youthful passions – and later with Antoine de Baecque, followed by Charles Tesson[*] and Jean-Marc Lalanne.[†] And let's not forget Jean Douchet.[‡] Today, after a period of rigidity and dogmatism marked by Jean-Michel Frodon's tenure, I'm pleased to see management led by Stéphane Delorme and Jean-Philippe Tessé. I don't agree with all their choices – not by a long shot, but they're less predictable, and today *Cahiers* feels quite lively.

How is the renewal of the editorial staff at Positif *carried out in practice?*

By natural selection, so to speak. What strikes me as very characteristic is the constant influx of new recruits and the departure of others. There are writers who have been there for a very long time. I've been there for fifty years,

---

[*] Charles Tesson (b.1954). French film critic.
[†] Jean-Marc Lalanne (b.1967). French film critic.
[‡] Jean Douchet (1929-2019). French film director and critic.

and Paul-Louis Thirard for almost sixty. There are some who have been contributing for thirty years, like you, for forty years, like Hubert Niogret or Lorenzo Codelli, for twenty years, ten years or three years. Some leave because cinema or writing about cinema no longer interests them. Like cinephilia in general, film criticism is often a young person's game. People like Kyrou didn't go to the cinema at all at one point in their lives. At fifty, they watch nothing but television. There are plenty of reasons for this, like having children to take care of, not wanting to go out in the evening, or just plain weariness. In general, people who read have always read and will continue to read until they die, or listen to music or look at paintings. But it's possible to have been crazy about cinema at one time, and then completely lose interest. I have found this to be the case even with hardcore cinephiles. Some are so hooked – like me – that they will probably push on with it until they die. But in any case, without anyone really noticing, because it's almost subliminal, this is what has maintained *Positif*'s vitality. This isn't at all what has happened at *Cahiers*, which has experienced a succession of distinct cycles. At *Positif*, our love of writing leads everyone to contribute with genuine empathy – until they are no longer able to. The result is a kind of permanent renewal and a constant thread running through our work. I'm not particularly fond of Edgar Faure,* but his famous expression "le changement dans la continuité" ["change in continuity"] is sort of what characterises our journal.

When we list all the articles you have published in Positif, *there are as many book reviews as film reviews.*

Yes, it's like an imaginary dialogue. One of my first articles was about a book by Robert Benayoun called *Le Dessin animé après Walt Disney*, published by Pauvert. I didn't yet know him personally, but found his work absolutely dazzling. The ability to admire, in my opinion, is a great quality. Vauvenargues wrote: "C'est une preuve de médiocrité que d'admirer modérément."] ["To admire with moderation is proof of mediocrity."] By all means make fun of me for getting all poetic on you, but I can't help it. Admiration inspires me to write.

---

* Edgar Faure (1908-1988). French politician.

The time of controversy

Some people miss the times when there was more controversy. Ours is much more an era of consensus. Do you think Positif *has suffered because of this?*

I wouldn't say that because in my case I've kept the polemical spirit alive in many of my editorials, and hopefully in this book as well. Some people criticise me for criticising my colleagues, which is odd when you look at the history of criticism. Read Michel Winock's biography of Flaubert and you'll see just how often literary critics taunted each other. I was recently reading Italian commentators of the sixteenth century who sent letters to Vasari accusing him, in his history of painters, of neglecting Venetian painting and not understanding anything about colour. These were endless controversies. And don't get me started on the nineteenth century... I really don't see why critics can tear apart directors but don't have the right to be outraged by absurdities from their own colleagues. When Serge Kaganski recently asked me why I was attacking Jacques Mandelbaum, a *Le Monde* writer, I explained that when he curated a retrospective of Holocaust cinema at the Cinémathèque française, which was accompanied by a printed catalogue, he ignored almost every fiction film on the subject, but chose to screen Antonioni's *L'Avventura* because three quarters of an hour into the film the character of Anna disappears, like the Jews did, or that Mankiewicz's *Sleuth* is one of the greatest political films ever made, or even that the shower scene in Hitchcock's *Psycho* is a reference to the concentration camps. I find all this so shocking, so obscene. What surprises me is that no one else was outraged. Keep controversy alive! I'll always kick out at things.

That said, it's true that there are fewer controversies these days precisely because critical thinking is in such short supply. We're immersed in such stunning mediocrity when it comes to the media. Our is a climate of consensus where everyone speaks well of everyone else and self-promotion overrides criticism. I sometimes have the impression that my young colleagues are surprised at my pugnacity, but I also think that we're in a much more cautious era, which could be explained by how tough it is to break into the job market. When I started, I had job security. I was a teacher, and that financial security allowed me to do what I wanted. Plus, I wrote voluntarily for a magazine, so there was no risk of me getting fired or losing my job. Obviously, in an extremely tough and competitive job market, you don't want to make enemies. I've made enemies, but at the same time it was easier for me because I could write whatever I wanted in *Positif* and had a job with complete autonomy and a salary. It's easier to be a provocateur in those circumstances.

Perhaps also at one time the stakes of cinephilia were different?

Yes. There is less ideology today, it's true. *Positif* was born at a time when France was a divided country. In the 1950s, the Church wielded considerable influence on censorship and people were turned away from seeing films. Prohibition codes even existed when it came to going into churches. With colonial wars in Indochina and Algeria, the military was also a significant factor. The political stakes were extremely high. The resurgence of far-right influence in intellectual circles was admittedly limited, but it nonetheless contaminated quite a few newspapers, while *Positif* at the time was anti-Stalinist and anti-right. Things were more black and white back then. Come to think of it, the Resistance was a mixture of right and left. Even though there were more leftists in the Resistance, Charles de Gaulle, who made the decision to leave for London and join the organisation, was a former royalist and supporter of Maurras.*

I think that nowadays we should be able to come together as democrats and defenders of freedom and transcend old divides. For me, the intellectual dividing line is between the partisans of any form of totalitarianism and, if not social democrats, then at least those people who accept the principles of freedom of expression and political plurality. We shouldn't condemn people to hell just because they vote for certain parties. It's possible to debate with right-wingers – although I'm excluding Le Pen† and the extreme right here – just as I would do with communists. It was my responsibility as an intellectual. I'm talking about grassroots communists: teachers, workers, artisans, people with strong convictions who did so much for France, people who were deceived and lied to and manipulated, and in the end became victims of their own ideology. But I wouldn't get into a discussion with a communist apparatchik or someone like Aragon, who knew all the dirty secrets, went along with it all, and lied to the people. And I wouldn't exchange views with a member of the National Front, no matter their place in society.

---

* Charles Maurras (1868-1952). French author and far-right politician.
† Jean-Marie Le Pen (b.1928). French far-right politician.

The journal of journals

When you contribute to the monthly "bloc-notes" ["notepad"] section in Positif, *it's clear that you're a close reader of other journals and magazines.*

People say I come off as aggressive and controversial towards my colleagues, but I take them very seriously. It's just that I genuinely believe in critical engagement. I read *Cahiers* every month, and I'm thrilled when more niche publications – which print around one or two thousand copies, and are often really very good – show up, though it's sad how frequently they disappear. Criticism nowadays is dwindling in the mainstream press. Aside from *Télérama*, *Le Monde*, *Libération*, *Le Figaro* and *Les Inrockuptibles*, there's hardly any space for genuine critical writing, where arguments can be expressed and developed. But when people claim that criticism is dying, that's far from the truth. There's never been as much critical discourse in France as there is today. The thing is, you have to hunt for it in the equivalent of medieval abbeys and monasteries – these small-circulation journals. There have been short-lived publications like the quarterly *Split Screen*, or *Brazil*, for example, which lasted longer but did eventually, sadly, disappear. There was a journal in Lille called *Tausend Augen*, a nod to Dr. Mabuse's "thousand eyes," and another in Toulouse called *Cinergon*. Some are more university-affiliated, like *Contre Bande* at Paris 1 Panthéon-Sorbonne, which no longer exists, or *L'Art du cinéma*, created by Alain Badiou and Denis Lévy at Paris 8 Vincennes Saint-Denis, which comes out every three months and is full of essays unrelated to current events on a theme that interests them. *Theorem* at Paris 4 Sorbonne-Nouvelle and *Éclipses* in Caen are still going. There's also *Trafic* in Paris, published by P.O.L, the former *Positif* publisher. *Vertigo* was once printed by one of our publishers, Jean-Michel Place. And then there's *CinémAction*, each issue of which is dedicated to a specific theme, *Études cinématographiques*, a fifty-year-old journal in the form of a monograph, and others like *La lettre du cinéma*, *L'Avant-scène* and *Jeune Cinéma*, which is similar to *Positif*. I find it all very exciting. So I spend a lot of time reading what other people write. It's very stimulating.

Are those kinds of publications competition for Positif *and* Cahiers?

I don't think so. Most of them are probably bought and read by people who also read *Positif* or *Cahiers*, and who read us because we're a complement to current events and can offer a deeper dive into things. On the one hand, readers of popular film magazines might go out and buy *Positif* or *Cahiers*, and on the other, readers of *Positif* or *Cahiers* might seek out more sharply detailed analysis.

Writer and reader

For several years now you've been writing fewer film reviews.

People ask me why I don't publish as many reviews as I did in the 1960s through to the 1980s. I do editorials, book reviews, reviews of exhibitions and festivals, sometimes historical articles, but it's true that I write less criticism. Why? Well, for one, more and more I've grown to enjoy reading what others have to say, whether it's the up-and-coming critics at *Positif* or people like Alain Masson, Vincent Amiel, Jean-Loup Bourget or others. It can be invigorating because they might write something more interesting than anything I might have to say. On the other hand, I continue doing interviews because I know I'm good at it. I'm glad I wrote all those books and articles, but these days I prefer to spend time interviewing because I just learn more when I'm doing it.

Are you tired of writing criticism?

I'm not tired, it's just that I have so many other things going on. The professional critics do important work and I wouldn't want to publish anything that wasn't as good as I know I can deliver, especially in the knowledge that other people can do the job just fine, and that I'll learn from them by reading their work. I prefer to give lectures, which are, in their own way, critical exercises.

You know very well, however, that Positif *remains strongly identified with your name.*

I sometimes suffer from my celebrity status! I have attained a certain notoriety because I've been around for fifty years. When Philippe Fraisse sent me the manuscript of his excellent book on Kubrick, *Le Cinéma au bord du monde*, I immediately thought big, and sent it to Philippe Sollers[*] – who I don't really know very well – for Gallimard's

---

[*] Philippe Sollers (1936-2023). French author and publisher.

L'Infini collection, because even though he's not actually that interested in cinema, I know that Sollers only has time for two directors: Hitchcock and Kubrick. He immediately read the book and published it. The book, however, which is a very significant work by a philosopher and writer, was practically ignored by the press. I spoke to Jean-Marc Lalanne about it, which led to a small but favourable article in *Les Inrockuptibles*, but other than that there was nothing. I was surprised that this book, copies of which were sent to many journalists, on a subject like Kubrick, didn't make more of a splash. There was also an extraordinary three-volume work by Pierre Berthomieu on Hollywood, published by Rouge Profond, that went nowhere – seven hundred pages each, two thousand photographs, a wide-ranging critical analysis of filmmakers about whom there is hardly anything written, informed by an understanding of music, painting and technology. Almost nobody talked about it, which I find scandalous. It's this sense of injustice that drives me.

Does this attitude of journalists reflect a general lack of public curiosity for books on cinema?

I recommended Philippe Fraisse to the Cinémathèque française for a conference on the occasion of the Kubrick exhibition. I met about fifteen young people in their twenties who had his book in their hands, waiting to get their copies signed by him. I said to them, "It was brilliant this conference, wasn't it?" They said to me, "We knew it would be. We read about it in *Positif*." The realisation that these young film enthusiasts were capable of grasping the significance of a writer that none of the professional critics had bothered to acknowledge really puzzled me. That fact that they knew more than the people whose job it was reflects an important shift in audiences, because when Truffaut, Benayoun, Rivette and Tailleur were writing, readers knew much less than they did, and so learned a great deal from them. Fifty years later, thanks to the growth of academic film studies, something which didn't exist back then, and the number of film books and people writing on the Internet, unimaginable knowledge can be acquired. These young people may not have such a developed cultural understanding of the world. They haven't necessarily all seen *Sunrise* and *The Rules of the Game*. They might be into Asian cinema, horror films or other things. But depending on their taste, they're able to develop a very serious knowledge of cinema, which means that many readers know more than the specialists who have a platform. And they're certainly more curious.

Shortly after that I went to Toulouse for a conference at the Cinémathèque and went to the cinema section of the Ombres blanches bookstore, one of the best in France. They had a stack of fifteen copies of Philippe Fraisse's book. The manager told me he had read it and constantly recommended it, and quite a few copies had been sold. So it's no longer some authoritative critic who boosts sales of a book, it's word of mouth. That's a very serious development. I have a lot of respect for what's being published. Recently, on my radio programme *Projection privée*, I hosted a fifty-minute conversation with a Finnish researcher, Taïna Tuhkuner, the author of *Demain sera un autre jour* [*Tomorrow is Another Day*] a book on Southern heroines in American films, from Lillian Gish to Elizabeth Taylor, and up to the present day. It's a sort of X-ray of Southern cinema, as well as a study of racism and society – an extraordinary piece of work published by Rouge Profond, the same publisher as Berthomieu, with a wealth of frame enlargements to support her theses. And yet, again, there have been practically no reviews of it.

THE PLEASURE OF TEACHING

High school

Positif has been something of a parallel activity for you, because from the very start of your association with the journal, you made your living as a teacher.

I've always been passionate about teaching. If I signed the IPES contract [Institutes for Preparation for Secondary Education], it wasn't about financial security, it was because I wanted to be a teacher. My own teachers had a big impact on me, and the writers I read had also somehow passed something on to me, so it made sense that I wanted to pass something on myself. In fact, passing things on has been the core of my life, whether it's film criticism published in *Positif*, writing books or speaking on the radio – it all comes down to a kind of pedagogy and didacticism, in the best possible way. A passion, a conviction, for this kind of activity has been the backbone of my career. But yes – it's true that my main activity, the one that allowed me to live and gave me such freedom, is teaching. It all started back in high school. I spent my secondary school internship at the Lycée Voltaire where, in the next room, Henri Agel* was preparing his students – including Alain Corneau – for the IDHEC exam.

Were you a French literature teacher?

No, I taught English. The first two years weren't easy. I got up at six in the morning and came home late at night. I changed at Creil station and got on another train to Mouy in the Oise. Ninety minutes of travel time each way – that's three hours a day. I taught at every level of high school, starting from the fifth grade, before asking to be transferred closer to home, and moved to the Lycée de Suresnes, where I taught until 1969. It's also where François Guérif worked. Once I invited Joseph Losey to present *Time Without Pity* to the first graders. I hadn't yet written my book about him.

Did you teach film?

Never, no. I just suggested showing the film and bringing in the director. The headmaster of the school didn't even bother showing up, and probably didn't even know who Losey was.

---
* Henri Angel (1911-2008). French film critic.

I started selecting films for Critics' Week at Cannes in 1968, which meant I was given accommodation in Cannes for six days. I was supposed to go for the second week of the festival, but ended up backing out, which turned out to be a good thing because May '68 blew up. Instead, I stayed in Paris with my students, who went on strike. The discussions in the courtyard were fascinating. Next door was the États généraux du cinéma français in Suresnes, where Marin Karmitz and Chabrol suggested that from now on all films should be free for everyone.* It was like a utopia had been born. I attended general meetings at the Odéon and the Sorbonne. It really got me fired up.

At university: Vincennes and Charles-V

How did you become a college teacher?

At the same time as Suresnes, the film department at Vincennes, which had just been established, asked me, through Marie-Claire Ropars-Wuillemier[†] and Roger Dadoun,[‡] to teach a class on Brazilian *Cinema novo*, because I had written a lot about those revolutionary films in *Positif* – the cinema of social and political protest, like *Antonio das Mortes*, *Terre em transe* and *The Guns*. My lectures on Latin American cinema, in 1968, were my first college experiences as a teacher. In April 1969, while I was still in Suresnes and Vincennes, I interviewed Losey and translated for him during daily debates at a retrospective at the Théâtre de la Commune in Aubervilliers.

Was that because you invited him to Suresnes?

No. We had stayed in touch since I had done interviews with him for *Positif* about *Secret Ceremony* and *Boom!* These hour-long meetings took place after each screening, in front of a huge audience. There was a young woman there I knew very well, Maryse Delarue, a university assistant professor who had prepared for the civil service exam at the same time as me, on rue de l'École-de-Médecine, in 1961/62, once I got home from America. I gave up after a year, but some of those people became civil servants and in 1968 created a UER ("unité d'enseignement et de recherche"/"teaching

---

* An opening meeting of distributors, directors, directors, technicians and critics, in May/June 1968.
† Marie-Claire Ropars-Wuillemier (1936-2007). French author.
‡ Roger Dadoun (1928-2022). French philosopher.

and research unit") for Anglophone studies. In my day there was just the Sorbonne, but after May '68 the Parisian system split into eight different universities. Paris 7 Jussieu had an annex, the Charles-V Institute of English on rue Charles-V, in the Marais, where these associates I had known at the Sorbonne had freedom to organise their UER. Maryse Delarue – the wife of Jean-Claude Delarue, also a teacher there, a future member of the Economic and Social Council – came to see me after one of the discussions with Losey and asked, "What are you doing, Michel? We read you in *Positif*. Are you a high school teacher? Why don't you come teach with us at the university?" I told her, "I don't have the qualifications. I don't have a doctorate. That world is closed to me. And what's more, I hate filling out forms." I certainly missed out on a lot because I didn't want to do the paperwork for this or that position. I'm very impatient by nature. Bureaucracy drives me nuts. So she said, "Look, we'll take care of that. It's clear how much you know about film," and two months later, in June 1969, I was summoned by two prominent Americanists, Michel Oriano and Michel Gresset, who told me it was possible for them to hire people who weren't certified if they brought something special to the table. "We know how much you know about American cinema," they said. "How about joining us as a full-time assistant, not just to teach cinema but also classes in American civilisation? Maybe a course on the relationship between cinema and American society. If you agree, you'll switch from high school to higher education." It was an incredible opportunity for me, a turning point in my life. That encounter at the Théâtre de la Commune in Aubervilliers really changed things for me. Once at the university, I taught eight hours of classes a week and supervised master's degrees by committee because I wasn't a professor, but no one else had the expertise in cinema and American culture that I did. I was also able to organise my classroom schedule, which isn't something you can do when you're teaching eighteen hours a week in a high school. With eight hours of university classes a week, I was able to go to a festival for a few days, then teach sixteen hours the following week. Starting in 1969, I began going to the Cannes festival. I had been to the festival at Venice because back then it was during the summer holidays. I spent a lot of time prepping classes and grading papers, but my new job offered unexpected flexibility for my work at *Positif* and later my radio programmes.

Were you teaching in lecture halls?

No, I had two tutorial groups, about forty students each. For example, I taught introductory courses in American cinema, starting with *The Birth of a Nation*. There was a small number of black students – maybe three or four per class – who were actually supportive of my screening the film. The whites, on the other hand, were outraged. They thought it was a despicable, racist film. "We like it," the black students said, "because it shows how people really perceived us." The greatest filmmaker of his era could talk about black people, praise the Ku Klux Klan, criticise the North, defend slavery, and paint a rosy picture of black people singing and dancing while their condescending slave masters acted all friendly. The black students were all for showing these kinds of films, as long as we analysed them instead of sweeping them under the rug. It was fascinating. We had 35mm prints and a large amphitheatre. Later, I used video as well. I took advantage of my contacts and relationships with filmmakers to bring them in for discussions: Elia Kazan, John Boorman, Robert Altman, Peter Brook, Joseph Losey. They all showed up and we had very instructive debates with students. They were all English speakers, since that was the focus of my course. It's always interesting to revisit films you love with a much younger audience and see their reactions. I noticed, for example, that among American filmmakers, Raoul Walsh's Westerns were well received. In the 1970s, people were highly politicised, especially students, and were extremely sensitive to issues of race, social class and sexism. But Walsh's brand of anarchism appealed to them. Take *Colorado Territory*, for example, where the woman and the man are equals. John Ford's films, on the other hand, didn't go down too well because they seemed more reactionary. The female characters in his films were always teachers, mothers or prostitutes. Students were very attuned to the representation of Mexicans in Howard Hawks' *Rio Bravo*, which they didn't like at all. I certainly looked at these films differently after these classroom experiences. I also taught classes on film noir, Westerns and comedy. For instance, I focused on the 1930s, from the Wall Street Crash and Prohibition to *The Grapes of Wrath* in 1940, which led to discussions about the Roosevelt presidency.

It also allowed you to teach English while introducing students to films.

I stopped teaching English and focused instead on American studies. Before that, for about four or five years, I taught English at high school, which I really enjoyed. What was noticeable was that students spoke English when they were younger, but as they got older, stopped doing so. I wondered about this odd phenomenon of losing familiarity with a language. Around the age of twelve or thirteen, they seemed to grasp the language much more easily than later on. At university, what really helped me personally was spending time on subjects other than cinema. I taught a course on the mythology of the American West: Jesse James, Calamity Jane, Davy Crockett. Another one was on urban planning and big cities, where I screened Henry King's *In Old Chicago*. Other classes were on international relations, American foreign policy, the U.S. Constitution, and American painting, which at that time was practically unknown, and still remains largely ignored. I talked about Eakins, Whistler, Bingham. Of course, I touched on the twentieth century and Hopper, but dealt mainly with the painters of the eighteenth and nineteenth centuries: Copley, the great landscape artists like Thomas Cole and Bierstadt, both from the Appalachian East Coast, and those from the Rockies who were influenced by German Romantic painting. Of course, all this sheds light on cinema as well. It was because of my knowledge of the transcendental philosophy of New England – Emerson and Thoreau – that I connected so quickly to the aesthetics and inspirations of Terrence Malick.

You were learning about all this as you taught it?

Yes. I have a huge library of Americana. I think, in any case, it's a truism: we're eternal students. Preparing for a course takes much more effort than attending it. The teacher has to work harder than the student! I learned so much because of my work as a teacher. I never took art history classes, for example, but for thirty years, from 1969 to 1999, I was a "student-teacher."

Your academic career is impressive, but you never worked your way up through the ranks, and never did a PhD.

That's a little complicated. I submitted two hundred pages to obtain the qualifications so I could supervise research work. That qualified me as a lecturer, after being an assistant and then an associate professor. My former mentor, Deleuze, in one of our conversations, said to me, "I read what you write and listen to *Le Masque et la Plume* – and I advise against pursuing a PhD. You could do it and easily become a professor with all that you've written, but you won't be able to do everything you do now. You're an associate professor, you have your tutorials to conduct and prepare. It's manageable. The minute you become a professor you'll have administrative tasks, meetings to attend. The bureaucratic work is overwhelming. I advise against it. It's going to cost you in the short term, but you'll see a return elsewhere." His suggestion was that I continue doing what I was doing. I could see the workload that my university colleagues had to deal with. The culture of meetings has become one of the major sins of our time. I've never seen so many people sit around so many tables and make so few decisions. At *Positif*, two hours a week are enough for us to sort out any problems. We don't hang around endlessly arguing about which ballpoint to buy.

In front of an audience of students

How did your classes work, practically speaking?

I don't think I've ever had more stage fright and anxiety than I did as a teacher. It was very different from appearing on the radio. There's no audience more demanding and ready to argue than a student audience, especially back in the 1970s.

But you're the authority figure...

Yes, but to maintain that authority, you have to keep them engaged. I really do think that, in a way, a teacher is an actor. They play a role and have to charm their audience by putting on a show and grabbing everyone's attention. There are professors who just read their notes – I've experienced that as a student. They're really quite unbearable, as are those who casually stroll into the classroom with their hands in their pockets. My teaching style – something I think I've brought into everything I've done since – is to prepare intensely, even write it all out, if necessary, but in a way that the overall structure, not the details, are crystal clear. Then I elaborate around this broad outline. It's what Deleuze did so beautifully. So – much like some very good films – it's about showing up with a script that doesn't include every single detail but that serves as a foundation on which we can build. That groundwork is the result of research and preparation.

As for classroom participation, it depends on the course and the audience. Letting students have their say was trendy after May '68, but that was never anything I emphasised. Some colleagues went big with that idea. There were slogans around, like "ne passez pas vos diplômes, ça ne sert à rien" ["don't bother getting a degree – it's worthless"], but these people had degrees themselves and were earning a salary, so they could afford to tell others not to do the same, which essentially meant being unemployed. It was the easy way out. There was also the theory that students should create their own curriculum, which I vehemently opposed. It was always self-evident to me that teacher had a lot to offer the student, and if I started asking, "What do you want to study this year?" they would have called out for *Jaws*, *The Godfather* and *Bonnie and Clyde*, but never *Greed*, because they had never heard of it. That was precisely my job: to introduce them to important work they weren't aware of. By definition, a good teacher knows more than the student. One of the most gratifying things that happens to me as a teacher is that years later, when I chance upon a former student in the metro, they never thank me for having shown a Coppola film. They say instead, "Ah, sir! What a revelation Stroheim's *Greed* was. Absolutely extraordinary!" Or Murnau's *Sunrise*. That's what struck them, because those were things they didn't even know existed. I always felt that it's the teacher's role to guide students. It's like in a debate, where it's important to give the floor to the audience, but first there has to be time to discuss the basic questions and big ideas. There's a danger of demagoguery, of populism, where everyone has their say.

I'm assuming your classes weren't just about the connections between film and society.

That's true. When they hired me, I made it clear that I was also going to spend time on aesthetics. You can't talk about *Citizen Kane* without dealing with storytelling and depth of field, because that's all part of it. Style and substance are inseparable. Even though my focus was on the relationship between cinema and American civilisation, we looked at the work in an aesthetic context. Discussing cinema and knowing a lot about American history and society really made a difference to the students. I knew what they were studying in other classes. Whatever anyone might say, it's an important way of framing the work under discussion. I read an article in *Positif* recently that claimed that all said and done, the most important thing about Resnais' *You Ain't Seen Nothin' Yet* isn't issues of death or theatre or memory, but the shot/reverse-shot technique. I disagree. It's like saying the only interesting thing in *The Brothers Karamazov* is the subjunctive tense. I don't buy into this formalistic viewpoint. It's as absurd as disregarding style altogether. We're drawn to a film or a book because the artist has captivated us with the form, but ultimately, the message of the piece is the real draw.

A unique community

What was it like at the Charles-V Institute of English?

Thrilling, like a commune, led by the brilliant Antoine Culioli, who was already a linguistics professor at the Sorbonne and gathered his former students to create the institute. He was its first president. Initially, it was a real, ideologically led community, inspired by ideas and rebellion of May '68. There weren't many hardcore communists, but hardly anyone leaned right. In general, they all shared a set of values, and they were truly the best in nearly every field: Richard Marienstras, one of France's top Shakespeare scholars; Michel Gresset, an expert in contemporary American literature who later supervised Pléiade's editions of Faulkner; Philippe Jaworski, who did the same for Pléiade's Melville and Fitzgerald editions; Elise Marienstras, Richard's wife, a major expert on Native Americans and constitutional issues; Paul Rosenberg, a leading figure in English Romanticism; Ann Grieve, a prominent translator of gothic novels and eighteenth-century authors; the psychoanalyst Liliane Abensour, married to philosopher Miguel Abensour; Rachel Ertel, a Yiddish scholar and translator of Isaac Bashevis Singer, among others. Then there was the renowned linguist, Marina Yaguello; Michel Oriano, a distinguished American historian; Marc Chénetier and Pierre-Yves Pétillon, also significant Americanists; Jean Guénot, another linguist and author of some remarkable books, including one on Céline; and Simone Chambon, an expert on Jack London and working-class American literature.

Was there a lot of discussion within the group?

We thrived on it. I didn't feel the kind of prejudice that sometime appears on campuses, like, "Oh, he does a radio programme and writes for a journal… That's not academic work. No footnotes!" They were actually quite interested in what I wrote. With my interest in culture in general, and my genuine curiosity in so many realms, I loved discussing things with them. They had nothing to do with journalism, but were never pedantic or elitist. They really did embody the best of what a university has to offer. Perhaps it stemmed from their Anglophone education. They had a freedom of thought and way of doing things that reminded me of my time on an American campus. What struck me most was the flow of ideas among very different people who all somehow had the same orientation. In the English department, I never experienced the kind of atmosphere I've heard about in other universities – all those petty rivalries and jealousies, like helping out your own doctoral candidates at all costs or trying to undermine a colleague's student. Those kinds of things would have made academic life really quite unpleasant, at the expense of the very reason we were all there: the cultivation and sharing of knowledge.

ON AIR:
THE RADIO EXPERIENCE

Birth of a programme (1): *Le Masque et la Plume*

You started doing radio in college?

Yes. Not many people know this, but it all started with Michel Polac.* He and François-Régis Bastide† created *Le Masque et la Plume* [*The Mask and the Quill*] together in 1955. They were friendly, but for some reason drifted apart after a while, maybe because Polac was an acerbic and rather quarrelsome person. They ended up with two shows that alternated: Polac's *Le Pour et le Contre* [*For and Against*] – the same format: four critics chatting about films, books, theatre – and *Le Masque et la Plume*, which continued with François-Régis Bastide. Polac was an inquisitive person, interested in underground journals, offbeat writers and alternative publishers. He noticed my articles in *Positif* and invited me to appear on the programme. Radio is a whole different ballgame, but what helped me, I think, is the fact that I was a teacher. That isn't to say all teachers know how to speak in public. I've known some who bored me to death. But on *Le Masque et la Plume*, someone like Jean-Louis Bory,‡ who taught at Henri-IV, was the epitome of the teacher-actor. His double act with Georges Charensol§ was wonderful – a classic clown routine. In any case, I started with Michel Polac and did maybe ten programmes, which went over so well that that when his competitor's programme came to an end a few months later, François-Régis Bastide asked me to join *Le Masque et la Plume*.

What year was that?

1970. So I found myself working with Charensol and Bory, who in their temperaments and political ideas were polar opposites. Charensol was frequently disparaged because he didn't measure up to Truffaut, Tailleur, Benayoun or Rohmer when it came to his critical writing. He had that subjective, empirical 1920s way of expressing himself, although was sometimes quite surprising, more so than Bory, whose tastes were fairly predictable, even though he did appreciate a variety of things, from the avant-garde to popular entertainment. Charensol, on the other hand, was truly unpredictable. He would gush over a

---

* Michel Polac (1930-2012). French writer and director.
† François-Régis Bastide (1926-1996). French writer and radio host.
‡ Jean-Louis Bory (1919-1979). French author and film critic.
§ Georges Charensol (1899-1995). French journalist and film critic who appeared, alongside Jean-Louis Bory on *Le Masque et la Plume* between 1964 and 1979.

highly innovative, groundbreaking film, and in the same breath rail against Godard. I always liked that about him. He knew an awful lot about literature and painting, and was almost the only film critic I ever met at exhibition openings or at the museum. He had written some of the first books on the Paris School painters of the 1930s – Soutine, Pascin, Rouault – and was rather anti-New Wave because they rubbished René Clair and Gérard Philipe, who were his friends. Bory was an exceptional critic. If you read one of his reviews in *L'Observateur*, you wanted to run out and see the film he was writing about. He was full of passion, and that excitement really rubbed off. The clashes between Charensol and Bory stole the show, so much so that sometimes no one even noticed I was in the same room. But *Le Masque et la Plume* was also a platform for Claude Mauriac, Pierre Billard, Robert Benayoun, Michel Aubriant, Michel Mardore and Michel Cournot – almost every leading writer of the day. The show was already very popular. Music played as we talked – Christian Ivaldi on the piano. It was a great atmosphere, with an eighteenth-century twist. Bastide even wrote about Saint-Simon.

Was it always recorded in public?

Yes, which was very important, because doing the show without an audience would have been more difficult. We see people's faces, we hear their applause. I've been doing the programme for over forty years now. What's amusing is that students researching *Le Masque et la Plume* who come to interview me announce: "You're the last survivor of the early years" – as if I'd been at Verdun.

Le Masque et la Plume today

How has the show evolved over the decades?

It really hasn't changed much. We've had three bosses. The first was François-Régis Bastide, then Pierre Bouteiller, who was more relaxed and detached. He didn't really like it when we got too excited. And finally, Jérôme Garcin, who, as I see it, was the person who brought the programme to a much bigger audience – about a million listeners. And it's striking how varied the audience is. It's France Inter's oldest programme and perhaps the most popular, but we also have twenty-year-old listeners. Jérôme Garcin edits the cultural pages of *Le Nouvel Observateur*. I really don't know how he finds the time. He goes to the theatre and ballet, he reads and reviews a fair number of books, he writes maybe three articles a week and goes to the cinema to see, at a minimum, the six films we talk about every fortnight. Like previous hosts, he shows great independence of mind, which makes him all the more likeable. He isn't part of any clique and his interests are all over the map. He gives his support to a lot of small publishers, like Finitude and Le Dilettante, while still making time for the big names – Grasset and Gallimard. His most decisive contribution to *Le Masque et la Plume* is that listeners have a say. He starts off at the start of the programme by spending seven or eight minutes reading their mail and involving the audience in our discussions. Hearing from us critics, then having the audience fire back, really ramps things up. That said, it's not always representative of public opinion because most people write letters only when they have a bone to pick.

Which would tend to suggest that the public is interested in criticism...

Paradoxically, I think that the growing success of *Le Masque et la Plume* is proportional to the general decline of the role of criticism in French intellectual life. It's precisely because the press has lost credibility and people are wary of proclamations from above that they prefer to think for themselves and listen to our programme. They say to themselves, "Here are these so-called experts who completely disagree about a film. There isn't some all-knowing authority out there. These people are supposed to know everything, and yet they can't agree amongst themselves! So I can make up my own mind." Another reason for the success of *Le Masque et la Plume* is that today, the media is flooded with promotional content. In many newspapers, everything is judged to be so excellent. A fairly charmless, run-of-the-mill French comedy can get three stars, and there's supposedly a masterpiece every week. Everything is homogenised. *Le Masque et la Plume*, by contrast, pulls things into focus, so much so that sometimes, when we throw our weight behind a film, an hour after the end of the programme, at 10 p.m. on a Sunday, there's a spike in attendance. Listeners trust us. Faced with the levelling of critical judgement in the media, the positions and freedom of opinion expressed on *Le Masque et la Plume* stand out. Sometimes we'll even give a bad review to a film that France Inter has helped produce.

Blasphemy on television

At one point Le Masque et la Plume *almost became a TV show.*

What happened is interesting. Patrice Leconte writes about it in his memoir. In the mid-1970s it did become a TV show. François-Régis Bastide would give the floor to each of us and we would talk about different films, and at the very end he would say, "Now, everyone throw in a line or two about a film we didn't have time to talk about." I'm last to go, so he says to me, "Michel Ciment, what about [Patrice Leconte's film] *Les vécés étaient fermés de l'intérieur* [*The Toilets Were Closed From the Inside*]?" And I say, "It's time to flush." Patrice Leconte and Christian Fechner, the producer, who are watching at home, have been waiting for an hour for us to talk about their film, and what do they hear? I felt bad because a lousy pun like that was just too easy, and since then I've liked some of Leconte's films. He said it was really unpleasant. On television, a comment like that can cause a much bigger stir than on the radio, and suddenly all these producers' associations were hollering, saying the show should be banned, claiming it was unfair competition, that because television was in the business of making programmes, it was diverting people from going to the cinema. As a result, Christian Defaye, a popular cultural talk-show host in Switzerland, said he would host the programme, and so – like Voltaire and Rousseau – we took refuge there. We would head to Geneva to record and discuss films with complete freedom. Several nearby regions played it – a cinema version of *Les Français parlent aux Français*.* It which lasted about a year.

Did you consider that to be censorship?

Yes, of course. A lot of people were surprised. But our Swiss adventures were very entertaining…

The Truffaut incident

Filmmakers were sometimes invited to Le Masque et la Plume.

François-Régis Bastide invited a director every three months or so. He once hosted Robert Bresson, but I wasn't around.

---

*A daily radio programme broadcast on the BBC from London between July 1940 and August 1944.

It was quite unique – Bresson talking with the audience and critics. Mylène Bresson, his widow, had the good sense to include a transcript in a book published by Flammarion. I remember a rather dramatic moment when Truffaut came to talk about *The Last Metro* in 1980. I said to him, "You were one of the critics who made me want to be a critic. I had such admiration for you, and used to read your work in *Arts* and *Cahiers*. But I was disappointed when I learned that around 1954-55, you published a dialogue with François Vinneuil in an extreme right-wing weekly." It was a series of four double-page spreads, a conversation between the two critics – young and old. Vinneuil was the pen name of Lucien Rebatet, a rabid anti-Semite who was sentenced to prison and stripped of his rights after the Liberation, one of the most racist and fascist journalists France has ever known. Barely ten years after the end of the war, just after he had been released from prison, Truffaut was fraternising with him. It's worth noting that according to Langlois, they were the two greatest film critics in France, and Rebatet – who was very attuned to issues of *mise en scène* – somewhat foreshadowed Truffaut's approach. Truffaut weakly defended himself, saying, "But I was very young..." Well, he was twenty-six or twenty-seven, and André Bazin, who had taught him and was very left-leaning, would never have overlooked Rebatet's wartime collaboration. Truffaut must have been aware of all this, even if he wasn't politically inclined.

He did later protest the war in Algeria.

Yes, but he made it clear that it wasn't for political reasons, that it had nothing to do with the war in Algeria, that it was in the name of "free will." Likewise, he defended censorship and even wrote, "La censure n'existe que pour les lâches" ["Censorship exists only for cowards"]. But when *La Religieuse*, made by his best friend Rivette, was subject to censorship, Truffaut immediately attacked the Gaullist government. In any case, an important scene in *The Last Metro* involves the critic Alain Laubreaux, the theatrical equivalent of Vinneuil during the war, who was also an anti-Semitic and homophobe, and who Jean Marais publicly slapped for attacking Cocteau – even if, as we learned later, Cocteau had the hots for Hitler! He's played by Jean-Louis Richard, and in the film is slapped by Depardieu because of his politics. I asked Truffaut if he was making a reference to Marais slapping Laubreaux. "And in a way," I asked, "isn't this a kind of contrition on your part? And now that

Vinneuil is dead, also an allusion to his conduct during the Occupation?" At that moment Claude Mauriac stood up and said, "What? Truffaut was a friend of Vinneuil's? I'm leaving. I refuse to be a part of this programme any longer." And he left. Martine de Rabaudy and Bastide had to run after him and bring him back to the studio. Truffaut said, "No, it's not like that. I was young and didn't realise..." I was told this part of the programme was cut because when I listened to the broadcast, it wasn't there anymore. I was also told that Claude Mauriac asked for the entire incident to be removed.

Circus games and commedia dell'arte

If there's one thing you must have loved at Le Masque et la Plume, *it's being able to sharpen your arguments to defend your point of view.*

I'm not saying I always buy into my opponent's opinions, but I do like a good argument. Some critics didn't last long on *La Masque et la Plume* because they were too rigid and ruthless in their writing but couldn't back up their judgements when challenged. It's easy to pluck quotes from Heidegger and drop them into an article to impress readers, but it doesn't work as well on the radio. A critic for a major newspaper never really knows how many people read their work to the very end, whereas when you're a teacher in a classroom or broadcasting in front of an audience, and you notice people fidgeting or walking out because they're bored, you very quickly know whether you're doing a good job or not. The feedback is immediate. Some critics at *Le Masque et la Plume* couldn't hold their ground. They struggled to articulate their ideas or got lost in the details or were unable to defend their arguments. They just kind of crumpled, followed the crowd, or went quiet if they felt like the odd one out. I never had that problem. It's easier to defend the indefensible when you write quietly in your corner than when you're on the radio with fellow critics poking fun at you.

At the same time, you do get worked up quite easily when you can't convince someone of something, which is great for radio, because it gives the whole thing a bit of a circus atmosphere.

That's true. *Le Masque et la Plume* is a bit like commedia dell'arte, in that everyone has a role to play. These days I'm the cinephile, the person who can make reference to an old film, who knows the work of a director and can explain how it has evolved over the years, who writes for *Positif*, the go-to journal, although to be honest I'm more interested in being polemical and combative, and asserting my tastes. Alain Riou,* for example, has a lively way of doing things. Jean-Marc Lalanne, who is very outspoken, used to write for *Cahiers* and *Libération*, and is now at *Les Inrockuptibles*. The provocative Xavier Leherpeur is kind of Bory's successor. Sophie Avon talks well and knows how to argue. Éric Neuhoff is sort of a 1950s-style dandy. He loves cinema, but above all he's a man of literature, and is passionately opinionated: "'I don't like it, I'm bored, it's awful!" Danièle Heymann, who represents the great journalistic traditions, wrote for *L'Express* for a long time before moving to *Le Monde*. She represents – in the best sense of the word – the sensibility of the dailies and weeklies. And then, of course, there's Pierre Murat, who writes for *Télérama*, which is definitely the most prescriptive mainstream weekly.

On-air responsibility

What do these fortnightly discussions contribute to your work as a critic?

It's actually monthly. We rotate within the group, as well as alternating with the theatre and literature crowds. I fully subscribe to something Truffaut said about Costa-Gavras, and I quote from memory: "Le rôle des *Cahiers*, c'est de montrer la limite des films politiques de Costa-Gavras, mais si on écrit dans *L'Observateur* ou dans *Le Monde*, on doit les défendre." ["*Cahiers*' role is to show the limits of Costa-Gavras' political films, but if you're writing in *L'Observateur* or *Le Monde*, it's vital to show your support."] What he meant was that you shouldn't express yourself in the same way – with the same tone and intensity – if you're writing for a journal with fifteen thousand readers as you would if you were writing for a newspaper that's read by a million people. You have a different responsibility. That might seem surprising, but it's actually not. Good films like *Z* and *The Confession* may not have the cinematic qualities of *Salvatore Giuliano*, but they play a real civic role in that they were important in raising awareness of torture and fascist coups d'état.

One time there was a discussion on the literary version of *La Masque et la Plume* about Rithy Panh's book *The*

---

* Alain Riou (b.1941). French film critic.

Elimination, which gave rise to his film *The Missing Picture*. It's an autobiographical story about the death of his family and the Cambodian genocide. One of the participants was asked what he thought of the book. He said, "I thought this was a *literary* programme. We shouldn't be discussing this book." I was taken aback by this way he completely brushed aside this extraordinary memoir, whereas he would have agreed to talk about some banal biography with no particular literary value. What he clearly didn't want to do, deep down as some kind of Parisian revolutionary, was to talk about the Khmer Rouge, question the value of communism, or make mention of the genocide of a third of the Cambodian population. Rithy Panh's aim with his book was not primarily literary. He wrote it with Christophe Bataille, and while it doesn't claim to be a masterpiece, there's real value to it.

Without changing my opinion, I sometimes significantly adjust the way I talk about the same film when discussing it in *Positif*, on *Le Masque et la Plume*, or in newspapers like *L'Express* or *Le Monde*, to which I have contributed, even though my core judgement remains the same across different media.

Birth of a programme (2): *Projection privée*

While appearing on Le Masque et la Plume, *you also became the producer of an interview programme on France Culture.*

I've always liked doing interviews and have recorded countless numbers of them. As early as the 1970s, I was publishing books of interviews. There was a programme by Serge Daney called *Microfilms*, which had replaced another programme by Claude-Jean Philippe called *Le Cinéma des cinéastes* on which I occasionally appeared, and I also used to appear on *Panorama de France Culture* hosted by Jacques Duchateau, a wonderful independent-minded producer, alongside Michel Bidlowsky. I would discuss books, art, and of course, films. Then Serge Daney, who had AIDS, stepped down because the weekly pace was too much for him, and Jean-Marie Borzeix, the director of France Culture, asked Michel Pérez if he wanted to take over, but Pérez, a close friend of mine who had written for *Positif*, was also dying of AIDS, so Borzeix asked me if I would consider the job. I hesitated because of my teaching commitments and thought a weekly show would be tough. At the time it was a shorter programme, around thirty to thirty-five minutes. Eventually I took the plunge and came up with a new name: *Projection privée* [*Private Screening*].

The Daney programme you were talking about – was it a talk show?

Yes, Daney was an excellent interviewer. My first broadcast, on 7 October 1990, was about Soviet cinema – not a very glamorous subject. The second was a conversation with someone who was practically unknown at the time I recorded our interview at a festival in Strasbourg: Dominique Besnehard, the agent turned producer.

So your guests are not exclusively directors?

Absolutely not. I wanted to mix things up. The first year I did episodes with the Taviani brothers at Rencontres du cinéma italien in Annecy; Patrice Leconte, who had perhaps forgiven me; Bachar Sabunsu, a Turkish filmmaker and theatre director who I discovered in Istanbul; Pierre Pitiot, who created Cinemed, a film festival in Montpellier; Christian Vincent, who talked about his first film, *La Discrète*; Farrokh Ghaffari, director of Tehran's cinematheque during the Shah's rule and a filmmaker in Iran before the arrival of the mullahs; filmmaker Alain Mazars to discuss his film *Lost Spring*, which he shot in China; and the Polish director Krzysztof Zanussi. You can see what I was aiming for: a Turk, an Iranian, Italian cinema, Russian cinema, French cinema, early cinema. There was an episode on Fritz Lang's centenary. The programme was really a survey of film history, and it was eclectic too: Brigitte Roüan, Jacques Doillon, Robert Kramer, João Cesar Monteiro, Micheline Presle, Isabelle Huppert, Andrei Konchalovsky, Geraldine Chaplin... I could go on! A thousand guests over a twenty-four-year period. I had complete freedom to invite whoever I wanted, and – it's important to add – unfailing support from the various people in charge after Borzeix: Patrice Gélinet, Laure Adler, David Kessler, Bruno Patino and Olivier Poivre d'Arvor.

Who was your audience?

We've never had more listeners than today, even though I've changed time slots four times. I'm now settled on Saturdays at 3 p.m. I have about a hundred thousand listeners: seventy thousand live and thirty thousand podcast downloads, which has completely changed the nature of radio. I get feedback from people in Tennessee and Japan. It's a very engaged audience. About two years ago the show was extended from thirty-five or forty minutes to an hour, and I incorporated ten-minute segments which allow me to cover other things, like a book or exhibition or DVD release. Four shows a month isn't enough! There's so much going on…

The joys of casting

Choosing guests can't be easy.

It's a bit like casting an actor in a film. It's not easy to get some of them talking. Directors often say that casting is 90% of their job.

You mean you direct them?

No, but they're sometimes intimidated and hesitant, especially the actors. It can be disappointing to read an interview with an actor in a magazine or newspaper, but if you talk to them about how they do their job – how they rehearse, if they watch rushes, how they interact with directors – much of the time you realise just how articulate they can be about what they do. There are some great actors who aren't necessarily geniuses, but let's not be unfair – plenty of them are surprisingly smart.

I always learn a great deal from my guests. There are the composers – Michel Legrand, Gabriel Yared, Alexandre Desplat, Bruno Coulais – who talk as we listen to extracts from their music. There are the cinematographers – Pierre Lhomme, Eric Gautier, Philippe Rousselot, Caroline Champetier – and set decorators, like Jacques Saulnier and Max Douy. Editors might be the trickiest. Some have made major contributions to cinema and are extremely creative, but it's also the most secret art because it goes by so unnoticeably. A lady in her fifties told me that she had listened to my programme with Hervé de Luze, who has edited films by Renais and Polanski. She said to me, "If I had heard that at nineteen, I would have become an editor! I didn't know that job even existed…"

Curiously, the episodes with the most listeners aren't those with the most famous guests. It turns out that in fifty minutes, we can really get to the bottom of things, and interviewees are grateful for that. Some of them, especially the technicians who work behind the scenes, people who aren't necessarily used to talking about their work, can be a bit anxious. Compare them with directors, who are always discussing things with collaborators, or writers who come to talk about a new book. But once they overcome their stage fright, they're happy to finally be talking about what they do, and they have great insight. I also have the pleasure, the honour, almost, of talking with people who rarely appear on the radio, like Philippe Garrel or Eric Rohmer – who appeared six or seven times. Alain Resnais, a fervent radio listener, was a regular guest. Just as some people like dogs and some prefer cats, there are television people and there are radio people. They don't always mix. Chabrol, for example, never listened to the radio. He watched television, mainly because – like Flaubert – he found it to be a remarkable storehouse of stupidity.

I've always invited people who aren't necessarily filmmakers whose work I like because France Culture is a state-run, public radio station. It's like Serge Toubiana at the Cinémathèque paying tribute to directors like René Clément, Robert Altman and Alain Corneau, who never got good reviews from *Cahiers*. When you work at the Cinémathèque française or Radio France, it's important not to reflect the policies of a particular journal. I did an episode with Jean-Jacques Beineix about his memoirs, and one with Claude Lelouch, who we aren't used to hearing at France Culture. And why not? Not only did he make films that I like a lot, like *The Crook* and *Happy New Year*, but he really did make an impact on French cinema. Actors adore him, and he always gets such good performances out of them. He has a lot to say about cinema, with an experimental twist all his own. He's always trying new things and operates the camera himself.

I have so many wonderful memories of these people. I recently did an episode with Marcel Ophuls when his autobiographical film, *Ain't Misbehavin'*, was screened at Directors' Fortnight at Cannes. Many people remarked on his outspokenness when talking about Arte, and his anger that they didn't broadcast his film in prime time. I also remember Lucian Pintilie, the Romanian filmmaker, a formidable polemicist who doesn't mince his words. Radio allows for a special kind of freedom.

What's the secret to a good radio interview?

Preparation. It's not so different from a regular conversation. And here again, my teacher training has come in handy. As I mentioned, you can't just walk in empty-handed. Let me clarify a couple of things. First, as much as I can be dazzled by twenty-five-year-old critics who write fabulously, I very much believe that when it comes to interviews, experience counts. Hours spent in the library and reading endless articles are no substitute. I'm thinking of someone like Carlos Diegues, one of the pioneers of Brazilian Cinema Novo, whose career I've been following since 1963 – that's fifty years now. It's obvious that if he's a guest on the programme, I'll talk to him about my experiences of Cinema Novo, a movement I'm very familiar with. I have a visceral, tangible knowledge that someone who has merely taken notes or perused summaries of films they've never seen simply can't replicate. Unless, of course, we're talking about just a single film. But most of the time on *Projection privée* we discuss an entire body of work, as when I invite a foreigner who's passing through Paris, like Andrei Konchalovsky or Krzysztof Zanussi. I've been following Konchalovsky since the premiere of *The First Teacher* in 1966 at Venice, and have witnessed all the ups and downs of Soviet politics. We can discuss the Khrushchev era or Brezhnev or Yeltsin. So there's my firsthand experience of things, which can be augmented by France Culture's archive.

What else is required for a successful interview?

The second important thing – and I always mention this to beginners – is not to ask questions that are too long. Don't confuse being a critic with being an interviewer. If a question is a piece of mini-analysis, you're missing the mark. Of course, there are filmmakers for whom this doesn't matter, because they have an answer to everything. You can ask them a twenty-line question and they'll respond with an impeccable two hundred pages. But most don't like to dissect their work. They might go along with it, but only reluctantly. So the shorter the question, the more you avoid hearing them say, "Well, you've said it all. What can I add to that?" Long questions take the pressure off them, leaving you high and dry.

And a third piece of advice is to not be afraid of silence. They say that nature abhors a vacuum, but the interviewer shouldn't be worried. When a film comes out and someone's done maybe seven or eight interviews before yours, they're bound to repeat themselves. The interesting thing is to get them to say something new. What happens if you let the silence linger? It's the interviewee who abhors a vacuum. If you jump into a new question right away, you miss out on what the silence might provoke. On the other hand, let the silence linger and perhaps the person you're talking to will come up with interesting ways to fill the gap.

So those are my three interview tips. As I see it, the interviewer's job is similar to that of the filmmaker, except that in this particular case, because we record for the exact duration of the broadcast, there's no editing.

The person being interviewed should feel that the interviewer has really put in the work, so they can trust them, relax, and let loose.

It's essential that the interviewee really feels listened to. It's a bit like wooing a woman – taking an interest in her, getting her to talk about herself. If someone feels that you're interested in their work, that you know and appreciate it, they'll open up. Jean-Loup Passek, director of the La Rochelle festival, who I knew well, wanted to do a Richard Brooks retrospective and asked for my help. I called Brooks in Los Angeles to tell him about the festival. I explained that La Rochelle is a port on the Atlantic, where part of *The Three Musketeers* takes place. He trusted me and agreed to attend. He landed in Nantes after a twelve-hour journey and I picked him up. He was already quite old and was exhausted when he arrived. The first interview was with *Ouest France*. Jean-Loup Passek says to me, "I don't have an interpreter. Can you translate?" Now, I don't want to criticise young journalists who are assigned all sorts of tasks, including surprise interviews, but the first question was, "Mr. Brooks, I haven't seen your films yet, but what was it like directing Humphrey Bogart?" I didn't bother to translate that bit. Coming all the way from Los Angeles for *that* – it's awful. It just kills the will to go on. It's vital to establish a climate of trust and credibility. Once the interviewee trusts the person asking the questions, they'll be more willing to open up.

Cinema seen by...

Something else you do with Projection privée *is invite personalities who aren't involved with film, like philosophers and novelists.*

It really broadens the mind. These are people who do write about cinema, but only occasionally, for example, Jacques Rancière, Clément Rosset and Marc Augé, who published a book about *Casablanca*. I invited Slavoj Žižek and Dominique Noguez, who have published extensively on cinema, also contemporary thinkers like Alain Badiou and Hubert Damisch. It seems to be a very French thing to do. It's not surprising that French and American films are consistently the most impressive in cinema history. There has been great Italian cinema, great German cinema, great Russian cinema, great Japanese cinema, but they were always confined to specific periods. This continuity applies not only to films made, but also the criticism written about them, especially for the past thirty or forty years. The first critics appeared in France in the 1920s, starting with Louis Delluc. Writers, thinkers and philosophers – Bergson, Malraux, Merleau-Ponty – have written about cinema. After the war, every film club published its own journal: the Catholics had *Télécine*, the Jean Vigo film club had *Jeune Cinéma*, the Fédération française des ciné-clubs had *Cinéma 55, 56, 57*, which leaned communist, the secular socialists had *Image et Son* and later *La Revue du Cinéma – Image et Son*. With the exception of *Jeune Cinéma*, all these journals have now disappeared. What a remarkable time it was! On *Projection privée* I've had the opportunity to speak with a range of intellectuals with very different ideas about film. Even though I think it used to be a big deal talking about cinema, an important cultural event, it's not the same anymore. The spark is gone. In the 1960s we were talking about Resnais, Antonioni, Godard, Losey, Bergman, Fellini, as well as the New Novelists.[*] It was part of the intellectual scene. I don't think we're there anymore today.

---

[*] A term applied to various French writers including Nathalie Sarraute, Claude Simon, Alain Robbe-Grillet, Marguerite Duras and Michel Butor.

THE BOOKS AND THEIR ORIGINS

Francesco Rosi

Your first interview for Positif, *done alongside your colleagues Goffredo Fofi and Paolo Gobetti, was with Francesco Rosi, in the May 1965 issue. In 1976, you published your book* Le Dossier Rosi.

We did the interview in Venice in 1964. I had seen Rosi's first film, *The Challenge*, which I liked, but hadn't yet seen his second, *I magliari*, which at the time hadn't been released in France. *Salvatore Giuliano*, which I discovered at the Bonaparte, on Place Saint-Sulpice, was one of the great moments of my life as a filmgoer, one I wrote about in *Cinéma-Textes*. I was overwhelmed by the film, not only by its mastery, its beauty and intelligence, but because it was the first time that I had seen such subtle political cinema. I was left with a series of lingering questions for which I had no clear answers, at the same time as being confronted with the equivalent of a poetic painting. *Salvatore Giuliano* is the most beautiful film that has ever been made about Sicily, its people and its landscape – the great writer Leonardo Sciascia recognised this – and explores the causes and consequences of a society's failings, the sequence of events, the zone of ambiguity where there are no clear answers. It's the opposite of propaganda, and makes Eisenstein, in contrast, look overly simplistic. He was a truly great artist, aesthetically speaking, but his films, bathed in Manichaeism, were really quite unsubtle. Rosi achieved what Eisenstein aimed for when he set out to film Marx's *Capital*. With Rosi, it felt like economics, politics, law – everything – was being explained through action and gestures, in a revolutionary chronological upheaval. I felt the same way about *Hiroshima mon amour* a few years earlier, although for different reasons.

So in 1964 I went to report from Venice for *France Observateur* and *Positif*. Some Italian friends of mine who were associated with *Positif*, including Goffredo Fofi, were there. Rosi wasn't screening a film but the previous year he had won the Golden Lion for *Hands Over the City*. I don't know why but he shot through town very quickly, and was there for maybe thirty-six hours. He immediately impressed me by the way he walked. He was burly man – not fat, but sturdy, strong, with sunglasses, wearing a cap, surrounded by three or four people with briefcases. He was always on the move, always doing something, like Nottola, the corrupt developer of *Hands Over the City*, played by Rod

Steiger, or later, Gian Maria Volonté in *The Mattei Affair*. They really had something of Rosi about them – his energy: always working, a man of action. He was a lot like his films. *Hands Over the City* is certainly critical of Nottola, but at the same time you sense that Rosi – even though in the film he denounces the character politically and morally – somehow respects his power and drive. Nottola is on the wrong side of society and politics, when he could have used his influence for good. That was the first impression I got of Rosi.

I called him and asked to meet. He knew *Positif*, since he's a big cinephile and I think he's always had a subscription. Many Italians of the time read the magazine because we covered cinema from that part of the world. Politically, the Italian Communist Party had no connection with ours. It was more open, and non-Communist leftists like Rosi connected with it much more easily. Plus, at the time Italy was producing such incredible films which combined visual beauty with a search for socio-political truths. Along with Pasolini, Zurlini, Bolognini, Olmi and De Seta, Rosi expressed this magnificently. And let's not forget Italian comedy.

At the time we didn't do much interviewing at *Positif*, so it was a tremendous opportunity. We sat down on a terrace of the Excelsior and did a great interview, my first with Rosi.

It was the start of a relationship that led to a book.

I liked his next few films, and we kept meeting up. We talked about *Many Wars Ago*, then *The Mattei Affair* and *Lucky Luciano*. Around the time of *Illustrious Corpses* in 1976, I suggested we talk about his early years. The book ended up being published thirteen years after our first meeting. I've never written a commissioned book in my life. The interview books I did with Elia Kazan and Joseph Losey were done in one go. In the case of Rosi, John Boorman, Stanley Kubrick, Jerry Schatzberg and Jane Campion, they evolved over time. I wrote about each of their films and met them along the way, and at a certain point decided retrospectively to collect the material together, add more, edit it all together, and publish them long after our first meeting. That's what happened in Rosi's case.

The duality of a Southern Italian

You and Rosi became friends.

I admire all the filmmakers I've written about, but I'm closer to Rosi than anyone else. We talk on the phone and see each other when I'm in Rome. I went to Cartagena in Colombia to do a "making of" documentary when he was working on an adaptation of Gabriel García Márquez's novel *Chronicle of a Death Foretold*. He's someone I greatly admire, no doubt because of the duality deep inside him – the interplay between rationality and reflection on the one hand, and emotion and sensitivity on the other. Reason and passion. And I find that Rosi, perhaps unusually for an Italian, has a rational streak due to his background in Naples, a land full of lawyers and rationalists, contrary to the clichés of the south: chaos and anarchy. Sure, there are plenty of quick tempers down there, plus superstition and exquisite opera, but the illustrious philosopher of history Vico, a great legal tradition and Enlightenment culture all left their mark on Naples. The place has been conquered by everyone: the Spanish, the French, the Normans before them. Rosi embodies this rational and disciplined side, like that of a lawyer. There are many great journalists of Neapolitan origin. At the same time, Rosi is all about fervour and fury. He can be explosive. You feel the presence of death. Corpses litter his films, including the one he planned to make about Julius Caesar. They're all over *Hands Over the City* and even *Carmen*. The only one devoid of dead bodies is his last film, *The Truce*, about the return to life after the concentration camps. In Rosi's cinema, passion and reason are never incompatible. Each feeds the other.

What were his politics?

Here, too, we stood together. He wasn't a communist – a rarity in Italian political cinema. He was a socialist, in favour of an alliance with the communists because, after all, Italy needed a government, hence there was an implicit understanding, just like there was in France at a certain point with Mitterrand's reformist *Programme commun*.* So he wasn't anti-communist, but he was

---

* A French reform programme, signed 27 June 1972 by the Socialist Party (founded by François Mitterrand), the Communist Party and the centrist Radical Movement of the Left.

fiercely anti-Stalinist and anti-authoritarian. In fact, sometimes the communists attacked his films, including *Illustrious Corpses*, because they wanted clear-cut answers and an obvious depiction of who the villains were. But Rosi showcased the ins and outs, broke down the different sides, and analysed the forces at play, never oversimplifying things. He showed that Mattei had to die, while refraining from asserting that the CIA had killed him, because he simply didn't know. He didn't create imaginary solutions. Interestingly, the communists, who criticised *Illustrious Corpses* for its lack of options, echoed the perplexity of Americans who, at the Cannes Film Festival, while appreciating *The Mattei Affair*, asked, "But who killed him?" Hollywood doesn't understand that a film might not provide an answer to that question. They were bewildered by the lack of a definitive conclusion.

I've always thought that there were connections between communists and American capitalism. American philosophy tells us that we're moving towards happiness, progress, and a better world – like communism, but in a different way. Both systems believe in progress. And it takes sceptical old Europe, which has seen it all, to cast doubt on everything. Even though many Europeans have fallen for what are essentially criminal utopias, European culture still thrives much more on ambiguity, and asks many more questions, compared with the United States, which has staunchly defended its capitalist dream, just as the communists did their communist ideal.

Elia Kazan

The second interview you conducted in Positif *was with Elia Kazan, which you recorded with Roger Tailleur in 1966. An obviously controversial personality, about whom you published your first important book, in 1973. What drew you to Kazan?*

For each book, my response is going to be the same: it was born of the shock I experienced either when I was already a critic or as a young filmgoer. Kazan lies somewhere between the two. His first film was *A Tree Grows in Brooklyn*, but at the age of sixteen I saw *On the Waterfront* for the first time, when it was released in France. With those performances from Marlon Brando, Eva Marie Saint and Rod Steiger, it really did feel like an earthquake. What really struck me about Kazan was his direction of actors. Obviously, I wasn't alone in feeling this. Many revered the Actors Studio that Kazan created and then left soon thereafter, where he trained a whole generation of actors: Montgomery Clift, Marlon Brando, James Dean, Paul Newman, and others. The revolution of Method acting impacted the whole world, though I wasn't aware of it at the time, as some of the films hadn't been released.

Seeing *On the Waterfront* for the first time was a profound experience. It was also an aesthetic shock. At a time when more and more films were being made in colour, Kazan shot his in black and white, in New York, on the docks, with extraordinary camerawork by Boris Kaufman. You could feel the steam, the characters' breath. Even though today it seems highly crafted, for a sixteen-year-old it felt so real. And it was also a love story, and a film about corruption. As I mentioned before, I've always been drawn to history, and the political critique of *On the Waterfront* fascinated me. This was all reinforced for me by Kazan's *East of Eden*, another revelation, thanks to James Dean. He fascinated everyone, even though we realise now he's probably a lesser actor than Brando. The use of Cinemascope and colour in *East of Eden* was extraordinarily inventive: the lyricism, the landscapes of the San Fernando Valley in California. And, notably, it's the story of a family. When you're an adolescent, family dynamics are crucial. You're no longer blindly following whatever your parents tell you. It's the period that precedes the discovery of love.

There were other magnificent Kazan films that perhaps impacted me even more aesthetically: *Wild River*, *Splendor in the Grass*, and a film that is utterly unique in American cinema of the era, *America, America*, with its personalised narrative style and the director's own voiceover over the credits: "My name is Elia Kazan" – like Orson Welles had done before him. When I say that Kubrick and Welles were the two greatest influences of their time, I could add that Kazan, sandwiched between them, had a comparable impact. He left a mark on an entire generation of filmmakers. It's debatable whether they were the greatest American filmmakers, but Kazan certainly left his mark on his era, if only because he filmed in New York, co-wrote his films, established a new school of actors, and delved into America's socio-political landscape, far from the entertainment-focused Hollywood films. Sidney Lumet, later Scorsese, Arthur Penn and Coppola all acknowledged their debt to him.

The uncertainties of a director

You first wrote about him in Positif *in 1964.*

An essay called "Les incertitudes d'Elia Kazan," published on the release of *America, America*. I was rather harsh in my judgement of his behaviour when he testified before the House Un-American Activities Committee, which caused quite a stir at *Positif*. People like Kyrou, who was of Greek origin – as Kazan was – and had fought on the side of the communists during the civil war, had no sympathy for him. I don't think he found Kazan's later films that bad, but there was some resistance. Benayoun, who adored Kazan and had written about *East of Eden*, backed me up. He also wrote about *A Face in the Crowd*, about a singer who might become president, which is a powerful and prophetic critique of showbiz politics and the mass media and foreshadowed the election of Ronald Reagan.

Did you avoid these political issues when you discussed the film at Positif*?*

No, we talked about it – which upset Kyrou and Louis Seguin. Even so, Kazan's films really got to them, and they acknowledged that even after Kazan's HUAC testimony, he continued – with even more vehemence, in fact – to attack false American values and the way society operates.

How did your first meeting come about?

The leading Kazan expert at *Positif* was Roger Tailleur. A few months after my article, his book on Kazan – one of the best I know about a filmmaker – was published. Tailleur didn't know Kazan, but they had corresponded, and Kazan let him know he was passing through Paris. He was staying at a small hotel near Madeleine and offered to meet. Tailleur rarely did interviews, but he asked if Kazan would give one. Since I had just written this significant article which he was good enough to say he found interesting, Tailleur suggested I accompany him. So we went to meet Kazan at the hotel, where he was at his typewriter, writing. He was at rock bottom, which wasn't like him, because he always seemed able to bounce back from things. Even though it had been well received in France, *America, America* had split the critics in the US, and although it received two Oscar nominations, it had flopped. What's interesting is that he was typing *The Arrangement*, his novel, which ended up selling three million copies and launched him on a new career as a writer. Kazan was like a phoenix who never stopped reinventing himself, moving beyond, immersing himself in something new, and always coming back strong. His wife had passed away the previous year, just after the filming of *America, America*, and he was with Barbara Loden. He introduced her to us, then we conducted our interview for *Positif*.

From *Wanda* to *Kazan by Kazan*

Barbara Loden later directed a beautifully unique film, Wanda, *in which she played the lead role.*

Wanda was screened at Venice in 1970, and Kazan came like a knight in shining armor to accompany his wife. The film, which was shot on 16mm and had a tiny budget, was well-received and won the Fipresci Prize. I did an interview with her, which wasn't published for another five years, when the film was released in France at Saint-André-des-Arts. I think it's perhaps the only major interview ever done with Barbara Loden because the film wasn't much seen in the United States. It's about a woman who is devoted to a man, which didn't fit with the feminist ideologies of the era. A DVD of *Wanda* was released thirty years later, which included a recording of the interview.

It was at Venice that I discussed the book project with Kazan. A series of volumes had been created in England under the auspices of the British Film Institute, in partnership with an English publisher, Secker & Warburg. They had already published Jon Halliday's *Sirk on Sirk*, so I said to Kazan, "Why don't we do a book like Truffaut's with Hitchcock, film by film, where I interview you?" I knew that the English wanted to publish it, and he seemed to like the idea. The following year, in 1971, I went to Sandy Hook, Connecticut, about seventy miles from New York, where Kazan had bought a country house with money he had made when he was an actor at Warner Bros. in the 1940s. His son Chris also had a house there.

How did you work together?

Every morning and afternoon we did a three or four-hour recording session, talking about his life. Before we sat down together, he allowed me to visit Wesleyan University, where he had deposited his archives. I think I'm the only person who was given access to it before his death. There were piles of correspondence. That's where I read all the memos from Darryl Zanuck around the time of *Viva Zapata!* and realised how exceptional a producer he was. Zanuck commented on every shot, the lighting of every frame, and asked for re-shoots, even if it meant spending more money. Thanks to this research, my questions to Kazan were much more informed. I think he was quite touched that a left-wing magazine like *Positif* took an interest in him. Even critics who could never be suspected of a conservative or right-wing bias looked beyond ideological differences. They didn't condone what he had done, but despite their reservations still admired his films. I think that made it easier for some kind of reconciliation to take place.

Reflections on McCarthyism

What were his feelings about what had happened all those years ago?

Kazan was anti-totalitarian and had no sympathy for McCarthy, but as a former member, he harboured a phobia of the Communist Party. He had been expelled in 1936 after eighteen months of activism because he refused to denounce his comrades at the Group Theater who were suspected of not being active enough in their pro-Soviet activities. His expulsion was voted on by sixteen people. Fifteen were against him, Kazan himself was the sole dissenting vote. Then came the Nazi-Soviet pact, which his former comrades supported, followed by revelations – by Koestler, Orwell and others – about Siberian labour camps, and then the invasion of North Korea by the Chinese communists, who imposed their ideology on the entire country, and the 1948 coup d'état in Czechoslovakia. And he snapped, and he informed. There are certainly things he did wrong, but we're not going to go into every detail here. Today it's certainly more acceptable to criticise Stalinism. But let's not forget that during the Cold War, American communist activists – including filmmakers and screenwriters – didn't utter a single word against Stalin. The people who condemned Kazan for his HUAC testimony said nothing about the informing that was going on in Soviet-controlled countries, where the result was often death. I know there were suicides during the McCarthy years, but the worst punishment meted out in the United States was a year in prison with a newspaper every morning and visits from spouses and friends. It was a long way from the Gulag or a dozen bullets in the head from a firing squad. The informing that went on in those totalitarian regimes was horrendous, but it was never once condemned by the American far left. I've never read statements from American Communists – many of whom were Jewish – expressing outrage at the anti-Semitism, the doctors' plots, or how Stalin liquidated Jews in the camps. It was a double standard that shocked me morally. We discussed this with Kazan. I reproached him for informing even while he condemned it when it happened in the Soviet Union.

He didn't hold it against you?

Not at all. I developed an extremely close relationship with him. Although he caused much suffering to others, he had himself suffered because, in reality, it wasn't an easy decision for him to make. He knew that after testifying his friends would distance themselves from him, and most of them did, though he remained close with Billy Wilder, Mankiewicz and left-leaning people like John Steinbeck and Budd Schulberg, who shared his anti-Stalinism. But ultimately, HUAC marked a turning point in his life, and he withdrew into himself. I think it fueled his anger because, deep down, it was the American system that had brought him to that moment. The producers never had to create a blacklist. People like Sam Goldwyn, Louis B. Mayer and Jack Warner could have said to McCarthy, "We don't care about your directives. These are talented people, and we'll continue to hire them." Their studios were privately owned, but they were so frightened that they showed absolutely no courage. They caved, just like Kazan. That's something no one ever talks about. The blacklist system was established, and for years Kazan was the scapegoat for all these powerful men who were even more responsible, since they'd had the power not to yield. If artists didn't comply, they lost their jobs, whereas the producers were masters in their own houses, and they wouldn't have been risking a lot if they had stood up to this fascist lunatic who was terrorising America. I've always despised scapegoats, anyone designated as responsible for everything. So for me, all of that made Kazan more likeable. As a result of the anger he felt at that time, he said himself that his subsequent films became much braver and more critical of an America with which he had temporarily collaborated. He was a liberal who challenged most of his country's values: sexual puritanism, capitalism, the media, and the rest of it.

For the love of Orson Welles

Even though Hollywood acknowledges Kazan's influence and importance, the industry has remained ambivalent towards him. Look at the controversy that ensued when he received his honorary Oscar.

An anecdote about Orson Welles, related to Kazan, is instructive. I conducted a press conference for Welles at the Ritz hotel, which went very well. It was tricky because he didn't want to do it in French, although he spoke it perfectly. He was known to correct his interpreters all the time – though that never happened with me. Afterwards, he said to me, "There's a conference at the Cinémathèque française in a few days. Would you come?" I was unwell at the time and couldn't do it, but if I had been there – and there's a film of it made by Pierre-André Boutang – it might all have been a bit different, because I would have challenged him. When I saw the recording, I was outraged. Three hundred students had come to listen to him. Someone asked him, "Mr. Welles, are you experiencing the same problems as described here two years ago by Elia Kazan, who wasn't able to make a film written with Budd Schulberg, about Puerto Ricans, because he couldn't find the funding?" "Young man," replied Welles. "Stop! Do not mention that name in front of me. That man denounced his friends." And there was thunderous applause. The audience was thrilled by the courage of this man as he attacked Kazan. Welles then added, "On the other hand, he's an extraordinary filmmaker." Once again, three hundred people applaud for this acknowledgment of Kazan's talent and artistic objectivity. Later, I worked on a second book about Kazan, *An American Odyssey*, an edited compilation – texts he had written, accompanied by photos – like the one I did on Losey called *L'Œil du maître*. I went back to his archive in Wesleyan, where I stumbled upon a beautiful drawing by Orson Welles dedicated "To Gadge" – Kazan's nickname since the 1930s – "With love. Orson. 1957." The man who was publicly attacked, in front of a crowd of youngsters who knew nothing about the stakes of that era, was handed a "with love" gift five years after his testimony before the House Un-American Activities Committee. Such a shocking double standard. After *On the*

Waterfront and *East of Eden*, by 1957 Kazan was back in the limelight. There had been rivalry between Welles and Kazan in the 1930s, in the theatre world, when Kazan was with the Group Theater and Welles was with the Mercury. They had also both worked in radio. And Welles, along with Kazan and Losey, was a Roosevelt supporter.

The man and the artist

Your partnership with Kazan lasted until the end of his life.

We remained very close. I must have about two hundred letters from him, some quite lengthy, up to four pages, always typed, extremely precise, discussing his private life, films he had seen, his projects and thoughts. He kept himself well-informed and read the paper every morning. He was concerned about what was going on in the world and was always on the side of the oppressed. He got Yilmaz Güney, the great Turkish filmmaker and actor, released from prison. Kazan arrived at Istanbul Airport and publicly said, "The most beautiful word in the Turkish language is 'freedom.' I demand freedom for Yilmaz Güney." He sent telegrams of support to imprisoned Brazilian filmmakers who were being tortured. He sympathised with Glauber Rocha and every left-wing Latin American filmmaker. Makavejev, the Yugoslav libertarian, embraced him, saying, "Yes, you were right to denounce those bastards. We, in Eastern countries, suffered terribly. So many people were tortured and massacred." He was admired by everyone he met because he had an extraordinary gift for communication. He would walk across Paris, even at eighty years old. From his little hotel near Étoile, he would walk down to the 9th arrondissement where I live, rue du Faubourg-Montmartre, and have dinner at my place. He would converse in somewhat broken French with the newsstand vendor, the fruit seller, and instantly establish a rapport. When you saw how he engaged with people, you understood why he was such a great director of actors. His job was to make each of them feel as if they were the absolute best in the world, and that, at that moment, he was working only with them.

A way to gain their trust, while also keeping a close eye on them.

During filming, he was always able to capture the unexpected, the accidental, on film. He mentioned this fantastic scene in *On the Waterfront* where Eva Marie Saint inadvertently dropped her glove. Another director might have said, "Alright, let's go again. Pick the glove up and hold it tight this time." But Kazan sees Marlon Brando picking up the glove, putting it on his hand – with the sexual metaphor it implies – and suddenly this object becomes imbued with emotion, with the relationship developing between this woman and her brother's murderer, with whom she falls in love. Kazan, like other great directors, knew how to embrace the unexpected. That doesn't mean good cinema is all about improvisation. But staying open to the unexpected is crucial.

What kind of person was he in private?

A very simple man, with no need for extravagance. He was happy to eat cheese, olives, tomatoes. He held onto that rural Anatolian essence, which is where he originally came from. He was a Greek from Turkey and stayed connected to his youth. He acted as a regular working-class guy in the theatre. He was always an activist. He couldn't find a producer for a project, and so, like Barbara Loden, he made a film on 16mm, shot at his country house for $50,000, called *The Visitors*. He had a cinematographer, a sound recordist, four unknown actors, and just one professional. The entire crew was only three people. They all cooked together. The film, one of the very first about the Vietnam War, could also be seen as him ruminating over his HUAC testimony – although he never apologised.

In the end, Kazan's work is full of tragedy. *The Visitors* also testifies to an incredible vitality and a remarkable ability to adapt. He mentioned that Deborah Kerr's costumes in *The Arrangement* – the big-budget flop that he adapted from his novel – cost as much as the entire budget of *The Visitors*. He felt he had returned to the filmmaking of his youth, when he made documentaries. How many famous American filmmakers, with two Oscars under their belt, invest their own money and go back to the basics? Most directors, as they get older, want bigger budgets because they want the best technicians and all possible safety nets in case something goes wrong. They want to feel completely safe. Not Kazan.

In the end, Kazan stayed somewhat outside the system. It was, at various times, both his downfall and his salvation. Maybe that's why you can relate to him.

Yes. And what I also liked was his intellectual curiosity across the board. He loved to talk, discuss, exchange ideas. He always wanted to know what was happening and watch films. He loved Tavernier's *The Judge and the Assassin* and Rosi's *Three Brothers*. He held Angelopoulos and Pialat in high regard. He was very down-to-earth, a filmmaker who captured the essence of reality. He had been shaped by Soviet cinema and loved Dovzhenko, Renoir and Rossellini.

Joseph Losey

Not long after you met Kazan, you encountered Joseph Losey, with whom you collaborated on a book of interviews.

I ran into Losey at a screening of *The Servant*, but we didn't talk that day. And then, in 1964, we met again at the Venice Film Festival, where he was screening *King and Country* – a beautiful, very modest, almost theatrical film, adapted from John Wilson's play *Hamp*, with Tom Courtenay and Dirk Bogarde. Along with *Uomini contro* and *Paths of Glory*, it's one of the great works of modern cinema about the First World War. But I was actually much more impressed by Losey's two previous films, *Eva* and *The Servant*. I didn't know much about his American films at the time, which were being distributed, but I had never fully appreciated them. I really liked the first films he made in England, especially *Time Without Pity*, but also *Blind Date*, *The Criminal* and *The Damned*, which is science fiction. He absolutely was a major figure of the modern era, as important as Antonioni, Godard and Bergman. Then there was *Accident*, which also made a strong impression on me.

 I went to see Losey in London with Bertrand Tavernier – who wasn't yet a filmmaker – to talk about two films which had been vilified by critics in 1968, especially in the United States: *Boom!*, written by Tennessee Williams, and *Secret Ceremony*, based on a short story by Argentinian author Marco Denevi, adapted by George Tabori, a great playwright originally from Hungary. Even some of the French critics were ambivalent. The two films were criticised for their baroque excesses and mannerisms, and their aestheticism. Losey was a victim of McCarthyism who was exiled to England and never worked again in the United States.

He was in a vulnerable position at that stage of his career.

I've noticed that filmmakers – it's probably true of almost all artists – are especially grateful and attentive to people who like their films when they're going through a rough patch. I think there are two reasons for this. Sympathetic critics are more easily noticed, because when everyone adores you, individuals blur into an admiring crowd. And also because filmmakers find it hard to accept failure, especially after having just created something. It's completely understandable. Your new film is like a newborn – it's the most beautiful of all, and you find it hard to take criticism. The worst thing you can say to a director is, "I loved your first film. It's your best." That really is an unforgivable blunder. Losey already knew Tavernier, whose first article in *Positif* was about *Time Without Pity*. Filmmakers are grateful. "He's interested in me even when everyone else has abandoned me!" As a result, Losey and I became firm friends. Even if, deep down, I prefer *Boom!*, I found *Secret Ceremony* to be a wonderfully intimate film that contains many of Losey's idiosyncrasies.

Back to grace

His career was about to change...

In March 1971, while I was in London, Losey asked me to come see his latest film, *The Go-Between*. I found it very moving, and called him. "Your film is fantastic. It'll be accepted at Cannes – and mark my words: it will be the highlight of the festival." Losey had just discovered that Fox had lost faith in the film and decided against distributing it, and he was very happy that I liked it so much. MGM ended up buying it and taking it to Cannes. He had also just made the very beautiful *Figures in a Landscape*, a kind of abstract existentialist parable, a fable about two men, played by Robert Shaw and Malcolm McDowell, pursued by an enemy in a helicopter, sumptuously photographed amidst the landscapes of Spain by Henri Alekan. A screening at the San Sebastián festival had been a complete flop and the film has been almost impossible to see ever since. Today, there are no prints and no one knows where the negative is. So Losey had endured three failures in a row and arrived in Cannes with zero expectations. Everyone was waiting for *Death in Venice*, which had been released in London and which I had seen there. It's not my favourite Visconti, but everyone was saying that a second Palme d'Or was going to him, after *The Leopard*. Robert Favre Le Bret, the festival president, insisted that the film was a masterpiece and that nothing could rival the combination of Thomas Mann, Gustav Mahler, Dirk Bogarde and Visconti. Moreover, Dirk Bogarde – Losey's favourite actor – had appeared in Visconti's *The Damned*. So *Death in Venice* is screened and get good reviews, but then, quite late in the competition, *The Go-Between* causes a critical storm. The jury loves it and gives it the Palme d'Or. Dirk Bogarde was very fond of Losey, but Visconti – who was Italian nobility and the father of neorealism – held for Bogarde a kind of hyper-cultural, imperial aura. They tried to convince Visconti that *he* was the real winner, since he was going to receive the festival's 25th anniversary prize – an award specially created for him. That was the truly supreme reward, they insisted, whereas the Palme d'Or, awarded every year, was fairly humdrum. He wasn't fooled, and never really got over it.

The book of Losey

It's only a few years later that Losey and you do a book together.

It was around the time of *Mr. Klein* in 1976 that we reconnected. *Positif* put the film on its cover, but no one really liked it at Cannes and it won no awards. Alain Delon didn't show up because of the poor reception the film had received. Patrick Thévenon, a critic from *L'Express*, who had attended a private screening in Paris with the cultural minister Michel Guy, wrote a scathing article about the film even before its release. But fortunately, overall, reviews were good and Losey felt reassured. To top it off, he was awarded the César for Best Film, even though at Cannes he had been completely shut out. Anyway, all this further strengthened our friendship.

My Rosi book had won the Armand-Tallier prize for the best film book of the year, and Stock, which published it and my Kazan book, were eager to do a third, so we talked about Losey. Eugene Braun Munk, a kind of agent, contacted him, and he said yes. He knew I had written a book about Kazan, as it had also been published in English, and kept asking me. "Any news from your friend Kazan? Have you talked to him recently?" He was a little paranoid. Once, when he was walking with Dirk Bogarde in a small town, they went into a cinema, and he said, "Let's get out of here – that's Kazan over there!" But it wasn't Kazan. He saw him everywhere! At the same time, he was very curious. The most surprising thing, in fact, is that he didn't cut me off because of my relationship with Kazan. He could have said, "If there's one person I don't want to do this book with, it's the man who admires Kazan and wrote a book with him." But he actually took a real interest. As for me, not only did I have boundless admiration for Losey, I also found him fascinating.

At one point my Kazan and Losey books were out of print, and late Jean-Marc Roberts, owner of Stock, told me he would reprint them on condition that they be published together in a single volume. This caused a bit of a stir in my relationship with Mrs. Losey, who didn't really appreciate that kind of cohabitation!

Peaceful coexistence?

Many things connected and set them apart at the same time.

It felt like a logical conclusion to these two books, even if I didn't conceive them that way. While interviewing Losey, I gradually realised that they had led parallel lives. I'm no Plutarch, but it truly was like the pairing of two great men. Both were born the same year – 1909. Both were members of the Communist Party. Both worked in theatre, politics and radio in late 1930s New York. Both headed to Hollywood – Kazan in 1944 with *A Tree Grows in Brooklyn*, Losey in 1948 with *The Boy with Green Hair*. Both had to deal with McCarthyism, albeit on different sides: one as a victim, the other as an informer. Then their careers diverged. Losey's took off after his exile in England, where he was able to work with some of the greats, including Harold Pinter. If he had stayed in America, he might have become a great director of crime films, like Don Siegel – that's a compliment, by the way – but he likely wouldn't have become as famous as he did in 1960s Europe. Whereas Kazan, post-*On the Waterfront* and *East of Eden*, never really had another major success. Most of his later films were commercial failures, and he stopped working, while Losey thrived. Their parallel careers are really fascinating. And both attended prestigious American universities. Kazan was at Williams, Losey went to Dartmouth.

But their backgrounds were diametrically opposite.

Kazan was the émigré, the son of a carpet merchant who didn't want him to become an artist. He washed trays in the university canteen to make money. Losey, on the other hand, was from La Crosse, Wisconsin, the same town as Nicholas Ray. He lived the high life, had lavish tastes, and suffered under McCarthyism. He ended up on the streets in London, sick to his stomach, without a penny, and had to start from scratch under a false name. There was a Losey Street in La Crosse. His was an "aristocratic" family in the American sense. Rachmaninoff played the piano in his childhood home and Mark Twain gave readings there. They read Proust and Racine. Losey lived very grandly and had exacting standards. When he dined at my place, I offered him a selection of fourteen different aperitifs. The one he asked for was always the one I didn't have!

How Losey thwarted Kazan

They met one another at the Cannes Film Festival, when Losey was president of the jury and Kazan was competing with The Visitors.

It was in 1972, shortly before my book with Kazan was released, and long before my volume on Losey was published. But I was already closely associated with both men, which made things a little difficult. It wasn't such a great idea for Maurice Bessy, Cannes' artistic director at the time, to invite Kazan to compete at the festival when Losey was president of the jury. That happened without anyone really noticing. Unsurprisingly, *The Visitors* didn't win any awards, but jury members Miloš Forman and Bibi Andersson told me about the deliberations. The majority liked Kazan's film and thought it absolutely had to be given a prize, but after a discussion where everybody spoke in turn, Losey recounted what Kazan had done during the McCarthy era. Kazan hadn't implicated Losey, but Losey was a victim of the blacklist, and in a lengthy speech he explained how people like Kazan had driven him into exile. Obviously, when you've spent twelve happy days with a jury president with as much authority and prestige as Losey, you're not going to insist that Elia Kazan wins an award.

In Losey's archives I found some paperwork, which I photocopied. Every member of the jury, including the president, had to fill out a form on which they recorded their thoughts about each film. I have it in front of me. Interestingly, Losey was actually very complimentary about *The Visitors*, even writing that artistically it was Kazan's best film, that he was extremely "skilful" and talented, more restrained than in his previous work, and that every element of the film, including the performances, blended brilliantly. Of the screenwriting, which was done by Kazan's own son, Losey wrote: "Good dialogue, but confused, probably due to the father-son dynamic." Of the cameraman Nick Proferes, who had also photographed *Wanda*: "Excellent, fluid, the best cinematography in the competition." Patricia Joyce, the female star: "Faultless. Perhaps the best. The one" – implying that she should be considered for the Best Actress award.

The film is about two soldiers, imprisoned for raping a Vietnamese woman, returning from Vietnam and seeking revenge on their informer. It was filmed in Kazan's own house and was written by his son Chris, and was clearly a story that Kazan felt very attached to. Losey's damning conclusion: "In terms of direction, it's the best. Also by far Kazan's best film. But the content and the ideas behind it are hopeless, somewhere between personal apology and the nation's current dilemmas."

Losey clearly saw a parallel between the film and what Kazan himself had done years earlier. He wasn't at all happy and was very much against giving the film a prize. Much later, Kazan wrote to me in a letter: "I have high regard for Losey. He's a great director, but I find it difficult to accept that he did what he did. Not for my sake, because I have already received every possible and imaginable honour. I don't need that kind of thing any longer, and I have no regrets about Venice or Cannes. But for my son Chris, whose first screenplay this was, it would obviously have helped him a lot if the film had been given a prize."

A leftist aristocrat

A story like that shows how contradictory Losey was.

It shows Losey's rather contradictory personality, yes. What's striking is that Kazan championed the oppressed, and victims of totalitarian regimes – both right-wing and left-wing – while Losey was largely unconcerned about all that. Mehdi Boucherie, the Shah's brother-in-law, had a production company that funded Welles' unfinished film *The Other Side of the Wind*. Kazan and Losey were both planning films with Boucherie. Of course, this was before the Shah's fall from power. Kazan met with a delegation of young Iranian students who told him about the torture and conditions in Iran. I know he withdrew from the project because of that.

An event that struck me, even though I really did respect Losey, was when, in the early 1980s, Rolf Liebermann, who directed the Paris Opera, asked Yuri Lyubimov, the great director of the Taganka Theatre in Moscow – kind of the Soviet Patrice Chéreau – to stage *Boris Godunov*. Brezhnev, in the meantime, for internal political and cultural reasons, had forbidden Lyubimov to travel. He was confined to his home and not allowed to come to Paris, so Liebermann brought in Losey. I was close to Losey, we met regularly, and I remember telling him the day before the dress rehearsal of *Boris Godunov* at the opera, "You were a victim of the blacklist. You couldn't work in your country. You were forced into exile. But Lyubimov can't even leave his country because he's on a Soviet blacklist. It would be an important gesture if tomorrow, in front of the international press, the diplomatic corps and the whole of Paris, you stepped on stage during the curtain call to say that you were a victim of the blacklist in the United States, that you're against all blacklists, and that you protest the one being practiced in the USSR that prevented Lyubimov directing this production." "That's a good point," he said. "I'll have to think about it." He didn't do it, of course, and until the end of his life never wanted to reassess his involvement with Stalinist politics, even during Brezhnev's time, despite everything we knew – the 20th Communist Party Congress, Solzhenitsyn, the dissidents. He always refused to criticise the Soviet Union. I'll never forget how he stuck to his guns, compared to someone like Kazan who, it's true, acted awfully at one point in his life, but after that, in his own way, lived a life of continual protest. In England in the late 1950s, Losey drafted a letter in which he disassociated himself from any involvement with communism. I think he was glad that the copy in his archive was never made public.

In a creator's private world

What was Losey like during your interviews?

They took place in his "small" four-room apartment on the ground floor in the rue du Dragon, which Jean Nouvel had sublet to him. It was very Loseyan. He found it all rather cramped, which meant he could savour the discomfort and complain about it. He had the means to afford a more spacious place to live. He was actually a tax exile. He owned a luxurious five-story house in London on the King's Road, near where he had shot *The Servant*, but he had to stay in France for tax reasons. I had gone to his house in London where I spent a few days going through his archives and reading his correspondence. I also went to the British Film Institute library to read the press clippings there. My book of interviews with him might be even more revealing than my Kazan book because Kazan had really been in control. He had been a teacher at the Actors Studio, he was a pedagogue and a master craftsman who was extraordinarily well organised and assertive, and said only what he wanted to say. I have the feeling that Losey, on the other hand really opened himself up.

He was less in control of you?

He drank a lot, which meant my problem was to stay lucid. He was a very good drinker and always wanted me to accompany him – as all alcoholics do. After long meetings on the rue du Dragon, we never managed to find the time to finish this enormous book of interviews, which eventually clocked in at fifty hours. At Christmas we went to Italy, which was typical Losey – in other words totally masochistic. We were in Fregene, by the sea, in the off-season, with all that wind and rain. At the same time, he hoped to work on a screenplay about Ibn Saud with Franco Solinas, screenwriter of *Salvatore Giuliano* and *The Battle of Algiers*, who had also written the first draft of *Mr. Klein* for Costa-Gavras. To begin with, he was insistent that he wanted to rent Rosi's house. Many wealthy Italians had houses in that area, thirty kilometres from Rome. They were these wonderful little buildings. He wanted Rosi's, but Rosi had no intention of renting it to him because he planned to spend his weekends there himself. That upset Losey. Eventually, he arranged for a hotel to open where the two of us stayed, and at nine in the morning we started with a vodka tonic – with very little tonic. He insisted I drink with him, so I rather discreetly poured it into the potted plants because I knew that after the fourth glass, I wouldn't even be able to hear what he was saying. He, on the other hand, was unaffected. We continued talking in Paris while he was shooting *Don Giovanni*, and the book was finally published when that film was released.

There was almost a Freudian-couch aspect to the interview process, which you sense in the book. He talks about childhood memories, his relationship with his father, with women. It's much more intimate and revealing. Kazan recounted a great deal in detail, some of which was already known, but Losey was notably more autobiographical. He was very articulate, and also a great analyst. It's bizarre how similar Kazan and Losey were in this regard. It's not very common in America to analyse your work and talk about yourself. Maybe someone like Coppola would have done so if he and I had done a book together, but the old directors didn't really talk about themselves – except maybe Huston, in a more anecdotal way. Losey's temperament was the opposite of Kazan's, in the sense that Kazan could stand around and chat with a greengrocer. I could never imagine Losey doing that.

Recognition from French cinephiles

French cinephiles played a significant role in acknowledging directors like Losey.

Yes, and here I would like to highlight the important role played in my own development by the person who led me to Losey: Pierre Rissient. Pierre had discovered him during his exile in England and brought his films over to show them in France, at a time when British critics weren't paying any attention to them. *Sight and Sound* summarised *Time Without Pity* in two lines, without even a critical note, in the "Also in cinemas…" section. They started paying attention to Losey when they realised the French were taking an interest. And that interest was initially sparked by Pierre Rissient and his friends from the Mac-Mahon cinema. They rediscovered Losey, who at first was very appreciative of their support, though he later distanced himself from the cinephiles who had discovered and championed him. They took that badly because once they latched onto someone – and this was one of Rissient's psychological traits – that person sort of became theirs. They expected him to seek their counsel and heed their advice. Perhaps because of the difficulties of being in exile in England, then later because of the gradual resurgence of his reputation, Losey aspired to a certain worldliness. He took pride in meeting Marguerite Duras and a prime minister. He was acquainted with high society, and then, nearing sixty, suddenly found himself in an intellectual circle where cinema was considered important. Rissient backed him until *The Servant*, and between Venice and Paris had succeeded in changing the critics' opinion on the film. But he disliked *King and Country* and from then liked only select Losey films, each time pointing out their faults – the bad choices made, what Losey should have done or not done. Not without a certain lucidity, it should be said. But I think that Losey wanted to free himself from these young people. The rupture actually came from both sides. Some of them he didn't want to listen to, the others he was sick of hearing from. The truth is that I wasn't a big fan of *Roads to the South* or *The Trout*, which are minor Losey films works. Eventually he returned to England to shoot *Steaming*, his final feature. But *Don Giovanni* and *Mr. Klein* were certainly standout films.

I recently learned a very interesting thing about *Mr. Klein*. In Marcel Ophuls' *The Sorrow and the Pity* there's a character called Mr. Klein, a shopkeeper who defends himself by saying, "First of all, I'm not Jewish. Despite my name, people think I'm Jewish, but I'm not and never have been. During the war I told this to everyone. I *proved* that I wasn't Jewish." It turns out that this man was a collaborator, at which he starts fumbling his words. Ophuls, with his interviewing genius, corners him. Costa-Gavras told me that when he wrote the script of *Mr. Klein* with Franco Solinas, that name came from Marcel Ophuls' film, as inspired by the ambiguity of that real-life character.

Stanley Kubrick

Your next book was about Stanley Kubrick.

That was a completely different endeavour from the previous ones. The book about Rosi was dossier-style, designed like one of his films, featuring interviews, documents, a timeline, statements, historical sources, even extracts from parliamentary debates. I was laying out the pieces of a puzzle. The interview books with Kazan and Losey were structured in the simplest way possible: a Q&A format, spanning three or four hundred pages. For Kubrick, I envisioned something different again. I felt that I had to demonstrate that Kubrick was an auteur, because it was around that time, just before *The Shining*, when he was first being recognised as a great filmmaker. *2001: A Space Odyssey*, *A Clockwork Orange* and *Barry Lyndon* hadn't gone unnoticed, and nor had his preceding films, but doubts lingered. The films were great, people said, but who was he really? And did anything connect the films, which were all so different?

The fact that he was always moving from one genre or subject to another bewildered critics.

Resnais, Huston, Polanski, Frears and many great American filmmakers all do the same – something we'll come back to.

In my Kubrick book is a beautiful line from Borges which sums up the situation: "Through the years, a man peoples a space with images of provinces, kingdoms, mountains, bays, ships, islands, fishes, rooms, tools, stars, horses, and people. Shortly before his death, he discovers that the patient labyrinth of lines traces the image of his own face." Borges was a free spirit and very fond of popular authors underestimated by literary critics, like Stevenson, who because of *Treasure Island* was pigeonholed as a writer of children's literature. Of some of filmmakers I've admired, it's only gradually that you begin to see the "face" emerge that Borges is talking about. I was certain that there were lots of connections between Kubrick's films: his obsessive interests, stylistic elements – like the backwards tracking shot and certain editing techniques – and, above all, themes I had already explored in *Positif*. In fact, that's what allowed me to get to know him.

Initial contact

How did it happen?

I first made contact I had with him was when I was in London and was looking for unpublished photos for *Positif*, because there weren't many of him and he allowed very few to circulate. I hadn't managed to get in touch with him directly, but did reach the London offices of Warner Bros. and was told that he would call me back at my hotel the next morning at 8 o'clock.

What film was this for?

It was after *2001*. I had written a long article about his work, which was the starting point of the book. I wanted to make connections between all his films and asked if he had photos from *2001* and others. There hadn't been a set photographer on *2001*, and though there was one on *A Clockwork Orange*, he never used one again after that. There were only images in 'Scope format. He told me he didn't have any photos, but said, "It's very easy. Organise a screening of whatever film you want, take a camera" – thinking that I was taking notes, he told me precisely what kind of camera – "set it to such and such aperture" – I know nothing about this kind of thing – "then stand about ten feet from the screen, take the photos, and you'll have the exact shot you need." Well,

I gave up on that one pretty quickly, and basically took his response as a no-go.

Could it all have ended there?

It could have, but on the phone I asked him about his next film. I'm thirty years old and really quite naïve. He tells me he's working on Napoleon. I ask him why Napoleon? "There are already dozens of films about him," I say. "You really want to make another one?" I didn't know that Kubrick always wanted to make the best film that was ever made in every genre he tackled. He wanted to create something very special – not because he disliked all other versions of the story. He just wanted to do better. "Have you seen a single convincing film about Napoleon?" he asks. I start to back down, but then, like any self-respecting cinephile, say, "Well, there's Abel Gance's *Napoleon*." "Really?" he says. "Do you like it that much? Okay – the triple screen, it's extraordinary for the time. The scenes filmed from a tethered balloon are amazing, and there are other extraordinary things from a technical point of view. But Napoleon is still the greatest strategist the world has ever known since Julius Caesar. When you came out of Gance's *Napoleon*, did you realise he was a military genius? Did you even understand how the battles were won?" "Well, not really..." I said. He tells me that the French Revolution is the greatest event in modern history since the Renaissance. "The way Gance shows us Marat brushing lice from his hair, Robespierre with his face covered in talcum powder, and Danton dead drunk singing at the top of his voice – do you think that really explains the importance of the event? It's a caricature. They don't come across as great men. It means nothing. A film shouldn't be just technically innovative. It should give us some understanding of the world." And then, to wrap it all off: "What's important about Eisenstein's films are their form. With Chaplin, the content is everything. The filmmaker who can combine Eisenstein and Chaplin would be the greatest of all." So ended our first conversation about Napoleon.

That's how it went every time I met him. He was an uncompromising interviewee. Actually, because he hated interviews, what he dreamed of was not having to answer questions at all. Instead, he bombarded you with questions and tried to extract as much information as possible. My luck, having initially wanting to be a historian, was that I knew the history well, so he was always asking me about

Napoleon. That's when he began to build his library of Napoleon books, which was displayed at the exhibition dedicated to him. There was an entire cabinet, probably including some of the books I recommended. I could talk to him about different French schools of history: the Bonapartists, the Marxists – like Soboul and Mathiez – and the diehard Napoleon enthusiasts. That's when, I think, he started taking me seriously. And additionally, he read my lengthy piece about him in *Positif*.

First interview

When did you meet him in the flesh?

Two years later, before he quit because he couldn't stand the way Kubrick constantly bothered him at two in the morning, Bertrand Tavernier was working as a press agent on *A Clockwork Orange*. I was writing for *L'Express*, which wanted an interview with Kubrick. My name was among those on a list of three or four. He had rejected everyone else. He was still giving a few interviews at that time, and I was one of the lucky ones who got to meet him.

Was this when A Clockwork Orange *was released?*

Yes. We met in a roadside café. Kubrick was already wary of interviews, although there had been a long and important one published in *Playboy* about *2001*. The production designer Ken Adam told me that when Kubrick went to London for a meeting with journalists to talk about *A Clockwork Orange* – he lived in a mansion about thirty miles away – he stopped three times to vomit because he was so anxious about having to answer questions. I think I'm the only one in the world he granted an interview to about *Barry Lyndon*. He must have liked the interview we had done for *A Clockwork Orange*. He did meet with Richard Schickel, who knew him well, but the interview was sliced into little pieces and quotes were used in an article in *Time* magazine. He complained of having been betrayed by journalists and insisted that any transcription be sent to him first so he could check it through. Several interviewers hadn't done so, and the transcripts didn't truly reflect what he had said, so he was very cautious. He respected academics more and knew I was a professor in Paris. He appreciated the serious preparation I did and appreciated the fact that I had interests beyond cinema, and that I could talk with him about philosophy, painting and other things.

Establishing trust

You were certainly one of the critics closest to him.

What emerged was... I wouldn't say a friendship. It wasn't the same kind of relationship as I had with Rosi or Kazan. But a certain closeness developed, a trust. He would call me three or four times a year to ask me what I had seen, what had been released, what I had watched at Cannes. He loved having copies of films sent to him without ever paying for them because he was worried about money. Later, for example, he asked me for information when he was preparing *Wartime Lies*, based on the book by Louis Begley, which he was going to shoot with Johanna ter Steege, an actress he had seen in Garrel's *I Don't Hear the Guitar Anymore* and *The Birth of Love*. It was a Holocaust story, about an aunt and her nephew who escape the camps. He called me to ask me for a list of Polish costume designers who could work on the film, and he wanted to know which filmmakers could help him. It was always something like that. Or: "Do you think we should put the *Barry Lyndon* poster on the Champs-Élysées roundabout or on rue Marbeuf?" He was always making enquiries, always focused on little details about advertising and locations of cinemas. "Is such and such a cinema in Saint-Étienne more of a parish hall where they might screen *Love Story*, or would young people go there to watch films?" The venue had to match the film. I would also call him to ask things, but I would never say I was a friend of Kubrick's.

Did you feel appreciated by him in a way?

I think, like the other figures we have discussed, that he was sensitive to the attention *Positif* and I gave his work. He was always a controversial figure, constantly under attack. Somehow he knew that *Positif* was a serious journal, and the questions I asked about the film he was releasing seemed to resonate with him. Shortly after our first conversation, he telephoned me because he had seen, on the cover of the hundredth issue of *Positif* – which included Renaud Walter's interview with him – the Romanian actress Adriana Bogdan, in André Delvaux's *One Night... A Train*, who had caught his eye. He thought of casting her as Joséphine. As we know, *Napoleon* was never made. That was around 1970.

Barry Lyndon was released a few years later. That was a whole other experience. In 1975, Claude Sautet and I were invited to the French Institute in London to show his latest film *Vincent, François, Paul and the Others*, followed by a discussion. As we had the afternoon free, we went to Leicester Square, a huge cinema, to see *Barry Lyndon*, which had been out for a fortnight. There was hardly anyone there – maybe fifteen people. It was a monumental flop. After the intermission, half the audience left. But we were absolutely bowled over by the film. No one in France had seen it yet. The reviews in the US had been bad, and even worse in the UK, where people wondered how an American Jew from the Bronx could possibly know anything about people living in stately homes in England in the sixteenth century. And casting an American as an Irishman? The film was savaged.

After the screening, I went to the Warner Bros. office. I was good friends with Julian Senior, the company's advertising manager in London. He was the one who arranged all the meetings with Kubrick, so I asked Julian to call Kubrick, since I still didn't have his number. I said to him, "Stanley, Claude Sautet, the great French filmmaker" – who he knew of, of course – "and I have just seen your masterpiece." "I'm touched," he said, "because the reviews have been bad and no one's going to see it." I said, "I can assure you that French audiences will like it. It'll be a triumph." I think it was the first time he took me seriously. Until then, for him, I was just a French intellectual writing about his films. I'm sure he didn't think I was a complete idiot, but he was always very practical, and the importance of box-office receipts was obvious to him, because they allowed him to maintain his artistic independence. My prediction came true, and the film was a great success in France and Italy, Spain and Portugal, although it didn't do well in Nordic countries and Germany. I think this experience sparked a decisive connection between us.

A publisher's commitment

And so you suggested a book?

My previous books had been published by Stock, but three years later, in 1978, I contacted Calmann-Lévy and met a delightful man, Alain Oulman. He was a very sensitive and refined person, who wrote songs for Amália Rodrigues. He was half Portuguese, half French, and had inherited – I don't know how – Calmann-Lévy. He pulled off quite a daring move, which was to produce a very fancy book with three hundred photos, including sixty in colour. There had already been a similar kind of book – the Hitchcock-Truffaut one, but they were two global icons! Kubrick was famous but far from the star he is today. It was all going to be very expensive. Kubrick immediately agreed, so I pulled together all the interviews I had already published with him and asked Kubrick to help with photos. He sent me some stills, and I found material at the Museum of Modern Art in New York and the British Film Institute, including images of *Fear and Desire* and *Killer's Kiss*.

I wanted to approach Kubrick in a new way, by showing the visual coherence of his cinematic world and making connections between the imagery, for example putting side by side the bulging eyes of Scatman Crothers in *The Shining*, those of tortured Alex in *A Clockwork Orange*, and the bewildered gaze of the cosmonaut in *2001*. I highlighted Kubrick's obsession with symmetry and how he used a handheld camera to break this symmetry and bring a touch of madness into an ordered universe. I brought together the masks in *The Killing*, *A Clockwork Orange* and *Barry Lyndon*. It seemed to me that, unlike the usual illustrations found in film books, which are nice to look at and aren't directly related to the text, the images in this Kubrick book should be a constant commentary on the text. There are wonderfully detailed analyses in the Truffaut-Hitchcock book, but very few visual comparisons. It was important to show the unity of a body of work that seemed fragmented and all over the place. The interplay between images and text was key to the book's design, which Calmann-Lévy was on board with.

"He'll call you back in half an hour"

Did Kubrick exercise any control over the book?

Years later I threatened John Baxter, a Paris-based Australian historian and author of several film director biographies, with legal action because he said in an interview about his own book on Kubrick that mine was an "authorized biography." First, it isn't a biography, and second, it wasn't supervised or endorsed in any way. Kubrick basically knew nothing about the book until it was published. Apart from the interviews we did together and which he reread – a completely reasonable request on his part – he knew nothing of its contents. The most curious thing is that for the English edition he modified the interviews. For someone so calculating and controlling, he didn't realise that by adding things and removing others, he was revealing something of himself. There's a PhD thesis in there somewhere... He wanted it known, for example, that he had taken photos of Montgomery Clift when he was a photographer, but removed other things that he thought might be too revealing. In any case, Baxter had no right to say what he did because I never sent the manuscripts of any of my books to the person concerned. Kubrick didn't know what the book would look like until I received the proofs. One evening when I got home, my first wife Jeannine told me that Kubrick had called and that he was going to call me back in half an hour. My heart was pounding because I knew he had just received the book. He had actually prevented Peter Cowie from publishing a book about him through Tantivy Press. When he read the manuscript, he wrote to Cowie, saying, "Not only will I not allow you to use any photos, but if this book is published, I'll sue." It never appeared.*

Kubrick had a soft voice. He coughed a little and cleared his throat. With a sort of shyness, and a hint of unease, he said to me: "It's the most beautiful book I've ever seen about a director. Do you think I would get a discount if I bought four hundred copies?" He never did anything small! I told him that Calmann-Lévy would give him a special price. He wanted to send a copy to every Warner Bros. office around the world!

Did the book's publication coincide with the release of a film?

It appeared at the same time as *The Shining* was released in France, which I had gone to see at the last minute, at a special screening in the London suburbs with the French film's subtitler, Isabelle Kourilsky, who did a lot of work for Warner Bros. It was just the two of us in the screening room. The film had already been released in the United States at 2 hours and 28 minutes. I really liked it, though maybe it was a little long – like the bit when Halloran comes back from his vacation in Florida, which Kubrick cut down for the two-hour international version. I asked Kourilsky:

---

* This book, by Neil Hornick, entitled *The Magic Eye*, was published by Sticking Place Books in 2024.

"How did you translate 'All work and no play makes Jack a dull boy' when Jack Torrance is typing?" She said she went with "Un tiens vaut mieux que deux tu l'auras" ["A bird in the hand is worth two in the bush"], which really didn't seem right to me. I asked why she had translated it that way. "Kubrick told me to use a proverb," she said, "and it's not important that it's different from what's in the English version." On the contrary, it seemed to me that this nursery rhyme was of *great* importance. Jack is the name of the main character. He works all the time. *All work and no play.* He has no fun, and he's in a state of collapse, consumed by sickness. I called Kubrick to tell him how much I liked the film and suggest that he change the translation to "Travail sans loisir rend Jack triste sire" ["Work without play brings Jack dismay"], which says everything about the character. He replied: "No, Michel. I don't get it. And I don't see the point of translating to the letter. It's a nursery rhyme that I chose at random. It doesn't mean anything special." A few days later, I'm reading some American reviews of the film. And what do I see? A takedown in *The New Yorker* by Pauline Kael, who had disliked Kubrick ever since *2001: A Space Odyssey*, and who closed her review with: "All work and no play makes Stanley a dull boy." She was a highly intelligent and rather cruel critic, and had found the perfect way to really get at Kubrick. She understood that it was a projection of his own fears of being trapped in his enormous house, working non-stop.

The taste of secrecy

Kubrick cultivated an air of mystery.

I later saw *Full Metal Jacket*, again during a secret session, with Michael Herr, author of *Dispatches* – an exceptional book about the Vietnam War. Having written the voiceover of *Apocalypse Now*, he had been hired by Kubrick to write a screenplay based on Gustav Hasford's book *The Short-Timers*. I was preparing a new edition of the Kubrick book and wanted to include testimonials from his collaborators. Before returning to my hotel, I accompanied Herr home to interview him. It was the last interview he gave about the film. I'm certain that Kubrick, as he often did with his collaborators, had asked Herr – who later wrote a delightful little book about him – not to talk. Likewise, Diane Johnson, the screenwriter of *The Shining*, gave only one major interview when the film was released, with Denis

Barbier, a French student enrolled at the University of Berkeley, where she taught. It was published in *Positif*, and was about as far from the usual press junket circuit as could be. Kubrick went out of his way to ensure that journalists couldn't contact the people he worked with. But as her student, Barbier just asked her to talk about Kubrick, and she did. I'm sure that Kubrick asked her never to do it again. Before the second edition of the book came out in 1987, I went to interview him about *Full Metal Jacket*. It was the first time we had met at his home instead of an office or restaurant. We had a long and very interesting talk, but then he said he didn't want the interview to be published, and that he preferred to write answers to a few questions of his own, which he did. They were interesting, but very short. He applied Nabokov's rule: write the answers first, then formulate the questions. Fifteen years later I did end up publishing the entirety of this conversation, which was extremely revealing. He said, for example, that he originally wanted to shoot *Full Metal Jacket* in Asia, but he couldn't find the 1930s German industrial-style buildings there which existed in Hue at that time, because they had been destroyed during the war. And then, coincidentally, he found exactly what he was looking for… in London, very close to his home, in an area that was going to be razed. So he planted palm trees and was able to blow everything up to re-enact the Vietnam War. I think, actually, that he had no desire to travel. He hadn't left home in thirty years. He must have felt that the interview was too revealing.

You never got a chance to discuss Eyes Wide Shut *with hm.*

No, but I did see the film shortly after he died, three days before it was shown to the international press in London. I watched it in the screening room at his house, and I also saw his grave, since he's buried in his garden. I liked the film, just as I do all his work. What's noteworthy is the confusion of the critics at the screening I went to. They didn't understand what Kubrick was saying with the film and how it connected to his other work. A long time before that, when I interviewed him about *A Clockwork Orange*, he told me his idea about adapting Schnitzler's short story. He had bought the rights but was never happy with the script, which I think is why, for the first time in a long while, he turned to an experienced professional screenwriter, Frederic Raphael. I'm certain that it was Raphael who came up with the character of Ziegler, played by Sydney Pollack in the film, who ties everything together and explains the whole scheme of the secret organisation.

Putting an end of the legend

What did the "Kubrick myth" look like up close?

I think I'm one of the few critics to have been gotten so close to Kubrick over such a long period of time – along with the British critic Alexander Walker and Gene D. Phillips, an American priest. The reality bore no relation to the mythology that sprung up, of a paranoid demiurge, cut off from humanity. Of course, I don't want to trivialise him either. He had a very real and intense family life. He adored his three daughters and his painter wife, Christiane, who created canvases as radiant and bright as his own films were dark and disturbing. He loved his home. He had two successive residences in England. The one I knew, the second, had eighty rooms, with editing suites, projection rooms and archival space. He had his professional life on one side, then crossed over into a bright family world, surrounded by large windows, seven cats and six dogs, all beloved and kept apart by fences. He saw a lot of films. Before there was satellite and he could watch them live, he watched baseball games on tapes that he had sent to him. He was particularly passionate about American politics and military. I remember that above his desk was a picture of the heads of the Pentagon at the time of the Vietnam War and, in his handwriting, "Shadows of Dr Strangelove." He was always on the phone with people from all walks of life. When it came to film, he and I talked casually about what was being made and cinema in general, but mainly he spoke with other directors and technicians.

He was really into the technical side of filmmaking.

He had long discussions with Spielberg and Polanski, who he met to talk about technique. It's been said that Spielberg was, in a way, Kubrick's heir, since he shot *A.I. Artificial Intelligence*, which was based on an original idea of Kubrick's. But actually, there are big differences between the two. Kubrick was fascinated by the extraordinary successes of Lucas and Spielberg, who emerged at a time when he was losing influence as an auteur director able to produce commercial hits, like his sci-fi trilogy, *Dr*

Strangelove, *2001* and *A Clockwork Orange*. After that, he sort of lost his connection with the public. He was fascinated by young filmmakers who used their technical skills to smash box-office records, and so revolutionise cinema. Kubrick never had megahits like Lucas and Spielberg did, simply because those two filmmakers were completely in tune with mass audiences, especially teenagers. Every time Kubrick made a film, he needed it to be groundbreaking and outshine every other film of the same genre. But at the same time, he couldn't resist indulging in his personal quirks. After the commercial failure of *Barry Lyndon*, I think he deliberately picked a horror film, *The Shining*, based on Stephen King's novel, because adaptations of King's other books had done well at the box-office. Kubrick wanted to make the scariest horror film ever. In the end, *The Shining* far exceeded King's vision. Kubrick transformed it into film about madness, creative struggle and artist's block, and while the film was a success, it wasn't as successful as everyone thought it would be.

Frederic Raphael, in his memoir about working with Kubrick on *Eyes Wide Shut*, says that at one point Kubrick asked him if he knew of a great film about the Holocaust. Raphael, spontaneously, replied, "Yes, of course: *Schindler's List*." And Kubrick said to him, "Actually, no. *Schindler's List* is how six thousand Jews were saved, when in fact the Holocaust was really about the murder of six million Jews." He implied that in the end, when it came to a Holocaust story, Spielberg had managed to find a happy ending.

The master of "film-brain" cinema

Was Kubrick a moralist?

Kubrick, as Deleuze said, created "brain-film" cinema. Kubrick is a great philosopher and a sceptic, an anti-authoritarian with a libertarian bent. In *Dr Strangelove* and *Paths of Glory* he mocks political and especially military leadership by showing the risks associated with it. Initially, the left embraced Kubrick with enthusiasm, *Spartacus* in particular. Many people think that he was the originator of that film, but in fact it was a commission. He was hired to direct a film he hadn't written, which had been started by someone else, and which he hadn't cast. He was quickly associated with the liberal American left and seen as an idealist and humanist.

He was rebellious.

Yes. And a great sceptic, critical of authority of any kind, be it moral, religious, military or political. Just watch *A Clockwork Orange*, or even *Barry Lyndon*, which is almost a Marxist analysis of society, about people being prevented from moving from one social class to another. This is the fate of Barry Lyndon, who marries so he can move up in society – but fails. Kubrick is clear-eyed about human beings. And he's steeped in Freud. It's not for nothing that Freud was banned in totalitarian countries. He was despised by Hitler and Stalin because he didn't fit into their purely socio-economic explanations of society, where, inevitably, once these problems are solved, humanity is saved. Freud teaches us that the animal within us is always lurking, ready to emerge any moment – which is what every one of Kubrick's films is about. For human beings, civilisation is a thin crust on the surface, and at any moment the famous "beast" that Brecht talked about could break through – although Brecht, a supporter of the Soviet regime and East Germany, seemed to ignore this basic reality when it came to his own life. Kubrick, on the other hand, really looked deep into the eyes of the beast. For him, humanity is constantly under threat. I think his films have therapeutic value. His father was a doctor, and Kubrick, in his way, is too. He's a doctor of the soul. He's warning the audience: beware! Remember that you're an animal too, because if you don't, irrationality can take over at any moment and overwhelm you with astonishing speed. Kubrick's co-religionists died in the camps. He had seen too much of what irrationality can unleash not to be wary of it. The battle between reason and irrationality is at the heart of all his films. As much as I feel close to Losey, with all the uncertainties and contradictions in his work – *The Servant* analyses human beings and their impulses, but with so much ambiguity – philosophically, I'm more in tune with the certainties of Kubrick's films.

Dinner with Kubrick

You gradually discovered that Kubrick is interested in everything.

He would organise dinners for Spielberg or Polanski, but also Nobel Prize winners, generals, chemists. Anouk Aimée, who was married to Albert Finney, confirmed all this for me. Ken Adam, who had been a set designer for both directors, told me about a meal between Kubrick and Mankiewicz. There's a topiary in Stephen King's novel, hedges in the shape of animals, but because that would have been more or less impossible to put on film, Kubrick replaced it with a maze, which he borrowed from Mankiewicz's *Sleuth*. Ken Adam told me that Kubrick, who was usually dazzling and very talkative, was basically silent throughout this dinner. He was impressed by Mankiewicz, and hung on him like a little boy. Despite their very different worlds, there are definite commonalities between their films when it comes to issues of manipulation and power.

Directing Actors

What also links Mankiewicz and Kubrick is an interest in directing actors.

Yes, because Kubrick, who could be said to be a monomaniac, an obsessive about form, certainly didn't treat actors the way Bresson did. He would be in ecstasy when working with them. He told me how dazzled he was by Peter Sellers' ability to transform himself. Malcolm McDowell told me that Kubrick burst out laughing and put a handkerchief in his mouth so as not to be heard when they were filming the final sequence of *A Clockwork Orange*, when McDowell is clacking his teeth in front of the Minister of the Interior, like a puppet.

And at the same time, they were both very demanding directors.

That's true. Kubrick never had any problems with Jack Nicholson or Peter Sellers, or most others. If he did have issues with a performer, it was when the actor couldn't remember his lines or was late or just not paying attention. That's when he could be hard on them. Watch the short documentary shot on the set of *The Shining* and see how he treats Shelly Duvall. Bresson and Sternberg are probably unique in their approach to actors. They wanted to mould and shape them, to have complete control over them. Kubrick was always open to what an actor did, to the unexpected and accidental. In *A Clockwork Orange*, for example, after two days of filming the rape scene in Mr. Alexander's house, Kubrick was at a loss. He had director's block. Then, suddenly, he asked Malcolm McDowell, "Any ideas? Do you know any songs?" And he begins to sing

"Singin' in the Rain." That wasn't Kubrick's idea – it came from McDowell. Kubrick immediately sends someone to phone and telex Metro Goldwyn Mayer to acquire the rights to the music, because otherwise there was no point in continuing the scene. Within two hours they had the rights, and Kubrick continued shooting what became one of the greatest sequences in any of his films. But it came out of a creative block, which I think is how most great filmmakers have worked, starting with Renoir and Pialat.

A film is never finished

Another characteristic of Kubrick was that he had difficulty finishing his films, which meant he made fewer and fewer of them.

John Boorman says that you never finish a film, it's taken away from you and released. Kubrick shared this trait with other directors, including, more recently, Wong Kar-wai, a specialist in indecision and hesitation. The fact that a film has to be released on a certain date forces the filmmaker to hand over their work. But if it were up to them, it would never be finished. We know that Leonardo da Vinci carried paintings with him for ten years without finishing them. It's a trait of certain artists, those in pursuit of the absolute – like Frenhofer in Balzac's *The Unknown Masterpiece*. Many filmmakers, even during shooting, are under constant pressure to deliver that so-called "useful" minute of cinema, especially when it comes to industrialised cinema made by large crews. Is there another art form where there is a need to be talented every minute of the day? A painter lacking inspiration can take a week off and go for a walk in the countryside, and a writer leaves home and returns in the evening, but with filmmaking, the director is forced to endure the demands of a shoot. Sydney Pollack, who worked as an actor on *Eyes Wide Shut*, said, "What's extraordinary about Kubrick is that his films don't cost more than Spielberg's, even if he shoots for a year." Kubrick's major problem was his obsession with time. Whenever possible, he minimised his crew so he could take more time. It allowed him to close down the set if he wanted, to stop shooting for three days if something wasn't right, and pick it up later or do take after take. Instead of having a crew of more than a hundred working for three months, like Spielberg, he preferred to have a dozen people for a year. He wanted to make films like certain silent directors had done. Chaplin would also shoot for a year, taking breaks and keeping himself open until inspiration struck. It's how some filmmakers work. Others are like clocks, always working and solving problems as they come. But ultimately, there's no reason to expect someone to be inspired all the time.

He never asked you to come and watch him shoot?

No one ever visited his sets, except maybe Alexander Walker, and he wasn't there for long. Kubrick didn't want any distractions. Anyway, I never much liked being on film sets. Occasionally, as I did on *Excalibur*, *The Draughtsman's Contract* and *Hope and Glory*, I would go and report for a newspaper. I was also on the set of Rosi's *Christ Stopped at Eboli*, Losey's *Mr. Klein*, and *Avanti!*, to interview Billy Wilder. Later, I was on Altman's *Short Cuts* in Los Angeles and Scorsese's *Bringing Out the Dead*. I've been on maybe twenty sets throughout my life, but it's always been as an outsider. I completely understand why [film scholar] François Thomas would want to follow a Resnais shoot from the first to the last day and write everything down. That makes you almost a script supervisor, recording everything. But coming in for a few hours, making the director feel obliged to chat with you when they have other things to do but want to be polite, watching a four-hour planning session – I don't think it's wildly useful.

"Required reading"

Your Kubrick book was a publishing phenomenon.

It was, compared with the Hitchcock-Truffaut book and Patrick Brion's *Tex Avery*. We sold about thirty thousand copies in France alone, plus there were Japanese, German, Spanish, English, Italian and, recently, Portuguese translations.

Of all your books, it's the one that has had the greatest influence on generations of film lovers and filmmakers.

Yes. It was especially popular in America, where Kubrick's reputation helped a lot. Alexander Payne told me that the book was on the curriculum when he was a student at the University of California. It was compulsory, required reading! Tarantino, James Gray and the Coen brothers all read it. In America, the new edition was published with some additions, and along with my work on Boorman, the Kubrick book is the most comprehensive I've done and involved the most collaborators. It all started because of how amazed I was when I saw *2001: A Space Odyssey*. It felt like a cinematic revolution. I had gone to the London premiere, several months before it was released in France, and afterwards wandered the streets for two hours. I couldn't make it back to the hotel to go to bed. I've never written a book on Resnais, but *Hiroshima mon amour* provoked the same feeling in me, that I was living through a moment of film history. I felt like I was watching *Citizen Kane* in 1941 or *Battleship Potemkin* in 1925 – a turning point in cinematographic language. I never had seen a story told that way, with flashes of memory, the editing that intercut the small and the big story into one, a feeling of a truly revolutionary film. *2001* was a little different because it really just came out of nowhere, and what strikes me about Kubrick is that he's a filmmaker without a clear artistic lineage or a direct successor. He's a meteorite that crashed into the history of cinema.

The inspirations of most great filmmakers are clear to see, like Renoir's connections to Stroheim and others, and Bergman's to poetic realism and Italian neorealism. But consider: what led to Kubrick? To *2001* and *A Clockwork Orange*? And consider also: who is Kubrick's heir? Many directors have been influenced by him, but there has never been a distinct Kubrick school of filmmaking, as there is with Godard. Plenty of directors have tried to emulate Resnais, even if very few went as far as *Hiroshima mon amour*, which has had a decisive impact on generations of filmmakers. Kubrick is without a predecessor or a successor, which is really quite phenomenal.

I can't end on Kubrick without telling you about an exchange I had in 1969 with Marguerite Duras at the Pesaro festival, where she was a regular guest. We would walk from the hotel to the screenings and talk. "You know," I said, "there's a wonderful film called *2001*. It starts with apes and continues with a journey in a spaceship. Then there's a completely abstract fifteen-minute sequence with experimental images which ends in a Louis XVI bedroom." She said, "That sounds extraordinary! But surely a film like that would never get a release." I assured her that it would, and had even been screened at the Empire Cinérama, and was one of biggest hits of the year. "I don't believe you," she said. "That's impossible." Six months later, I met Duras at Éric Losfeld's bookstore, Le Terrain Vague, where she occasionally stopped in. She said, "I finally saw the film you recommended, at the Champollion." She had seen it on a tiny screen – the smallest in Paris – and had liked it a lot.

John Boorman

How did your book on John Boorman come about?

The same way as my other books did: it was born from the vision of a film, in this case *Point Blank*. Boorman's first film, *Catch Us If You Can*, was never released in France. A press agent from MGM France on rue Condorcet telephoned me to let me know about the release of a new film starring Lee Marvin. I thought Marvin was extraordinary, and had seen several films of his: *The Dirty Dozen*, *Cat Ballou*, and before that, of course, Fritz Lang's *The Big Heat* and Ford's *The Man Who Killed Liberty Valance*. He was an icon. So we went to this press screening, four or five of us from *Positif*, including Benayoun and Tailleur. We didn't know anything about it, except the director's name: John Boorman. And we sat and watched this absolutely stunning gangster film like nothing we had ever seen before, and more innovative than most everything made since. It's unlikely that a film like *Point Blank* could be produced in Hollywood today. At one point, the studio executives even considered sending Boorman for treatment because they thought he was crazy to make such a weird film. Every sequence was shot in a dominant monochromatic tone. The studio didn't know what to make of the narrative, but Boorman had the support of Margaret Booth, the great editor at MGM, who had re-edited Stroheim's *Greed* and was still around. "Over my dead body," she said. "They'll have to go through me if they want to mess with this fantastic film." Lee Marvin, whose contract gave him absolute control over the film, said, "I delegate all my powers to John Boorman." The film has also been influential on Americans like Coppola and Scorsese.

The most comprehensive work (and man)

You were vindicated by Boorman's next films.

Hell in the Pacific seemed to me astonishingly audacious, with these two soldiers, an American and a Japanese, who don't understand each other and for two hours, on a desert island, say almost nothing to each other. Then *Leo the Last*, also utterly unique, and *Deliverance* – more classical in its approach but still very impressive. It went on and on. I thought *The Heretic*, a disaster in America and around the world, was extremely imaginative. Scorsese loves the film, which is one of his guilty pleasures. Pauline Kael considered its visuals worthy of the greatest German films of the 1920s. Then there was *Excalibur*, a great success and a great film. My Boorman book came out at the time of the release of *The Emerald Forest*. The success of the Kubrick book helped a lot. Not only did I convince Calmann-Lévy to publish a book on Boorman, but I knew it needed to be a visually impressive object. As with Kubrick, I wanted to show the unity of Boorman's work as he moved from a Western to a philosophical fable like *Leo the Last*, from a horror film to *Zardoz*, which is a science fiction, from a thriller to a war film. It's even a visually richer book than the one on Kubrick, with more colour photos and testimonials from collaborators. There's one interview chapter per film. Boorman was talkative, and the book came out exactly as I had hoped. It wasn't as successful as we thought it would be, despite good reviews and a prize from the British Film Institute. I'm proud of it because I think it's perhaps the most comprehensive work I've done, even if we could have added more illustrations.

Romantic and lucid

As with Kubrick, Boorman's cinema is visionary, yet tinged with disillusionment.

Boorman is very different from Kubrick. He's a man possessed, a romantic who simultaneously turns his back on romanticism. His characters build castles in the air and dream of great achievements, which ultimately leads to their downfall. Lee Marvin realises that his quest is in vain, that he isn't going to find solace in killing people or letting them die in order to deal with his wife's death. The result of the macho expedition undertaken by the four urbanites in *Deliverance* is that one is sodomised and another dies, and in *Excalibur*, the Grail is so obviously unattainable. Boorman is brilliant at depicting human illusions, our capacity to fantasise and create imaginary worlds. He's driven by this wild audacity, which means that some of his films work and some are courageous failures. There's a fascinating mix of lucidity and poetry in him. And he is probably, of all the filmmakers I have met, the most complete. He's a Renaissance man, a family man and an athlete who can ride a horse, a man of boundless culture, someone interested in the times in which he's living. The book is actually subtitled "A Visionary in His Time" because all of Boorman's films are deeply embedded in politics and society, but not in the same vein as Ken Loach, because for Boorman, dreaming is a vital part of life. The book's subtitle juxtaposes the amateur poet of myths, dreams, imagination and adventures in distant lands with the auteur who deals with racism, capitalism and all the problems of society today. It encompasses both the external and internal worlds.

There's a sense of completeness about Boorman. I find him not dissimilar to what I have long admired in Surrealism, in Breton's ideas. He cultivates the past while always being open to new techniques, which he talked about with Kubrick, who was equally interested in such things. He's also a gentleman farmer who cultivates trees. Ten thousand have been planted on his property. The man does his own gardening! A great traveller, too. Absolutely fearless. They're always talking about Herzog, but Boorman's shoots have often been unimaginable expeditions. He risked his life in the South Pacific, he lived through the Los Angeles earthquake, he filmed in the Chattooga River for *Deliverance*. He never put his crews in harm's way, as Herzog did, but they were intensely ambitious undertakings nonetheless. For *The Emerald Forest*, he spent six months in the Amazon among the Indians, cut off from anywhere. He's in the great tradition of British adventure writers like Conrad, Stevenson, Kipling. I also admire the way he gets straight to the point, the simplicity of the style he uses in *Queen and Country*, his new autobiographical film, a sequel to *Hope and Glory*, which he made when he was eighty. Matisse wrote in 1948: "J'ai toujours souhaité que mes œuvres aient la légèreté et la gaieté du printemps qui ne laisse jamais soupçonner le travail qu'il a coûté.' ["I have always wanted my work to have the lightness and joy inherent in spring, and that no one would suspect the work it required of me."] The lesson we draw from late films – like John Huston's *The Dead*, *7 Women* by Ford, or *The Immortal Story* by Welles – is that in the autumn of their lives, great artists manage to rediscover the freshness of spring. After virtuoso works like *Point Blank*, *Hell in the Pacific* and *Excalibur*, Boorman had nothing left to prove, and his style became serene and minimalist, without showing the hard work it took.

He's also someone who fought for his convictions.

He's politically engaged, but doesn't wear blinders and never simplifies things, which makes him similar to Rosi, who takes a great interest in politics without expressing strong opinions. In *Beyond Rangoon*, Boorman very much sides with Aung San Suu Kyi, and *In My Country* deals with the reconciliation trials in South Africa. He always shows an insatiable interest in the world as it is. And as a human being, he has a wild sense of humour. He's a delightful man – very generous, enthusiastic about others. I have a deep admiration and genuine sympathy for him. Actually, I feel the same way about all the filmmakers I've worked with. I never had to suffer the humiliations that Benayoun experienced when working with Jerry Lewis, or Emmanuel Carrère, who, at the age of 25, tentatively handed Herzog the first book ever written about him, and was promptly snubbed. Carrère wrote about this in a book. Herzog mocked the comparison with Caspar David Friedrich – which was, in fact, completely justified.

Mediation

When you have a filmmaker's trust, do they follow your advice or recommendations?

What I enjoy is bringing together artists I admire. I remember introducing Boorman to Bartabas' equestrian theatre. Back in 1979, I suggested he watch Boulez and Chéreau's *Ring* production at Bayreuth, which I had found so exciting the previous year. Boorman later acknowledged how much of an influence it was on *Excalibur*. I also went with Kazan to see Chéreau's staging of Marivaux's *La Dispute*, which left a strong impression on him. One time at Café de Flore, Chéreau asked Kazan if he would teach some classes at Théâtre des Amandiers, but Kazan, who had long since stopped teaching, declined. I also remember discussing Emily Dickinson with Jane Campion during one of our initial meetings for an interview about *Sweetie*. She confessed to not knowing much about Dickinson's poetry, but later told me she had read a lot of Dickinson while writing the screenplay for *The Piano*.

Jerry Schatzberg

Your book on Jerry Schatzberg is different...

Schatzberg is also one of Pierre Rissient's discoveries. When his first film, *Puzzle of a Downfall Child*, premiered at the San Francisco Film Festival, people hated it. They said it was boring and wondered what a fashion photographer was doing making films. Rissient, pushing back against almost everyone, insisted it was an important film and brought Schatzberg to Paris so the film would get a second chance. Rissient later showed *Panic in Needle Park* and *Scarecrow* in Cannes, and of course Schatzberg won the Palme d'Or. Marc Bernard, a friend of Rissient and press officer at Fox, teased us with twenty minutes of *Panic in Needle Park* before its Cannes debut. It was staggering, Pacino's performance in particular. It was one of his very first films, thanks to Schatzberg, and it was after seeing it that Coppola cast Pacino in *The Godfather*. Schatzberg was constantly ignored by the American intellectual elite.

You've already mentioned your altercation with Andrew Sarris over Scarecrow *at Cannes.*

It wasn't at Cannes that I discovered the film. In 1973, I was passing through New York on my way back from Washington, where I had given a talk with Marc Ferro, and I went to see *Scarecrow* in a cinema. I was absolutely dazzled and immediately interviewed Schatzberg again to talk about the film. He was delighted when I told him it would be a sensation at Cannes. It was Losey and *The Go-Between* all over again.

Schatzberg's career is somewhat puzzling.

His first three films were extraordinary. Maybe the only comparison is Losey, when he made *The Boy with Green Hair*, *The Lawless* and *The Prowler* back-to-back. Even Coppola's and Scorsese's first films aren't as good. Schatzberg is unique. There's no other case of an American filmmaker since the war asserting himself with three films of such striking mastery. From the start, the American press, however, as it sometimes does, missed the mark.

What was it about Schatzberg that the press didn't like?

He was a fashion photographer and had been the companion of Faye Dunaway, who played a model in *Puzzle of a Downfall Child*. Everyone said how lacking in imagination he was. But the film is actually extremely sophisticated. Formally speaking, it was really quite innovative, much more like what was being done in Europe than the usual realism and classic American action cinema. The critics thought the film was pretentious and simplistic, but if they had actually watched it, they would have realised that Schatzberg – who was a newcomer to cinema – had done extraordinary things with the subject matter, one he was very familiar with. He was inspired by the nervous breakdown of a top model – Anne St. Marie – and had recorded her on tape. Despite earning a lot and always being at the centre of attention, the moment their age becomes apparent and their beauty begins to fade, models get depressed. The most beautiful women often doubt their beauty. When they look in the mirror, they always find something wrong. It was a story that meant a lot to Schatzberg, and with the help of a great screenwriter, Carole Eastman, who worked under the name Adrian Joyce – she wrote *Five Easy Pieces* for Rafelson and *The Shooting* for Monte Hellman – he made a unique film. When they saw his second film, *Panic in Needle Park*, the critics doubled down, saying he had no distinct style, even though it depicted the drug world close to where he lived in Manhattan and that he had documented as a photojournalist. When *Scarecrow* won the Palme d'Or, the Americans were even more annoyed, because once again the French were ahead of the game. I would never say that every one of his subsequent films are uninteresting. I like *The Seduction of Joe Tynan*, *Sweet Revenge* and the wonderful *Honeysuckle Rose*, with folk singer Willy Nelson. *Reunion* and *Street Smart* are excellent. But they aren't on the same level as his first films.

An exhibition and a book

How did the project get started?

In 1982, I suggested to the Centre Pompidou that they do an exhibition of Schatzberg's largely unknown photos – he had taken countless pictures for *Look*, *Vogue* and *Harper's Bazaar* – and include excerpts from his films on television screens.

The photos were grouped into several categories. There are portraits of personalities like Polanski, Fidel Castro, the Rolling Stones, his famous shots of Bob Dylan, his portrait of Willy Nelson in *Honeysuckle Rose*. There are his fashion photos, which he was most known for, along with *Puzzle of a Downfall Child*. He had a house in Upstate New York, so there are countryside shots reminiscent of Walker Evans: wooden buildings, landscapes, all comparable to *Scarecrow*, also city shots of subways and streets that echo *Panic in Needle Park*. I published a book at the time of the exhibition called *De la photo au cinema* [*From Photo to Film*]. His photographs fill half the book, the other half contains my commentary and past interviews, plus a new one about his beginnings and his transition from photography to cinema. I'm rather proud of this book, which remains the only one in the world about Schatzberg, and was the last big photo book published by Les Éditions du Chêne.

Theo Angelopoulos

You originally met Theo Angelopoulos through Positif?

Here again, *The Travelling Players* was one of the great moments of my life as a filmgoer. It was at Directors' Fortnight, at Cannes in 1975, where the film had been rejected for the competition. This was before Gilles Jacob came on board. Under Maurice Bessy's control, the festival was all rather traditional. He was a close friend of Chaplin and Welles but wasn't too interested in contemporary cinema and ignored a lot of films. Pierre-Henri Deleau [who came in to run Directors' Fortnight] was much younger and a lover of new kinds of filmmaking, so he shook things up. Directors' Fortnight had been established in 1969, and over the years has helped launch the careers of many significant filmmakers. Scorsese, for example, with *Mean Streets*, and also Herzog, Oshima, Fassbinder. It was an incredible place for new discoveries, including Angelopoulos' third film, *The Travelling Players*. It's four hours long, and the screening started at ten at night. You know how tired festival-goers can get, especially at Cannes, but at two in morning there was a standing ovation that lasted twenty minutes. Not a single person had left the cinema. The film is a masterpiece, deeply moving in its use of Brecht's ideas, and with exquisite cinematography by Giorgos Arvanitis. I had liked Angelopoulos' early films *Reconstitution* and *Days of '36*, but wasn't expecting a film of this magnitude. Angelopoulos is one of my favourite directors, and he's never disappointed me. Critics rank some of his films higher or lower than others, but he never made a bad one. I did interviews with him for each of them. He kept going until that stupid accident when he was hit by an off-duty policeman on a motorcycle. He was doing some sort of scouting on a freeway ramp and wasn't wearing a fluorescent jacket. He died almost instantly. It's a huge loss.

Recognised as an artist, unknown as a man

Publicly, he always seemed unhappy.

He wasn't exactly popular outside his circle. It was common knowledge how grumpy he was. When he didn't win the Palme d'Or for *Ulysses' Gaze* in 1995, when Kusturica's *Underground* won instead, he made a very public scene. It was all the more difficult for him because the president of the jury was Jeanne Moreau, who had acted in his *The Suspended Step of the Stork*. Actually, it showed just how sincere he really was, because every director who doesn't win a prize feels the same way – they just don't let on. Angelopoulos made the mistake of letting it show. He was uncomfortable in public and a very different person in private. He loved good food, he was affectionate and very loyal. Among the filmmakers I got to know and write about, he was the one who never failed to call me when he was in Paris so we could meet up. He had studied at the Cinémathèque française and had even been a student at IDHEC before quitting because they criticised his long takes. He spoke French fluently and enjoyed showing me his films in preview screenings in Athens and doing interviews with me, which perhaps helped him see his films in a different light. He had great intellectual rigor but was a bit of a melancholic soul. He had been a staunch communist, but then reality hit, and he struggled with the loss of those ideals. It became a major theme in his films.

You collaborated on your Angelopoulos book.

I did it with Hélène Tierchant, a young journalist who had written a few texts in *Positif*. She wrote the critical analysis and I did the interviews. One day I'd like to expand the book, which only goes up to his early career.

In the footsteps of a new world

You published an anthology which synthesises your long-standing interest in American cinema.

It appeared in 1981, under the title *Les Conquérants d'un nouveau monde* [*Conquerors of a New World*], which is the French title of a film by Cecil B. DeMille called *Unconquered*. The book was done at the request of François Erval, one of the co-founders, with Maurice Nadeau, of *La Quinzaine littéraire*. He was, like me, a Jew of Hungarian origin. He worked at Gallimard and read *Positif*, and was a friend of the producer Anatole Dauman. He wanted to publish a book by me, so I suggested a collection of essays on American cinema. The first of its three parts is called "From Vienna to Hollywood," which recalls my own roots and connections to Central European culture. There's an essay in there on *Sunset Boulevard*, which leads me to investigate the notion of the auteur, with texts on Frank Capra, Orson Welles, Howard Hawks, Elia Kazan, on the West and its myths – particularly King Vidor's *Our Daily Bread*, John Ford's *My Darling Clementine*, Abraham Polonsky's *Tell Them Willie Boy Is Here* – and Terrence Malick's *Days of Heaven*, an image from which is on the book's cover. That film seems to me a reverie about America's grand myths. It's a book I value a great deal because it's composed entirely of essays. I plan to republish it with additional texts I've written on American cinema over the past thirty years.

Stroheim, the magnificent imposture

We're going to backtrack a little and talk about the monograph you wrote on Stroheim.

I had been writing for only four or five years at the time. I was grateful for support from veterans who weren't much older than me but were established figures, like Claude Gauteur and Claude Beylie, who also wrote for *Cinéma-Textes*, and Claude-Jean Philippe, who congratulated me on my Kazan piece in *Positif*. They noticed what I was doing. Every month *L'Avant-scène* published a film script accompanied by a monograph about a director or actor, under the title "L'Anthologie du cinéma." They later compiled these into volumes for subscribers. When they asked who I wanted to write about, I chose Erich von Stroheim, who I had been fascinated by ever since I saw a big retrospective of his work at the Cinémathèque française ten years earlier. One problem was Denise Vernac, his widow, who was very protective of his legacy. Knowing I was working on a book about him, she had Lotte Eisner ask that I not mention he was Jewish. An outstanding Belgian historian, Denis Marion, had done some research and published an article in which he revealed that in the Vienna civil registry, Eric von Stroheim was actually named Benno Stroheim, born in a working-class district of the city. He had no noble background at all and completely fabricated his own mythology, claiming his mother was the lady-in-waiting to the Empress, that he was in the Imperial Cavalry, and that he left Austria for the United States following a duel during World War I. It was all untrue. I loved his films, and the stories he told made him all the more fascinating. This book also allowed me to reconnect with my family and origins. Billy Wilder, who directed Stroheim twice as an actor, in *Five Graves to Cairo* and *Sunset Boulevard*, told me that Stroheim had a strong accent typical of the Vienna suburb where he came from and that he even annotated his scripts in Yiddish. They were from the same world. Wilder was born in Austria-Hungary, where his father ran restaurants in train stations. The rumour was that Stroheim wasn't born in Austria but present-day Poland, because the Austro-Hungarian Empire encompassed many nationalities and faiths. In fact, he spent his youth in Vienna. I realised that Stroheim, my first choice for a monograph, was also an Austrian Jew. Later, I discovered that Schatzberg was of the same origin, and Kubrick too, who was partly of Central European Jewish descent through his grandparents. And Mankiewicz, who I made a documentary about, came from Poland.

The *Mitteleuropa* spirit

Your attraction to Vienna is obvious.

I've always been fascinated by the city, which in my opinion was the capital of the beginning of the twentieth century – even more so than Paris. At the turn of the century, you had twelve-tone music, architecture, the first works of sociology, the birth of psychoanalysis, a significant artistic movement in painting, and a lot of great writers. It was the site of many ruptures in art, science and other fields, and was a much more revolutionary city than Paris.

Could you elaborate on this idea of the Mitteleuropa *Viennese spirit?*

In much of the literature, and later in the cinema, that came out of Vienna – Lang, Sternberg, Wilder, Preminger – what stands out is the important role that Jews played in cultural and intellectual life. They were protected by the Emperor Franz Joseph, whereas the mayor of Vienna, Karl Lueger, was a wild anti-Semite. Lueger's ideas, incidentally, influenced a young Austrian named Hitler. The Jews had a special position because they were both integrated and excluded. They had no right to be soldiers or landowners, but they still wielded considerable influence and were held in high esteem. They could attain a certain renown, but remained outsiders, which meant they maintained a critical distance. What they didn't foresee was the collapse of this civilisation, which was multi-ethnic – a sort of precursor to the American melting pot. The Jews who left for America carried with them the memory of the collapse of a culture that was one of the most brilliant in the history of the West, and which in the space of a few years crumbled following military defeat, the dissolution of an empire, and the resurgence of national identities. They experienced society's fragility, fostering a critical attitude – a consistent trait in Jewish thought which didn't just influence artists, but also a psychoanalyst like Freud and an economist and philosopher like Marx, who found more acceptance in America than in Paris. When they arrived in the United States, they found a confident new empire steeped in Enlightenment ideals. The American Constitution referenced Greeks and Romans more than Europe did. America gained independence, had its revolution, and established democracy before France did – though not without the stain and catastrophic flaw of slavery. Their pre-French Revolution Constitution was founded on democratic principles. And while established American filmmakers – Catholics from Italy like Capra, Irish like John Ford, natives like Hawks and Walsh, going back to Griffith and DeMille – had an optimistic vision of humanity, the emigrants who arrived had witnessed atrocities, first the collapse of the Austro-Hungarian Empire, then the rise of Nazism, and were in a better position to exercise a critical eye over the contradictions of American society. Fritz Lang's first film after arriving in the United States was *Fury*, about a lynching and the kind of mob violence he had lived through in Berlin. Wilder's *Double Indemnity* laid bare themes of greed and obsession with wealth. These individuals cultivated a socio-cultural critique while embracing their American identity with joy and pride. It's a generation that laid the groundwork for the emergence of modern American cinema.

They were immigrants, like your father.

I've realised that in addition to my interest in filmmakers of Austro-Hungarian origin, almost everyone I've been drawn to is also in some way a migrant or an exile, people like my father who travelled before settling down. Part of my father's family went to England and the other part to Argentina. Because of immigrations quotas, my father was arrested at the border when he went to join his older brother in England, and ended up becoming more French than the French. His brother was more English than the English. There were their adopted countries. Interestingly, Kubrick came from America to live in England – like Losey, but under very different circumstances. Kazan is an Anatolian Greek who emigrated to the United States. Always this mixing of cultures, this cosmopolitanism. Wilder and Lang both left Vienna via Germany and finally reached Hollywood via Paris. All of this resonates deeply with my internationalist sensibilities. I have never felt stuck within the boundaries of French culture, even though it has been a crucial part of my life. I've always been drawn to the interplay between cultures. In matters of politics, I'm an ardent supporter of a unified Europe. I have enjoyed my travels across Europe, and also the United States, Asia and beyond, and have always been curious about foreign literature: Italian, English, German, Russian, South American. It's no coincidence that I started with Stroheim and that my most recent book is about Jane Campion.

Jane Campion

You have followed her filmmaking from the very beginning.

The foundation of the book is my interviews with her over the years, our discussions about the feature films she has made to date, including the *Top of the Lake* television series. Like everyone else, I discovered her at Cannes, thanks to Pierre Rissient, who spotted her as a film student in Australia. He suggested to Gilles Jacob that he show her shorts at the festival. She isn't just the only woman to have won the Palme d'Or, she's one of the greatest filmmakers in the history of cinema and a director whose tastes align exactly with my own. Her work is inspired and refined, and manages to reach a wide audience, all while maintaining an original cinematic style. Watching *Sweetie* again, her first film, you realise how daring it truly is, even though Wim Wenders' jury preferred *sex, lies, and videotape*. It wasn't a bad call, but *Sweetie*, which received no awards at Cannes, might have been just a little too audacious.

The books I didn't write

Are there any books that you always wanted to write? And are there any you refused to write?

When Gallimard asked me for a biography of Godard, I turned them down because I didn't have the guts to write a 900-page book about someone who was going to spit in my face when I finished it. I prefer talking to people I would like to meet again over dinner. There was this Surrealist game: "Would you open your door to...?" Everyone in the group would answer: Would you open up to Gérard de Nerval? To Herman Melville? Goya? Sometimes they were very scathing: "No, I'll never forgive him..." Godard is a very important filmmaker, there's no denying it, but I didn't want to write a book about him. I didn't have to think for a second about it.

The subjects of your books are almost exclusively European or Anglo-Saxon.

You might be surprised that I haven't done any monographs on, for example, Chinese, Turkish or Indian filmmakers. It's possible to do an interview with someone after doing homework and accumulating some background knowledge. In my book *Petite planète cinématographique* are interviews with filmmakers from all over the world: fifty directors, forty years, thirty countries. But for a real in-depth analysis, for a book – as I did for Rosi, Kubrick or Boorman – I think you absolutely have to speak the language. Angelopoulos and Rosi spoke French fluently. Moreover, Greece and Italy are European countries, and are sufficiently close my own culture and the political problems of the Mediterranean: dictatorships, fascism, communism, socio-economic inequality. It's much easier for me to dive into their worlds than to take on a filmmaker from Taiwan or Sri Lanka. I would feel quite lost. So that's why my books are about

Americans, an Englishman, a Greek, an Italian, a New Zealander. I would have liked to have written about a French filmmaker, but it's a matter of priorities. I speak English, I know the culture and Anglo-Saxon world well, which gives me an edge. There are already plenty of excellent books on French filmmakers written in French.

It's not too late. Who would you want to write about?

My dream would be to take a few years and write a book on Alain Resnais, because not only did I host him a few times on *Projection privée*, we were good friends and spoke regularly on the phone, and I did interviews with him for *Positif*. But more than all that, he's just an exemplary filmmaker. He was, until his death, the greatest working French director. He started in 1946 with trips to painters' studios, which led to his short films. And what shorts they are! I'm thinking of Roman Polanski and Jane Campion – rare filmmakers whose perfect, singular short films anticipate their features. Resnais was forever reinventing himself. He was constantly questioning things, or at least always exploring new paths. I sometimes say that Resnais is the Kubrick of European auteur cinema. He's as unpredictable as Kubrick, and always coming up with new ideas. *Muriel ou le Temps d'un retour* and *Pas sur la bouche*, *La guerre est finie* and *Cœurs*, *Je t'aime, je t'aime* and *Stavisky* – it's a body of work of extraordinary variety, with – at the same time, as with Kubrick – a common thread, ongoing obsessions and recurring themes. He also had the good fortune of being backed by great producers who took risks when they financed his films, from Anatole Dauman to Jean-Louis Livi, who worked on his final films.

About fifteen years ago at the French Institute in Madrid, I ran a seminar that I called "Les incipits d'Alain Resnais" ["The Beginnings of Alain Resnais"], where students analysed the first four minutes of all his films. It was fascinating to see how, in just a few moments, he set the tone. Parallels with other films were immediately evident. What really draws me to Resnais is the richness and diversity of his work. His films are unquestionably about the imagination and dreams, as with *Providence* and *Je t'aime, je t'aime*, which delve into the realm of fantasy and science fiction. But they're also political, and for a long time he was associated with a certain kind of commitment. *Night and Fog* is about the concentration camps, *Hiroshima mon amour* the atomic bomb, *Muriel* the war in Algeria, *La guerre est finie* the Spanish Civil War. He's a man of his time, deeply introspective and a poet at heart, plus a great director of actors. Some critics didn't much like his recent work, but I think that actually it brought out something we never quite grasped when we first saw *Stavisky*, for example. He's exploring his childhood, when he would often go to the theatre, and the fact that he wanted to become an actor. In a way, all Resnais' recent work is a Proustian madeleine, even his adaptation of Henry Bernstein's *Mélo* and his penultimate film, inspired by Anouilh, *You Ain't Seen Nothin' Yet*. There's an atmosphere in those films that brings to mind poetic realism of the late 1930s – the time of his adolescence.

Have you ever thought about taking the idea for a Resnais book to a publisher?

I was actually working on a Resnais project – a small volume in the "Découvertes Gallimard" collection, which had published two books of mine, one about Lang and the other on American crime cinema. Unfortunately, the collection was discontinued in 2013, and the book never materialised. It would have been fun to write for a wider audience – playing with imagery and making visual connections, as I did with Kubrick and Boorman, with a filmmaker equally suitable for such treatment, whose work leaves some people scratching their heads. I certainly wasn't going to write a book that I hoped would revolutionise how people see his films, certainly not after Jean-Louis Leutrat and Suzanne Liandrat-Guigues' *Alain Resnais: liaisons secrètes, accords vagabonds*, or, before that, Robert Benayoun's *Resnais, arpenteur de l'imaginaire*.

You actually published that book by Benayoun.

Yes, in a collection I created at Éditions Stock, which included Jean-Loup Bourget's *Le Mélodrame*, Alain Masson's *La Comédie musicale*, Robert Parrish's memoirs, a book by Jerry Lewis, two books by Jean-Pierre Jeancolas on French cinema, and two books by Petr Král on slapstick.

Along with Claude Sautet, Resnais was one of the French directors you were most friendly with.

He was incredibly polite and courteous. I never heard him speak ill of a colleague. He was very interested in young filmmakers, including Arnaud Desplechin, who returned the compliment. And above all, he loved actors. Critics tend to underestimate the importance of actors, perhaps because they don't know how to talk about them. I'm the first to admit it's one of my shortcomings. In America, there are texts by James Naremore, and in France – though I don't really like the word – "actorial" studies by Christian Viviani, Michel Cieutat and Christophe Damour, among others, who write very well about actors. But more often than not, the actor's work is ignored. And yet, when you talk to most great directors, you realise how even those labelled as formalists are fascinated by actors. You might think that Resnais was more interested in editing or camera movement, but no – he was always drawn to actors. He adored their voices, like a musician would. Think of Emmanuelle Riva in *Hiroshima*, Ingrid Thulin in *La guerre est finie*, Albertazzi and Delphine Seyrig, who's almost singing in *Last Year at Marienbad*. And of course, Sabine Azéma, who lit up his work.

DOCUMENTARIAN

We talked about Positif *as a hub for critics who don't want to make films themselves, but you have actually made a few documentaries yourself, which can be seen as an extension of your work as a critic. There's the "making of" about Rosi you mentioned, plus the three films you made about Elia Kazan, Joseph Mankiewicz and Billy Wilder at the start of the 1980s.*

With Antoine de Gaudemar, I made the documentary *Once upon a time: A Clockwork Orange.* We filmed inside Kubrick's house and outside at his grave, and interviewed his wife and brother-in-law/collaborator Jan Harlan, as well as actors he worked with, including the extraordinary Malcolm McDowell and Warren Clarke, who played one of the Droogs, and production assistant Bernard Williams.

Why didn't you make more films?

I could have, but I made the ones I did because I knew producers and people who were willing to invest in the projects and get them moving. Spending a year negotiating, making deals, trying to find the money, waiting for television stations to sign on – that's absolutely not for me. There were too many other things I was working on. Still, I did enjoy making these films, which were done quickly and efficiently. When people interview me, they sometimes bring a crew of six people, who spend two hours filming a ten-minute interview. Director Annie Tresgot and I made the first of those films, the one about Billy Wilder, in three days, with Gary Graver, Welles' cinematographer on *The Other Side of the Wind*, and a sound engineer. There were three filming locations: his small house at Trancas Beach, his office in Los Angeles, and his apartment. It was the same thing for the Elia Kazan film, *Outsider*, which I also made with Tresgot, along with the extraordinary Quebec cinematographer and Direct Cinema pioneer Michel Brault. We shot over three days, at the Actors Studio in New York and fifty miles away in the Connecticut country house where he filmed *The Visitors*, then in his place in New York, and also Hoboken, where he shot *On the Waterfront*, and in a cabin on Long Island. It also took three days, including travel. For *All About Mankiewicz* it was even simpler because he didn't move. We shot with Luc Béraud, who directed, in the garden of Mankiewicz's house, also over three days, but this time with two cameras.

Portrait of a "60% perfect" man: Billy Wilder (1980)

The first of these documentaries is about Billy Wilder.

It was a stroke of luck. He agreed mainly because of Tresgot, a talented filmmaker and a friend of Michèle Firk from *Positif*. She had been Wilder's intern on *Love in the Afternoon* when she graduated from IDHEC, and he had a soft spot for her. I also knew Wilder because I had done interviews with him for *The Private Life of Sherlock Holmes* and *Avanti!*, films which had been poorly received by critics and audiences in America. He was touched that we were interested in him despite this alleged decline. He was quite friendly but didn't particularly care for critics and didn't like being in their company. Annie was our ticket in. I remember him being very hands-on, almost directing the film. Don't get me wrong – Annie made the film, but he brought in I.A.L. Diamond, his writer, and with that little stick he always had, the one that drove Raymond Chandler nuts, they re-enacted a writing session for us: Wilder pacing, Diamond typing his suggestions. When the two of us were on the beach and he was flying a kite, he teased me about French critics flattering directors. Wilder was in control of everything. He knew exactly what he wanted to do and not do. We filmed his extraordinary collection of paintings, which he later sold – he didn't want it to be scattered after his death, though he ended up buying more.

One of the most enjoyable moments of those three days was one morning when he said to me, "We're having dinner tonight in your honour. I know you French critics don't really care about actors, so I didn't invite any." I said, "Audrey Hepburn would have been nice." He said, "No, no. For you, it's the directors who count, so I invited William Wyler and George Cukor." Audrey, Wilder's second wife, who he was married to for forty years, cooked. Wilder stood there watching Cukor and Wyler, who was originally from Alsace, saying, "Look at Wyler! He really does look like a Strasbourg cheese merchant. I invited them because I like to feel young." Wyler and Wilder explained that people always confused them. Fans would tell Wilder that the chariot race in *Ben-Hur* was the best thing he had ever done, or they would say to William Wyler, "*Some Like It Hot* – what a fantastic film!" It was awkward correcting them and suggesting that perhaps they didn't know that much about the films they claimed to love. Both men eventually got so weary of it all that instead of being rude, they would just accept all compliments, no questions asked. Wilder finished the story by saying, "Manet, Monet! What's the difference?" After dinner, George Cukor dropped me off at my hotel in his chauffeur-driven car. Wyler was also very funny. Cukor, Wilder and Wyler – an evening of immigrant Jews. Wyler said he had shown one of his films to producer Samuel Goldwyn, famous for his absurd pronouncements – called "Goldwynisms." He had brought his eight-year-old son, Sam Jr., to a screening, and at the end Goldwyn said to Wyler, "Willie, this is the first time I haven't understood one of your films. There are flashbacks. It's not at all clear what's going on." He turned to his son and asked, "Sam, did you understand?" And the son replies, "Yes dad, it's clear" – and he tells the story to his father, putting it in chronological order. Goldwyn, furious, bangs on the table and says, "Okay, but we don't make films for eight-year-olds!"

Was he pleasant to work with during the shoot? Wilder was known for being quite cruel at times.

I think he was genuinely moved that we liked his films. He wasn't really into irony. I remember later, around 1988, I taught a summer class in Santa Barbara. I was with Evelyn, who became my second wife, and we went to lunch with Wilder – who was a real gourmet – in a delightful Italian restaurant. Evelyn wanted pasta carbonara, but I said, "Come on – there's plenty to choose from. We make carbonara at home. Pick something else." And Wilder said, "Why are you telling her that? Women are all the same. At five o'clock she'll ask you why you stopped her from eating the pasta she wanted." Billy Wilder's marital tips. He was charming.

Elia Kazan, Outsider (1981)

So your first experience as a documentary filmmaker was a success...

And was followed shortly thereafter by Kazan, who was very close friends with Wilder. They met in Hollywood when Kazan was an actor, and had great admiration for each other.

This was in the late 1930s?

Yes. Apparently they were dating the two Dowling sisters, one of whom later became Pavese's mistress. Wilder said he dated a lot of American girls so he could learn the language. But it's not as if I needed Wilder's backing to make the Kazan film. He was immediately won over by the idea, and appreciated Tresgot's professionalism and precision. He was generous in opening his doors to us. Michel Brault did beautiful work – I remember being amazed by what he caught on film. We shot Kazan, tense and nervous, walking, as he always did, around Columbus Circle, near Lincoln Centre, at dusk, and I was convinced that there wasn't enough light. And five minutes later there wasn't. But Brault managed to get a wonderful twilight shot. Annie found a beautiful piece of Stravinsky to accompany the scene.

Kazan was less hands-on than Wilder?

Yes. He was originally an actor, but knew he would never be a great actor, and since he was ambitious, he decided he wanted to be the best director there ever was instead of a mediocre actor. He knew he was never going to be a star because of his looks. He gave very good performances, but they were second fiddle roles in gangster films like *City for Conquest* and *Blues in the Night*, two Anatole Litvak films. Kazan was always very comfortable in front of the camera.

He was also a celebrated teacher.

He taught at the Actors Studio, and thanks to him I attended the lessons of three famous teachers: Ellen Burstyn, Joseph Mankiewicz and Arthur Penn, who was rehearsing scenes with the actors. De Niro, who had made *The Last Tycoon* with Kazan a few years earlier, agreed to be interviewed there. We also filmed with the man who had been Kazan's bodyguard during the filming of *On the Waterfront*, when there were threats from the mafia and corrupt unions.

All About Mankiewicz (1983)

Your third film was about Joseph Mankiewicz.

That was really thanks to Kazan. Mankiewicz had immense respect for him because he revered the theatre. He wanted to write a book, which he never finished – like many things he started – on seventeenth-century actresses. He had actually invented the Sarah Siddons Award for *All About Eve*, which was a tribute to a great actress of the eighteenth century, who Joshua Reynolds once painted. The award was sitting on his mantlepiece when I interviewed him for the first time. He respected Kazan because he had done so much theatre work, which Mankiewicz never had the guts for. He once staged an opera, *La Bohème*, but could only dream of directing theatre. For him, Kazan was the king of Broadway in the 1940s and 1950s.

That's surprising. Cinephiles often pit Kazan's naming names during McCarthyism against Mankiewicz's stand as the head of the Directors Guild, refusing to endorse the anti-communist loyalty oath pushed by Cecil B. DeMille.

You're right, but it's not as straightforward as it seems, because a few days later Mankiewicz ended up signing that oath himself. Huston, Bogart and lots of non-communist liberals went to Washington to support the Hollywood Ten, but ended up so disgusted by their behaviour that they wanted nothing more to do with them. The Hollywood Ten, who were members of the Communist International, described America as fascist. The real dictator, of course, was Stalin. Communists like Abraham Polonsky, Dalton Trumbo and John Berry held a grudge against Kazan, understandably so, as they were direct victims. But among liberals like Wilder and Mankiewicz, I never sensed any hostility toward Kazan. In the 1950s, a film like *On the Waterfront* – with Brando righteously fighting the corrupt unions – could even be seen as Kazan drawing parallels with his own experiences. Two years later, anyone could have seen it was just self-justification. But surprisingly, the non-communist American press, even the liberals who praised the film, made no mention of it, while Lindsay Anderson, who was British, and wasn't even a communist, published a scathing ideological analysis of *On the Waterfront* in *Sight and Sound*. Anyway, there's no doubt that Mankiewicz and Kazan were friends. Kazan admired Mankiewicz's cinema, so different from his own – more cerebral, intellectual, with a more thoughtful and less introspective English-style approach to directing actors.

Surprisingly, Mankiewicz taught at the Actors Studio.

Kazan didn't like seeing him so bitter and withdrawn, so he tried getting Mankiewicz out into the world by inviting him to teach. It didn't last long because Mankiewicz didn't see much value in rehearsing aspiring actors or sharing his knowledge. He was quite self-absorbed, much like his characters. He lived in New York state, not far from Kazan, in his secluded Westchester home. Much like Kubrick, Mankiewicz rarely gave interviews or liked commenting on his films. Despite being a great intellectual, he was part of a true Hollywood tradition. Viennese directors like Wilder, Preminger and Lang were more talkative in comparison.

How did you meet him?

He agreed to be interviewed for *L'Express* when *Sleuth* was released in France in 1972. I was driven to this manor that looked like a scene out of one of his films: ivy-covered walls, a massive barn and a huge office. It was like something out of *Dragonwyck*. Gothic, filled with thousands of books, all his awards and Oscars, a prominent portrait of his father – who was a literature professor at Yale – above the fireplace, and a fierce storm outside that added to the atmosphere. It might be the most impressive interview of my life. I watched the tape roll as he spoke almost in a monologue. I probably asked a maximum of eight questions, each followed by a profound discourse on adaptation or the actor's paradox. It was masterful. I was captivated. All I wanted to do was film him.

Your documentary is one of the rare occasions when he allowed himself to be filmed.

He did a few written and radio interviews, but besides our documentary, the only film of him is about thirty minutes of footage shot by Jean Douchet during a press conference at the Avignon festival. I asked Luc Béraud, who made *Like a Turtle on its Back* and is a real cinephile, to direct it. I warned him that we would need two cameras because otherwise he wouldn't be able to cut, and that Mankiewicz would talk for half an hour without stopping. We set out to make a one-hour film, as we did for Kazan and Wilder, but he was so captivating that we split the film – *All About Mankiewicz* – into two parts. The first was him talking about other people, the second was him talking about himself. Given his extraordinary career as, successively, a screenwriter, producer, then a director, he could talk as much about Hollywood as about himself. He was well placed to discuss the studio system because he had become a director at a time when renowned screenwriters were beginning to direct their scripts. This was the 1940s – an important moment in Hollywood's evolution towards more freedom, or at least more autonomy for filmmakers who wanted to exercise more control over their scripts. In the second part of the documentary, he talked about the films he wrote and directed. The film might never have been finished, but sometimes my impatience serves me well. We started filming in Berlin in February 1983, in the snow. As Mankiewicz had once been a correspondent in Berlin, where he had worked on silent film intertitles, it was a fitting setting. The main part was supposed to be filmed in April at his home in New York. Everything was arranged with the producer Klaus Hellwig, who worked on the Wilder documentary, but a few weeks before the New York shoot, Mankiewicz wanted to cancel. His wife Rosemary called me and said they wanted to postpone until the summer. "It's not possible," I told her. "Everything is planned. We already have the plane tickets." So we went ahead, and shortly after we finished filming he found out that he had throat cancer. He was a heavy pipe smoker. If we had postponed that interview, the film – which I think is an important document – wouldn't exist. He died a few years later.

How was he during filming?

Compared to Wilder, and especially Kazan, who were full of non-stop energy, always on the move and forever improvising, capable of catching me off guard, Mankiewicz resembled his characters. He spoke beautifully, but barely moved. He told me things I had already heard from him, but it was fascinating to see him speak, with that mischievous glint of his, that hint of irony. There was clearly more he wanted to do – this was ten years after *Sleuth* – but I couldn't see him making another film. Kazan, on the other hand, even years later, met with Juliette Binoche and travelled to the Middle East with a plan to make a film for Anatole Dauman, then for René Cleitman. *Beyond the Aegean Sea* eventually became a novel, but he was clearly totally invested in the project and quite capable of shooting a new film. Wilder too, but he only wanted to work under familiar conditions in Hollywood. At one point he thought about filming a Hollywood saga, a bit like *Sunset Boulevard*, which he was going to call *The Foreskin Saga* – a pun on Galsworthy's *The Forsyte Saga* – about a Jewish dynasty in Hollywood.

Unmade films

Let's say a producer came to you saying: "I'd like to produce a documentary about a filmmaker. Anyone you want." Who would you choose?

I had plans to make a film about John Huston with the support of Hellwig, who died young. I had met Huston several times at Cannes, notably once in Cap d'Antibes with my Swedish friend Jan Aghed, and another time, on my own, at the Carlton. At our first meeting we talked extensively about *Fat City*, and the second time about *Wise Blood* – two great films from his later period, and then about *Under the Volcano*, his Malcolm Lowry adaptation. I found him quite phenomenal, a larger-than-life character. He was tall, mischievous, funny, overflowing with anecdotes, and didn't take himself too seriously. I dreamt of going to his island at Puerto Vallarta, Mexico, where he had taken refuge among the monkeys and crocodiles, with his mistresses, his cooks and crew. He led an exceptional life. He really was an adventurer. Later on, I thought about writing a biography of him, my first, but I dropped it because I realised that American biographies have the kind of financial backing I would never get. I would have had to put a temporary halt on all my other work in order to do the project justice. I don't know how Pascal Mérigeau managed to publish his monumental book on Jean Renoir while writing his weekly column at *Le Nouvel Observateur*. And it still took him five years! With everything I do, the intensive research, the expensive trips, interviews with people Huston knew, re-watching all his films, re-reading… I'm just not cut out for that. A French publisher gives you 3000 Euros, while an American one might offer $100,000 to cover travel, time spent, expenses. There's no comparison. They can afford it because the print runs are different. There are great biographers in America – Joseph McBride, Patrick McGilligan, Todd McCarthy – who write fantastic books, but they invest themselves totally in it. It's all they do for years at a time.

Huston is an interesting case because he's one of the few directors from the Golden Age of Hollywood who, until his last film The Dead, *in 1987, produced a body of work that – while uneven – was nonetheless significant.*

In 1987, I published the book *Passport to Hollywood*, which includes my interviews with Huston, Wilder and

Mankiewicz – three screenwriters who became directors. After Preston Sturges, Huston was the second American screenwriter to become a director when he made *The Maltese Falcon* in 1941. Then there was Wilder with *The Lost Weekend* in 1943, and Mankiewicz with *Dragonwyck* in 1946. And within five years there were plenty of others, like Delmer Daves and Richard Brooks. As Wilder said, "I became a director because I was fed up with making the bed, only for another director to jump in and do the screwing." That's why he became a director. *Passport to Hollywood* contains the interviews I did with these filmmakers, Wilder and Mankiewicz in particular, and transcripts of the filmed material too, alongside interviews with three European filmmakers – Wim Wenders, Roman Polanski and Miloš Forman – who, years later, made films in Hollywood. I wanted to know what perspective they had on America compared to that of their predecessors.

THE FESTIVAL SCOUT

Light and shade

I like to describe critics as "scouts." It seems to define the profession as I see it. "Scout" in the double sense of the term. On one hand, the critic is there to shine a light, to clarify and analyse what is sometimes obscure, and avoid making it even more obscure with illegible jargon. Someone said we should make what is clear more complicated and explain what is confusing. "Making clear things complicated" matters because sometimes there are hidden complexities in what seems to be obvious. Exploring these complexities can make something obvious more interesting.

In classicalism, for example?

Yes, it's about diving into areas which the smooth surface of the work doesn't reveal. I'm also talking about being a "scout" in the sense of someone who ventures to the frontlines, to uncharted territory, to undiscovered forests, and unearths unknown talent. It's part of the thrill of cinema, and has happened to me a few times. For example, when I saw Peter Greenaway's *The Draughtsman's Contract* at the Venice Film Festival, his first feature, I was captivated. And then, two days later, I listened to an interview with him and discovered how wonderfully clever he is in analysing his own work. An intellectual thrill followed the artistic one. When I saw Makavejev's first films at festivals, especially *Love Affair, or the Case of the Missing Switchboard Operator* and *Innocence Unprotected*, they were also revelations. They didn't look like anything I had ever seen before.

The whims of John Ford

I remember Makavejev at the Montreal festival in 1967, the year of the Expo, when all the top talents of the new generation were brought together. Monte Hellman and Glauber Rocha were there, and three masters who were being feted: Jean Renoir, Fritz Lang and John Ford. They showed a restoration of a Fritz Lang film, the only one he made in France, after he left Germany and before he arrived in America – *Liliom*, which had been unavailable for a long time. Also screened was Renoir's neglected *La Marseillaise*. I told the organisers, "There's no John Ford film. He's disappointed." No one, in fact, was paying much interest in the old man. The organisers had other things to do, so they asked if I would accompany him for a couple of days. I wasn't yet thirty and adored Ford. I went to see him in his room. The festival organisers had given him a novel, *Valley of the Dolls*, so he wouldn't get bored. When a charming young woman came up to the room to offer him this book, he got up, naked, and threw it out the window. I wanted to introduce him to all the young filmmakers, so I invited him to a screening of Makaveiev's *Love Affair*. "He really is a very important new filmmaker," I said. He came, was very quiet, and sat down next to me. The film begins with erotic engravings where we see people making love. A woman is seated on the knees of a man who takes her from behind. Ford told me, "That's definitely not the right way to have kids." It got worse – there are nude scenes. He took out a cigar, because he didn't want to appear rude and leave the room on his own, and once he lit up, they escorted him out of there. I remember one time at the same festival Renoir coming out of the elevator, misidentifying Ford – with his black eye patch – and hugging him with a resounding "Fritz!" Lang, another famous patch-wearer, was also there that year. His patch was on the other eye.

The organisers wanted to show a Ford film, so I suggested they get a copy of *Young Mr. Lincoln*, with Henry Fonda, from Toronto. The film was barely known at the time. Eisenstein had written about it and Roger Tailleur had published a long essay about it in *Positif*, but the film had never been seen widely. I said to him, "Mr. Ford, they're paying homage to you tomorrow evening. We're going to show *Young Mr. Lincoln*." "What?" he says, "that's not one of mine!" I thought it might be his age or the fact that was so deaf, which he played up when he didn't want to hear something. I wasn't quite sure what to say. "It's the film where at the end Lincoln goes off up the hill. You shot it for Darryl Zanuck at Fox." He says, "I don't remember. I don't know this film. I never made it." I kept coming back to Henry Fonda, forgetting that he had fallen out with Ford because he had left-wing views and Ford was very right-wing, although he remained a free spirit and had pushed back against Cecil B. DeMille during the McCarthy years. He was a cantankerous Irishman, but more Irish than right-wing, so he was capable of independence of mind and rebellion against any dictate. I mentioned Fonda several times. He finally replied, "No, it was with Alice Brady." She played Lincoln's mother. He certainly had a good sense of humour.

The sun rises on the East

You visited some interesting festivals in the East.

I followed Czechoslovakian films from the very start – I was at Karlovy Vary in 1966. Czech cinema was flourishing until Soviet tanks put an end to the Dubček experiment in 1968. I saw films like *Black Peter* by Miloš Forman, *Daisies* by Věra Chytilová, *Intimate Lighting* by Ivan Passer, *Diamonds of the Night* by Jan Němec, *Closely Watched Trains* by Jiří Menzel. It was an extraordinary generation of filmmakers who worked closely with great writers like Bohumil Hrabal. There were Surrealist groups in Romania and Yugoslavia, and I established strong connections within the Czech community. The intellectual climate was exciting. Among the great Yugoslav filmmakers, Makavejev was brilliant with collage. He was closely tied to a specific cinematic era but struggled to adapt to narrative cinema. It was easier for Forman to go from *Loves of a Blonde* to *One Flew Over the Cuckoo's Nest* because his filmmaking had well-developed characters, strong narratives, and a sense of drama reminiscent of Chaplin – qualities he successfully transported to Hollywood. He was able to adjust to the new landscape. Makavejev's references, on the other hand, were Eisenstein, Dziga Vertov, Boris Barnet and avant-garde Soviet cinema. His cinema was characterised by collage techniques and juxtapositions that were all over the place, and he found it challenging to negotiate the turn towards a more conventional, classical cinema, as industry and audience preferences shifted through the 1980s.

The Moscow festival was famous.

I went there in 1969 and did the first major interview with Tarkovsky – virtually the only one he gave – on *Andrei Rublev*, which at the time was banned. Luda and Jean Schnitzer, two Frenchmen who could speak good Russian, accompanied me and interpreted. I was able to speak at length with Tarkovsky, who incidentally had just seen *2001: A Space Odyssey* and didn't like it. I think he was already preparing to respond to Kubrick's film with *Solaris*, his own science fiction film. The Moscow festival screened *2001* in 1969, a year after its release, and awarded it something like the 25th prize. They gave prizes to everyone. *2001* was bottom of the list – and it didn't do any better at the Oscars. It was July, and some journalists had asked to watch the

Moon landing on television, but surprise, surprise – there were no televisions that worked. It was political, of course. There was no way the Russians wanted to watch their space rivals triumph, but it backfired, because people said, "The Americans are on the Moon, but the Russians can't get a television working!"

I did an extensive piece on Soviet cinema for *L'Express* – eight or ten pages. The Russians were very generous. I went as far as Tbilisi in Georgia, where I met Iosseliani, and Yerevan in Armenia, where I discovered Pelechian's incredible documentaries. I went to Riga and Tallinn and checked out local production. It was an intensive, three-week investigation. They were shocked by my article, and felt I was ungrateful because they had made all those trips possible but I didn't hold back from talking about censorship and the social unease I had seen. When I was young, books like Gide's *Return from the USSR*, which went completely against the tide of his fellow travellers, left a mark on me. I admired his courage, especially later, when members of the Académie Goncourt returned from the USSR without a word about what they had seen – the imprisonments, the suicides – just so they could sell their books there. I found it remarkable that a man like Gide, who in 1937 had stood on the Kremlin balcony in Red Square alongside Stalin, quickly realised what was really going on: the oppression, especially the persecution of homosexuals who were locked away in camps. After being treated like the global icon he was, with red carpets and all that pomp, he came home and told it like it really was, with incredible candour, and immediately cut himself off from many of the people who supported him in France. Figures like Aragon or Éluard could have learned something from him. There was actually no shortage of testimonies about Soviet Russia at that time. Just look at the books by Panait Istrati, Ante Ciliga and, later, Orwell and Koestler. There was such willing ignorance. People just didn't want to see the truth. I'm not comparing myself to Gide, but I've always believed that the role of a journalist is to testify as honestly as possible to what they have seen. Sartre arrived at the Red Square in 1954 and said, "I breathe the air of freedom," and when he got home from the United States, described it almost as if it were a fascist country. After my article was published, Sovexport summoned me and gave me a dressing down. It wasn't a big deal. No one tried to bomb my home.

Festival discoveries

Your work as a scout is done mainly at festivals?

When it comes to the discovery of new talent, festivals – and their artistic directors – have become more important than critics. But when I began as a critic, around 1963, in Cannes, there was only Critics' Week, and that was it. Apart from that, there was only the official competition. During my initial experiences at the Venice festival in 1964-65, a pompous old fascist, Luigi Chiarini, ran the place, and he showed only fourteen films. That was it – no other screenings, only those so-called masterpieces. There were no genre films, for example. We didn't have nearly as many opportunities to make new discoveries. At the time, critics travelled a lot more, like Georges Sadoul and Robert Benayoun going to Hollywood and smaller, faraway festivals like Mar del Plata in Argentina. They really were explorers who brought back important news. Nowadays it's the people who run the big festivals who are doing this kind of thing. They have the means that newspapers no longer have. And these people are themselves sometimes former critics or experts on cinema. Charles Tesson, for example, who heads Critics' Week, used to review Hong Kong films for *Cahiers du cinéma*. Edouard Waintrop, a former critic for *Libération*, runs Directors' Fortnight. The new head of the Locarno Festival, Carlo Chatrian, is also a former critic, as is Alberto Barbera in Venice, and before him Marco Müller. Barbera also directs the Cinema Museum in Turin, just as Thierry Frémaux, the author of a book about *Positif*'s Lyon years, is simultaneously the artistic director of Cannes and heads the Institut Lumière.

The Cannes trifecta

The most famous example is Gilles Jacob, a critic who took control of Cannes in 1978.

He was well known in France as a critic, and created the magazine *Raccords* at the end of the 1940s, shortly before *Cahiers* and *Positif*. He wrote for *Cinéma*, *Nouvelles littéraires* and *L'Express*, and in the early 1960s published a book called *Le Cinéma moderne*, a quite remarkable collection of essays. His appointment was a turning point in the way festivals were run. Maurice Bessy, who ran Cannes, had been a journalist at *Cinémonde*, but it was Jacob who brought film criticism into the world of major festivals. He also shook up Cannes because he understood, with his deep knowledge of cinema, that it was time for change and that the festival couldn't just coast on past achievements. There had obviously been great films selected and given prizes at Cannes before his arrival, like *La dolce vita*, *The Leopard*, *The Go-Between*, *The Mattei Affair* – and so many others. The groundwork was there, but a new direction was sorely needed. Jacob responded to the pressure of Directors' Fortnight, which was established in 1969 after May '68, when the SRF [Society of Film Directors] got permission from the festival to create a parallel event, which has become increasingly influential. Jacob particularly wanted the festival's official competition to be more discerning in its choices, while also somehow retaining its glamour and maintaining its status as a professional event. It's this threefold perspective that gives Cannes its influence and power, making it the greatest festival in the world.

It's always going to be difficult to please everyone all the time.

Some people want Cannes to only show blockbusters – meaning no films like *When Father Was Away on Business* – and invite only big stars. Others lean towards experimental cinema by fringe filmmakers. Then there are the business folks who don't watch any films and spend all their time making deals. The place is a convergence of parallel worlds, but that's its strength: it brings together glamour, money and art. That always seemed like the right mix to me. I have a horror of total purity, extremists and fanaticism. Run after the audience too much, Max Ophüls said, and all you'll see is their backsides. It would be the death of Cannes if it catered only to the mainstream or became all about star power. If money reigns supreme, that's also a death knell. Conversely, it would be suicidal if Cannes became overly elitist. The festival works in the same way that a juggler is able to catch several balls at once. Everyone wins, because you can see Spielberg's latest or an appearance by Alain Delon, then at eight in the morning you might discover a new *sex, lies and videotape*, which won the Palme d'Or and overnight launched the unknown Soderbergh – who by now has made twenty-five films in twenty-five years. Or Kusturica's *When Father Was Away on Business*, or even *Reservoir Dogs*, which screened out of competition, and now, of course, Tarantino is a darling of the festival. There was very little talk of Belgian cinema in the mainstream media before the Dardenne brothers and their two Palmes d'Or, for *Rosetta* and *The Child*.

The Promise was screened at Directors' Fortnight.

Yes, it did its job of discovery, but what really propelled them globally was *Rosetta*. I'm talking about the major kinds of events at Cannes that a certain puritanical clique would like to rob us of, the kind of people who would kill Cannes stone dead if we listened to them, because at a certain point the international press and the public would lose interest. We all know that there are great films of all sorts, some made on shoestring budgets, others costing millions. You can't judge the quality of a film by its budget, or even solely on the director's reputation.

Festivals for cinephiles

Has the shift that began at Cannes spread to other big festivals?

You could actually say that the Cannes model served as an example for Berlin, which has its Forum, as modelled on Directors' Fortnight, and Panorama, which is the equivalent of Cannes' Un certain regard, created by Gilles Jacob to pull the rug out from under Directors' Fortnight's – a kind of parallel event, now with a jury and prizes, which makes it possible to select twenty more films, thus doubling the number of feature films in the official selection. Similarly, the Venice Film Festival created sections that approximate Un certain regard – Orrizonti – and Directors' Fortnight – Giornate degli Autori – while also having its own Critics' Week. So the pattern was really established by Cannes. More proof that these days festival directors have replaced film critics as the most important prospectors of new work is the book that Phaidon published a few years ago. *Take 100: The Future of Film, 100 New Directors* features a hundred directors from the last fifteen or twenty years who have made their mark on cinema. Fifty years ago, a book like that would have been entrusted to ten film critics for their perspectives, but here it's festival directors who weigh in.

Changes like this resulted in unexpected Palmes d'Or, like When Father Was Away on Business in 1985, when Miloš Forman was president of the jury.

It was Emir Kusturica's first Palme d'Or, before *Underground*. I loved the film, which I wrote about in *Le Matin*, and was very happy it got a prize because Kusturica is one of those great discoveries to have emerged from Yugoslavia, following the lead of Pavlović, Djordjević, Makavejev and others. The triumph of his film was a turning point in the media's attitude to Cannes. The press screening of *When Father Was Away on Business* was at eight in the morning, and only a few people showed up. Most critics didn't bother. They didn't know Kusturica's first film, *Do You Remember Dolly Bell?*, and his name meant nothing to them. There was one particular film magazine whose writers hadn't seen the film, so there was panic on the day of the awards when Miloš Forman announced that it had won the Palme d'Or. "What are we doing? What should we say about it?" After that, journalists got up in the morning, no matter where a film was from. This kind of surprise began happening more often, where films by unknown directors from unexpected countries ended up with the Palme d'Or. The jury was clearly no longer to be trusted... Forman must have appreciated the sense of liberty of Kusturica's film, its glorious mix of laughter and drama. Don't forget that Forman had been a student at FAMU, the famous Czech film school, years before Kusturica.

I'm reminded of an anecdote about his first film, *Do You Remember Dolly Bell?* One day in 1981, two journalists from the former Yugoslavia came from Sarajevo to see me in Paris. "Mr. Ciment, for ten years, we've been translating and publishing your articles and interviews from *Positif* in our Sarajevo magazine. We're embarrassed because we never told you about it until now. We don't have a penny because we can't get foreign currency out of Yugoslavia, and we don't know how to thank you for you permission – which we never asked for... But what we can do is offer you a week in Dubrovnik with your wife. We'll fly you out and put you up in a luxurious five-star hotel on the Adriatic, all expenses paid." I set off for Bosnia, and they were waiting for me at the airport in Zagreb. "Excuse us," they said, "but actually we aren't going to go straight to Dubrovnik. We would like to show you a film by a very talented young filmmaker from Sarajevo." It was June or July. They read *Positif* every month, so they knew I went to a lot of festivals, including Venice. The film they showed me was *Do You Remember Dolly Bell?*, which showed a lot of promise, so I called the people at Venice, who screened the film, which won the Silver Lion. I'm sure they would have taken it anyway, but it was clear that these young journalists, and the producers of the film, seemed to think that if I liked Kusturica's film enough, I could get it into Venice. I always wondered if their invitation was just a sneaky way of getting me over there because it was easier than asking me if I would come to Zagreb to watch a film. I mentioned it to Kusturica once during a meeting in New York, but he didn't say anything, perhaps because Scorsese was there, and it was a bit embarrassing. I probably shouldn't have told the story in public. I really like his subsequent films – *Time of the Gypsies*, *Black Cat, White Cat* and *Underground*. He was one of the few great European filmmakers to emerge in the 1980s.

The other side of the coin

Kusturica's prize at Cannes highlighted the growing importance of cinephilia.

Yes, even though there's something a little worrying about this kind of progress. We've shifted from a Malthusian approach, in Venice, for example, where in the 1960s there were very few films, to today, where we're drowning in choice. Look at Toronto, with its 350 films, which is just ridiculous. It makes the critic's job completely impossible. I expect a festival director to make choices, even if it means getting caught out if he lets a great film slip through his fingers. It's too easy for a festival director to say he missed nothing when he showed *everything*. In reality, most films go unnoticed by the press because there isn't enough time to watch them all. Who, if not the press, is going to let the world know about what's going on at a festival? Even the people who buy films for distribution can't see all 350 films at Toronto. It leads to a typical modern-day trend – a drab homogeneity, where no one wants to take a side or express their preferences. Everything gets labelled as "good," everything is deemed "interesting." I *really* don't like it. The Cannes Film Festival, *the* major festival, actually showcases the fewest films. If we consider all the new films in the main sections, there are less than ninety. I'm not including restored films or those for sale in the market. A diehard festival-goer watching four or five films a day could get through roughly half the films shown at Cannes each year. That's impossible in Berlin and Locarno, where they show between a hundred and fifty and two hundred new films.

Five films a day? That doesn't sound like a good idea for a critic.

It's sometimes useful to watch a film again and re-evaluate it. I've been doing this for fifty years, and what I've noticed is my growing impatience. When I was young, I would tell myself that I had to stick with a film that started badly because it might improve after half an hour. Back then, I still had hope. But when you've seen as many films as I have, you get to know the formulas and how the stories are going to unfold, and you have a sense of what the filmmaker is doing, and it's clear that after ten minutes the film isn't going to get any better. It's just irredeemably bad. There might be rare cases of a film improving, where after half an hour, all of a sudden, it gets better, but the more films you've seen, the quicker you realise that this isn't going to happen. It's like in Robert Bresson's *Four Nights of a Dreamer*, where the characters watch a parody of a non-existent film within the film itself, and one of them realises they have been tricked into seeing it, so they decide to leave. If I have to write about a film, or even mention it in passing on *Le Masque et la Plume*, I always stay to the end, but if I know I'm not going to be writing about it or talking about it publicly, and it's really a lost cause, and there's another film that's starting in fifteen minutes, I'll leave. On the other hand, and perhaps this is a bit odd, I rewatch many more films today than when I was young. When I really like a film at Cannes, I might watch it a second time there, then back in Paris go to a press screening and see it again when it's released. It doesn't happen very often, but I sometimes see a new film three or four times.

I might criticise Cannes quite regularly about certain things, like how it selects films and the awards it hands out, but it's always been the festival with the highest proportion of quality films every year. Its various sections make it possible for us to see a third or even half of the great films of the year, which we end up featuring on the cover of *Positif*. The major festivals – Cannes, Venice, Berlin – are also essential for a specialised journal like ours, which doesn't have the means to travel the world, to do interviews with filmmakers who live a long way away, which makes it impossible for us to catch up with them when their films are released. Festivals allow us to sketch out the contents of the next few issues, because we already know what's worth covering.

A critique of *homo festivus*

What else has changed since you've been going to festivals?

I find the shift in the attitude of festival-goers over the years a bit unsettling. There used to be really extreme reactions in Venice or Cannes, and I remember press screenings in Venice in the 1960s – the first festival I ever attended – when all the great Italian films, including those which subsequently won the Golden Lion, were booed by half the room. It might be Visconti's *Sandra*, Antonioni's *Red Desert* – which played out of competition – or Fellini's *Satyricon*. We and our French colleagues defended films which seemed important to us, while the Italians criticised Fellini for distorting history and Antonioni and Visconti for their aestheticism. It really was wild. *L'Avventura* was booed at Cannes, *Hiroshima mon amour* was jeered, *The Mother and the Whore* and *La Grande Bouffe* were controversial, to say the least, and *Mr. Klein* and *Van Gogh* were not well received. Today, such strong responses to great films – or any film, for that matter – are rare.

There seems to have been an evolution of sorts, one that cultural commentator Philippe Muray defined as *homo festivus*, to the point where partying is mandatory. Everyone, on command, on a set date, must have fun, and Cannes and Venice have become those moments when "we have fun." We're at the epicentre of everything, the biggest festival in the world, where we watch films and hang out with stars and the world's press. Cannes, after the Olympic Games, is the most publicised event on the planet. Just being there gets audiences excited, and in that party atmosphere, every film is given a standing ovation. Even Directors' Fortnight has completely changed. It's nothing like it was when Makavejev's *Sweet Movie* was greeted with outraged howls and he was called an anti-communist because he said it was the Soviet army that had carried out the Katyn Massacre. Communist representatives of La Société des réalisateurs de films [the Society of Film Directors] insisted he was a scumbag CIA sellout, when actually what he was saying turned out to be true. And there were *real* scandals. Today, no matter the film, whether it's at a gala screening or at Directors' Fortnight, there's unanimous agreement. Everyone rejoices and applauds themselves just for being there. Cannes itself becomes the event, not the films being screened.

Would you rather some masterpieces were booed?

Perhaps, yes. Because back in the day, when people didn't like *L'Avventura* or Bresson's *The Trial of Joan of Arc* or Wenders' *Kings of the Road* or any other genuinely innovative new film, they didn't hold back. When their snobbishness or close-minded thinking prevented them from enjoying a film, they weren't shy about letting you know. There have always been old-fashioned, conservative types who just don't get it. Why should our generation be any more in the know? There are still plenty of people today who can't handle films that push boundaries, but they don't speak up anymore. There are two things at play here. First, as I said, everyone is having a blast because they're at a festival and love being in the sanctuary of cinema. And second, there's that little voice in your head saying, "I might be wrong here... This film might actually be brilliant." And in the end, we stop passing judgement on everything.

Juries

How does a film critic end up on a festival jury?

For me it began in 1976. I wasn't quite forty years old when I was invited to participate in a jury at Berlin. That was a festival I didn't usually attend because *Positif* had a German correspondent, Alexandre Alexandre, who collected film posters and lived in Paris, and was a well-known journalist back home. He must have liked my work because although I had never met him, he recommended me for the jury. At the time, the festival in Berlin was run by Alfred Bauer, who had created it and been in control since 1951. Back then it was held in June, in West Berlin at the Zoo Palast. It was certainly an exciting experience, the first of many, and I've been on perhaps thirty juries since then. They're an opportunity to spend ten days not just watching films but also meeting with unexpectedly interesting people. I know that for some people on a jury, someone who isn't a critic, having to watch as many films in ten days – two per day – as they typically would in six months can be daunting. But for me, it's perfectly normal. Being on a jury is a chance to spend time not only with filmmakers but also writers, actors and everyone else – people I wouldn't normally have the chance to interact with. We sit and chat about any number of things and share what we've been watching. The best thing is seeing the films that I've been lobbying for championing over others. Overall, I don't recall any disagreeable experiences or being disappointed in not having been able to convince anyone else of my preferences. There's often a tinge of regret, but on the whole our discussions were always positive, and the final decisions were always ones that I felt were fair.

Do you have any particular memories of that first jury you served on?

Some filmmakers – Georgiy Daneliya, Márta Mészáros and Shuji Terayama – I already knew. The big problem was that things needed to be discussed and we had to communicate through interpreters. The jury president was a very good director, Jerzy Kawalerowicz. I remember that the Golden Bear was awarded, with my enthusiastic support, to Altman's *Buffalo Bill and the Indians*, which isn't considered one of his best films but impressed us more than anything else we had seen. After its screening in Berlin, we learned that the producer, Dino De Laurentiis, had re-edited the film and cut together a shorter version, and so, in a rather unusual move, we announced that the Golden Bear had been given to the version that had been screened in Berlin, and that no other version could claim the award. That definitely helped ensure the release of the full version. Altman didn't show up because at the time he was making three films a year, and the Golden Bear ended up on Dino De Laurentis' desk in Rome. I hope Altman managed to retrieve it…

The untouchables

Did you feel any pressure during your first time as a juror?

For the first and only time in my life I received a dubious gift: a bottle of vodka, delivered to my hotel room, from the Polish delegation. There was a Polish film in competition and Jerzy Kawalerowicz, a Pole, was president of the jury. It was a cheap trick to try and buy me off with vodka. Poland received no awards that year.

The more significant the gift, surely the more inclined you would have been not to give any awards.

Absolutely, yes. There was also the issue of *Pocket Money*, Truffaut's film which was in competition and which I didn't think was a major work, certainly not as good as some of his previous films. Perhaps a bit controversially, I argued that Truffaut deserved either the Golden Bear or nothing at all. We weren't going to give a consolation prize to such an important filmmaker. It was a bit of a twisted argument and in the end the film got nothing. Then I got a phone call – the only time something like this has happened. It was a rough start to my jury duties! The representative in Germany of Unifrance Films, the organisation responsible for distributing and promoting French films abroad, was on the line. She let me know that such comments were unbecoming and that as a representative of France, it was expected that I would advocate for French cinema. I replied to this charming lady that, unlike her, I wasn't being paid by the government or the cinema industry to promote French cinema, and made clear that I was an independent critic and my judgement was free from any influence or national bias. It's true that I might have had a little hand in spreading the rumour that French jurors, especially directors, won't stop negotiating until it's certain that France is going home empty-handed. Italians, on the other hand, endlessly critical of their cinema at home, won't stop until they're sure Italy gets an award. Like noisy football fans, they're quite the nationalists abroad.

Group strategy

Your thoughts on Truffaut suggest that a jury member must also be a strategist.

There's certainly an element of group psychology involved. You can sense who the more influential members are. A private discussion with someone between sessions can sway the vote. It's a bit like chess, but it's not just a simple mathematical formula. Psychology plays a part. All in all, it's enjoyable and often exciting. I do like those kinds of discussions.

Does that mean that in all your years on juries, you never felt pressured?

Not really, although the second time I was on the Venice jury, the president of the Biennale, Gian Luigi Rondi, strangely enough, appointed himself head of the jury. He was a kind of cardinal of the profession, a very old critic who had been around since the end of the war, close to the Vatican, very conservative. The Biennale oversees all the artistic sections of Venice – there's a biennale of architecture, of painting, of visual arts. The film festival, also run by the Biennale, takes place every year. Rondi was a strange character. He never watched the films with us. It's said that inside his Rome apartment there was a chapel. There, in the basement of the Palais du Cinéma, he also had his own chapel – a small projection room, where he watched films on his own. We deliberated and very quickly came up with a list, at which point he showed up, quite upset, and said, "This is awful. There's no Italian film here. I'm president of the Biennale. You've put me in an impossible situation, in front of everyone! Help me, Michel. Do something!" He was practically in tears. I wanted to say to him, "You put yourself in this situation. You didn't have to declare yourself president of your festival's jury." Eventually, it turned out that there was a film in competition, an adaptation of a novel by Sciascia, *Una storia simplice*, a decent film but not terribly interesting, featuring the great Gian Maria Volonté. I suggested we give him a career Golden Lion. Italy thus saved face, and Rondi was relieved.

The critic's role on a jury

Two years after Berlin, in 1978, you were a member of the jury at Cannes.

It was Gilles Jacob's first year as general delegate of Cannes, and he wanted me to be on the jury. It was also the year of my fortieth birthday, which was celebrated at the festival with a birthday dinner where I was given a splendid book, Robert Delevoy's *Le Journal du symbolisme*, signed by my colleagues on the jury. I must have let slip my love for painting during our discussions. Back then, there was a critic on the jury every year, a tradition that has unfortunately disappeared. Without boasting, I think that film critics like me can be useful on a jury. You might have jury members who, for whatever reason, don't know much about international cinema. Maybe they've never seen a Korean or Turkish film and need a bit of guidance.

So the critic can play the role of a teacher.

Yes – even with his fellow jurors. I remember at Venice, two years later, I had to explain who Theo Angelopoulos was to my fellow judges, including critic Andrew Sarris and George Stevens Jr. of the American Film Institute. Angelopoulos' film *Alexander the Great* was being screening to people who had never heard of him. Along with Margarethe von Trotta, who is very knowledgeable about cinema, I told them about his other films, like *The Travelling Players* and *The Hunters*, and that he was one of the greatest living filmmakers. We even began discussing the meaning of Angelopoulos' work with them. He ended up being awarded the Golden Lion for Experimental Film, awarded to works that use… let's call it unconventional and unique cinematic language.

I think that if you're going to put three young actresses on a jury, as is done these days for reasons of glamour, it's not a bad idea to include someone who can enlighten them a bit about the context of the films they will be judging. That year at Cannes I spent a lot of time with Liv Ullmann, who was also on the jury. I could tell that people like her – honest, sensitive – needed someone to talk to about the directors and the films, because they felt a genuine responsibility. They didn't want to make a mistake or feel unsure about things, and it can be reassuring if a critic of a certain standing, someone respected, agrees with their point of view or not. The unfortunate tendency of big festivals – which have followed Cannes' lead – is to no longer include a critic on the jury because compared to a star, or even a beautiful budding actress, it's not very glamorous. That's not the only change I'm not too happy with. In 1978, the festival was still held in the old Palais, which is now a modern four-star hotel where, paradoxically, Directors' Fortnight takes place. It's like the Overlook Hotel in *The Shining*, built over an old Indian cemetery. It all used to be very different. We were all always more or less in the same place, in close proximity to each other, and all drank at the Blue Bar, where people would come talk to us. These days the jury is almost invisible for twelve days, surrounded by bodyguards and driving around in armoured cars.

So no one knows which way they're going to vote?

It's all so over the top. They're completely cut off from everyone, except at official dinners. I was very friendly with Konchalovsky, who was also on the jury that year.

I first discovered him in 1965 with his masterpiece, *The First Teacher*. Alan Pakula, a producer turned director, who I had interviewed for *Positif* about *All the President's Men* and *Klute*, was also there. There was also a film journalist called François Chalais, the producer Harry Saltzman, and a charming old gentleman, the great French production designer Georges Wakhevitch. Swiss filmmaker Claude Goretta, a contemporary of Michel Soutter and Alain Tanner, all of whom I admire a great deal, was also there, as was Franco Brusati, an Italian filmmaker who had a big hit with *Bread and Chocolate*. What a great jury that was! On the third day, more or less, we saw Ermanno Olmi's *The Tree of Wooden Clogs* and unanimously decided that it was our favourite. During our second meeting, halfway through, Olmi was still top of the list. No film had dethroned him. And at our final meeting, we unanimously gave him the Palme d'Or. We weren't allowed to discuss our decision with anyone, but people wanted to talk to us about it anyway. All we could say was, "I'm listening to what you're saying, but can't tell you what I think." And so they would say something like, "In any case, *The Tree of Wooden Clogs* is definitely not going to win, because Cannes is diplomatic. They spread the awards around. Every country gets a chance, and last year's winner was an Italian film produced by RAI about peasants" – it was the Taviani brothers' *Padre Padrone* – "so you're not going to give it to Olmi's film. That's just impossible." Well... that didn't stop us from awarding him the Palme.

I've never felt pressured. Jury deliberations always took place in the presence of Gilles Jacob. They lasted four or five hours, and he never intervened in any way in our discussions. He was there simply to make sure that the rules were followed and that we wouldn't do a three-way tie and give the award to multiple films, that kind of thing. It was all very calm, and the final decisions were almost always unanimous. We gave the directing prize to *Empire of Passion*. It was the first time that Oshima had been in competition, because his scandalous and intensely erotic *In the Realm of the Senses* hadn't been selected.

Though he had been at Directors' Fortnight.

Yes, with several of his previous films.

For or against ties?

You had an opportunity to award a tie.

For Best Actress we split the award. Jill Clayburgh won for *An Unmarried Woman*, a film about female emancipation, a subject very much in tune with the times. She was very popular at the time in the United States.

And won the Oscar for the same role.

Isabelle Huppert also won for her sensational performance in Chabrol's *Violette Nozière*. Actually, she could just as well have won the previous year for *The Lacemaker*, so it was a way of correcting that oversight.

That film was directed by Goretta, your comrade on the jury.

When filmmakers don't win an award, they're sometimes put on the jury the following year by way of consolation. Clayburgh took it pretty badly! The big Hollywood star was offended at being considered as good as a relatively unknown French actress she had never heard of. It's ironic really, because thirty-five years later, if anyone remembers Clayburgh today it's because she shared the Best Actress award with Isabelle Huppert. She was a big star back then who became a footnote in the history of cinema. *Sic transit gloria mundi.*

Jury ties are quite common.

There were others that year. The Grand Prix was split between Skolimowski's *The Shout* and Marco Ferreri's *Bye Bye Monkey*. I was invested in that decision because Skolimowski was one of my favourites. I had written about *Identification Marks: None*, his graduation film, in *Positif* and since then had followed his work and had interviewed him. *Walkover, Barrier, Le Départ, Deep End* and the glorious *Moonlighting* with Jeremy Irons – that's quite a career. He came to see me at the closing dinner of the festival and whispered in my ear about how absurd he thought it was that I, a critic he thought was intelligent and good judge of cinema – and for good reason, since I liked his films – would make him share this prize with Marco Ferreri, who, okay, was an original, but who scored an absolute zero when it came to film directing. As for Ferreri, he didn't even bother whispering anything. He was so unhappy he stayed in his room.

He sulked?

No one saw him, even though he had won the Grand Prix, which is second only to the Palme d'Or. I thought he would be delighted, but he was mad with rage.

The director of a film that ties with another might feel flattered, or maybe insulted because they're forced to share.

I could understand the upset in 1973 when *Scarecrow*, one of the great American films of the 1970s, shared the Palme d'Or with Alan Bridges' *The Hireling*, which, like its director, is completely forgotten today. Placing Skolimowski and Ferreri on the same level seemed absolutely fair to us, though neither of them were happy.

Surveyor of the Croisette

That reminds me of another story about Ferreri. In 1973, he showed *La Grande Bouffe*, which I like a lot, at Cannes. A few days later *Scarecrow* was screened, which I liked even more and which I really fought for. I've since lost the habit of strolling down the Croisette, but I used to do it back then, sometimes until three in the morning – meeting people, chatting, discussing, sometimes with jury members. So I'm walking along and see Ferreri sitting on the terrace of the Carlton, and he gestures for me to come over because he has something to tell me. I had always liked his films, and had written about *Dillinger is Dead*, which I love. He was a major figure in Italian cinema. So there he is, sitting – ironic, sarcastic – and he says to me, "Why are you so into this fashion photographer, this Jerry Schatzberg? Look over there..." and he points to an American warship in the bay. "Fascist America has sent a warship to support *Scarecrow*. They're sitting in the bay, trying to influence the jury. I heard you were defending it." I said, simply, "I really like your film, but *Scarecrow* deserves the Palme d'Or – even more." I left him, rather flustered, sitting there. Taking a cue from Skolimowski, I thought *La Grande Bouffe* was an extraordinary and explosive film, more than *Scarecrow*. But aesthetically, in terms of lighting, framing – in short, the direction, the craft in Schatzberg's film was superior to Ferreri's, which shone in other ways.

Back then I really believed in my skills of persuasion, but today I'm that much older, and it's become something of a lost cause because people are so impervious to new opinions, so these days I don't bother, though I did get angry with Jacques Deray and Jean-Claude Carrière, who were on the jury when *Excalibur* was in competition and it only got a consolation prize, the award for the *meilleure contribution artistique* [best artistic contribution]. They preferred Wajda's *Man of Iron*, which, in my opinion, was a wholly political decision. It's one of Wajda's weakest films, much less interesting than *Man of Marble* and many other films in competition that year.

As a jury member, would you have been okay with a Michel Ciment type roaming the Croisette pushing his picks on you?

Not exactly pushing them on me, no. I'd make up my own mind anyway. But I would actually like it if someone knowledgeable took the time to make a case for a director.

Venetian Dolce Vita

Two years after the Cannes jury, you took part in your first Venice jury, which also ended with a tie for the big prize when the Golden Lion was awarded to Louis Malle's Atlantic City *and John Cassavetes'* Gloria.

That wasn't a big surprise. *Atlantic City* is one of Louis Malle's best films, one of the rare cases of a French filmmaker really succeeding in the United States. And *Gloria* may not be the first film that comes to mind when you think of Cassavetes, but it's still quite remarkable. Cassavetes couldn't be in Venice because he was filming. It wasn't as if he refused to be there – he sent a thank-you telegram. But Louis Malle was very classy and came to pick up his Lion. He said he was extremely happy and flattered to share this prize with a filmmaker he admired and who had started out much like he had, at the end of the 1950s. It was, once again, a very brilliant jury. The president was that great lady of Italian cinema, screenwriter for half of the important Italian filmmakers of her time, especially Visconti: Suso Cecchi d'Amico, daughter of a great literary critic of the 1930s and 1940s. A personality, an authority, an incomparable cultural treasure. Then there was Marlen Khutsiev, named after Marx and Lenin, director of *I Am Twenty* and *July Rain* and one of the young Russian filmmakers who followed the Stalinist thaw, the exceedingly film literate Youssef Chahine, and Umberto Eco, who hadn't yet written *The Name of the Rose* and was then known as a semiologist and philosopher, also fantastically cultured. Of everyone, I knew Margarethe von Trotta the best. She had acted in Volker Schlöndorff's films before becoming a director herself.

I've always loved the Venice festival, which hasn't changed much in forty-five years. It's amazing. New screening venues have been created, but the atmosphere remains just as idyllic. It's the end of the season and everyone is just strolling around. People talk to each other, no one's in a rush. The place isn't full of police and there aren't even paparazzi. It has a real seaside resort feel to it. Berlin and Cannes, in comparison, have become wildly complex and bustling behemoths. There's no time to see anyone. In Venice, everything happens within a fairly compact space, and anyone can run into the jury. I keep telling the people who run Venice, and who seem to want their festival to be more like Cannes and Berlin, to stay true to themselves. It's one the greatest festivals in the world. They always screen fascinating films and you can do your "shopping" just like anywhere else, but there's a very special way of doing things in Venice.

The critic can shop for films, but not the industry. There's no film market for producers, buyers and sellers at Venice.

That really doesn't matter to me. What's important is that films are seen and discussed. The starting point in Venice is cinema, not money. In Cannes, of course, that's everyone's immediate obsession: How many films have been sold? For how much? To how many countries? Don't get me wrong: the business side is important, but it's wonderful to spend twelve days immersed in film. And there's no need to make those treks you have in Cannes between the Palais du Cinéma and other screening venues, trying to squeeze through crowds of people who are just there to spot celebrities they don't even know.

Other festivals, other juries

You have also been a jury member in many other festivals, each with their own unique way of doing things.

I couldn't list them all – there have been so many memorable moments. I was on a jury in Locarno with Abbas Kiarostami, Alexandre Sokorov and, as president, Nanni Moretti. Since the 1960s, Locarno has been known for its wonderful retrospectives. Every morning, we watched two films by Boris Barnet, Ozu or Preston Sturges, then had a salad on the terrace, and in the afternoon went to see two films from the competition, which were usually very interesting. They would often pick up films that had been shown at Directors' Fortnight or Critics' Week in Cannes but hadn't gotten enough attention. A wonderful Korean film, *Why Did Bodhi-Dharma Go East?* by Bae Yong-kyun, which went unnoticed at Cannes, became a sensation at Locarno, winning the Golden Leopard. And then in the evening, outdoors on the gigantic Piazza Grande, there was a big show – an action film or a comedy with stars. It was great. Today they play 250 films, and I always feel like I'm missing the day's big event. It was extraordinary being a member of the jury in Pusan, Korea, alongside Jiang Wen, who had just screened *Devils on the Doorstep* at Cannes and who spoke freely about the Chinese regime, which had banned his film. Smaller festivals can also be very stimulating because I get to explore all these countries whose films I have been watching. At Karlovy Vary, I was a juror with István Szabó, who I had written about in one of my very first articles. In Romania, at the Cluj festival jury in 2012, I was immersed in Romanian cinema, which was undergoing a renaissance. In Istanbul, I was a juror with the great German theatre director Peter Stein. In Chicago, I found myself sitting with Chantal Akerman, whose delightful company and humour I enjoyed. I even suggested she should add more of that humour and whimsy to her films, because I can't say I was too captivated by Delphine Seyrig's housework in *Jeanne Dielman*.

Have other filmmakers surprised you while serving on a jury?

Sokurov was somewhat of a lone ranger. Compared to him, Kiarostami and Moretti seem conventional. He had this "Russian madness" about him, and he kept us on our toes. But he didn't contribute much to the awards.

Unfunny games

Do you recall any controversies or conflicts?

I had a rather unpleasant time with Michael Haneke's film *Funny Games* when I was part of the seven-person Fipresci jury at Cannes. In the first round, three finalists emerged as the best film in competition: Atom Egoyan's *The Sweet Hereafter* and Abbas Kiarostami's *A Taste of Cherry*, each with two votes, and *Funny Games*, which had three. In the second round, Kiarostami's supporters rallied behind Atom Egoyan's film, so his film won by four votes to three. Everything went smoothly. The president of Fipresci at the time, Derek Malcolm, the English critic from *The Guardian*, was chair of the jury. *Time Out* magazine later wrote that I had threatened to resign if *Funny Games* received the award. Malcolm had to write a letter stating that this was a complete fabrication. Three years later, I received a rather aggressive letter from Haneke in which he brought up this supposed threat of resignation, also accusing me of preventing the publication of an interview with him in *Positif*. This was all completely untrue. It was an interview that Michel Cieutat, a Haneke enthusiast, wanted to do before we had seen the film, so there was no guarantee it would be published. As it turned out, *Funny Games* divided the editorial staff, with a slight majority against, so we decided not to publish the interview and instead – in a rare move – publish two reviews of his controversial film: one positive, by Philippe Rouyer, one negative, by Alain Masson. Personally, I could appreciate Haneke's technical brilliance, but morally speaking I found the film highly questionable. There is never any emotion or empathy towards the victims, unlike, for example, *A Clockwork Orange*. I later came to admire Haneke's films *Code Unknown*, *Caché*, *The White Ribbon* and *L'Amour*, and while I hold his work in high regard, I still have strong reservations about *Funny Games*. But I never threatened to resign from the jury if my opinion didn't win out. When you agree to be on a jury, you have to be ready to go along with the decisions made, even if they don't match your own preferences.

Festivals versus Oscars

Despite everything, isn't there an element of arbitrariness in prizes?

When you look at the lists of awards handed out by major film festivals, especially Cannes, I don't think there's anything to be embarrassed about. The range of awards given includes a multitude of truly great filmmakers – even if Bergman never won the Palme d'Or. I think it compares pretty well to the Oscars, which I've never quite understood. Such a fuss around the globe, year after year, as if the American film industry rules the world. Consider that Chaplin, Sternberg, Fritz Lang, Lubitsch, Hawks, Vidor, Walsh, Hitchcock, Kubrick, Cassavetes, Altman and Malick never got their due at the Academy Awards, while people like Barry Levinson, John Avildsen, Richard Attenborough, Robert Benton, Anthony Minghella and Mike Nichols all won Best Director Oscars. As Godard said, even the "professionnels de la profession" [the "pros of the profession"] aren't always the sharpest judges. So take awards with a pinch of salt.

Is this evidence for your suggestion that critics, not just industry professionals, should be on juries?

Being in the industry doesn't automatically mean you have special insight. Speaking of awards, let's talk about the survey that *Sight and Sound* magazine has done every ten years since 1952, on the best films ever made. In the last referendum, from 2012, the most recent film in the top ten list was *2001: A Space Odyssey*, made forty-four years earlier. In 1962, *L'Avventura*, made two years earlier, was on the list. It's as if critics have become more and more cautious in their evaluations, and need more of a distance to make up their minds. There are fewer and fewer recent films on the list. What's interesting is the impact of DVDs on how films are appreciated. Twenty years ago, there were hardly any silent films, but three are listed in the last survey: *Sunrise*, *Man with a Movie Camera* and *The Passion of Joan of Arc*. What's also striking is how few comedies there are. There seems to be a prejudice against them, including in festival competitions. The last comedy to win the Palme d'Or at Cannes was Altman's *M*A*S*H*, more than forty years ago.

Is comedy considered a less respectable art form?

Even though it might be one of the most challenging of all genres, being a successful maker of film comedies doesn't usually lead to critical recognition.

In general, I get the impression that genre films aren't considered as serious as so-called auteur films.

Yes, but what's interesting is that at Cannes, for example, thanks to Thierry Frémaux, over the past decade we've been seeing more and more genre films in the official selection.

Festival programmer

You were part of the selection committee for Critics' Week at Cannes.

From 1968 to 1972. We reviewed films from all over the world. It was a hands-on realisation of my interest in contemporary cinema.

Who else was on the committee with you?

There were two critics from *Cahiers*, Jean Narboni and Michel Delahaye; Bernard Cohn and me from *Positif*; Albert Cervoni, the excellent communist critic of *France nouvelle*; Nelly Kaplan, who started out as a journalist; the American Gene Moskowitz, French correspondent for *Variety*; Jacques André, a very likeable critic from the South-West; and the Portuguese critic Novais Teixeira, also a correspondent in Paris. The rule was – and still is – to select only first or second feature films. Most of the time they were debut films and we didn't know anything about the directors. We screened Philippe Garrel's *Marie pour mémoire*, Otar Iosseliani's *Falling Leaves*, Robert Kramer's *The Edge*, Alain Tanner's *Charles, Dead or Alive*, Barbet Schroeder's *More*, Jean Eustache's *La Rosière de Pessac*, Denys Arcand's *Dirty Money* and *Kes* by Ken Loach, who had made only one feature film, *Poor Cow*, which was unreleased in France.

Did you serve as an official or unofficial adviser to Gilles Jacob?

Neither. At Cannes, it was always a bit difficult to know who was really involved in the decision-making process and even who was part of the selection committees. It was shrouded in mystery. But Jacob liked to surround himself with critics and listen to people he thought were knowledgeable about cinema. A true stateman isn't afraid to surround himself with qualified people, which benefits both him and those he works with. Jacob had a formal committee when it came to French cinema, but in the 1980s people like Pierre Rissient, Pascal Mérigeau, Jean de Baroncelli, Guy Braucourt, Max Tessier and I were regularly asked to screen foreign films and give our opinion. I remember, for example, discovering Kiarostami. I was enthusiastic about *Where is the Friend's House?* at Locarno, and when Kiarostami's new film, *And Life Goes On*, was shown to the group, we were all impressed. Baroncelli said, "It's a bit excessive to compare him to Rossellini," but two years later Kiarostami received the Rossellini Award at Cannes. Rissient played a crucial role in bringing filmmakers like Lino Brocka, King Hu and Jane Campion to Cannes. Jacob had worked alongside Maurice Bessy for a few years before being officially appointed general delegate, and was already very active. He was preparing Cannes for a shift towards more demanding auteur cinema.

You were involved in the official selection of some festivals.

Mainly Berlin, for about twenty years. I was an adviser to Moritz de Hadeln* for French films. This gave rise to epic battles because we didn't always see eye to eye, but in general we ended up agreeing, and very often he endorsed my choices.

How did it work?

I would watch films for two or three months starting in October or November, and in early January he would come to Paris and I would give him a preselection of six or seven titles, noting my preferences. I particularly remember François Ozon's big international breakthrough, *Water Drops on Burning Rocks*, adapted from an early Fassbinder play, which was in competition and made a significant impact at the festival. I also recommended two films that won the Golden Bear: Bertrand Tavernier's *The Bait* and Patrice Chéreau's *Intimacy*. When Hadeln left Berlin for Venice, he asked me to be his advisor. I was quite pleased that he selected Noémie Lvovsky's *Feelings* because it's a beautiful comedy, a genre that doesn't end up in competition very often. But I wasn't at all enthusiastic about Jacques Rivette's film with Sandrine Bonnaire, *Secret Defense*, with its endless train journeys. The producers

---

* Moritz de Hadeln (b.1940). Director of the Berlin Film Festival (1980-2001).

were indignant, saying, "How dare you refuse Rivette! It's ridiculous!" It reminded me of Godard's statement against Clouzot, Clément and René Clair who, according to him, had monopolised the French presence in festivals for fifteen years. Rivette had been automatically selected for forty years, and I thought it was time for a change. The final decision, of course, rested with the artistic director. This was one of my various roles at Venice. I advised on retrospective programming, and then, around 2000, Dieter Kosslick succeeded Hadeln to run Berlin. He's a man of great initiative, a good networker too, and succeeded in revitalising the festival and building audiences. He's a great communicator, like Thierry Frémaux at Cannes. They're the new generation of festival directors who are constantly in the field, in screening rooms, engaging audiences, always with a lot of enthusiasm. I worked with Kosslick for several years, but in terms of taste, we weren't always on the same page. After a certain period of time – as always happens, it's the Peter Principle – I was "promoted" and became part of an official committee of three people, along with Peter Cowie and Palestinian actress Hiam Abbass. It was a transition that ultimately led to my departure. But I was relieved, and we parted on good terms. It's true that I'm not one to mince words. Even though Kosslick was the boss, I would voice my disagreement – and sometimes my persistence got on his nerves.

You were being a bit of a pest?

I was. It was embarrassing for me because I would come out of a screening telling the directors or producers that I loved their film, only to have the film not be selected. It made me look bad, and I felt like I wasn't really making a difference. I'm happy to put in the work if it leads to concrete results. For instance, I strongly recommended Philippe Lioret's film *Welcome*, and pushed hard for it to be in competition. Faced with my relentless persistence, they eventually placed it in the parallel Panorama section, where it was a big success. The press said it was one of the best films at the festival, and it was sold to forty countries. Being right when your boss thinks otherwise is even worse than pestering him.

REFLECTIONS AND CLARIFICATIONS

Doing criticism

How does Michel Ciment write a film review?

I used to take notes while watching the film, but was never happy with the result. I can't write in the dark. Being of an impatient temperament – which hasn't improved over time – I tended to leave words unfinished. I admire my colleagues who I see bent over their notebooks taking notes during a screening, but they miss too much of the film. At the beginning of a screening, I sometimes start writing, but give up fairly quickly, especially if it's a film I like, because I know I'll see it again. So I watch the film first, then think about it. When I was writing more reviews than I am today I would watch it a second or third time. I'm not able to do what my friend Alain Masson does: see a film once, without taking notes, then write a review with impressive precision, acuity and accuracy. I need to revisit and re-examine the film a second or even a third time.

Even sometimes to prepare for an interview?

Yes. When doing the radio programme, I always re-watch a film that we're going to discuss, then pull notes and ideas together. If I do that, the writing comes very quickly. I'll mull it over later in the day and practically write the whole thing in my head. I even sometimes get out of bed at midnight to jot things down. But most of the time, after making notes and generally thinking about the film, I'll finish the final text the next day, or even a couple of days later. When it comes to my books, the ones on Kubrick or Boorman for example, the process was similar to that of a film director. To write about *Barry Lyndon*, for example, I immersed myself in the eighteenth century. Given Kubrick's psychological and philosophical makeup, I first tried to understand why he might be particularly interested in the eighteenth century and chose to make *Barry Lyndon*. Then, little by little, I realised that there are references to the eighteenth century in several of his films: the castle in *Paths of Glory*, the room in *2001*, the portrait at the beginning of *Lolita*, even *A Clockwork Orange* in a way – the clothes they wear, the Droogs in period costumes. And then it dawned on me that the eighteenth century was the era when the Enlightenment gave way to butchery and the Reign of Terror, when reason clashed with madness. I started reading Jean Starobinski – a free-thinking scholar I greatly appreciate, one of the most important commentators on painting, literature and philosophy. I found his illustrated books and essays on the eighteenth century very enlightening. I was also familiar with English painting of the time – Hogarth, Gainsborough – which surely inspired Kubrick. I did the kind of research that he would have done, looking at work by Chodowiecki, who was from Poland, and Zoffany, who I knew nothing about. It turns out they were major painters of English society of that time. My thoughts on symmetry in Kubrick's work connects to his fascination with the eighteenth century.

Did you re-read Thackeray's book?

Of course. The film is very faithful to the book, which is relatively obscure. I chuckled when someone in Téchiné's *The Brontë Sisters* asks, "Have you read Thackeray's *The Luck of Barry Lyndon*?" Kubrick's film had come out a few years earlier. In reality, at the time, people would have referred to Thackeray – a nineteenth-century writer who wrote about the eighteenth, played by Roland Barthes in Téchiné's film – as the author of *Vanity Fair*, which was a much more widely known book. It's like asking, "Have you read Flaubert's *The Legend of Saint Julien the Hospitaller*?" instead of *Madame Bovary* or *Sentimental Education*. They're the kinds of anachronisms I love to spot. It's a bit like "this little corporal will go far" when you spot young Bonaparte.

In praise of the imaginary

Something we talked about in relation to Rosi and Kubrick was the blend of rationality and a taste for the imaginary in your work.

I like filmmakers who stress rationality but take it as far as it can go – into irrationality. Many of the great realist writers of the nineteenth century – Balzac, Théophile Gautier, Maupassant, Mérimée and others – played with that moment when extreme rationality comes up against what seems incomprehensible, and tips over into madness or the fantastic. It's interesting that the English Gothic novel – *The Castle of Otranto*, *The Monk*, *Vathek*, all written at the end of the eighteenth century – made its first appearance during the Enlightenment. There's also Goya's famous etching, "The Sleep of Reason Produces Monsters." This shift in European history starts with a moment of intellectual brilliance that ends in the bloodbath of the Great Terror. It all appeals to my taste for the rational and the fantastic. With Victor Hugo, you've got *Les Misérables* on one hand, then séances and the great metaphysical questions on the other. It's the notion of myth woven into the very essence of man, which ties in to my mythological interest in Boorman, who is of English origin but lives in County Wicklow, Ireland, his adopted home. Boorman takes a Jungian approach. His cinema is that of the archetype, of dreams and the imagination, with a dose of realism. In psychoanalysis, this is what drove a divide between Freud and Jung, which David Cronenberg represented brilliantly in *A Dangerous Method*, with his amazing Mankiewicz-like dialogue and conversations between the two men. I discussed this with Cronenberg. In my opinion, rationality prevails among filmmakers of Jewish origin, like Kubrick, Polanski and Cronenberg. When they make fantasy films, they're always governed by rational thought, whereas Christian filmmakers are Jungian, and the imagination prevails. Think of Fellini, Malick, Boorman, Lynch. It's a radically different orientation, even though they're all connected to the fantastic.

And within Michel Ciment, critic of Jewish origin, educated as a Christian, do we find the two coexisting?

Yes! Nature and nurture. From that point of view, Surrealism is the answer because it encompasses both rationality and imagination. André Breton's prose is extremely classical and structured, and goes hand in hand with his fascination with mystery and the unknown. For him, reasoned thought is close to magical art, which explains his interest in Australian aborigines, Eskimo masks and African rituals. Someone like Losey also embodies that duality. He may not have been Jewish, but his cinema, while employing rational psychological analysis, also delves into mysterious and unsettling rituals. Just take a look at *Secret Ceremony*. Some of his finest films were collaborations with the Jewish writer Harold Pinter. Look at the deadly nightshade in *The Go-Between* and the descent into a shadow world at the end of *The Servant*.

Irrationality in life and in the grand narrative of history leads to barbarism. But in art, can it lead to creation?

Kazan used to say that in the 1930s, you became either an artist or a gangster. Kubrick spoke of the artist channelling his impulses and transforming them into something creative. He transcends them instead of letting them express themselves in savagery. Art as a sublimation of instincts.

Breton, by the way, like Aragon, was originally a doctor, but he had a deeper understanding of things and delved into this darker side of human nature, which can be dangerous but also rewarding. It's like the Yugoslav animated short *Tamer of Wild Horses*: to tame our inner demons, we first need to recognise them. From the point of view of *Positif* – and me too, actually – consider the somewhat academic but not entirely unfounded distinction between the Méliès and Lumière traditions. With *Workers Leaving the Lumière Factory* and *Arrival of a Train at La Ciotat*, cinema was initially about recording reality. Then we get Méliès, who makes his phantasmagorical *The Four Troublesome Heads* and *A Trip to the Moon*. These are two branches of cinema, but we shouldn't push this binary too far, because in imaginary films there are often realistic elements, and – more rarely – realism can have moments that feel strangely surreal. But what has always struck me, and what characterises *Positif*, as well as my personal tastes in cinema, is that I have always appreciated the great directors of the imagination – Murnau, Boorman, Michael Powell, Kubrick, Fellini, Polanski, Tim Burton, Terry Gilliam, Tarkovsky, Buñuel – more than realistic filmmakers like Ford and Hawks, and in France, Jean Renoir, Jacques Becker, Claude Sautet, Maurice Pialat. It's clear that Lumière's way of doing things has always been appreciated everywhere. Nobody ever objected to *The Crowd*, *Rome Open City*, *City Lights*, *Caesar and Rosalie*, *Loulou* or the Dardenne brothers' films, all of which belong to the realist tradition, which also takes in Truffaut's *The 400 Blows* and even *Breathless*. All these films were greeted with almost unanimous acclaim, whereas the great filmmakers of the imagination have always faced criticism and controversy, and have had sometimes rocky careers. This is understandable because what is realism, really? It's films that make people think, "Yes – that's how life is." I'm simplifying things here, of course, because art isn't just about representing reality, although with a realistic film you empathise with the marital problems the characters are experiencing and perhaps recognise yourself in the young boy from *The 400 Blows*. We should be careful not to oversimplify Bazin's idea of la "fenêtre ouverte sur le monde" [the "open window to the world"], but it's about being able to relate to what is happening around you. We take to the streets and capture everyday moments on film, like De Sica's bicycle thieves and shoe shiners.

As opposed to artifice?

Especially when compared to the kind of imaginative cinema which asks us to step inside someone's head. Everyone dreams differently. Someone might claim that if ten people are looking at a city intersection, none of them see the same intersection, but they will more or less identify it as such – with the policeman in the middle and the mother with her pram wanting to cross the road. When it comes to the imagination, it's about entering into someone's dream life or the fantasies that someone puts on the screen. Think about Fellini's wonderful *Book of Dreams*, in which he records all his dreams in drawings. His films are translations of them. I think it's less common that someone embraces the worlds of Tim Burton, Tarkovsky, Boorman, Lars von Trier, *2001: A Space Odyssey* or *Barton Fink*, or even some of Almodóvar's films. Fellini was booed in Cannes and Venice. Buñuel's *Belle de jour* was heckled. After Cannes turned him down because the film wasn't artistic enough, he went to Venice and three months later won the Golden Lion. It's almost a rule that audiences are divided over filmmakers of the imagination, and that the real battles of Hernani have revolved around idiosyncratic works that allow the imagination to flourish freely.

Alain Resnais, for example…

Every one of Resnais' films has aroused indifference and enthusiasm. Compare, for example, the reception given to *The 400 Blows* in 1959 at Cannes to that of *Hiroshima mon amour*. Everyone loves and has always loved *The 400 Blows*, which is a very good film. It's normal for disruptive, revolutionary works to provoke strong reactions. Marcel Achard, president of the jury, openly stated – and by the way he had the perfect right to do so, since the film wasn't in competition – that *Hiroshima mon amour* was absolute rubbish. Micheline Presle, a member of the jury, responded by saying that it was a masterpiece. I would never praise a film just because some people criticised it. That doesn't automatically make it better. That's not how it works. I'm just saying that big, imaginative works often rub some people the wrong way.

The evolution of French criticism

Has film criticism in France evolved since you began writing it?

There was infinitely greater diversity when I started out, many more outlets than today. Newspapers would come and go. There used to be so many of them, which meant a plurality of opinions. Years later, I reacted against what I called the Bermuda Triangle, which referred to the fact that at a certain point, the influential criticism, written by people who really knew what they were talking about, all emanated from a single trend and a dominant belief system. Back then, you had *Les Lettres françaises*, the cultural magazine of the Communist Party, edited by Aragon, which published remarkable critics like Michel Capdenac and Paul-Louis Thirard, who was also a critic at *Positif*. The excellent Albert Cervoni wrote for *France Nouvelle*, the party weekly. There was *Arts*, of course, where Truffaut was very active. There was even a far-right press where some very good writers wrote about cinema, and there was a lot of space in the weeklies, like Robert Benayoun in *France Observateur*, which became *Le Nouvel Observateur*, *L'Express* and *Les Lettres nouvelles*, where Louis Seguin and Roger Tailleur wrote, in addition to *Positif*. All sorts of different ideas and divergent tastes were expressed. There were also lots more journals, often offshoots of film clubs: *Cinéma*, *La Revue du Cinéma* and *Image et Son* – which have merged – the Catholic *Téléciné*, the Mac-Mahon *Présence du cinema*, and of course *Positif* and *Cahiers du cinéma*. It was an infinitely more varied landscape, and all made for a healthy climate of controversy and debate. And you didn't see rating systems everywhere, except in *Cahiers*, which came up with the idea. Ratings are a good idea in a journal, but their widespread use has done damage because today people just look at the number of stars without reading the reviews. And there were fewer interviews and reports from film sets than today.

Every major daily newspaper gave their critic plenty of space.

Each newspaper had its own critic. Every day in *Le Monde*, for example, Jean de Baroncelli wrote about a film, or Henry Chapier in *Combat*. They were sometimes assisted by one or two colleagues, but there really was only one lead critic, which meant that the reader – a bit like with *Le Masque et la Plume* today – would get to know a particular critic's sensibilities and make decisions based on their personality. When you're familiar with a critic's tastes, you can either follow their recommendations or, if you prefer, take the opposite view and go see a film they didn't like. In the world of theatre, for example, people used to read Jean-Jacques Gautier in *Le Figaro*, who was very conservative and didn't like Audiberti, Beckett, Ionesco or Adamov – basically none of the great playwrights of the 1950s. So if you didn't share his tastes, when he criticised a play, it could be an encouragement to go see it. It's not so much about disagreeing with a critic, it's about understanding where they stand on things. If you have a collection of different critics writing for the same newspaper, a group that's all over the place with their opinions, it can be difficult for the reader to decide whether or not they want to see a film.

Is the Bermuda Triangle a fantasy?

I would like to come back to this phenomenon you call the Bermuda Triangle.

In the 1990s, there was a moment when *Cahiers du cinéma* began to influence weekly magazines and even daily newspapers. In the 1950s, *Cahiers* was a genuinely significant journal that made real discoveries and defended directors who the majority of critics didn't hold in high regard. Take Hitchcock, for example, who was seen as a low-brow entertainer, certainly not an auteur. *Cahiers*, in particular Truffaut, deserves some credit here. But over the decades, following *Cahiers*' success, and as it gained international recognition – thanks in part to the New Wave filmmakers who emerged from its ranks – some of *Cahiers*' writers and their followers ended up in influential positions in daily, weekly and monthly film publications, which led to a homogenisation of tastes. Readers would end up reading more or less the same predictable opinions, with the same filmmakers being praised and everyone else regularly panned. It's what I call the Bermuda Triangle, which was more than a triangle really. It included *Cahiers du cinéma*, *Libération*, *Les Inrockuptibles*, *Le Monde* and a few writers from *Télérama*. This uniformity of taste, in my opinion, has had a harmful effect.

So today things are less diverse and more scattered?

The Bermuda Triangle, or its equivalent, doesn't really exist today. Did I play a role in breaking it up and helping to spread things out, or did that happen naturally? Or was I wrong and just imagining things? I don't think so...

In any case, at the time it caused a stir.

It's what got Patrice Leconte fired up back in 1999, when he went on a famous rant against what he believed was a threat to French cinema from the press, and the ARP [Société civile des auteurs-réalisateurs-producteurs] backed him. The problem was that he didn't name names and his arguments weren't specific enough, so in the end most of the critics quite understandably circled the wagons in retaliation. He definitely had a point about a particular trend in French film criticism, one that actually doesn't exist today. For about ten years now we've seen this structure break down, and you're now able to read divergent opinions on film in newspapers like *Libération* and *Le Monde*. But there does still exist what Philippe Noiret called *la carte* ["the card"], which is a badge that a happy few filmmakers seem to have. It protects them, while others still have to deal with serious criticism of their work.

When the critic becomes a director

It was a kind of after-effect of the unconditional auteur theory, where certain designated directors could do no wrong.

Yes. The critics of *Cahiers* who became filmmakers in the 1960s stopped writing film criticism and were replaced by a new generation of writers. I don't want to sound paranoid and suggest there was some kind of conspiracy, but it seems there was a deliberate effort to pull certain filmmakers into the spotlight at the expense of others. Just as the New Wave was building momentum, Jean-Luc Godard famously declared, "Dorénavant c'est nous qui irons dans les festivals. C'est nous qui représentons le cinéma français" ["From now on, we'll be the ones attending the festivals. *We* represent French cinema"], and essentially pushed aside an earlier generation – directors like Clouzot, Clair, Carné, Clément and Autant-Lara, who were largely dismissed as representatives of "quality" French cinema. They knew there was no longer room for everyone at the table, and if there were only so many spots available for French cinema, they would be given to Truffaut, Godard and their friends. Similarly, the new critics of the 1960s felt that if they wanted to have a say in what was happening in French cinema, they needed to snub certain filmmakers and push them aside. These filmmakers – even if they belonged to the New Wave generation – weren't part of the old *Cahiers* editorial team. They weren't Truffaut or Godard or Chabrol or Rivette or Rohmer. Some curious things happened as a result. Take, for example, the early films of Michel Deville, like *Tonight or Never* or *Adorable Liar*, which had been well received and praised in *Cahiers* by Rohmer and Jean Douchet. In many ways, if you ask me, Deville, with his flirtatiousness and breeziness and free-form approach to filmmaking was much more representative of a New Wave spirit than Chabrol's *Le Beau Serge*. Stylistically, Deville was closer to Pierre Kast or Doniol-Valcroze, both former *Cahiers* contributors. But *Cahiers* dismissed Deville, and Sautet, Rappeneau, Malle and Cavalier too – though they did begin to show an interest in Cavalier much later, when he became a somewhat marginal filmmaker, starting with *Thérèse*, which was a turning point for him, and later his Super 8 films, at which point they dubbed him a hero.

Has this mindset been perpetuated as a kind of tradition?

In the 1970s, a new generation of critics, some from *Cahiers du cinéma*, started making films – people like Téchiné, later Benoit Jacquot, then Olivier Assayas. A new generation of filmmakers began being treated with absolute disdain by *Cahiers*, directors like Bertrand Tavernier, Alain Corneau, Claude Miller, Patrice Leconte. Their cinema was nothing like the old "quality" cinema of Clouzot and Autant-Lara. It was completely different. But Tavernier's choice to work with Aurenche and Bost, who had been Autant-Lara's screenwriters, was the last straw. His films were never going to measure up, and he was practically accused of trying to turn back the clock, even though that wasn't what he was doing at all. What's puzzling is that later on, films by Tavernier, Corneau and Miller were automatically damned, but Téchiné's *The Brontë Sisters* and *My Favourite Season*, Jacquot's *The Wings of the Dove* and Assayas' *Les Destinées sentimentales* were praised, even though they worked with professional screenwriters, made films that were basically classical in form, and cast famous actors. Why were some considered great while others were criticised? I think there's something profoundly unfair in such judgements.

Did you feel like you were fighting against this unfairness?

If I talk about the childlike spirit of the filmmakers I admire, I could just as well be describing myself, in the sense that children have a deep sense of injustice. They can't stand it when something unfair happens. And I've always felt that way when a good filmmaker falls into obscurity or is automatically misjudged.

Classicism and modernity

Just as we differentiate between modern and contemporary art, so the birth of so-called "modern" cinema, which took place in the 1960s, is now almost itself history.

It's mind-boggling to think that there are now more years between us and the New Wave than there were between the New Wave and World War I. I remember that during the New Wave era, in the early 1960s, filmmakers like Delluc, Epstein and Dulac from the early 1920s seemed truly ancient to us. When I watched *Breathless* in 1960, I sensed that *Sunrise* or *The Wedding March*, even *M* or *The Blue Angel*, were from a different era. And yet here we are, still stuck in this idea of so-called modernity, half a century after the New Wave. I really admire the contributions of the New Wave, and I'm not one of those who think it killed French cinema. No question it breathed new life into it. But that doesn't mean French cinema was completely moribund up to that point. I recently read an article by François Margolin in *Le Monde* about the extension of the collective agreement, stating that the New Wave finally put French cinema on the map.* But films like *The Wages of Fear*, *Beauties of the Night*, *Fanfan la Tulipe*, *Pig Across Paris* and *Forbidden Games*, not to mention *Les Enfants du paradis*, drew millions of viewers worldwide, including in the Soviet Union. And yet fifty years later the myth of the New Wave still stands. I remember a journalist very much caught up in this orthodoxy who discovered a retrospective of Henri-Georges Clouzot at the Florence Film Festival, where Aldo Tassone was doing an amazing job promoting French cinema. He came out of *Quai des Orfèvres* and *Le Corbeau* expressing his enthusiasm – and his surprise. He had never seen these films before because he had been told they were

---

* "La convention collective qui va tuer les films d'auteur," *Le Monde*, 15 July 2013. The collective convention is a set of rules relating to feature film production in France.

boring "quality" French films. It's high time we looked past this idea. It's worth noting that even though it's headed by Serge Toubiana, a former editor-in-chief of *Cahiers du cinéma*, which was at the forefront of this witch hunt against traditional French filmmakers, the Cinémathèque française wouldn't hesitate to mount a René Clément retrospective. And thank God, because it's important to know that a film like *Knave of Hearts*, for example, from 1955, preceded the New Wave by three years. I'm not saying it's *Breathless*, but there was a rare freedom in the way it was filmed – the camera was hidden away in a small car driving through London. In addition to being arguably Gerard Philipe's best role, it's a film of astonishing amorality and modernity. Regardless of my appreciation for Chabrol, if today you watch a film that helped inaugurate the New Wave, *Le Beau Serge*, you realise that *Knave of Hearts* is a much better film.

Avatars of Italian cinema

Once again, it's the radical positions that bother you.

Some critics are extremely conservative and stuck in the past. They can't seem to move forward. Yet even as I push back against it, I've always felt that the past is absolutely necessary. One of the reasons for the decline of Italian cinema from the 1980s onward, its lack of renewal, is that an entire generation of new filmmakers, led by people like Bellocchio – who is currently one of Italy's greatest living directors – was influenced by Maoism and wanted to take down the old masters. His friend Goffredo Fofi, who had been associated with *Positif*, was in the same vein and wrote an astonishingly brutal book called *Padri e Padroni*, in which he demolishes all the greats of his era, including Visconti, Rosi, Antonioni, Fellini. I think this entire movement cut Italian cinema off from its roots. Nowadays, the problem with Italian cinema is the opposite. Filmmakers have gone back to the old ways of doing things and are trying to copy what was happening fifty years ago – comedies, political dramas, period pieces, you name it. But the films are never as good as the old ones. The new filmmakers started by killing off the old guard, but now they're trying to fill their shoes, and as a result, their political films aren't as good as Rosi's, their existential films aren't as good as Antonioni's, their period dramas aren't as good as Visconti's, and their comedies pale in comparison to those of Risi, Comencini, Monicelli and Lattuada. If American cinema is thriving, it's because Tim Burton, the Coen brothers and

Tarantino don't make the same kind of films as Scorsese or Coppola did, and no one even thinks of comparing them. And those filmmakers didn't make the same kind of films as Billy Wilder or Otto Preminger. The same is true for French cinema. Today, Ozon, Bruno Dumont, Desplechin and Kechiche don't make the same kinds of films as Godard, Truffaut or Chabrol do. Similarly, those directors, for good reason, didn't make films in the same vein as Autant-Lara, Clément or even people they admired, like Tati, Renoir and Bresson. There has been a genuine renewal. True continuity is about inventing new forms. That is what has always interested me about film directors: maintaining a connection without living in the shadow of what was done before, yet without completely erasing the past.

The death of cinema

You don't subscribe to the eternal refrain that announces the death of cinema?

I would never say, as Susan Sontag did, that cinema is dead. I consider it to be very much alive, otherwise we wouldn't spend evenings and years studying it and talking about it. And we wouldn't continue with *Positif*. Cinema dead? I don't believe it for a second. In the 1980s, Godard and Daney announced the death of cinema. I remember a telling incident at Venice in 1987 – the decade when cinema was supposed to be mortally wounded. Alain Tanner held a press conference after the screening of his film *La Vallée Fantôme* and declared that cinema could no longer tell stories or present characters. It was over. His protagonist was a director in crisis, and to me he seemed to be taking his own creative block, his inability to continue making films like *Charles, Dead or Alive* or *La Salamandre* as a sign that cinema as a whole was dying. It's as if he had taken his specific situation as a universal example, as if he were in his room, at his window, looking at the Swiss mountains around him, all covered in snow, and thought that the entire world was frozen. When it comes to aesthetics, there's a danger of making your personal experience a universal truth. But while it's snowing in Switzerland, in Copacabana people are dancing the samba on the beaches of Rio. Daney – who was unfortunately seriously ill at the time – may have been identifying his own illness with cinema. It's also a symptom of our excessively narcissistic era. American sociologist/philosopher Christopher Lasch wrote an excellent book in the 1970s about this phenomenon, a few years before it actually happened. He predicted and analysed it accurately, calling it "the culture of narcissism." We're in an era where people take their own condition as valid for the entire world. It reminds me of the great Hungarian playwright Ferenc Molnár, author of *Liliom*, which inspired films by Frank Borzage and Fritz Lang. He would work all night, writing until four in the morning, then would go to sleep. One day he was summoned to court as a witness, so he had to get up at 7:30 to be in court at 9. He went out into the streets of Budapest, and seeing the crowds exclaimed, "So many people!"

But isn't this part and parcel of what we call "modernity," where cinema becomes more about the first-person experience than just telling stories? When Fellini made 8½, he said the same thing as Tanner did.

Yes, but at the same time I think that the great filmmakers of the 1960s continued to tell stories. There's that famous conversation between Clouzot and Godard where Clouzot said, "A film must have a beginning, a middle and an end," and Godard says, "Yes, but not necessarily in that order." It was a joke, but it was true. I consider Godard's greatest work – which, incidentally, was poorly received by *Positif*, although I wasn't in agreement with that point of view – to be *Le Mépris* and *Pierrot le fou*. Those two, and films like Bergman's *The Silence*, Fellini's *La dolce vita*, Losey's *Accident* and *The Servant*, and even Resnais' *Muriel* and *La guerre est finie*, all told stories, but they told them *differently*. The relationship between story and audience wasn't always the same. But cinema went further still and became very solipsistic. It folded in on itself, closed itself off. To come back to narcissism, it aligns with this form of artistic practice where, eventually, we not only make fun of not having a relationship with the audience, we brag about it. We're happy about it! Not being successful is almost a guarantee of authenticity, which I think also ties in with narcissism. What's unfortunate is that the critical period of the 1970s, when cinema was analysed through monolithic scientific frameworks, has been replaced by hyper-subjectivity – especially in France. With blogs, it's even more pronounced. It's the triumph of subjectivity, of "I like it/I don't like it," which is really the opposite of what we had known before. The truth must be somewhere in between. For me, criticism is a mixture of research and a relatively objective approach, and at the same time an expression of taste and a personal relationship to the work. It's a combination of the two that makes a good critic. Quality criticism is neither absolute objectivity, which doesn't exist, nor hyper-subjectivity, which ultimately reflects the reader's own narcissism.

Steve McQueen and the avant-garde

A recent revelation in global cinema, at a time when people often say such discoveries are becoming rare compared to previous decades, is Steve McQueen.

You raise an interesting point because, without getting too nostalgic, I find it difficult to name any really major discoveries in the past ten years. Jeff Nichols in the United States is practically the only American filmmaker who has emerged. Maybe Cristian Mungiu, the Romanian who won the Palme d'Or with *4 Months, 3 Weeks and 2 Days* and also made *The West*. And certainly Nicolas Winding Refn with his *Pusher* trilogy, then *Bronson* and *Valhalla Rising* before *Drive*, which made him an international name. There's Nuri Bilge Ceylan from Turkey, Steve McQueen from Britain, Bruno Dumont from France, the Russian Zvyagintsev, and the great Koreans directors. That's not a lot of people. When you look at the 1960s, in the space of ten years we had Glauber Rocha, Ruy Guerra, Carlos Diegues, Jacques Rozier, Dušan Makavejev, Lucian Pintilie, Alain Tanner, Michel Soutter, Miklós Jancsó, Pierre Perrault, Bernardo Bertolucci, Marco Bellocchio, Nagisa Oshima, Francis Ford Coppola, Miloš Forman, Roman Polanski, Jerzy Skolimowski, Andrei Tarkovsky, Andrei Konchalovsky, Otar Iosseliani, Sergei Parajanov, John Boorman, Richard Lester, Karel Reisz and Ken Loach. It's amazing really. These aren't people we discovered afterwards and rehabilitated. Almost all of them were immediately recognised as important filmmakers. I don't think you could make a comparable list covering the past ten years. So there's undoubtedly a shortage of major discoveries. There are still great filmmakers at work, and cinema deserves to be explored, otherwise we wouldn't publish *Positif* every month. But I do think there's been something of a decline.

Steve McQueen's trajectory is unique.

He's a fascinating case because his background is in the experimental, in avant-garde cinema and the visual arts.

Since 1992, he has made about twenty films of five or ten minutes each, before directing his first feature film, *Hunger*, in 2008. There was recently a major exhibition in Basel of his short film installations, projections and photographs. It would have taken you three days to watch it all. For example, there was a film called *Five Easy Pieces* in which he urinates in the visitor's eye, so to speak. In *Cold Breath* he strokes his nipple as it gets hard. In a film about Charlotte Rampling called *Charlotte* there's a four- or five-minute close-up of her eye. This question of the experimental is interesting because, in my view, no matter how successful his installations are, no one could look at them and predict what Steve McQueen might do in his three full-length films.

If I had to decide between the two modes of expression, I wouldn't choose the avant-garde. For a great critic like the American Annette Michelson, who wrote in *Artforum*, the greatest film ever made is Warhol's *Sleep* or Stan Brakhage's work, which is radical underground cinema. Everything else is outdated, nineteenth-century art that tells stories with characters and has narratives with beginnings and endings. It couldn't possibly compare with experimental cinema, which, in her view, is worthy of contemporary painting. But I find it hard to subscribe to such a position.

It's a line that has been pushed since the 1920s.

The Surrealist poet Robert Desnos loved Chaplin, Stroheim and classical Hollywood storytelling even though he was a groundbreaking author of literature. In 1929, in the seventh issue of *Documents*, he published a text entitled "Avant-garde," which reads: "Un respect exagéré de l'art, une mystique de l'expression ont conduit tout un groupe de producteurs, d'acteurs et de spectateurs à la création du cinéma dit d'avant-garde, remarquable par la rapidité avec laquelle ces productions se démodent. Son absence d'émotion humaine est le danger qu'il fait courir au cinéma tout entier." ["An exaggerated respect for art and a mystique of expression has led a whole group of producers, actors and spectators to the creation of a so-called avant-garde cinema, remarkable for the rapidity with which its productions become obsolete, for its absence of human emotion, and for the risks it obliges all cinema to run."] Here's a man who represents an avant-garde movement and who – like Artaud, Breton and other Surrealists – loved Keaton and Murnau, but didn't have a preference for experimental cinema. Which reminds me of a good anecdote. In 1969, there was an Otto Preminger retrospective at the Cinémathèque française. A young man, a very aggressive *soixante-huitard*, stood up at the press conference and said, "Mr. Preminger, your kind of cinema is dead! These films of yours, with Hollywood stars, with stories, adaptations of novels – it's old-fashioned. It's dead cinema and no longer has any good reason to exist. Underground cinema is the future, the kind we make in New York at the Factory." Preminger replied with a single line: "I'll make underground films when I'm dead."

This really is my problem with the work of someone like Straub, who is revered unconditionally by some people, who consider him the greatest creative force of the twentieth century. Initially, the revolutionary novelty and originality of great works of art can understandably elicit resistance, but thirty or forty years later they have been assimilated into the mainstream. Stravinsky's *Sacre du Printemps*, which caused a scandal in 1917, was performed fifteen years later without any problem. In 1913, Picasso's *Les Demoiselles d'Avignon* caused a terrible fuss, but people were lining up around the block to see his exhibitions as early as the 1930s. Everyone today reads Proust, who sold very few books during his lifetime. What troubles me is avant-garde work which, fifty or sixty years later, has no more of an audience than when it first appeared. A film like Straub and Huillet's *Othon*, which when it came out was declared by some people to be a key moment in the history of cinema, I'm sure wouldn't reach a bigger audience if it were released today. This is what troubles me. I refuse to be told, "You don't understand *Othon* because you don't like modern art." I liked a good many films that left their mark on modernity, like *The Mother and the Whore* and *Kings of the Road*. But those films, which were at times puzzling, eventually became classics. I don't believe in the eternal cult of the damned. Great works, even the most misunderstood ones, eventually gain recognition, especially when it comes to the performing arts. When I saw eight hundred people in La Rochelle, silent and captivated by *Hiroshima mon amour*, fifty-five years after it was made, it's a testament to the hard work of the critics and the audience's knack for embracing work that remains bolder than most of what's being made today.

From the gallery to the cinema

Going back to Steve McQueen, he's now a highly rated visual artist.

It's true that he has been successful with gallery exhibitions, but I really do think that it's narrative cinema he's most interested in and wants to continue doing, and which has given him a worldwide reputation. He won the Caméra d'Or at Cannes for his first film, *Hunger*. His favourite actor, Michael Fassbender, won the Best Actor award at Venice for his second film, *Shame*. And his third film, *12 Years a Slave*, won the Oscar for Best Picture. *Hunger* is about the Irish Civil War and a prisoner who goes on a hunger strike, featuring an extraordinary verbal exchange, a twenty-minute scene where a chaplain presents his arguments to a terrorist inmate. It's absolutely extraordinary. *Shame* paints the portrait of a character consumed by sex – just the frenzied act, without any emotion or attachment.

A "sex addict."

We can all think of politicians who fit that description… It's also a thrilling film, just like *12 Years a Slave*, which shows the daily life of slaves as no one has ever done before.

Do we have to choose between the two forms that McQueen works in?

Everyone has their preferences. It reminds me of a story about Abbas Kiarostami, who presented a video installation at the Centre Pompidou, a single static shot of a baby sleeping for ten minutes. At one point, when the audience was ready to proclaim it as his greatest film because he had discarded all characters and any notion of a narrative, and that his cinema was finally worthy of Warhol and this film was the pinnacle of his work, Kiarostami himself said it was deadly boring and couldn't bear to watch it a second time – thus pulling the rug out from under his admirers. I don't condemn the avant-garde. And it's true that after you get know American cinema through the emotions of the characters, the sense of rhythm, the narrative richness, the play of light and colour, the symbolic grandeur of the image, the talent of the actors, you might then be drawn towards more abstract forms. But ultimately, what has always captivated me as a viewer is narrative cinema, even if that narrative takes wholly original forms. Consider *Le Mépris, L'Avventura, Accident, Mulholland Drive* and many other great films.

The limits of minimalism

There is also the question of minimalism, which always seems to be very popular with critics.

Minimalism, for many critics, is the way to go. Over the past few years, we've seen the festival successes of filmmakers like the Lithuanian Sharunas Bartas and the Argentinian Lisandro Alonso, with his film in which a man spends fifteen minutes cutting a shrub. It wasn't an oak, fortunately, otherwise we would have been there for three hours… The starting point of this approach was clearly Chantal Akerman in 1975 with *Jeanne Dielman, 23, quai du Commerce, 1080 Brussels*, a three-hour-and-forty-minute film in which Delphine Seyrig does the dishes and peels potatoes in real time. This kind of cinema is beloved by critics because even though audiences might find it boring, the critics can throw out commentary and interpretation. Béla Tarr has certainly made some wonderful films full of sublime imagery, but five hours can be a bit much. Many commentators who like this kind of cinema typically deploy a whole arsenal of profound assumptions about films that, for the majority of the public, are plain monotonous and repetitive. On the other hand, when you watch the kind of intricate films made by directors like Fellini or Altman, you think of Rodin's sculptures of Victor Hugo and Balzac. There's a sense of the demiurgic power of the artist. At the end of the twentieth century, around 1998, there was a literary movement called "Les moins que rien" [The Less Than Nothing], launched by the *NRF*. Everything in it was extremely minimalist. A hundred years earlier, *NRF* had been at the forefront of literary debates. It seemed as if a kind of exhaustion was manifesting itself because it was possible to label a literary movement as "less than nothing." Today we barely remember it. But you know how it is in France… You have to be constantly inventing movements and issuing manifestos to be taken seriously.

There's a constant need for dogma.

It's something Lars von Trier understood, though he fairly quickly abandoned his Dogme manifesto, which prohibits tripods, artificial lighting and the construction of sets. Minimalism is often preferred over the abundance, fecundity and grandeur of the great visionary filmmakers, writers like Tolstoy and Shakespeare, and painters like Rubens and Titian. What appears to be dry and lacking in inspiration can fuel interpretation far more readily than creative power alone.

The Tate Modern and the rubbish bag

In your opinion, is contemporary art more susceptible to deception than in previous eras?

Perhaps. This is what my friend Jean-Philippe Domecq, and also Jean Clair, have suggested. Clair is one of those thinkers who has been very important to me. He's always swimming against the tide, exposing impostors and snobbery, and has written many major works on painting, as well as having been director of the Picasso Museum and created extraordinary exhibitions at the Centre Pompidou, including one on Vienna called "L'Apocalypse Joyeuse" ["The Joyful Apocalypse"] and another on Marcel Duchamp. No one could ever accuse him of a lack of knowledge. He takes nothing at face value. Without denigrating many talented contemporary artists, there are certainly some current absurdities which would never have happened in the nineteenth century. At the Tate Modern, for example, a rubbish bag was put on display, the work of a contemporary artist – doubtless an important figure, who, I'm sure, had been generously paid. One evening, a cleaner threw away the bag. Scandal! Threat of dismissal! The artist eventually jumped to the cleaner's defence and said he would recreate the work. It took a week to fill a new trash bag because a delivery the very next day wouldn't have justified the price the Tate Modern paid for it. No matter what you say, you can't imagine someone throwing away an Ingres or Delacroix canvas because they thought it was rubbish. This doesn't mean there isn't great contemporary art, but there's a lot of confusion these days. The difference between a rubbish bag displayed at the Tate Modern and a rubbish bag thrown out onto the street often comes down to the review of an art critic who has declared the former a piece of art. This is what Kubrick – an innovative artist himself – mocked in the sequence from *A Clockwork Orange* with the woman who has a plastic penis sculpture in her house. When Alex starts touching it and rocking it, she tells him not to touch it. "It's a very important work of art!" Today, a well-meaning bourgeoisie that would have scoffed at Van Gogh or Gauguin and so avoid being called ignorant is gushing over rocks, crumpled newspapers and rubbish bags at biennials, unable to distinguish them from genuinely innovative art on display. But there are far fewer objective criteria now. Why would today's curators be more insightful about contemporary art than someone living a hundred years ago? Isn't the idea of inevitable progress, of humanity growing more intelligent and peaceful, heading towards radiant happiness, contradicted by the facts? Who's to say our judgement is so much more advanced than that of our predecessors?

The value of creativity is often measured by the immediate and official recognition it generates.

In Ardèche, I had a neighbour called Ronald Blaes, a painter who was tangentially part of the Cobra movement. He's from Belgium, and makes extremely haunting and powerful canvases. I gave a lecture at the museum in Saint-Étienne on painting and film, then had lunch with its director, Bernard Ceysson, who was intrigued that a film critic was so interested in painting. I explained to him, "You know, in the region where I live there's a painter whose canvases are bought by local professors, notaries, lawyers and doctors. He's very talented and has a certain notoriety around the small town where I live. But no museum has ever purchased one of his paintings and he has never received any critical coverage, except in the local press. Since you're just a three-hour drive away, it would be great if you or one of your colleagues visited his studio and bought some of his work, if you like it." If he really appreciated my judgement on art and knowledge of painting, he could have made the effort to visit at least once or send one of his colleagues. But he never did. If it had been a text by Philippe Sollers or Philippe Dagen, or some of his paintings had already been purchased by Claude Berri or another prominent collector, Ronald Blaes would have received immediate recognition. I know that no one went to visit Van Gogh and Gauguin's studios either, and I'm not suggesting that Blaes is on their level. But his art hasn't ever been seen by the gatekeepers, which suggests that the art world's networks aren't much more perceptive than they were in the late nineteenth century.

Criticism isn't always right

Would you say that cinema is somewhat shielded from this phenomenon?

Somewhat, yes, because, ultimately, it reaches a broader audience. Contemporary art operates within a circle of about a dozen critics, several museum curators, a few sincere buyers and many speculators, who store art in vaults to drive up its value with the support of art critics. Cinema is shielded from this to some extent because of the balance that exists between the audience and critics. Criticism isn't all-powerful when it comes to film. It allowed people like Buñuel, Antonioni and Bergman to become widely known and successful after relatively niche careers of ten or fifteen years. On the other hand, there have been some great filmmakers rejected or underrated by critics. In the 1950s, for example, John Ford was held in low regard. In France, with a few exceptions like Tailleur and Mitry, people stopped talking about him. Neither *Positif* nor *Cahiers* particularly liked him. And yet audiences flocked to his films. Something similar happened with Kubrick. This is what gives cinema its vitality. It doesn't allow itself to be locked in the hands of experts. I'm not saying that the audience is always right – contrary to what producer Adolph Zukor claimed in the title of his memoir. And neither is the critic. But sometimes the audience can open the eyes of the critic, and the critic, as a scout, can alert the public to work it will enjoy.

Does it all come back to Stanley Kubrick?

Kubrick had many ardent defenders, but at the same time many critics pushed back. I don't mean to suggest that he's a minority taste. The general public is well able to understand his philosophical intentions. It's there for the taking. There are certainly books they can read about Kubrick, but his cinema is completely comprehensible without them, unlike some work, for which a user manual is mandatory. What would the Tate's rubbish bag be without some explanatory commentary? In essence, it's the contemporary art critic who explains why the bag exhibited at the Tate isn't the same as the one you put outside your front door every morning. Without the critic, the layman would have no way of determining the artistic importance of that bag.

Perhaps there are moments in art, and cinema too, where it's healthy to shake things up – like Dada, for example.

Yes – Duchamp's "Fountain." The question then arises: what's the point of redoing Duchamp's "Fountain" a hundred years later? Duchamp had a great sense of humour, which I'm not sure would be completely appreciated today.

There's a piece of graffiti from May '68 that I really like: "Méfions-nous des avant-gardes éclairées, il y a des pannes de courant." ["Beware of the enlightened avant-garde. There are power outages."] That was prophetic, anticipating everything that happened in the 1970s, with the triumph of jargon-filled, exquisite and absurd [*"précieux ridicules"*] "learned men" [*"hommes savants"*] – as there were very few women – whose commentary tainted all criticism, to the extent of rendering it completely unreadable.

Even in its earliest days, with its ties to Surrealism, Positif *never championed so-called experimental cinema.*

The magazine was wary of the avant-garde, of excessive esotericism, of deliberately obscure work, at the same time as rejecting commercial cinema that catered to the masses. In his 1934 essay "Style and Medium in the Motion Pictures," the great German aesthetician, philosopher and art critic Erwin Panofsky, who was a great admirer of Hollywood – unlike Adorno and the German theoreticians of the Frankfurt School – wrote: "While it is true that commercial art is always in danger of ending up as a prostitute, it is equally true that noncommercial art is always in danger of ending up as an old maid." *Positif* has consistently maintained a measured stance, avoiding two pitfalls: on the one hand, the potential to fall into the trap of certain media outlets that uncritically praise banal, easily digestible films, and on the other, the perils of a certain kind of criticism that, at one point, excessively favoured pretentious and inaccessible work. This position also resonates with the sentiments of the Surrealists of the 1920s, who recognised Louis Feuillade as a greater genius than Marcel L'Herbier. Interestingly, Feuillade's films have aged much better those of L'Herbier. How many so-called "artistic" literary works are now unreadable, full of convoluted prose, while Jules Verne and Alexandre Dumas, more popular authors, still provide immense pleasure?

The martyrology in question

Isn't it sometimes difficult to make a clear distinction when screens are being flooded with such uninteresting commercial films and innovative filmmakers are struggling to do their work?

Obviously there have been artists who were prevented from doing their work, but I believe we must fight against the mythology of the tormented creator, at least in the performing arts, which are, by definition, designed for audiences. It's true that Rimbaud wasn't being recited in schoolyards in 1870, and that his importance was recognised only much later. But can anyone name a great opera composer who was never performed during their lifetime and whose work is now regularly performed? Monteverdi, Mozart, Wagner, Verdi and Puccini were always greatly admired. Are there any truly great playwrights who weren't staged during their lifetime? Ionesco's and Beckett's theatre was innovative compared to that of Giraudoux or Anouilh. Yet from the start *The Bald Soprano* caused a sensation and is still being performed forty years later. *Waiting for Godot*, a revolutionary work, was successfully staged. Consider even Van Gogh. Most of his major work, where his genius is fully expressed, wasn't painted in Holland but during the three years between his arrival in Paris and his suicide in Auvers-sur-Oise. He was starting to get noticed at the time of his death, and if he had lived he would probably have been as lauded as Monet, Degas, Renoir or Gauguin.

There were certainly filmmakers who faced a string of misfortunes.

The tragic death of Jean Vigo, for example. We can only wonder what might have been he hadn't been afflicted by tuberculosis. He was very upset to see *L'Atalante* tampered with and re-cut. But the undoing of great filmmakers can sometimes be partly of their own making. Welles significantly contributed to his own downfall by running off to Brazil to shoot a film, leaving *The Magnificent Ambersons* unfinished, and later by abandoning the filming of *The Other Side of the Wind* after burning through the money given to him by his Iranian investors. Michael Cimino made two magnificent films, but who forced him to make a dud like *The Sicilian* with an impossible script and a lead actor who couldn't act? You can't blame all this on "the system." I don't want to sound overly optimistic, but I think it's dangerous to tell young filmmakers that "the system is flawed" because the "system" in this case – Hollywood studios – allowed Ford, Lang, Walsh, Minnelli, Preminger, Anthony Mann and countless others to produce all their great films. Ozu, Mizoguchi, Naruse and Kurosawa had brilliant careers, despite the rigid studio system in Japan. In Italy, despite all the production challenges, Fellini made twenty films and Visconti made fifteen. They directed as many films as there are great Tolstoy and Dostoyevsky novels. It might be Rossellini's fault that he was able to make great films for ten years. When he created his television series like *Blaise Pascal* or *Acts of the Apostles*, it was because he had lost interest in cinema.

For or against the system

Some filmmakers are better at working the system than others.

The great Hollywood directors knew how to manoeuvre their way around producers. John Ford, for example, would travel more than a thousand miles from Hollywood to shoot films like *Judge Priest* and *Steamboat Round the Bend* because he wanted greater creative freedom. He knew he didn't need a lot of money and didn't have to ask for blockbuster-style resources. When Cimino, on the other hand, overspent three times the budget on *Heaven's Gate* and celebrated his hundredth day of overruns with champagne, it was clear he was heading for a fall. John Huston, on the other hand, managed to make small films that meant something to him in between his big-budget ones. They might not have made a lot of money, but they weren't a bottomless pit either. It's also a matter of temperament. People enjoyed working with Huston, who was full of colourful stories, had a good sense of humour, and didn't moan about things. He also never went over budget, so he could have a flop now and then and they would still give him another chance. Someone who's never satisfied, always arguing and demanding a fancier hotel room, who hates the food, nitpicks the script and mistreats actors – their career might be a bit more problematic. Having a black-and-white attitude doesn't help. Even though making films is extremely difficult and the director must fight for what he wants, it also requires a kind of intelligence when it comes to the system that not everyone possesses. Being talented as a filmmaker isn't enough. You've got to be adaptable when it comes to dealing with people, you need good risk assessment skills, an understanding of the economics of cinema, and the ability to adapt to the resources at your disposal. There's a real complexity to it. Maybe we should rewrite the history of cinema with a more practical outlook, instead of just focusing on the struggles and hardships.

Speaking of which, in your first article for Positif, *on Orson Welles, where you discuss his allegiance to his own ideas when it came to adapting Kafka, we can already see the seeds of what you later wrote about Kubrick – that in the world of cinema, an author can remain true to themselves while navigating the intricacies of the film industry.*

The parallels between Welles and Kubrick are striking, not least because they're probably the two individuals who have had the most profound impact on subsequent generations. Welles directly influenced filmmakers of the 1940s and 50s, just as Kubrick did on those of New Hollywood directors of the 1970s and 80s. And yet they walked completely different paths. Welles, at the age of 25, was given everything he needed, including a blank studio check, complete control, and the opportunity to hire actors from his own theatre group and the choice of the most prestigious collaborators when it came to the screenplay and cinematography of *Citizen Kane*. Kubrick, on the other hand, began at the same age by making a war film with a bunch of amateurs in a vacant lot. He had no resources, so he did everything himself: the script, editing, photography, production. Then, at the end of his life, he shot *Eyes Wide Shut* by reconstructing New York on a set in a London studio. Welles, meanwhile, did all he could to prevent the collapse of *The Other Side of the Wind*. It's a fascinating story, but why? Because Kubrick had the kind of intelligence I was talking about. It isn't enough to have Welles' extraordinary talent. You also need an understanding of the system you're moving through. Kubrick knew that when it comes to cinema, being a great craftsman isn't enough. You have to be a producer at the same time. That's the main difference between Welles and Kubrick. And between these two extreme cases, there is room for every possible position.

Filmmakers make fewer mistakes than critics

Can you offer some clarification on positions you consider excessive when it comes to film criticism in France?

Critics from certain newspapers or weeklies, even those who write for specialised journals, have, over time, become disconnected from the average reader and have seen their influence dwindle. These days, critics are in the habit of championing filmmakers who belong to a clique or exclusive group, or who simply like to stand out from the crowd. This loss of influence has, in turn, fueled a kind of indifference towards the reader. Critics, sensing their diminishing impact, feel emboldened to express extravagant opinions. It's a shift that marks a departure from the sense of responsibility that characterised traditional film critics. These seasoned critics understood the importance of striking a balance in their judgements, being cautious in their opinions, and avoiding extreme positions. It's a vicious circle, because when critics feel that their influence is waning, they might feel empowered to write whatever they please, further widening the gap between them and their readers.

Speaking more broadly about film criticism, it seems to me that when we look at the history of taste, it's clear that at one stage or another in their careers, many great filmmakers have faced rejection. I've come to the conclusion that, in the end, the great filmmakers have made fewer mistakes in their creative work than the critics have when evaluating that same work. At one point it was all ad hominem attacks, like saying that Glenn Close looked like a menopausal Swiss cow. That's just a little bit too removed from the realm of film criticism. Or Jean Becker being accused of making a film that's sympathetic to Vichy France, or that Philippe Harel hates himself, or that the Serbian filmmaker Paskaljević did to his characters what Milošević did to the Kosovars or the Bosnians, or that Stephen Frears should be ashamed of directing *Philomena*. They're all comments that tarnish the image of the critic.

The opponent's point of view

Your perceived shortcomings in your colleagues don't stop you from reading them. Is that a way of overcoming your biases?

The criticism that I have crossed swords with, that I've waged war against – at the same time I think it's some of the best that's being written. That's what's so disheartening. It's not as if these people don't know anything about cinema or don't know how to write. The team at *Libération*, for example – Olivier Séguret, Didier Péron, Gérard Lefort and Philippe Azoury, who has since left – are genuine connoisseurs. And at *Les Inrockuptibles*, Jean-Marc Lalanne, Serge Kaganski and at one point Frédéric Bonnaud, are clearly remarkably knowledgeable about cinema, and very often I feel a great affinity with them. Let me take this opportunity to remind you that I am still an avid reader of film journals. I enjoy reading opposing opinions. I've always read *Cahiers du cinema*, and know that Charles Tesson, who was at one point its editor-in-chief, regularly reads *Positif*. Just as controversy is healthy, I think it's healthy for critics to read one another. I couldn't imagine seeking solace in a self-indulgent reading of *Positif*. It's also enriching to read the foreign press to stay informed, American magazines like *Film Quarterly*, *Film Comment*, *Sight and Sound* and *Cineaste*. There's no way of seeing everything and discovering it all on your own, and there are so many different ways of writing about things. The fact is that I haven't changed much since I was seventeen, when I used to read *Cahiers* and *Positif*, even though, of course, I'm infinitely more in agreement with the magazine I write for. In 1997, I published *La Critique de cinéma en France* with Jacques Zimmer, who wrote for *La Revue de cinéma-Image et Son*, which I think is quite unique. It's a history of French film criticism, an anthology with a selection of forty or fifty important texts from the 1920s onwards, and a list of critics with details of their publications and commentary on their work. Unfortunately, it's now out of print and should be updated. Zimmer and I were committed to representing all opinions and found a way to do this by having the briefer entries about *Cahiers* contributors written by *Cahiers* contributors, and those about *Positif* contributors written by *Positif* contributors. That might all sound too much like mutual admiration, but in the end it seemed to be the best compromise, so as to avoid pointless conflict in the future. The book was an initiative of the Syndicat de la Critique de Cinéma [the film critics' union].

Criticism is not dead

There's a recurring debate that arises from time to time: what's the point of criticism? Criticism is dead. What is said about cinema has also been said about film criticism.

No, it's not dead and remains important – just as cinema isn't dead either, despite claims made in 1929 and nearly every decade since. There are plenty of reasons for this. Audiences absolutely need criticism, complete with its hierarchies and evaluations. Everyone wants to know if they should go see this or that film. The strange thing is that this reliance on critics can lead audiences to dislike them, meaning they would rather not rely on them, even though, deep down, they do. Beyond this rather primitive psychological reading, I think that criticism still has an important role to play, though not so much – as it used to be – in terms of the box-office. It's lost a lot of credibility over the years, perhaps due to cronyism or the occasional off-the-mark judgement. Some very good critics, who wrote in niche magazines that printed maybe ten thousand copies, used to have thought-provoking and offbeat perspectives. But the moment these paradoxical, highbrow and entirely unconventional viewpoints start showing up in mainstream media, trampling on films that everyone loves, readers begin to feel left out. It all feels a bit too cliquey and sectarian, so they stop following recommendations and stop going to see those kinds of films, the result of which is that criticism has lost much of its clout. I remember, for example, one week in Paris when two auteur films were released: Tsai Ming-liang's *Face*, produced by the Louvre and screened in competition at Cannes, and *Kinatay* by Brillante Mendoza, who won the directing prize at the same festival. Both got rave reviews in *Le Monde*, *Libération* and *Les Inrocks*, but in two weeks the first got an audience of only 4,600 and the second 6,800. I did a rough calculation just for fun: if you added up all the readers of those magazines, you'd get about one filmgoer for every six thousand readers. That means that out of 6,000 people who read a glowing review, only one actually bothered to go see the film. It's a far cry from what was happening back in the Sixties when, if someone like Jean de Baroncelli said, "I think Louis Malle's *Le Feu follet* is a masterpiece" – and he used the word "masterpiece" three times a year – the crowds flocked to see the film because his word carried serious weight and credibility. That could never happen today. I don't think anyone has the influence of someone like Jean-Louis Bory, who persuaded hundreds of thousands of people to head to Saint-André-des-Arts and watch an Alain Tanner film. It's not just a case of losing credibility, it's also about media overload. These days, television is all about interviewing stars from big blockbusters, many of which are produced by the television networks themselves, which are being screened in hundreds of cinemas.

Box-office paradoxes

Advertisements now take up a lot of space in newspapers.

They drown out everything else. And there's also this obsession with numbers, where many newspapers publish the box-office results of the week, which means that only the biggest hits ever get a mention. Even if *Le Monde* devotes a page to a film that's playing in only one cinema and calls it a masterpiece, that film will disappear into oblivion the following week because only the top ten highest-grossing films ever get a mention. *Libération* is the only paper that might remind readers in a small side note, "By the way – we highly recommend this film we talked about last week…" In other words, highly praised films are forgotten if they don't make money. We constantly make fun of the United States, where everything is always about money, but it would be unthinkable for *The New York Times* to discuss box-office receipts. They review the film and don't concern themselves with ticket sales. Here, it's a significant issue because films are left to fend for themselves – a symptom of an increasingly market-driven society. Imagine a food critic saying, "This place serves amazing food, but it's always empty. You should go check it out!" Most people probably wouldn't bother. When you tell people that a fantastic film isn't getting any attention, but a brainless one is doing well at the box-office, audiences are more likely to want to see what all the fuss is about with the silly film. So criticism doesn't carry as much weight these days.

There are exceptions.

Sure, there are some surprising exceptions. When a million people go see Asghar Farhadi's *A Separation*, a subtitled Iranian film by a virtually unknown director with no known actors, or when seven hundred thousand viewers see Jeff Nichols' *Mud*, which received unanimously positive reviews, the press is partially responsible. But in these cases it's because these films broke out of the critical bubble, and everyone – from radio stations like France Inter to fashion magazines like *Elle* – was singing their praises. And you know what really helps get people into cinemas? Things like *Le Masque et la Plume*, with its healthy argument and debate. When participants are unanimous in their praise for a film, listeners know that this is a genuine, spontaneous burst of enthusiasm.

Does film criticism really make a difference in the long run?

It can play a considerable role in gradually establishing the importance of certain filmmakers whose films, when they started out, were being screened in one, two or three cinemas. Think back to the Sixties, to Antonioni, who eventually hit it big with *Blow-Up* and even won a Palme d'Or, or Buñuel, who began by making films like *Los olvidados* and *Él* before moving on to the incredibly successful *The Discreet Charm of the Bourgeoisie* and *The Phantom of Liberty*. With *Scenes from a Marriage* and *Fanny and Alexander*, Bergman managed to attract huge audiences. All this is partly thanks to the work of film critics, who are a counterbalance to the marketing machine. It's the producers churning out mediocre films and relying solely on advertising, mass distribution and journalists happy to jump on the band wagon who long for the absence of critics.

Everyone's a film critic

Film criticism in magazines is being steadily displaced by what are basically promotional articles.

I think newspaper editors are becoming increasingly resistant to that kind of thing. Maybe one of their critics recommended a film that they disliked... But more seriously, this is a version of Truffaut's famous line: "Toute personne a deux métiers: le sien et critique de cinéma." ["Everyone has two professions: their own, and film critic."] One of the great glories of cinema is that it is an extraordinarily vibrant art form that sparks debate and gets people fired up. *Everyone* has an opinion about films. If a newspaper editor, accompanied by his wife, sees a film he dislikes, one his critic raved over, he's going to get into the office and say, "My wife and I thought the acting was terrible! How could you recommend that?" But he would never confront his economics editor and debate the merits of an article about sugarcane – because who cares about sugarcane! Most people don't have an opinion on painters and wouldn't be able to give you a single name of a painter exhibited in a prominent Parisian gallery. And yet I was a professor for thirty years and saw battles between students, with Woody Allen on one side, Spielberg on the other, one group for Antonioni and another for Fellini. I never heard of a single argument between Joseph Beuys' supporters and those of Murakami or Damien Hirst. In the nineteenth century, moderately cultured audiences might be for Ingres or for Delacroix. They were for or against Flaubert, for or against Balzac. People argued about painting and literature. Even though it's less potent today than it was in the 1960s or 70s, cinema – and this is the beauty of it, and one of the reasons why I'm so passionate about it – is an art form that remains at the heart of public debate. We *discuss* films. Abdellatif Kechiche's *Blue Is the Warmest Colour* immediately provoked reactions for or against. There were controversies surrounding Lars von Trier and Almodóvar. People *argue*. Cinema is a living art, and critics clearly have a part to play in keeping it that way. Long after their deaths, new books on Hitchcock, Ford, Bergman, Antonioni, Buñuel, Welles and Truffaut continue to be published. They may be gone, but their films live on.

The cocktail that kills

What about the argument that there is less space for critical writing because, in the end, readers aren't all that interested?

In that case, I get the feeling that newspaper bosses aren't really giving any thought to readers. They say it doesn't interest the readers because it doesn't interest them. They're too busy playing power games with politicians and trying to exert influence at Matignon, the Élysée Palace and the Quai d'Orsay to read an in-depth analysis of the latest Kechiche film. There's also the risk of ruining a dinner party if you end up sitting next to a celebrity or director who says, in the middle of the meal, "Who's the idiot on your newspaper who trashed my film?" That can be awkward… It's much easier to run with a profile or a report from a film set and offer almost ironclad praise for every film that comes out, rather than publish a critical review that stirs the pot and creates friction with celebrities at cocktail parties. That said, there are still newspapers like *Le Monde*, *Libération*, *Télérama*, *La Croix*, *Le Nouvel Observateur*, *Les Échos*, *Le Figaro* and *Les Inrocks* which continue to exercise their freedom and critical duty – even if I don't always agree with them. Without that, we would fall back into what journalism was like in the 1930s, which is exactly why Georges Charensol established the Association amicale de la critique cinématographique, so he could fight back against a press that was in the pocket of the film companies, taking bribes and shamelessly pushing their own agenda. They claim they're bowing to public pressure, but there's no question in my mind that newspaper readers appreciate long-form analyses and good old-fashioned criticism. I don't see why in the United States, the so-called land of illiterates, a widely read weekly like *The New Yorker* can give Pauline Kael six pages to write admittedly debatable but brilliant film criticism, while such a thing seems to be impossible in France, the self-proclaimed land of culture and the intelligentsia. I read in the *New York Review of Books* – a bi-monthly, general culture magazine which talks about nearly everything – an eight-page critique of *Avatar* which we translated and published in *Positif*. Eight pages! Which French newspaper would publish an eight-page analysis of *Avatar*? I'm talking about mainstream media here, not specialised journals.

The example you're using is one of the most publicised films ever.

Even films like that don't get properly reviewed in newspapers. But you're underestimating readers if you think they don't want eight thoughtful pages on *Avatar*. If an article is interesting, well-researched and thoughtful, it will find readers.

A visual art

It's not easy to break down how a film is directed.

Let me go back to the example from my early days picking films for Critics' Week in 1969. Since I was an English teacher, I was asked to provide simultaneous translations for some films that arrived without subtitles. Some productions had tiny budgets and weren't even sure they would make it to Cannes. I remember that for Ken Loach's *Kes*, after about fifteen minutes I just gave up. I could see the film for what it was. I saw the extraordinary performance of the boy, I saw the imagery, the Midlands landscapes – but I didn't understand a word of the dialogue. Feeling a bit discouraged, I asked Gene Moskowitz, who wrote for *Variety* and who spoke fluent French, to take over for me, but he found it just as difficult as I did. As Bernard Shaw once said, "The British and the Americans are two great peoples divided by a common tongue." After about fifteen minutes, Moskowitz threw in the towel too and said, "Sorry folks, I don't understand it either." And what happened at the end of the screening? We selected

Kes for the festival, of course. This proves yet again—it's one of my pet theories—how much cinema is a visual art. We understood the story: the little boy with his falcon, his relationship with his family, his connection to the landscape, and the beauty of the film, the authenticity of what we see on the screen – it all left no doubt. We knew we were in the presence of a highly talented filmmaker, and selected *Kes* without any discussion. Is it stating the obvious to think of cinema as a visual art? Actually, it's the kind of thing that's barely mentioned. You can read a long review in a newspaper which makes no reference to the visuals. What strikes me is that even though I have the greatest admiration for the great writers of dialogue, like Mankiewicz and Éric Rohmer, what remains most vividly etched in my memory is not "Atmosphere! Atmosphere!" [from Marcel Carné's *Hôtel du Nord*] or "Nobody's perfect," despite the genius of those filmmakers. Instead, it's the child's carriage on the Odessa Steps in *Battleship Potemkin*, Rosebud in the final shot of *Citizen Kane*, the cosmic journey in *2001*, Giuliano's bloodied corpse, images from films of the Coen brothers, Tim Burton, Fellini. It's visual memories that remain.

An entire tradition of criticism is unaccustomed to commenting on images and sounds.

I'm basically at a disadvantage because I come from a literary generation, and the language of images didn't come naturally to me. Computers, television, video games – it's a real visual education that children are receiving. These days a twenty-year-old has an understanding of cinema that's much more visual than my generation ever had. Most established critics are concerned only with a film's plot. Almost their entire reviews are about what's going on in the story – character psychology, that kind of thing. It's all very literary. Sometimes you wouldn't even know they're talking about a film because there's so little mention of form. It's like talking about *The Passion of Joan of Arc* without mentioning that it's shot primarily in extreme close-ups. You would have no idea what the images look like after reading a review, whether, for example, a film is edited quickly or with long, continuous shots. You would be none the wiser about the music or performances, which our colleagues at *Positif*, like Michel Cieutat and Christian Viviani, write about so well. Typically, there's a sprinkling of moral or ideological commentary, depending on the critic. If a film doesn't sufficiently highlight class struggle, it's repugnant. If it does, it's brilliant. What I mean is, this kind of critical writing revolves mainly around storytelling, psychology and ideology. Today's good critics, including the young writers at *Positif*, have a more visual approach to the reading of a film.

Do you mean that in most critical writing, the work of the director is largely ignored?

It's rarely analysed. Our work is all the more difficult because it involves finding verbal equivalents for a medium that is primarily non-verbal. This is even more obvious when it comes to silent cinema. How can you convey images through language? The ideal would obviously be to show excerpts and analyse specific sequences, which is done on some television programmes, and there's a lot more of it happening on the Internet – but still not enough. It's very tricky when it comes to writing about this kind of thing. Plus, critics can fall victim to their own hallucinations. I remember, for example, Jean Mitry, a very respected historian, was convinced he had seen a sequence from *The Grapes of Wrath* that had since vanished from the film. It turned out to be all in his head…

The cinema as a witness to history

This question of the visual reignites the age-old debate about form and substance.

I think we should pay equal attention to what a film it trying to tell us and the aesthetic expression by which it achieves this. Chabrol wrote a very good text about modest stories in which he argued that Fritz Lang's American crime saga *You Only Live Once* might be better than *Metropolis*. He's not entirely wrong, of course. Remember, it's possible to give the story of a film too much focus. You can paint a still life like Chardin and still be a tremendous artist. There was a time when formalism took over and the subject matter of a film really didn't much matter. What I've always found interesting about cinema as an art form of the twentieth century is that it's the great chronicler of its era. In a way, it took the place of well-known historical paintings. With the advent of abstraction, there was almost no figurative painting being done. In the seventeenth century, for example, there was Velázquez's great painting about war, *The Spears of*

Breda, and Rubens chronicled the events of his time. But it's undoubtedly the nineteenth century that made the greatest impact, with Goya's *The Third of May 1808*, Delacroix's *Liberty Leading the People* and Manet's *The Execution of Maximilien*. Cinema has documented the great moments of the twentieth century, and even some of those at the end of the nineteenth. American cinema, for example, has always been closely tied to the history of westward expansion, and like Italian cinema has narrated the history of the country. You could say that *Battleship Potemkin* contains timeless images of the Russian Revolution, *The Grapes of Wrath* evokes the Great Depression, *Objective, Burma!* is the story of the fight against the Japanese in Southeast Asia, and Chaplin's *The Great Dictator* is about Hitler. Cinema has a knack for connecting with history.

Are you talking exclusively about fiction cinema?

Yes, because fiction films reach a broader audience, even though today some documentaries are seen by large numbers of people on television. I'm talking about fiction and its interpretation of history. In fact, when it comes to the nineteenth century, I wasn't talking about photography but painting, which is also a form of historical fiction. French cinema, unfortunately, has never been that interested in documenting the nation's history. There have been many more films made in Italy and America that bear witness. The American philosopher George Santayana said, "Those who cannot remember the past are condemned to repeat it." That doesn't mean Italians and Americans have avoided repeating their mistakes, but the emphasis of history in their national cinema has had an impact on public opinion. There's a wonderful Peter Brook line: "We talk of Beckett's world, or Giacometti's world, but we don't talk of Shakespeare's world because Shakespeare *is* the world." Benayoun published a text in 1961 in *Positif* entitled "Pour un bilan positif du sujet" ["A Positive Assessment of the Subject"]. This was at a time when the New Wave was making films about young girls coming of age, which is entirely commendable, but – in line with Chabrol's text – it justified a tendency to disconnect cinema from history. Any number of charming New Wave films were in stark contrast to the great Italian cinema of the same period, which, through the work of directors like Visconti, Rosi and Monicelli, or even the sweeping epic of *La dolce Vita* and others, was truly engaged with society. There's an amusing anecdote where two great writers playfully swap roles. It's a conversation between Zola and Mallarmé, during which each pretends to speak in the other's voice. It's quite funny for anyone familiar with Mallarmé's formal aesthetic obsessions and Zola's emphasis on content. Zola said, "But really, Mallarmé, everything is of equal value in art. You can write a book about a diamond just as well as one about shit. It's not the subject that matters." And Mallarmé replied, "Yes, that's true. But diamonds are rarer." Some of the filmmakers I have written about, especially in my books, are connected to history. They never shied away from "big themes."

Perhaps I've been much influenced by my culture and the books I've read, because I have always loved Balzac, Zola, Dickens, Tolstoy – many great novelists who explored the nineteenth century and who were witness to major historical events. Think of Stendhal's account of the Battle of Waterloo and Tolstoy's depiction of the Russian campaign. I'm talking about filmmakers like Rosi and Kazan, of course, but also John Ford – who unfortunately I never wrote a book about – whose cinema recounts the entire history of America, not just the West. I greatly admired Wajda, for example. Consider his entire body of work, from the Polish resistance in *Kanal* to the recent portrayal of *Katyn*, where his father was killed by the Soviets, through *Man of Marble*, *Man of Iron* and his extraordinary recent film about Lech Walesa. Whether he lived through events himself or depicted them forty or fifty years after the fact, he truly is a chronicler of Poland. The same goes for Jancsó in Hungary or, obviously, Angelopoulos in Greece. In France we had Jean Renoir, especially in the 1930s, though after the war his cinema went in a different direction. I'm not just thinking of *La Marseillaise* or *La Grande Illusion* but also *The Crime of Monsieur Lange*, which is about the Popular Front. Currently, Tavernier – who is passionate about history and a great admirer of Italian and American cinema – is one of the few French filmmakers who makes historical films. He's taken his interests and turned them into genuinely personal and original films. Think back to the era of silent film in France, as exemplified by Léon Poirier's *Verdun: Visions of History* and Abel Gance's *Napoleon*, where there was a genuine commitment to historical narratives. This has always interested me, perhaps because, as I explained earlier, I started out by wanting to become a historian. I reconciled my interest in history with my non-exclusive interest in grand cinematic artistry that engages with history.

The pitfalls of didacticism

One can nevertheless be critical of certain films for their preoccupation with "big themes," much like one can fault academic painters for being didactic or overly illustrative in their approach.

That's true. I don't appreciate propaganda or cinema that tends to be excessively didactic. The directors I've just mentioned don't make those kinds of films. I very much dislike one-dimensional films, for example those that plainly oppose fascism but without any complexity, that fail to ask any questions and lack any enlightening or aesthetically valid analysis. At some point, we swung the other way and got caught in an unconditional condemnation of "big themes," but that doesn't prevent me from being a great admirer of Bresson, Rohmer or even Woody Allen, currently the world's foremost comic filmmaker. Altman criticised him for not having any black characters in his films, despite them all being set in New York. But this is an example of someone being put on trial for a film they *didn't* make. It doesn't bother me in the slightest that with the exception of *L'Arbre, le Maire et la Médiathèque*, Rohmer doesn't deal with modern day politics, choosing instead to make films in the vein of Marivaux and Alfred de Musset's *No Trifling with Love*.

Some of his films deal with historical events.

True. He has made four or five historical films, like *L'Anglaise et le Duc*, in which he expresses an aversion to the French Revolution. But if he hadn't made those films, I never would have thought to criticise him, because that was never his goal. You can't blame him for not filming in the slums. That said, coming back to Rosi, one thing that has forever irritated me is that in his press conferences there is never a single question on form, notably Pasqualino De Santis' superb cinematography. I remember the Venice press conference of *Many Wars Ago* where only the subject matter was discussed. At the same time, maybe that's the price to be paid for an artist like Rosi. His films deal with such powerful and thought-provoking realities that perhaps we should put aside their aesthetics. Critics have never been much interested in discussing form, and given the opportunity – and there certainly are plenty when it comes to Angelopoulos and Rosi's films – they avoid doing so. It's a problem, I feel. Filmmakers who deal with "big themes" should be prepared for it to backfire on them, meaning that aesthetics take a back seat.

When it comes to your reservations about propaganda, how do you rank Soviet cinema?

The heyday of great Soviet cinema didn't last long, about ten years, until the early 1930s. I recently rediscovered Eisenstein's *Battleship Potemkin*. I had already seen *October* in London, with the original music by the great German composer Edmund Meisel, who was almost Eisenstein's alter ego, his artistic companion, and who died in a car accident in November 1930 and was replaced by Shostakovich. I had never found *October* to be as captivating as *Potemkin* or *Ivan the Terrible*, but that day in London I was completely enthralled by the score – which underlines the importance of seeing silent films with live music, which is happening more and more. In 2005, in Berlin, I saw *Potemkin* again – which I know by heart – with Meisel's score, and I was able to see the film in a completely new light. I realised how amazingly homoerotic it is. The cannon pointed towards the sky is a kind of phallic discharge. Shirtless sailors swing sensually in hammocks. The music definitely pushed it in this direction. I'm not saying that Eisenstein wasn't a political filmmaker, but the 1905 riots was actually subject matter that was assigned to him. It was a commission he accepted. I'm sure he sympathised with the spirit of the revolution, but at the same time the film does convey certain hidden aspects. It seems that Eisenstein's homosexuality came to light in Mexico when he was filming *Que Viva Mexico! Potemkin* is clearly a loaded film, with another layer of meaning. Dovzhenko was the other great Soviet filmmaker I admired, much more than Pudovkin. For me, he represents lyricism, nature, pantheism. *Earth* is full of collective farms, but the film is more Virgil than anything else. The people in it are all being oppressed. In his rather distressing journal, Dovzhenko makes clear the heavy hand that was bearing down on him. With his magnificent *Alexander Nevsky*, Eisenstein succeeded in making a thinly veiled propaganda film, but I would agree with Kubrick: there's no great political depth to it.

Style of images and style of ideas

Can you say what makes a great filmmaker?

I don't exactly know. There's a famous essay by Balzac that I like, which he wrote after [Stendhal's] *La Chartreuse de Parme* was published to general indifference. Not many people read that book, even though Stendhal dedicated it to "the Happy Few" who appreciated his work, hoping that recognition would come fifty or a hundred years later. Balzac's essay is a wonderful tribute from one great creator to another, ignored by his contemporaries, in which he defines three styles. There's the style of images, which is that of de Chateaubriand. There's the style of ideas, as exemplified by Stendhal. But there's also a third style, where the image connects to the idea and which Balzac claimed as his own way of doing things. Of course, he took the opportunity, while praising Stendhal, to place himself on a pedestal. Many of the filmmakers I admire are in this third category. Filmmakers like Rivette have a style of ideas, and others like Tarantino have a style of images. And then there are those who blend images with ideas. Once again, I come back to Kubrick. You can imagine a filmmaker like, say, Luc Besson, who in a science fiction film would include a shot of a bone flying up in the sky and a shot of a spaceship. But there's this extraordinary moment in Kubrick's *2001* where the bone that the primate throws up into the sky is transformed, with an edit, into the spaceship. It's a leap in time of thousands of years, a way of showing that the great stages of humanity are tied to technology. The bone is an instrument of power and death which the monkey uses to kill the tapir, then thousands of years later comes the conquest of space. The juxtaposition of these two images triggers an idea. This is where what has always impressed me the most is manifested: the ability to generate ideas through images. It dovetails with Italian Renaissance painting. Leonardo da Vinci used to say that painting is a mental thing, a *cosa mentale*, and that his discovery of perspective also inspired him to dream up flying machines. It's like this fusion of technical craftsmanship and artistic creativity. Many of the filmmakers I most admire have this knack for connecting images with ideas.

Long live eclecticism!

Is a filmmaker's eclecticism compatible with the auteur theory?

I remember an interesting round table in the summer of 1987, just before the Locarno festival, in Ascona. The subject of the debate was "Qu'est-ce qu'un auteur?" ["What is an auteur?"]. I was invited along with Jean-Luc Godard, Freddy Buache, founder of the Cinémathèque suisse, Theo Angelopoulos and Moritz de Hadeln, director of the Berlin Film Festival. Godard began, brilliantly as usual, with a framework of formulas. "There are two types of films," he explained. "There are films *of*, and films *by*.

The films *of* are the films where after a few minutes we immediately recognise the filmmaker's signature style. The films *by* are those where screenplay was handed to the director, who shot it in a relatively anonymous way." I asked him, "That's all very interesting, and it's certainly a stimulating idea, but allow me to apply it to you, since you screened your *King Lear* – as produced by Golan and Globus of Cannon Films – at Cannes, and which, right from the start, is clearly a film *of*. We see seagulls on the edge of Lake Geneva. We hear overlapping dialogue and Mozart. Personalities, including Norman Mailer, are interviewed. There are snippets of quotes, inserts of photos, wordplay and pun. We're unmistakably in the realm of Godard. It's a film *by*. Your film and Shakespeare's play are the only two totally unique versions of the King Lear story. I'm not talking about adaptations, like the ones by Kozintsev or Peter Brook, who filmed the text of the play. But as much as your *King Lear* is *by Godard*, so *King Lear* is *by Shakespeare*, because if you had watched *The Taming of the Shrew* the night before, *A Midsummer Night's Dream* the night before that, and before that *Macbeth*, *Love's Labour's Lost* and *Julius Caesar*, you would see that these plays are so diverse and different from each other, and yet they are all unmistakably *by Shakespeare*." The Swiss who were present, and who were rather taken aback that someone could be quite so flippant with Godard, told me, "We didn't quite understand what you meant." It was inconceivable to them that someone would contradict the master. At the end of this panel discussion, Godard asked me to have lunch with him. During our meal, we talked about numerous films, including those by Boris Barnet, who Godard was really into. It was a conversation shot through with cinephilia. He asked me about Robert Benayoun, even though Benayoun had spent his life unfairly criticising and belittling him. Godard wanted to know how Benayoun was, because he'd had a stroke and Godard was worried about him. All this got me thinking. Why is it that people who for centuries have been dubbed "geniuses" – Shakespeare, Rubens, Mozart, who all tackled diverse subject matter – are now criticised for their versatility?

Is this a flaw of modern criticism?

I'm wondering. The genius, until Delacroix, was the one who could do everything: paint flowers, portraits, mythological scenes, landscapes, still lifes, battles, interior scenes. They said that Rembrandt was a genius, and Titian, Velázquez and Rubens too. But at what point did what we define as genius become – pejoratively – eclecticism? An artist was accused of having no personality and jumping from one subject to another. It's the concept of a "signature," which began in the late nineteenth century. Artists were expected to have an immediately recognisable style and subject matter. This is a very European idea, and is especially French – the sanctification of the auteur who finds himself almost doomed. By painting three thousand black canvases, Soulages is a prisoner of his own "signature." If he started doing figurative work, no one would understand what's going on. Bresson is a genius, but all he does is "Bresson." He can't do anything else. At *Positif* we've never been afraid of throwing our support behind someone who can keep us on our toes, someone constantly surprising us with different perspectives, with shifts in attitude and genre.

Eclecticism risks being labelled as inconsistency.

I'm reading Isaiah Berlin at the moment. In his book *Russian Thinkers* there's an essay I love called "The Fox and the Hedgehog." Berlin references two lines from the Greek poet Archilochus, which I wasn't familiar with: "the fox knows many things, but the hedgehog knows one big thing." Then he writes about writers and thinkers – although we can equally apply the idea to filmmakers – and the "great chasm between those, on one side, who relate everything to a single central vision, one system, less or more coherent or articulate, in terms of which they understand, think and feel – a single, universal, organising principle in terms of which alone all that they are and say has significance – and, on the other side, those who pursue many ends, often unrelated and even contradictory, connected, if at all, only in some de facto way, for some psychological or physiological cause, related to no moral or aesthetic principle. These last lead lives, perform acts and entertain ideas that are centrifugal rather than centripetal; their thought is scattered or diffused, moving on many levels, seizing upon the essence of a vast variety of experiences and objects for what they are in themselves, without, consciously or unconsciously, seeking to fit them into, or exclude them from, any one unchanging, all-embracing, sometimes self-contradictory and incomplete, at times fanatical, unitary inner vision. The first kind of intellectual and artistic personality belongs to the hedgehogs, the second to the foxes." Sternberg,

Hitchcock, Bresson, Cassavetes and Bruno Dumont are hedgehogs. Renoir, Buñuel, Michael Powell, Altman, Frears and Bergman are foxes. And Kubrick, to me, is a hedgehog disguised as a fox.

What I don't appreciate is one-size-fits-all thinking – the ideas you're supposed to embrace, the established norms. Take Bertrand Tavernier's *The Princess of Montpensier*, which was screened at Cannes. *Cahiers* published an article wondering why it was even in competition. And yet internationally it was judged to be among the top-rated films of the year, and most French critics also liked it. The prevailing notion is that a period costume drama must be conventional. But I can't help but wonder what would have happened if Bangladesh had presented a film for the first time at Cannes, about a religious conflict, the story of a Sunni landowner who wants to marry off his daughter against her will to the son of a notable of the same faith, though she would rather be with a young man from the neighbouring Shiite community. That's basically the plot of *The Princess of Montpensier*, which is about intolerance during the Wars of Religion. And what if it had been shot with a shaky handheld camera so it's all low lighting, grainy visuals, and shots of the backs of heads? I bet that same press would have raved about this groundbreaking revelation and hailed the film as a masterpiece.

A permanent enemy: prejudice

Isn't it difficult to free oneself of all prejudices?

A critic obviously can't help but have prejudices. There's a "horizon of expectation," as Hans Robert Jauss puts it, from which many critical errors have been born. We're faced with something that isn't as we thought it would be. The trick is knowing how to break loose. When Jane Campion directs *The Portrait of a Lady*, is the brilliant director of *Sweetie* going to go all textbook because she's adapting a classic period piece with Nicole Kidman? The problem is that you've already stopped watching if you think she's making a James Ivory film. We had fun at *Positif* trying to predict the kind of critical storm that would blow up around *Portrait of a Lady*. It didn't disappoint. But when you look at that film today, it's a very accomplished work and is absolutely a Campion film, even if it's a Henry James adaptation. The historical, cultural and contextual reality is very different from that of *Sweetie*, but there's no less energy or conviction. To be a critic means to fight against one's prejudices – which I'm not immune to myself.

Do you ever change your mind and think more favourably about a filmmaker?

Benoit Jacquot is a good example of that. I didn't really like his first five or six films, including *Closet Children* and *The Musician Killer*, which critics raved over but for me were made under an ill-absorbed Bressonian influence. Lacan considered Jacquot a major revelation. Then there was *The Wings of the Dove*, based on Henry James, and a Louis-René des Forêts adaptation, *The Beggars*, two films that seemed very traditional to me. But then, at a certain moment, his films began to evolve in a very interesting way. They became something very different. *La Désenchantée* with Judith Godrèche, *La Fille Seule* with Virginie Ledoyen, then the films with Isild Le Besco and other costume films that certainly weren't traditional, like *Farewell, My Queen*, of course, but even before that *False Servant*, with a quartet of dazzling stars, or *Princess Marie*, for television, about Marie Bonaparte. So for me, he became a French filmmaker of great significance, one of the best of the last twenty years. I could have continued to keep my distance, but there was definitely some kind of rupture and evolution. No one's asking him to disown his first few films, and he knows himself that his cinema has changed a lot. I don't understand why people can't give a director a second chance.

Take Claude Miller, whose first film, *The Best Way to Walk*, rubbed critics the wrong way. They never warmed to him, no matter what he did and how successful he was, whether it was making *La Chambre des magiciennes* in a hospital room or co-directing *I'm Glad My Mother is Alive* with his son. That's what really annoys me. I might have disliked certain films by Claire Denis, but others, like *Friday Night* and *White Material*, are tremendous. Someone like François Dupeyron, for example, doesn't have the status he deserves simply because he's always doing something original. He changes register. He takes risks. And as a result, he doesn't always succeed to the same degree – and that's just fine. But he's a fascinating filmmaker, and the cult of the auteur stymies us from seeing his films for what they truly are.

I can detest Spielberg's *Tintin* or *War Horse* and at the same time love *Minority Report*. Some filmmakers are uneven. Some people change register. Others, like Chabrol, alternate between the very good and the less good – as he knew it himself. Critics should be able to readjust their glasses each time and not let themselves get trapped in a meaningless style war. You could never say that *Coup de torchon* is traditional and Truffaut's *The Last Metro* is modern. I appreciate some Truffaut films a lot, like *Shoot the Piano Player*, *The Man Who Loved Women*, *The Woman Next Door*. But some of his films just aren't as good as Autant-Lara. There's more vigour, singularity and audacity when it comes to depicting the Occupation in *Pig Across Paris* than *The Last Metro*.

An example of critical bias: British cinema

Can you give an example of how a critic might fight against their prejudices?

What often annoys me when it comes to film criticism are prevailing trends that give rise to clichés, like Truffaut's famous aphorism that the words "cinema" and "English" are incompatible. Godard took up the same idea more than thirty years later in *Histoire(s) du cinéma*. This dogma comes from two men, it should be said, who didn't have good experiences working in England when they filmed there – *Fahrenheit 451* for Truffaut, *British Sounds* for Godard. Truffaut made an exception for Hitchcock, but still thought Hitchcock's English period markedly inferior to his Hollywood work. How can anyone seriously parrot that idea these days in any kind of authoritative way out of reference to two legends? Even today, when a lacklustre British film is released, critics inevitably evoke Truffaut. I find it astonishing, especially when we consider the profound contributions to cinema made by individuals like Humphrey Jennings in the realm of documentary filmmaking, and the creative prowess of directors like Michael Powell, Carol Reed, Alexander Mackendrick, David Lean, Karel Reisz, Lindsay Anderson, John Boorman, Mike Leigh, Stephen Frears, Ken Loach, Peter Greenaway and others. English cinema continues to astound, not least due to the talents of contemporary female directors like Lynne Ramsay, Andrea Arnold and Clio Barnard, who just released *The Selfish Giant*. Ramsay's *We Need to Talk about Kevin*, featuring Tilda Swinton – an actress who, through her physicality, acting and eccentricity, embodies the quintessence of British genius – was misunderstood in France. The French think the English are homogenised and conformist, while in reality they're really quite wild. That's what I've always liked about them. The French are much more middle-class in comparison. The English working class, unlike the French, don't aspire to become middle-class, hence the very direct nature of Cockney speech. On buses, people will address you, talk to you, call you "darling."

They have a tradition of irreverence too.

There are rows of houses that all look the same, but inside are people with green hair. In the 1950s and 1960s, after having long since been buried, a great spirit appeared that was reminiscent of the English Renaissance, of the seventeenth century, of Congreve's and Sheridan's licentious Restoration theatre. Obviously there had been the war, rationing and restrictions, and before that Queen Victoria and a hundred and fifty years of Puritanism. But all of a sudden, what escaped from the bottle again was the kind of English genius that had always existed and that so fascinated me. I found England a much more liberated place than France, especially when it came to women. I lived *À nous les petites anglaises!* The first time I ever really spent time with girls was when I was fifteen in England, which would have hardly been imaginable in the bourgeoisie France of 1953. British cinema remains largely unknown, no doubt because of stereotypes about English conformity.

Britain's Free Cinema was contemporaneous with the French New Wave and preceded by the Angry Young Man movement.

It's often been said that what was new about the New Wave was that critics were becoming filmmakers, but actually that had always been the case. The masters of French silent cinema – Louis Delluc, Germaine Dulac, Marcel L'Herbier – were all critics and essayists. The Italians Antonioni, Visconti, Lizzani, De Santis, Lattuada, Risi, Comencini had all been critics. And in the early 1960s, it was the same thing with the Free Cinema movement, which emerged at almost the exact same time as the New Wave, with Karel Reisz and Lindsay Anderson's first documentaries. This unfair snub of British cinema is nothing more than a dismissive line from two former critics who were also very talented filmmakers.

It must have particularly annoyed the lover of Anglo-Saxon culture in you.

I have a special relationship with England. Along with Italy, it's the place where I go most often. Unfortunately, I don't read Italian fluently, but all the Italians I know speak French, which makes things easier. I went to England at a very young age to learn the language. When I was thirteen, I spent the summer with a family in Leigh-on-Sea, on the Channel, and even learned to play cricket. There's no doubt that British cinema has played an important role in my life.

"Not bad for a first film"

What other clichés of film criticism should we kick against?

I'm wary of "Not bad for a first film," as if a first film is inevitably going to be riddled with beginner's mistakes. It always seemed a ridiculous idea to me, given the number of remarkable debut films across film history. It's more difficult to succeed with your seventh film than your first. When someone is genuinely talented and makes their first film, they aim high. I never thought much of directors who play it safe with their first film. Anyone who acts that way at the age of 25 or 30 is likely to play it safe for the rest of their life. If you make your first film at that age and haven't yet had any commercial or critical failures, or been treated badly by the industry, you're more likely to dive in headfirst with even more guts and try to make the most epic film ever. As the great Portuguese novelist António Lobo Antunes recently said, "When you write a novel, you want it to be the most beautiful novel ever written." There's none of this "I've always wanted to make a little film or write a little book because I'm not especially ambitious." Take a look at *Citizen Kane, Strike, Hiroshima mon amour, The 400 Blows, Lola, Breathless, Pather Panchali, Knife in the Water, A Generation, Fists in the Pockets, Hunger, The Boy with Green Hair, They Live By Night, Reservoir Dogs, Puzzle of a Downfall Child, Ossessione, Badlands, sex, lies and videotape, Saturday Night, Sunday Morning, This Sporting Life.* Even if there have been filmmakers who have been slow to establish themselves, like Bergman, Kazan and Kubrick, whose early work doesn't hint at future greatness, the number of brilliant first films is impressive, not to mention one-offs like Leonard Kastle's *The Honeymoon Killers* and Charles Laughton's *The Night of the Hunter.* The condescending attitude of old-time critics toward newcomers stems from the belief that young folks are automatically less capable than anyone in their golden years. Big mistake.

The last film is the best

On the other hand, there are diehard fans of the "ultimate masterpiece."

Yes, the idea that a filmmaker's last work is their greatest, which is also a legacy of the auteur theory. But it's impossible to generalise. It's often true in music, literature or painting because those are solitary arts, but with cinema, the ups and downs can lead to caution, fatigue and a gradual disconnect from the world. The filmmaker becomes more and more isolated, less aware of what's going on around him, less attentive to technological developments. In the same way that unconditional praise for a debut film isn't always justified, neither is going all-in on a director's supposed ultimate magnum opus.

You generally steer clear of generalisations.

Generalisations that don't leave room for exceptions.

Sartre called it the roots of racism.

Not being able to see things from someone else's point of view. There are filmmakers who have consistently created remarkable work throughout their careers with very few missteps, like Fellini, Resnais, Bresson, and Kubrick. But there are also many great directors who hit their creative peak over a period of a decade, like Rossellini, from *Rome Open City* to *Voyage to Italy*. Pabst too, and Carné, between *Jenny* and *Gates of the Night*. More recently Bob Rafelson.

Other filmmakers endure and have productive later years.

That's true. Think of the late-career work of Ford and Buñuel. As much as I enjoy discovering new and emerging talent, I'm equally moved by the final years of some of the great filmmakers who are – to paraphrase Shakespeare – in the winter of their contentment, or rather, sometimes, the winter of their discontent. As de Gaulle once said, old age is a shipwreck. But it can also be an incredibly fertile period where you feel as if you've been engaging with an artist's work for decades and yet are surprised by its ongoing renewal. I discovered Buñuel at fourteen or fifteen with *Los olvidados*, and a quarter of a century later, when I saw *The Phantom of Liberty* and *That Obscure Object of Desire*, it wasn't the uncanny that gripped me but the profoundly familiar, the feeling of being in touch with his universe and at the same time being amazed, moved and touched by the surprises it has in store. The uncanny, as Freud called it, is the feeling you get when you're in a familiar place and yet there's something indefinable about it. It feels like you're there for the very first time, although you're also sure that you've been there before. This is the sensation evoked by the work of an old master, where you reach back and explore, but nothing quite looks the way you remembered it. I find that very moving. It's why I was never one of those who fetishised B-movies. "Minor masters" are fun, no doubt, but what sets them apart from the work of a genius? It's that the truly great filmmaker can make you see life in a different way. It's like someone taking you on a car ride, a Kiarostami-style journey through the mountains, and when you come across a landscape you think you know, they say, "Wait, look there, around the bend in the road. See that cave?" Or you enter a church, and they point out, "Did you ever notice the gargoyle in that corner?" Perhaps that's one definition of an auteur, someone with an idiosyncratic perspective. Think of the extraordinary work that Fellini did in his later years. Bergman and Resnais too, and John Huston, with his sublime final film, *The Dead*. Altman died after *A Prairie Home Companion* in 2006, a wonderful film with Meryl Streep about a radio programme. At eighty, Polanski made *Venus in Fur*. Alain Cavalier created *Irène*, about his late wife, a *memento mori* forty years after the fact. Or Agnès Varda's *The Gleaners and I* and her self-portraits, which are wonderfully youthful, yet imbued with the wisdom that comes with old age.

Not to mention the doyen of doyens…

Manoel de Oliveira, yes – with *Eccentricities of a Blonde-Haired Girl* and *The Strange Case of Angelica*, both inventive and wonderfully liberating.

The cliché of the flawed masterpiece

Critics today seem wary of expertise.

Every era has its clichés, but throughout the history of art, expertise was always welcomed. People talked about Michelangelo's expert illustrations and Delacroix's use of colour. Being a master of one's art. The mastery of Flaubert's novels or Chekhov's plays. Today, that's frowned upon. The trend is to like the *"grand film malade"* ["flawed masterpiece"], as Truffaut described Hitchcock's *Marnie*. But Truffaut never made any claims for *Marnie*, and never said he preferred it to *Vertigo*. What he said was that *Marnie*, with all its flaws, was still captivating – and he was absolutely right. This has transmogrified into the idea that a filmmaker who demonstrates great mastery of cinematography, acting and editing is seen in a very negative light. What we're talking about here is the notion that accidents, chance, imperfections, the hole in the canvas and improvisation are signs of a lively and contemporary approach. I'm not at all sure that today, in France, *Barry Lyndon* would receive the same reception it did thirty-five years ago because it's a good example of perfection. Kubrick, like many great filmmakers, is a true master. On the other hand, I also adore Cassavetes, who is a master of a very different kind. I don't see why everything should be standardised or something should be ignored, and why anyone would close themselves off from beauty because of certain principles or in the name of a theory. I just don't accept that. However tempting it is, the job of the critic isn't to define what cinema should be. But it is certainly true that in my appreciation of great filmmakers, I place very high on the list anyone who has mastered all aspects of filmmaking. Cassavetes, for example, is an extraordinary director and is remarkable in his direction of actors and the truth he finds in them, but I wouldn't say I get much visual pleasure from the cinematography and visuals in his films, which is just as much what cinema is about. I tend to admire most those versatile filmmakers who have a wide skillset with more than one string to their bow – Fritz Lang, Kubrick, Ford, Bergman, all-around creators who, at the same time, explore society and humanity and its relationship to the image, and the connections between sound and image. The greatest playwright in the history of theatre is Shakespeare, whose work has it all: lyricism, metaphysics, tragedy, comedy, society and history.

Maybe the reason for this stereotype of the critic is fear of not being sufficiently attuned to originality. No one wants to turn into a stuffy, academic critic.

Yes, but I also think that critics want to fill in, with their knowledge and analysis, the gaps left by artists. It seems relatively easy for a critic to shine when reviewing films like Abel Ferrara's *Mary* or *4:44 Last Day on Earth* by finding all sorts of hidden depths that will be missed by the average filmgoer, who then showers praise over the critic for unearthing so much. But when faced with a work that proudly displays its richness and complexity in an accessible way to a general audience, the critic might feel a bit frustrated for not being able to play the role of decoder. Take, for example, masterpieces by directors like Mizoguchi, Altman and Buñuel.

Does academicism exist in cinema?

Of course. There are lots of academic films. They recycle existing forms and slavishly imitate. They redo what has already been done, much as in the nineteenth century when artists looked at the Old Masters and tried to mimic their style. So many films have absolutely no sense of novelty. To avoid falling into that trap, Kubrick was always battling against his own tendencies, trying not to leave his signature mark on a film. After *A Clockwork Orange* he made *Barry Lyndon*, which some would call an academic film because it was inspired by paintings. But it's not that at all. It still completely baffles critics.

Those who know before they know

A variant of the received idea is the trend, which by definition can appear and disappear just as suddenly.

It's interesting to note that alongside the dogma of the auteur theory, it's possible to draw a geography of cinephilia. All of a sudden, certain film industries become important – and rightly so. The emergence of Kiarostami, Makhmalbaf, Panahi, Ghobadi and others caused a stir about Iranian cinema. The same thing happened with Taiwan and Argentina. I do recall an exceptional filmmaker, Roy Andersson, who showed *Songs from the Second Floor* at Cannes in 2000. It was like nothing anyone had seen before, and it came from Sweden, a country that wasn't really on the film map, so it got a lukewarm reception and, annoyingly, was ignored by most people.

The critic always runs the risk of being influenced, either by themselves or by others.

It's all about biases, narrow-mindedness, and what you already know in advance. "This is what's going to be important at the next Cannes Film Festival…" – without knowing anything at all. No one has seen the films yet. And there's something else that annoys me about film criticism today, which proves it's becoming less and less important: this obsession with scoops and celebrity news. Let's not forget the column inches that were published to promote Baz Luhrmann's *The Great Gatsby*. Warner's press office told us that there was no way to see the film before its premiere at Cannes, which was on the day of its release, and that they hadn't even seen it themselves. They said Luhrmann was re-editing and remixing, and that we had to wait for the festival screening. End of story. While they were telling this to the "serious" critics, they were sending journalists to New York, all expenses paid, promising them interviews with DiCaprio and Luhrmann if they liked *Gatsby*. When they got there and saw the film, they were convinced it was a major piece of work and wrote three, four, eight-page articles to celebrate the event, which were published to coincide with its release. The rest of us, meanwhile, who were told the film wasn't ready, knew just how bad it really was. The same evening in Cannes, I was at dinner with some colleagues who had been on this press trip, and they were saying, "It's odd, because I loved the film when I saw it in New York, but today I've hardly met anyone who likes it." I think they had talked themselves into it. They had convinced themselves. There was even a statement made by Alex Masson on his *Fiches du cinema* website which caused quite a stir in film circles, lamenting the fact that film journalism is becoming more and more standardised and that criticism is playing a less important role. Major American production companies are flying journalists to Cancún in Mexico, showing them trailers and clips of films that haven't even been edited yet, and sitting them down with directors and actors. Later on, as the films are released, these interviews are released. The promotional strategy has evolved beyond any sense of conventional advertising and has become significantly more efficient and profitable. What looks to the average reader like a newspaper's genuine interest in a film is actually the end result of an invitation to spend time with a celebrity. It makes you wonder if we've gone back to the 1930s, when film journalism was about nothing other than selling the public on a film.

The same thing has happened in politics, where journalists travel with politicians.

So-called "embedded" journalism. It's almost incestuous.

Difference or connection

Why should a critic take a film's success into account?

There's an entry in Gide's journal from 1927 where he writes that he saw *The Gold Rush* again. "Communion possible et dont il sied de profiter. Cela est si bon de ne point mépriser ce que la foule admire." ["It would be a shame to miss this possibility of connection. It is so good to be able not to scorn what the crowd admires."] Ten years later, Malraux writes: "Il y a deux manières d'être un homme parmi les hommes. La première consiste à cultiver sa différence, la seconde à approfondir sa communion." ["There are two ways to be a man among men. The first is to cultivate one's difference, the second is to deepen one's connection."] It might be my Janus-like nature, but I do like contrasts, and welcome them within myself, not least a love of both tradition and modernity, or between the two options that Malraux talks about. That doesn't mean you should somehow be forever enhancing your sense of connection. I certainly sometimes want to steer clear of the crowd, like at the end of Dino Risi's film *In the Name of the Italian People*, when football fans scream like savages in the streets of a small town because their team won. I also understand why left-wing writers like Victor Hugo make a distinction between the "populace" and everyday people. Just as human beings are capable of the worst and the noblest of things, the crowd can be driven by generous feelings or collectively lose all sense of reason – like lynching a black man or shaving the head of a woman who slept with a German soldier. Resnais had the courage to show this, at the risk of shocking many, in *Hiroshima mon amour*.

New media

It's often said that the Internet and digital culture are a threat to film criticism. Is Positif *under pressure in this respect?*

No. What's at risk from the Internet are magazines that contain short interviews, photos and cursory film reviews.

Internet users prefer browsing the web for that kind of information instead of buying a magazine, even if it isn't very expensive. *Positif*, on the other hand, publishes detailed historical pieces and long interviews – the kinds of things you won't find online. You won't find twenty-six pages on Michael Curtiz or Henry Hathaway, René Clément or Jacques Becker on the Internet. We cater to a niche audience. It's almost as if we're living in the Middle Ages, where all around there's an increase in stupidity, ignorance, "clickbait," populism, quantity over quality. There are still safe havens – like monasteries. In the United States there are all those wonderful universities isolated in the Midwest, surrounded by cities and shopping centres that contain not a single bookstore or cinema. They have university publishing houses, fabulous libraries and vast cultural resources that serve as strongholds of resistance. As for online film criticism, people sometimes ask me about blogs. In the United States, respected critics like Todd McCarthy or Dave Kehr were let go by their newspapers and their columns discontinued, so they turned to blogging. Roger Ebert, among many others, has a blog. I assume that they are read by a good number of American cinephiles. What's missing in France is a Michelin guide for blogs. There are hundreds of them. How do we know which ones are any good? There should be a committee of experts who read them and do what we do for cinema: rate them and provide information about the ones worth reading. I don't doubt that a good number of these film enthusiasts and connoisseurs – some of whom are more cultured than many journalists – are currently writing interesting blogs. It's a shame they don't send their articles to *Positif*…

What about the fact that people can now download and watch films on their phones, and that this might become the primary mode of consumption for young audiences, possibly even replacing cinema? Does that make you feel nostalgic?

I'm sceptical about the cinematic pleasures gleaned from watching *2001: A Space Odyssey* on a mobile phone or even a computer. That kind of viewing experience will tend to diminish people's visual perception, which means they may no longer appreciate the difference. I'm certainly concerned that many future filmmakers and film students might stop going to places like the Cinémathèque and settle instead for watching films on a tiny screen, like their mobile phone or computer. For quite a few young directors, though fortunately not all of them, framing – which delineates what is on screen and what isn't, and is clearly a fundamental aspect of the work of directors like Lang, Kubrick, Antonioni and Godard – is considered less and less important. I'm not saying that in all great films it's the framing that is most important, but from the silent film era onwards it's always been an essential element. If every image you look at is low resolution on a small screen, you're going to end up forgetting about how crucial framing is. In many contemporary films, the visuals fall short. If a film does contain interesting imagery, it risks being labelled as too traditional. But expertly composed images are a vital part of most of the films I like. Digital technology has changed everything. Cinema, as a performing art, has always been distinct from painting and literature in that it requires significantly more resources than a canvas and palette or a pen and paper. It has more in common with theatre and, to an even greater extent, opera. Nowadays almost anyone can make a film, which has led to an abundance of work that needs to be sorted through so we can separate the wheat from the chaff – which is a monumental task. It's an entire project unto itself. For better or for worse, these new digital films are very different from what historically has been produced by the industry.

Series mania

There's a growing debate about the inventiveness of television as compared with mainstream cinema.

The kind of filmmaking which emphasises the political and social context of the story and the depth of the characters is now found largely on television. It's no new phenomenon: Hitchcock made films for the small screen. In the United States, mainstream cinema caters mainly to teenagers, with films full of special effects, or crude or overly sentimental comedies. This is at the expense of the kind of filmmaking that, in my opinion, brought glory to Hollywood – cinema made by great directors who addressed the issues of their time and presented complex characters to the audience. Some of this inventiveness and originality has shifted over to television, where it's said that some of the best work is now being done. But personally, I think the best films by directors like Paul Thomas Anderson, Malick, Soderbergh, the Coen brothers, Tarantino, Tim Burton, Michael Mann, Cronenberg and James Gray still have more artistic ambition and formal complexity compared to what is happening on television. Their films are aimed at adult audiences, people who these days have little interest in the average American film, since the filmmakers I just mentioned represent only the tiny, visible piece of the iceberg, and everything below the surface is artistically mediocre. These days, weary adult audiences watch television, and as a result some interesting filmmakers – like Fincher and Scorsese – have begun working in that medium. David Lynch broke new ground with *Twin Peaks* and Jane Campion recently made *Top of the Lake*. But I find it reassuring that two of Woody Allen's biggest ever hits were recent films of his: *Midnight in Paris* and *Blue Jasmine*.

Politics and politicians

What sparked your still keen interest in politics?

That politics has always interested me is reflected in my writing and the choice of filmmakers I have focused on, people who were all in sync with their times. An ability to talk about the world is something I appreciate in certain directors. Almost all the filmmakers I've written books about, and those whom I greatly admire and haven't written books about – like Buñuel or Fellini – were never exclusively wrapped up in their own personal problems.

I can speak from experience, having heard you discuss current events at gatherings with as much passion as you do cinema.

I even dabbled myself. After more than twenty years of the right in power, I joined the socialist party, in the writers' section, where I encountered Gérard Legrand, a Surrealist who wrote for *Positif*. Bernard Pingaud, who I respect a great deal, was also involved. And I spent time with historian Michel Winock, who was associated with the reviews *Esprit* and *L'Histoire* and who has written extensively on the history of France in the nineteenth century and today.

What sort of things were you involved in?

Well, I wasn't putting up posters, but I did attend meetings because I really did want a change. I found the stranglehold on French political life by the right – first the Gaullists, then Giscard d'Estaing, from 1958 to 1980 – absolutely stifling. Then I threw my weight behind Mitterrand. But after a few years I broke away because I was disappointed with certain pieces of the socialist agenda, especially during the second seven-year term. When you find yourself at odds, you either conform or step aside – and I chose to step aside. After campaigning for Mitterrand's re-election, I went independent, although have remained on the left and vote social democrat.

The authorities in France have always sought to integrate cinema into cultural policy.

True, but what's paradoxical is that the non-righteous left, of which, it's fair to say, *Positif* is a part, has never really been listened to. Without there being any hostility, we've actually been ignored by left-wing governments. They have always thought that the left possessed the ultimate truth in matters of culture, and since most intellectuals and artists voted for them, they made no effort with us. What they liked was being fashionable. I never asked for anything and never went knocking on any ministry door to ask for a handout or official role. Maybe because I was involved in politics myself and *Positif* was a world-famous magazine, we might have been approached more often, but in fifty years I've only been twice asked to get involved in any kind of commission at the CNC [Centre national du cinéma et de l'image animée]. The first time was under Giscard d'Estaing, for the *commission d'avance sur recettes* [a government committee that gives pre-production grants to filmmakers], the second time was very recently, under Sarkozy, for a heritage commission about films. There's a kind of snobbery on the French left, coupled with an indifference to people who, like us, aren't aligned with the latest trends and dominant currents.

A certain conformity?

Exactly. On the other hand, the right claims that when it comes to politics, power is almost a God-given entitlement for them. They consider it scandalous that a Mitterrand or Hollande could be elected, since the only kind of legitimate political power is that held by the right. But culture, traditionally, is left-leaning, and in this case people on the right have certain insecurities, which means that as a general rule they steer clear of cultural issues, while still continuing to hand out money. Even though it's a left-leaning journal, *Positif* has continued to be financially supported by right-wing governments, perhaps because of the inferiority complex of conservatives. Today, both left and right are equally uninterested in culture. Our current politicians don't read or go to the theatre, with rare exceptions like Martine Aubry or Laurent Fabius. Overall, there's no longer much of a difference. Sarkozy tried – he read Proust and Dostoyevsky and watched Dreyer's films to catch up after his marriage to Carla Bruni, but he wasn't fooling anyone. Today there's a kind of uniformity. Many politicians who come out of ENA [École nationale d'administration] are more interested in the world of finance and business than in culture. And they hardly ever go to the cinema.

It's also a generational issue.

Yes. People like Léon Blum, de Gaulle, Pompidou and Mitterrand had a broad education. Compare this to Hollywood today, where producers are Harvard Business School graduates and real estate, oil or car magnates. The moguls who used to run the studios were relatively cultured, as they thought that making a film of *Anna Karenina* was the best way of pushing Tolstoy on an audience. Even if they didn't read much themselves, they at least listened to people who did. And they knew a thing or two about cinema. Tyrannical and vulgar they might have been, but they took a genuine interest in the films that John Ford and Frank Capra were making, and they respected the great directors they worked with. Today, the gatekeepers in Hollywood don't have a clue. There's a famous story about Fred Zinnemann meeting a young producer at Columbia who had his feet up on his desk and was smoking a cigar. "So Mr. Zinnemann," says the producer. "What have you done?" "You first..." says Zinnemann. Broad cultural education has been largely abandoned in favour of specialisation – and this isn't just an issue when it comes to politicians. It's a problem with French education in general that, as far as I can see, has seeped in from America, where people are absolute experts in their field but often don't know a thing about anything else. A scholarly American book about French cinema in the 1920s referred to Paul Valéry as "Ambroise Valéry," making quite clear that the author had no idea who Valéry was, had to look up his name, and picked the one that no one uses. This shift towards specialisation is fairly recent because when I was at Amherst fifty years ago, we were studying everything from Freud and Tolstoy to Marx and Melville. We got a well-rounded education – something that has disappeared today.

While retaining your left-wing convictions, I imagine that politically, you must have gone through some moment of soul-searching that influenced your work as a critic. I'm thinking especially about what took place in Eastern Europe.

My unwavering anti-totalitarian stance never prevented me from siding with the left-wing. Unfortunately, when it comes to creativity in Eastern Europe, every glimmer of hope and opportunity for freedom proved futile. Again and again the Iron Curtain slammed back down – until the Soviet empire disintegrated. Before that, you would see regular waves of dissent in Eastern European cinema. We must acknowledge that compared to Nazism and even fascism, communism did allow for a level of artistic expression, although it was suppressed, trampled upon, and under tight control, while still funded by the state. What did Nazism produce in terms of art? Nothing. There were mass killings under both regimes – tens of millions of people. But I draw a significant distinction between the initially generous ideas of communism and the racist, deadly doctrines of fascist ideologies. Miloš Forman, one of the Eastern European filmmakers who best summed up the situation, compared communism and capitalism. He said that communism is like living in a zoo. You get fed every day, but you're in a cage. Capitalism, on the other hand, is like the jungle, where the strongest preys on the weakest. That's the kind of clarity that contributed to his success as one of the few Eastern European filmmakers who made it big in Hollywood, winning two Oscars.

In praise of mavericks

Looking back, I've never gone along with the crowd. Sure, I love the classics of Ford and Walsh, directors who thrived in Hollywood, who managed to carve out unique paths. But what really gets me excited are the mavericks, the genuine individuals. This applies to great writers too. In my everyday life as a critic, and also when it comes to history and politics as well, I've always been drawn to rebels. I've never been one to follow trends or just do what everyone else is doing. It's not about rebelling for the sake of it. I like judging things on their own merits and confronting the facts without getting bogged down by preconceived notions. Someone who has left a lasting impression on me is George Orwell. I'm not saying he's on the same level as Henry James or Conrad, but his independent spirit resonated with me. Books like *Animal Farm* and *1984*, about Stalinist surveillance, and his journalistic pieces, in which he criticises the Stalinists who were killing Trotskyists during the Spanish Civil War, are classics, and show his unwavering commitment to truth. It's no wonder that Simon Leys is also a big Orwell fan.

Another contrarian spirit...

I was shaken by his book *Chairman Mao's New Clothes*, published by Champ Libre in 1971, which denounced and laid bare the mass death and sheer absurdity of the Cultural Revolution and the Great Leap Forward. This was at a time when an entire French delegation was rushing to Beijing to sing Mao's praises, and the *Le Monde* correspondent Alain Bouc was writing positive things about him. Leys was a Belgian sinologist who lived in Australia and was banned from entering China. A first-rate translator of Chinese literature, he knew the country intimately and couldn't bear what Mao was doing. What set him apart was his deep love for the Chinese people as individuals. As Ingmar Bergman put it, there are people who love humanity but can't stand Peter, Paul and John. Leys said that it's more important to love people individually than to claim to love humanity abstractly while putting people into extermination camps. In Cambodia, Pol Pot outdid even Mao in terms of mass death. It took Mao three decades to do what Pol Pot achieved in three years.

Which other thinkers have influenced you?

I really liked Jean-François Revel. I remember reading his books back in the 1950s and '60s: *Pourquoi des philosophes?*, *La Cabale des dévots*, *Le style du Général*, *Contrecensures*. He was a leftist who at one point was an advisor to Mitterrand, an art critic at *L'Œil*, and editor of the Libertés and Libertés Nouvelles collections at Pauvert. But he was more than that: he was a philosopher and a political commentator, always independent-minded and fiercely anti-totalitarian. There's also the historian Tony Judt, an Englishman who lived in America and for years wrote for *The New York Review of Books*, which I have been reading for four decades. He wrote a lot of book reviews in which he discussed Vietnam and criticised America, but he never glorified any authoritarian regime, like Sartre did. Judt also wrote books about the responsibility of intellectuals. He stood up for Camus and Raymond Aron, thinkers who got the boot from the establishment for going against the grain when it came to totalitarianism. And I mentioned already someone I recently stumbled upon, Isaiah Berlin, an English philosopher with Russian roots. He's also someone who rejects one-size-fits-all thinking and is wary of ideological systems and the dangers of utopia. These few individuals I've mentioned – and there have been others – have been invaluable to me because they refused to follow trends and arm themselves with the usual slogans. They always went back to the basics and maintained a real spirit of protest. There's a journalistic aspect to these philosophers I identify with, which is why I am friendly with Jean-Philippe Domecq, who has written for *Positif*. He's primarily a novelist and art critic, and was heavily criticised because he spoke out against blind admiration for contemporary art. We chat often because we both share a resistance to tunnel vision and conformist groupthink.

Did you ever co-write anything?

Yes, but only political pieces, nothing on film. Domecq and I published a text together in *Libération*, but the subsequent election of François Hollande took the wind out of our sails, because we talked about how a desire for defeat seems to drive the left, and that it often finds ways to lose because ultimately it's afraid of power. We got some criticism for that. I deeply believe in certain left-wing values, but at the same time what holds me back and brings me closer to Kubrick's point of view is that I find it difficult to believe in the linear progression of humanity. The left, fundamentally, thinks that civilisation is moving inexorably towards an ideal society. This was also Marx's point of view. We moved through serfdom, then capitalism and the bourgeoisie. The apotheosis of all that is peace regained, happiness and harmony among all peoples, which will come about through the monopoly of the means of production, the abolition of private property, and the single party. I never believed in any of that. How is it then that the twentieth century is probably the deadliest in history, with the carnage of two world wars, fascism, Nazism, Stalinism, and all the totalitarian regimes that stem from communism: Mao in China, Pol Pot in Cambodia, the Kim dynasty in North Korea, Ceausescu in Romania, Castro in Cuba? After these hundreds of millions of deaths, how can we continue to say that humanity is heading towards a brighter future?

Did your political reading influence your work as a critic?

As a critic, I have opinionated, sarcastic and ironic feelings when it comes to any kind of conformist way of thinking. This is also linked to my interest in Anglo-Saxon culture. Jean-François Revel and Simon Leys, one French, the other Belgian, are also influenced by a relativism, empiricism and a sense of democracy that are characteristic of Anglo-Saxons. What I mean is that America, after the horrendous experience of slavery, eventually elected a biracial president, which is an achievement that deserves recognition. There were a hundred million Asians in the USSR, and I have never seen a single one of them play a crucial role in its political life, whereas many mayors of major American cities have been black.

The importance of speaking out

I get the impression that you admire people who speak out even within their own circles.

The kind of author who subscribes to an ideology but isn't a slave to it, who won't hesitate to call out one of his own. Take Bernard Frank, for example. I was a big fan of his columns in *Le Monde* and later in *Le Nouvel Observateur*, and his beautifully written books *En soixantaine* or *La Panoplie littéraire*, about Drieu la Rochelle, who wasn't exactly on his side, and *Un siècle débordé*. He was a staunch leftist, an outstanding thinker, always with a strong independent streak. We crossed paths at Frédéric Vitoux's place. I'm also thinking of journalists like Jacques Julliard of *Le Nouvel Observateur*, a leftist who picked fights with everyone and openly denounced what, in his opinion, was wrong with the world. Or Philippe Val from *Charlie Hebdo*, who dared to think that terrorism wasn't the solution to all problems. He was the editor-in-chief but sometimes stood apart from certain aspects of the magazine.

I wonder if I haven't played a similar role myself at *Positif*, where initially I agreed with almost everything that was being published, but eventually began defending the likes of Demy and Godard, who weren't in everyone's good books. After a while, I wondered, "Why are we so down on Bresson, Dreyer, Hawks and Hitchcock?" So while being almost completely in agreement with the journal and its choices, I felt a certain freedom of manoeuvre. I've never been a joiner. To me, it's a kind of a mafia mentality, the idea that blood is thicker than water, and that if a family member is a criminal, they have to be protected no matter what. That's just not for me. This is the whole problem of fundamentalism, of defending a party, an ideology, a religion – at absolutely any cost. As American patriots put it, "My country right or wrong." Nationalism has never appealed to me, even though I feel very French and would never turn my back on my country.

A critic's life

Is it easy to live with Michel Ciment?

Not easy at all. I mean, is it easy to live with anyone? Let me take this opportunity to emphasise the importance in my life of my two wives, Jeannine, then Evelyn, both of whom shared my interest in cinema. How could it have been otherwise for a monomaniac like me? Jeannine was on the *Positif* editorial board under the name of Isabelle Jordan, and made considerable contributions. She wrote some excellent articles and did translations, too. She helped and supported me a great deal. It would have been impossible for me to live with someone who wasn't interested in cinema. I can't imagine separating my love life from my passion for film and the arts. The occasional disagreement or clash of opinions with the person by one's side and sharing one's life is essential. I've always been fond of strong women who don't hold back, even though I am sometimes annoyed when we don't see eye to eye. After all, I like to persuade people of my point of view. My wife, in a way, is my first reader. Even if I don't make a habit of reading my work aloud to the person I live with, we discuss films and I bounce my ideas off her. I don't separate the emotional and sexual from the intellectual. At the same time, love isn't something that we have complete control over, and you might well find yourself having a passionate affair with someone with views very different from your own, though I suspect that this is untenable over time. If a couple has a chance together, a minimum of shared tastes and opinions is required.

The same for friendship?

Absolutely. I have some great friends – you're one of them – with whom I can talk about anything. We're always throwing ideas around. I've been discussing any number of things with Michel Sineux, now retired in the south of France, since adolescence. Of course, there's something inexplicable about it, as Montaigne and La Boétie suggested – "parce que c'était lui, parce que c'était moi" ["because it was him, because it was me"]. Friendship, at its core, certainly during adolescence, is some kind of prelude to love. Even if you're into the opposite sex, a strong friendship with another man sets the stage for the concept of a couple, of sharing and harmony. That said, if I could offer people advice about their love life, I wouldn't recommend taking a woman – or a man – to see a film on a first date, because if you sell it as being the most beautiful film in the world, and the person you're falling for walks out of that sublime work saying they were bored to death, it's hardly a perfect start. It's a better bet, later on, knowing that she actually likes going to the cinema, and once you've found some common ground, to take her to see your beloved film with confidence.

Animation and comics

Is film criticism hereditary? Your son Gilles has also become a regular contributor to Positif.

Gilles was born in 1962 and grew up in an environment teeming with filmmakers and *Positif* critics who practically set up shop in our house, since we held our weekly meetings there. He also started writing early on, particularly about animation – one of his great passions, alongside his love for comic books. He could have gone the route I did and become a cinema devotee, but he took a different path, diving headfirst into the world of comics. He is one of the leading experts in France, and ran the Cité de la bande dessinée in Angoulême with a team of seventy – curating the museum, organising exhibitions and inviting authors. One significant influence on Gilles' early interests was the fact that *Positif* had always been passionate about animation. The early contributors to the magazine read a lot of comics, and Benayoun and Tailleur were avid readers of Li'l Abner. Alain Resnais, who shared *Positif*'s sensibility, created the magazine *Giff Wiff*, which was dedicated to comic books, and wrote about Milton Caniff. *Positif* was always drawn to the visual arts, and one of the things that drew me in was an interest – stemming from Surrealism – in painting and animation. It's interesting that back in the 1950s and '60s, when I started writing, every prominent critic was interested in animation. Bazin and Godard, like Benayoun and Tailleur, would go to Tours to see films by Norman McLaren, Jiří Trnka's puppet films, Tex Avery, Walerian Borowczyk and

Jan Lenica, Stephen Bosustow and Nedeljko Dragić, Len Lye – the founders, the great practitioners and innovators, of this kind of cinema. Everyone was talking about it. Nowadays, among leading French critics, hardly anyone attends the Annecy Film Festival. Occasionally, when it's Miyazaki or Pixar, a generalist critic might deign to write about these films because they're so successful they can't be ignored. But there's barely a mention of new talent. Even on *Le Masque et la Plume* animation is hardly ever talked about because the reviewers don't go to see it. They don't know how to talk about animation, which is surprising, since it's both a cinematic and graphic art. A film critic has to take an interest in painting and be capable of switching from one to the other. That was a digression, but one that I find very important in understanding the evolution of film criticism.

In the field (1): programming a cinema

The image of a film critic is often that of someone who sits in an ivory tower, far from the public's reach. But actually, at one time, Positif *programmed unreleased films in a cinema, which is how I discovered Oshima's* The Ceremony, *at Le Quintette Positif in the Latin Quarter. Then there were "*Positif *weeks" at the Olympic, hosted by Frédéric Mitterrand.*

Positif would showcase unreleased films, many of which we discovered at festivals. We showed a different film every day, for weeks. The cinemas generously provided us with space and our critics would host a discussion after each film. In 1969, for example, Fox didn't want to release John Huston's *A Walk with Love and Death*, but after we programmed it and pulled in an audience of more than a thousand in a single day, they released it in cinemas. We also showed Lucian Pintilie's *The Reenactment*, and after it did well, the cinema kept it as part of their regular lineup. This great filmmaker later became the spiritual father of the new Romanian wave: Puiu, Porumboiu, Mungiu. We also released important films like Zulawski's *The Third Part of the Night*. When the producer Albina du Boisrouvray saw the film, she was so enthusiastic that she asked Zulawski to direct *That Most Important Thing: Love*. There was Irving Kershner's *Loving*, a talented but somewhat forgotten filmmaker, with Eva Marie Saint, George Segal and Sterling Hayden – one of Claude Sautet's favourite films. We also screened Oshima's *The Ceremony*, which Anatole Dauman later distributed before producing *In the Realm of the Senses*. We had to abandon the initiative after a few years because the journal itself had to be our primary concern. Many such films were subsequently released thanks to independent distributors.

In the field (2): creating a festival

You helped to create a film festival.

A very important moment for me. In 1988, I bought a house in Ardèche. I got to know some people from the region, including Jean-Marie Barbe, who at the time was organising a horse festival and wanted Sergio Leone to attend, and created the États généraux du film documentaire in Lussas. A few years later, I was approached by my neighbour Simone Lainé – who had helped me find the house – a very active painter and sculptor, and Jacques Daumas, director of a cinema in Aubenas, who has since acquired several more. They had the idea of creating an event. It wasn't exactly a festival, since there was no competition. The concept was to organise "Rencontres du cinéma européen" ["Encounters of European Cinema"] in Aubenas for a week and bring personalities I had met through my work at *Positif*. Lainé did all the organising and logistics, and Daumas programmed the films in his cinemas. My role was to oversee the artistic direction and choose the guests. Over eight years, we experienced tremendous growth. In a town of 13,000 residents, we had 2,000 attendees in the first year, and by year eight we were up to 14,000. We brought in filmmakers for tributes and premieres – Mike Leigh, John Boorman, Lucian Pintilie, Stephen Frears, Volker Schlöndorff, Francesco Rosi, Marco Bellocchio, Theo Angelopoulos, as well as French directors and actors like Claude Miller, Bertrand Tavernier, Nicole Garcia, Nathalie Baye, and many others. Even an American friend joined us, Jerry Schatzberg. The two-hour discussions I conducted after the screenings would draw a couple of hundred people. But, as is often the case, success attracts attention, and at one point there was an attempt to reduce Lainé's working days and, consequently, her already meagre salary. They tried to impose unacceptable conditions on her so she would step aside and others could take her place. I had warned them that if it unfolded this way, I would resign. And that's what I did.

In the field (3): a documentary portrait

You remained friendly with Simone Lainé, which led to another project.

A few years later she came to see me, saying, "I found a producer, Magali Chirouze, who is going to back a documentary I want to make about you." It wasn't my idea – I would never have thought of it. She went on to make this documentary which involved her interviewing me and following me about. Simone filmed me at my various places of work, so it's not just me talking for an hour. In Cannes, she filmed the interview we did – you and I – with Turkish filmmaker Nuri Bilge Ceylan, and the 2008 masterclass I did with Tarantino, then visited the Cinémathèque française with us, a place that was so important to me when I was young.

It's at a different location now.

Today it's in Bercy, yes. She filmed an episode of *Projection privée* with Arnaud Desplechin, who she also interviewed, as well as Joel Coen, Tarantino, Atom Egoyan, Bertrand Tavernier, Gilles Jacob, Thierry Frémaux and Wim Wenders. She even captured a meeting of the editorial board of *Positif*. The documentary, which was seen widely at Berlin and other international festivals, is entitled *Michel Ciment, le cinéma en partage* [*Michel Ciment: A Shared Cinema*] – just like this book. I love that title. It sums up one of the driving forces of my life.

Do public events help you reach people who aren't normally tuned in to your radio show?

Absolutely. It's wonderful being able to expose people to new things. In 2013, for example, in Angers, I suggested to Claude-Éric Poiroux, director of the Premiers plans festival, to invite John Boorman, one of the important figures from the late 1960s to the 1980s, who had faded from the spotlight, while people were still talking about someone like Brian De Palma, who, in my opinion, is a lesser director. Boorman is admired by his peers, from Scorsese to Coppola, and I watched as screening after screening of every one of his films was packed out with eight or nine hundred people. Most of them were discovering gems like *Leo the Last* and *Exorcist II: The Heretic* for the first time. There's nothing more rewarding. A young man later told me he had bought all of Boorman's films on DVD and became a fan. New trends emerge and take over, and someone like Boorman is forgotten by critics. It's great to be able to bring this cinema back to life.

Even if it wasn't initially your idea, being the subject of a film enables you to pass on life lessons.

Yes. Thierry Jousse also made a documentary about Jean Douchet, and I would like to see films made about critics who played an important role in America – Andrew Sarris, for example, or even English critics like Philip French. There's already a documentary by Todd McCarthy about Pierre Rissient, and the Cannes Film Festival showed another one about Roger Ebert in 2014. I'm sometimes criticised for arguing with fellow critics, but it's because I have such a high regard for this profession. That's why when criticism loses its way, when it strays from its true purpose, I think about the definition offered by T.S. Eliot – not only a great poet himself but also a great essayist on poetry, an admirer of his contemporaries, and a translator of Saint-John Perse: "the common pursuit of true judgement." I love this idea of searching for something together and engaging in dialogue. As I've said before, I read what others write. It's this passion for my profession that sometimes makes me critical when it's not practiced with the integrity I expect. It's like being unhappy in love.

Work partners (1): press agents

Let's talk about the intermediaries between films and critics. You work with press agents, who are hired by distributors to promote the films they are selling.

Relationships with press agents are important. There was a sort of golden age in France, as encapsulated by three people. First, in the 1960s, the duo of Bertrand Tavernier and Pierre Rissient. They were masters of publicity, both when it came to re-releases of classics and new films by French and international directors. Together, they revolutionised the job. I never experienced the previous era, which mainly involved organising corporate screenings, which meant gathering three hundred journalists in a cinema on the Champs-Élysées and handing out press kits.

Which is how things still work when it comes to big Hollywood films.

Exactly. Tavernier and Rissient did something entirely new. They were both cinephiles, with a remarkable knowledge of cinema history and a genuine sensitivity that allowed them to recognise the importance of new directors. I'm thinking of Michel Deville and Claude Sautet in France, but also the future New Hollywood directors like Scorsese, Rafelson, and also people like Makavejev and Skolimowski. They organised *"fragmentées"* ["segmented"] press screenings, carefully choosing who would attend each one based on the critics' tastes and affinities with each other. Right after the screening, Tavernier and Rissient would ask the critics questions because they wanted to gather immediate reactions so that no one would be able to backtrack. It was masterful.

And somewhat manipulative?

Undoubtedly. But we didn't mind being manipulated because they were right. They were championing talent, not mediocrity. In their personal relationships with journalists, they set a new standard when it came to the job of the press agent which I don't think has ever been surpassed. And their love of cinema often matched ours at *Positif*. The third person in this dynamic, who was involved with Italian cinema, was Simon Mizrahi. We worked hand in hand with him because *Positif* had collaborators like Goffredo Fofi and Lorenzo Codelli, two Italians from different generations. Codelli lived in Italy, while Fofi, who worked for various Italian publications, lived in Paris for several years. They were interested in Italian comedy – not just the usual big names. Before them, starting in the 1950s, when Benayoun was writing about Totò,* the press was very down on comedy and barely covered it. The Italian critics, who were essentially Marxist, didn't have much of a sense of humour and had no time for comedy, which they blamed for having corrupted neorealism – when, in fact, it was an extension of it, in a different form. When you watch those comedies today, they're like X-rays of Italian society. And in France, it was truly terra incognita. Mizrahi used to write press kits with excellent interviews, which would still be worth publishing today. They were as good as those in specialised journals.

---

* Totò (1898-1967). Italian actor and comedian.

Since those three individuals – Tavernier, Rissient and Mizrahi – there have been many press agents of all kinds. I won't rank them here. I've had good relationships with some of them, not because they're more accommodating or friendly to *Positif*, but because they're also cinephiles, which shapes their preferences. They don't push too hard and try to convince us of anything because they know we have our own opinions. They don't spend ten minutes on the phone trying to change our minds because they know it won't make a difference. Rather than get anxious trying to convince us that a particular film is great, they would rather work closely with *Positif* on another film. That kind of approach makes it all much easier for everyone. At the same time, what I appreciate is that press agents aren't just bureaucrats. There's a strong sense that they know about the films they're promoting. The public doesn't know them and their names are buried at the end of a film's credits, but they're serious film lovers, and their work ties into the dense network of French cinephilia – from producers to exhibitors, via the festival directors, distributors and press agents. We aren't talking here about people who haven't a clue. There's a genuine love for cinema going on.

So establishing a friendly relationship with a press agent isn't akin to making a pact with the devil?

Not at all. It's like being "friends" with a director. What matters is maintaining independence of judgement. If the director isn't happy because you don't like his films anymore, if he doesn't want to see you anymore, well – that's how it goes. You have to accept that.

Work partners (2): distributors and exhibitors

Which brings us to another controversy. Distributors sometimes complain that a bad review published before a film's release is unfair, that it's a kind of abuse of trust, or an abuse of privilege on the part of the critic.

There was an outcry over freedom of the press when Patrice Leconte said that negative reviews from critics shouldn't come out before a film was released. It does occasionally happen at *Positif* due to a lack of coordination or slip-ups. Personally, I find Leconte's position a legitimate one. A film isn't really being given a fighting chance, especially one by a young filmmaker who spent three years making it, if three weeks before its release a critic pre-emptively diverts audiences by announcing that it's an absolute dud. While it's perfectly fine to sing the praises of a film before its released, there should be some sort of understanding in the press that bad reviews won't surface too early. I tried to get this rule passed by the Syndicat de la critique française when I was president for a few years, but failed. This isn't a problem for daily newspapers because they review a film the day it's released, but for weeklies, and especially monthlies, it's not a great system.

American studios are now going so far as to agree not to show anything to anyone before the day of a film's release.

They're very serious about that kind of thing, which is understandable. I don't see why it's so surprising. Press screenings are a privilege, not an obligation. We're invited to see films in advance so we can write about them. Obviously, we need complete freedom to write what we want. The distributors can't interfere with that. But they show us films in advance so that if we do like something, we can make plans. If we don't like something, we shouldn't take the opportunity to bash it before it comes out.

What about your relationships with distributors and exhibitors? Some of them reach out to you and read Positif *to keep up with what's going on.*

The cinephilia of the profession, in France, among independents, is really quite striking. The traditional divide between intellectuals and critics who look at films from an artistic perspective, and businesspeople in production, distribution and exhibition focused solely on profits, is disappearing. Steven Soderbergh criticises modern-day American producers for what he sees as a genuine lack of love for cinema. All they want to do is churn out formulaic stuff, the usual sequels and remakes. They're all wary of anything new, when, in fact, of course, that's what makes things interesting. I've met some fantastic independent distributors, highly cultured, in England, Italy and even the US. But it seems to me that there are more of them right here in France than anywhere else.

They listen to your opinion?

Absolutely. The late Fabienne Vonier and Éric Lagesse from Pyramide, Alexandra Henochsberg from Ad Vitam, Margaret Ménégoz and Régine Vial from Films du Losange, Stéphane Célérier from Mars Films, Michel Saint-Jean from Diaphana, Jean Labadie from Pacte, Alexandre Mallet-Guy from Memento Films, Carole Scotta, Laurence Petit and Caroline Benjo from Haut et Court, Jean-Michel Rey from Rezo, Sophie Dulac and, until recently, Marin Karmitz from MK2, himself a former director, who produced and distributed filmmakers like Kiarostami, Pintilie and Chabrol. They all have a remarkable knowledge of cinema. I think it's a bit of a chicken and egg question. Which came first? We critics do our thing, and the distributors are likely to have read us and keep an eye out for certain things. When I came back from Venice, where in 1982 I recorded an interview with Peter Greenaway in the garden of the Hotel Quattro Fontane about *The Draughtsman's Contract*, I was determined to find a distributor for the film and immediately called Karmitz. Jean Labadie was working for him at the time. He saw the film and he decided to take it on – with great success. This kind of cooperation would seem completely natural to me. And through the CNC [Centre national du cinéma et de l'image animée], the government also participates with the *avance sur recettes* system and by supporting festivals, distribution, co-productions, and the restoration of old films, that kind of thing. At all levels, in all sectors, there is a real love of cinema.

Disagreements, resignations

Any example of you walking away?

There have only been two instances when I haven't been able to express my opinion. The first was in *Magazine littéraire*. Jean-Jacques Brochier, the editor, a real film enthusiast, asked me to write reviews of film books. He was very friendly with the publisher André Balland, who published what were sort of photo novels based on great classics like *La Grande Illusion* and *Les Enfants du paradis*, comprised of frame grabs and dialogue. They weren't very good because they really didn't capture the spirit of the films. Brochier asked me to review the series favourably, to help Balland, and I refused. Our working relationship ended by him telling me that I could continue writing articles from time to time, but that never happened. The second example was when I was writing for *Les Nouvelles littéraires*, which was edited by Jean-François Kahn. The report I filed from Venice was completely re-written, with sentences added under my byline. I wrote a letter of resignation saying that I would never again write for *Les Nouvelles littéraires*.

Any examples beyond journalism?

It has happened. Maybe I'm too impatient – a word that often comes up. Impatience is one of my flaws, but it has also allowed me to accomplish a lot, to take the plunge without overthinking, like in radio, for example. At the same time, I don't regret the radical decisions I've made. When I was elected to the board of directors of the Cinémathèque française, Claude Berri, who I admired, was president. He was a great producer, director, cinephile and, notably, unlike many producer-directors, he had no desire to overshadow the talents he produced. Take Coppola, for example, who founded American Zoetrope and brought filmmakers like Michael Powell, Dušan Makavejev and Wim Wenders to California and produced their work. Some projects never saw the light of day, and Coppola even forced Wenders to completely reshoot *Hammett* because he wasn't happy with it. Berri, on the other hand, probably knew that Pialat, Polanski and Chéreau – all of whom he produced films for – were greater talents than he was. He didn't let his ego get in the way. Moreover, he knew how to alternate between artistically ambitious films and popular comedies, which allowed him to make a lot of money. Essentially, he understood the economics of cinema and the balance needed to survive as a producer. But when he took over the Cinémathèque and decided to dedicate space at Bercy exclusively to exhibitions of contemporary art – of which he was a collector – I saw a conflict of interest. With thousands of potential subjects for cinema exhibits, Berri chose to start with paintings, for which there are hundreds of private galleries in Paris, not to mention museums. It was just unthinkable to me, so I told him that if he continued with this, in the name of cinema I would resign from the board of directors. Berri invited me to lunch at his place and we talked for a couple of hours. I stood firm, as did he – a man of conviction. I remember being in Berlin when I learned that the board had given his plan a stamp of approval, and I sent in my resignation. Some people criticised me for this, but ultimately the supervisory authority, the Ministry of Culture, which provides 95% of the Cinémathèque's budget, dropped his idea. Berri passed away shortly after.

I really did like him, and had a lot of fondness and affection for him. He was a fascinating man, and his autobiography is an excellent book. I would have liked the board of directors of the Cinémathèque – which included various directors and some remarkable people, and which I re-joined twenty years later, in 2014 – to have backed me, but too often the tendency is to dodge conflicts and clashes, to avoid asserting one's positions. But I've always thought that if you have a certain belief, you should remain true to it.

Both in your critical and non-critical activity?

Absolutely. This probably comes from the fact that I have always known great freedom in all my activities: teaching, criticism, journalism. At the same time, I'm always open to feedback. When I worked at *L'Express* for five or six years, for example, doing long articles, reports from film shoots and profiles, I very much appreciated the perspective of Danièle Heymann, who edited the culture pages. Very often she corrected my mistakes and made useful suggestions. She was a fantastic journalist with a real talent for making things concise. If the text was too long, she would make cuts in a very clear-sighted way. Her insights were always spot on and I don't ever remember arguing with her. She would never ask me to make changes for ideological reasons, only to improve the text.

Any other examples of you walking away?

I slammed the door of the Syndicat de la Critique de Cinéma behind me when I was president, even though it was all going well. I managed to change the practice where only the secretary general, the second in command, got to travel the world to programme Critics' Week while the rest of the selection committee stayed in Paris, watching hundreds of films. I suggested that travel responsibilities be shared among all the members. Some of them, especially three or four people who were all friendly with each other, didn't like that idea and voted against me. I didn't expect everyone to agree, but it felt like settling scores. At one point, someone even told me, "We voted against you to teach you a lesson, as a warning." I said, "Alright then, I resign." It was a rather onerous job, and unpaid to boot.

**GRAND
CINEMATIC
PLANET**

The anthology you published a few years ago, Petite Planète cinématographique, *includes half a century of interviews recorded across the globe. I would like to take this as an opportunity to revisit your encounters with remarkable filmmakers worldwide.*

That title is a tip of the hat to Chris Marker, who came up with the "Petite planète" collection for Éditions du Seuil. My aim with the book, published at the end of 2003, was to pull together my discoveries in various countries. Not every country is represented because the idea was to pick conversations with fifty filmmakers from thirty countries over a forty-year period. It was my Christopher Columbus phase, exploring uncharted territory, in parallel with rediscovering cinema history. It reminds me of the original title of Eisenstein's film *The General Line: The Old and the New*. I enjoyed bringing people of different generations together. In Paris I introduced Glauber Rocha to Kazan, who hit it off.

Bresson, Godard, Pialat

Why the three French filmmakers you picked for the collection: Robert Bresson, Jean-Luc Godard and Maurice Pialat?

Because their names felt less predictable compared to what you might find in *Positif*. I could have gone with Claude Sautet, Michel Deville and Alain Cavalier, or even a modern master like Alain Resnais, but I hadn't done a solo interview with him.

Bresson made the list because he was the trailblazer of modern French cinema. He started back in 1943 with *Angels of Sin* and *Les Dames du Bois de Boulogne*, but really shook things up later with *Diary of a Country Priest* and *A Man Escaped*. His modernity manifested itself in an incredibly unique way, in the same way that Orson Welles revolutionised American cinema with *Citizen Kane* in 1941. My interview with Bresson came about because the American Film Institute wanted to publish something in their magazine *American Film* when his final film, *L'Argent* – which shared the Jury Prize at Cannes with Tarkovsky – was released. It was remarkable to meet him on Île Saint-Louis [where he lived]. I published the full version in *Positif* thirteen years later. Initially, Bresson wanted a shorter version and removed several fascinating things himself. He had a thing for asceticism and short sentences. I remember asking him about the rumour that he never went to the cinema.

He sort of embraced that myth, although some people had told me they had seen him there. I said, "Obviously, you don't go to the cinema…" He said, "Don't be so sure. I do! Just yesterday…" And he leaned in and whispered: "Please, stop the tape recorder… I took my niece to see a film, a spy film… James…" "James Bond?" "Yes! That's the one. James Bond. It was *For Your Eyes Only*. So… you're not recording this, are you? There's one stunning sequence in that film. I was really impressed: a ski chase with the snow flying all around, which was really magical… You aren't recording, are you?" He asked me that four times because he must have wondered: what would a semiotics expert who studies Bresson year-round at the University of Nebraska think if they found out he enjoyed a James Bond film? But then again, it's not really that surprising because what turned Bresson off in other people's films was anything that felt theatrical, especially when professional actors "acted." He absolutely couldn't stand that. There's a sense of abstraction in that chase sequence – something physical, tactile – which brought back memories of his youth, when Surrealists were watching Jean Painlevé's scientific documentaries and anything that distanced cinema from literature and theatre. I have always had immense respect for Bresson. When I joined *Positif*, the second generation of writers, people like Kyrou and Benayoun, were adamantly against him, probably because of his Catholicism – even though at the start, Bernard Chardère wrote some outstanding articles about Bresson in three consecutive issues.

And the interview with Godard?

It was quite a remarkable meeting, after several decades of silence from *Positif*. His *Histoire(s) du cinéma* both fascinated and annoyed me, and I wanted him to meet with me and a young colleague, Stéphane Goudet, for a genuine back-and-forth. Godard was extremely friendly and available. He did his best to answer all our questions, even those that weren't necessarily complimentary. What was supposed to last an hour ended up lasting three, at the end of which I told him I had a screening and that I had to leave. He said, "Ciment rend l'antenne!" ["Ciment leaves the airwaves!"]

The third Frenchman in your anthology is Maurice Pialat.

To me, he was an essential figure in the French cinema of his era, and at the time never got the recognition he deserved.

At *Positif*, we immediately applauded *L'Enfance nue*, his debut feature, which I saw in 1969 with Roger Tailleur at Venice, where it was in competition. After that, we ran extensive interviews with him about *We Won't Grow Old Together* and *The Mouth Agape*. I was genuinely passionate about his work. We used to have frequent phone conversations, and he had this habit of constantly downplaying himself, which allowed him to criticise other filmmakers. Putting himself down somehow gave him a sense of freedom. He used to say that he learned more from people who spoke ill of him than from those who praised him. He had pretty brutal things to say about his contemporaries, with only a few exceptions, like Sautet, who he respected for his professionalism and craftsmanship. Because he wasn't embraced by the New Wave – even though Truffaut helped him make films – Pialat felt marginalised, as if he wasn't part of the right crowd. I think he held grudges against that generation.

You interviewed him at a time when he was giving very few interviews, around the time of his film about Van Gogh.

I think mine is the only major interview he gave on *Van Gogh*. The film was fairly poorly received at Cannes and won no awards, unlike *Under the Sun of Satan*, which won the Palme d'Or. I would have preferred it to be the other way round, because *Van Gogh* is a much better film. I remember after its showing at Cannes the security people were doing the usual thing of stopping people from going down the main stairs, and everyone had to exit through the side doors. Nicolas Seydoux from Gaumont and Pialat left by themselves. I went around the barriers and rushed down to catch him at the bottom of the stairs. I had known him for quite some time, and said, "You've created a masterpiece. An amazing film!" And he comes back with, "What – this film? It's nothing special." Right in front of a shocked Seydoux! That's so Pialat. The tough exterior some artists put up, like Wilder's snarky, biting style, or Pialat – fiery and confrontational. They're really just hiding great sensitivity and deep emotions. It's a defensive mechanism, so they don't get hurt. They attack so as not to be attacked.

You never saw the scary side of Pialat that people talk about?

No, because I don't spend time on film sets. I never had any issues with Pialat. We always got along fine, maybe because *Positif* wasn't a big supporter of the New Wave at first. I do remember Pialat's last time in public, at the Angers festival, which was running a retrospective of his work and where he was doing a public talk with Serge Toubiana. He was on dialysis, and greeted me by praising *Positif* and criticising *Cahiers*. Typical Pialat. If I had been in Toubiana's place, he probably would have praised someone else in the room.

Eastern Europe

Can we come back to your ongoing interest in Eastern Europe, something we touched on when talking about festivals?

I've always been drawn to what's happening in Eastern Europe. In my youth, the first major movement was from Poland. When I was seventeen or eighteen, it was Wajda's *Kanal* and *Ashes and Diamonds*, and Zbigniew Cybulski's acting, which reminded us of the Actors Studio. Andrzej Munk's films too. Then came a new generation, with Polanski and Skolimowski, who was more influenced by the French New Wave and made films with such independence. Following the Poles, Hungarian filmmakers emerged in the 1960s, notably the extraordinary cinema of Miklós Jancsó, with his intricate camera moves, István Szabó – whose first film, *Age of Illusions*, I wrote about in 1965 – István Gaál and Zsolt Kézdi-Kovács.

Hungary must have a special place in your heart, considering your roots.

I remember in the 1980s when I would go to Budapest for a few days with Gilles Jacob – who had recently been appointed general delegate of the Cannes Film Festival – to watch Hungarian films that might be selected for the festival. There were two key figures there: the director of Hungaro Film, István Dósai, and his assistant Klára Kristóf. They were remarkably intelligent, diplomatic and shrewd, and they reminded me of my father. The Hungarians were unique in the Soviet bloc in maintaining a space for private enterprise. They called it goulash – not gulag! – socialism, and had managed to ensure that their people were the least hungry in Eastern Europe. They had developed a subsistence economy where there was relative freedom, more so than in other countries that had experienced repression. Maybe because of the upheaval in 1956 and the events in Budapest, the Russians realised they needed to give the Hungarians some leeway to prevent history from repeating itself. In any case, Hungary is a non-Slavic and very dynamic country, shaped largely by Germany. As it was part of the Austro-Hungarian Empire, the initial influence of Austria, then Germany, was significant. From the Germans they adopted a form of organisation and efficiency that set them apart. When we wanted information on Russian or Polish films, it was no use writing to organisations there because they were completely disorganised. They could never tell us anything. The Hungarians, on the other hand, had all their press kits ready a month before Cannes. Every year they invited people to come and watch their films, and when Gilles Jacob and I did so, the Hungarians never put undue pressure on us. They were smart, and knew very well what was good or not. They didn't waste our time with uninteresting work that they knew we would never select for Cannes. And then at *Positif* we had a correspondent in Poland, Boleslaw Michalek, who was a great critic and a friend of Wajda, and who later became ambassador to Rome. Petr Král, who was a Czech Surrealist and had left Prague after the 1968 invasion, was part of the journal's editorial board. In fact, there were Surrealist groups across Eastern Europe. Karel Teige, for example, a great art critic and philosopher, was at the forefront of Czech Surrealism.

Satyajit Ray

One of the first interviews you did for Positif *was with the great Indian filmmaker Satyajit Ray.*

And one of the first articles I wrote was about *The World of Apu*, the third part of Ray's trilogy. I got to know him later when he came to Paris and I did a really good interview with him for a television programme. I followed that with a comprehensive interview about his career. Visiting him in Calcutta was unforgettable. He was like royalty – tall, majestic, and spoke very refined English. As a young man he had studied with Rabindranath Tagore, the great Bengali Nobel Prize-winning poet. Bengal was the most cultured part of India. His house was like a library, with books everywhere. Besides being a filmmaker, he was a musician, writer and illustrator. It was all very impressive. I remember an evening in London in 1973 with him and Marie Seton, the great English historian who had written a book on Eisenstein and was working on one about Ray. The British filmmaker Lindsay Anderson was there, but he was behaving quite terribly to the *Sight and Sound* critic John Gillett, openly mocking him. I could see that Ray was torn because he owed a lot to Lindsay Anderson, who wrote about him when he was a critic. Anderson was aggressive towards everyone and criticised the Cannes jury for not giving an award to his film *O Lucky Man!* "They gave the prize to a photographer's film, *Scarecrow*," he said with complete disdain. Definitely not your typical reserved Brit…

The importance of Satyajit Ray's early films isn't much acknowledged today.

Back in 1955 and '56, what did we know about Asian cinema? It was basically just Kurosawa's *Rashomon*, which won the Golden Lion at Venice in 1951, and Mizoguchi's films *Ugetsu*, *The Life of Oharu* and *Sansho the Bailiff*, which all won prizes at Venice. We knew a little about other Japanese directors like Kinoshita and Naruse, but that was pretty much it. Then along comes Ray's *Pather Panchali* at Cannes, and it's a big hit. John Huston had recommended it, just like he did later with Buñuel's *Nazarin*. It got a minor prize at Cannes, but the next year, Venice – which seemed to have a thing for films from the east, it's where Marco Polo was born, after all – gave the second part of the trilogy, *Aparajito*, an award. Ray then made two other films before directing *The World of Apu*. He had been Renoir's assistant on *The River* and was at the forefront of independent Indian cinema, which today we hardly talk about anymore. Western critics are only interested in the song and dance of Bollywood. The Bengali Mrinal Sen and Shyam Benegal, and Govindan Aravindan and Adoor Gopalakrishman of Kerala, are all overlooked. In a way, great men like Ray always have a dark side. Another great Indian director, Ritwik Ghatak, was making films at the same time as Ray, and they were friends. Ray was more of an English-style liberal, a humanist. Ghatak was a Marxist activist and a rebel who died of alcoholism. He made a series of masterpieces, and yet almost no one in the West ever heard of Ghatak when he was alive. We discovered, over time, that he was Ray's equal. If Ray, in any of his many international interviews, had said, "You know, there's a genius in Bengal named Ritwik Ghatak," the critics would have raved about Ghatak. But Ray never said anything like that. It reminds me of François Truffaut, who greatly admired Claude Sautet and invited him to watch his rushes and early cuts of the films. He wrote the foreword to *Vincent, François, Paul and the Others* in *L'Avant-scène*: "Français, français, français, Claude Sautet est français." ["French, French, French, Claude Sautet is French."] He admired him unreservedly, while allowing *Cahiers*, as usual, to rip his films apart. There was a lunch in New York with Truffaut, accompanied by Helen Scott, his translator, and the critic Vincent Canby, of *The New York Times*. When Canby asked him about Claude Sautet, Truffaut simply said, "Let's move on." Just a word from him praising Sautet as one of the great French filmmakers would have made the New York critics – who always follow French trends – take notice. We had to wait until 2012 for *Max and the Junkmen* to triumph at Lincoln Centre, and *A Heart in Winter* too, at the Brooklyn Academy of Music, in a tribute to *Positif*. But a simple word from Truffaut would have had much more impact, just as Ray might have done for Ghatak.

Encounters with Asia

Asia has been an important part of your work as a critic.

The Middle East too – Iran and Turkey. It's all about looking for new discoveries, but not just chasing exoticism for its own sake, and not just going after the most obscure films because it's trendy to do so. But if, in terms of revitalising national film culture, the 1960s and '70s were dominated by Europe, the United States and Latin America, there was subsequently a bit of a downturn. On the other hand, starting in the 1980s, Asia produced a really significant number of new filmmakers. It was only ten or even twenty years after they first began making films that we discovered the early films of Imamura and Oshima, which had been made around the same time as *Breathless*. Apart from these older Japanese filmmakers whom we recognised only belatedly, there was the fifth Chinese generation with people like Chen Kaige and Zhang Yimou. Their later work might have been disappointing, but for a time they were at the forefront of a real renaissance. And don't forget the Hong Kong filmmakers like King Hu and his magnificent sword-fighting films like *A Touch of Zen*, and later Wong Kar-wai, when he was making very different films. Taiwan has given us at least three greats: Edward Yang, Hou Hsiao-hsien and Tsai Ming-liang. So yes, Asia has always interested me. I was even given a grant from the Japan Institute to go over and interview Imamura who, for me, was perhaps an even greater filmmaker than Oshima. He certainly had a longer career. Oshima was a more conceptual filmmaker, closer to Godard and certain aspects of the

New Wave, while Imamura was more like Buñuel. He had a materialistic side, but also a taste for animal metaphors, a sense of rebellion, and a touch of Surrealism.

Oshima was always much more famous than Imamura.

Yes, although in the end he won two Palme d'Or awards and Oshima didn't get any. This reminds me of an anecdote when Imamura's *The Ballad of Narayama* was in competition at the same time as Oshima's *Merry Christmas Mr. Lawrence*. We knew there was a Japanese contingent at Cannes, and festival officials sent someone to tell them who had won the Palme d'Or. Because all Japanese apparently look the same to some French people, this festival representative walked up to Oshima to tell him he had won, not realising that there was another Japanese team just down the beach. *Positif* published that long Imamura interview I did in Japan. He had started a film school and was spending a lot of time there. That's where I interviewed him, with a translator. What surprised me was that despite the years-long American occupation of Japan, or maybe because of it, there was a kind of resistance among the Japanese to learning English. Practically none of these Asian filmmakers spoke any language other than their own, except in Hong Kong, of course, which was still a British colony. Chen Kaige from mainland China had studied in California and spoke English. But I often had trouble with interpreters during interviews, especially with Asian directors. Sometimes I would ask a question and the response would last ten minutes, but it felt like most was lost in translation. It's frustrating. You almost want to come back with a language teacher to get everything right. I've always much preferred doing interviews in French or English.

Jia Zhang-ke

You have traced the career of Jia Zhang-ke, the Chinese director of Still Life *and* A Touch of Sin, *from his earliest films.*

I first discovered Jia Zhang-ke in Nantes, at the Three Continents Festival, an event that has greatly contributed to the discovery of Asian, African, and South American cinema. It's where I saw *Xiao Wu*, which is a kind of modern take on neorealism, shot entirely on the streets and really quite fresh in its approach. What happened to Chinese cinema is a bit strange. The previous generation, known as the Fifth

Generation – major filmmakers like Zhang Yimou and Chen Kaige – had lost its edge, changed direction, and ended up as official, government-backed filmmakers. On their heels came filmmakers like Jia Zhang-ke, today the greatest Chinese fiction director, and Wang Bing, an important documentarian. After *Xiao Wu*, Jia Zhang-ke made *Platform*, *The World* and *Still Life*, all visionary films that depict Chinese society with all the many changes taking place, both in terms of the fast-paced economic growth and the growing gap between rich and poor. They're also about how difficult it is for young people to find love these days. I like the fact that he makes personal films, but they speak to wider issues. Jia is also a writer, and we have published some of his work in *Positif*. His films are very dark, but he's extremely smart, friendly, funny and creative. I ran into him in Shanghai, where his film *A Touch of Sin* played – which is odd, because it's quite critical of China and won't ever be released there. It's one of those mysteries of the Orient… What's really going on? Why did the authorities decide not to censor him and let him show his films abroad? It won the best screenplay prize at Cannes, which is odd because, of course, while the film is wonderfully written, its qualities are mainly visual, and it probably didn't get the prize it deserved. I don't think he's the type to just go with the flow and give in to the sirens of conformity. I hope he's able to get the resources he needs to continue making films.

Korean quartet

And then there's the recent emergence of Korean cinema.

Korean cinema has probably produced more important filmmakers than anywhere else over the past fifteen years. Think of Lee Chang-dong, the director of *Oasis*, *Secret Sunshine* and *Poetry*, who is also a novelist. He's a bit more under-the-radar than some, but his work is incredibly subtle and poetic, and he's an excellent director of actors. Bong Joon-ho is the highly original filmmaker of *Memories of Murder*, *The Host* and *Mother*. And there's also Park Chan-wook, as bold and crazy in his films, known for *Sympathy for Mr. Vengeance* and *Old Boy*. There's the Korean Rohmer, Hong Sang-soo, who shoots films faster than his shadow, one or two per year, always a variation on the same theme: someone quite aimless, perhaps a filmmaker, in love with one or two women. This Korean quartet ranks among the very best of contemporary filmmakers.

What about that rather strange character Kim Ki-duk?

He's known for his intense, sometimes violent and biting style, like in *Spring, Summer, Fall, Winter... and Spring* and *3-Iron*. He's not so popular in Korea, but did win the Golden Lion in Venice, an award none of his compatriots ever received. I also had a great time at the Pusan Film Festival, where I was on the jury. Watching Korean films there was incredible, a real eye-opener. It was globalisation in the best sense of the term, unimaginable fifty years ago: a festival where crowds of passionate young people flocked to see films from all countries. Every screening of the most radical and freshest international cinema was packed. There are really no more borders today. Films circulate with incredible speed – except perhaps in India, where there are eight hundred films made every year. I've already mentioned Ritwik Ghatak, an important filmmaker, completely unknown outside of India, who died at the age of 65.

Two Turks

Among the filmmakers you have championed over the years is the unique case of Turkish actor and filmmaker Yilmaz Güney.

What was special about my encounter with Güney was that he was in prison at the time. He was a big star of Turkish adventure films back in the '60s, then directed a few films and ended up with a long prison sentence. He wrote scripts, which he directed from his cell. He planned the shots, cast the actors, explained all the camera movement. His old assistants would bring these ideas to life on set. That's how *The Herd*, co-directed by Zeki Ökten, ended up winning the Golden Leopard at Locarno. I connected with Güney around that time. In 1982, I spoke to the Cannes selection committee about *Yol*, co-directed by Serif Gören, which had been shot but not yet edited. I had to meet him secretly in France, where he was hiding out. It was like meeting with a Russian dissident. I did a long interview with him. Güney couldn't make it to Cannes, but he still won the Palme d'Or – by remote.

He wasn't exactly a political prisoner, right?

He was just a regular prisoner. But he was definitely an agitator. He was Kurdish, so he was no friend of the Turkish authorities. It's unclear if he was arrested for an actual crime that was committed on a film set or if it was just to sideline him because of his political activities. He was very popular and always caused a stir.

He ended up making a film in France?

He shot a film about a prison – *The Wall*, produced by Marin Karmitz in France in 1983 – and then died.

A more recent revelation is Nuri Bilge Ceylan.

When I saw his second film, *Clouds of May*, in a small cinema in Berlin, before its official premiere, I was just blown away. It was so original and sensitive, and visually stunning. It turns out he was a great photographer before he made films – just like Schatzberg. I met him a few times later, and he really delivered on his promise. I think a critic should always be on the lookout for new talent, and my travelling has been vital for that. I sometimes got to know countries through their films long before I had visited. It was years after I wrote about *The Guns* and *Black God, White Devil* that I ever went to Brazil. I went to Japan decades after first getting hooked on Mizoguchi, Kurosawa and Naruse. And I really got to know the Philippines by going there during the Hong Kong festival to meet Lino Brocka, who took me around Manila. It was like seeing in real life what I'd been watching in his hyper-realistic films. He even ran a theatre school.

Federico Fellini

You met Fellini several times. What memories do you have of him?

I liked Fellini's early films, although had some reservations. I preferred *Il Vitelloni* and *Il bidone* to *La Strada* and especially to *Nights of Cabiria*, which I found annoyingly sentimental. He was clearly a great filmmaker, but he really started to fascinate me only with *La dolce vita* and especially *8½*, which is a masterpiece of modern cinema, then films like *Satyricon*, *Amarcord*, *Orchestra Rehearsal*, *The Clowns*, *Casanova* and *And the Ship Sails On*. As a person, Fellini kept himself at a distance. Everyone was writing about him, and he had his entourage, so I held back. In Venice, *Satyricon* had been booed and he had been dragged through the mud by Marxist critics. This was 1967, by the way

– the peak of protest and upheaval. Fellini spoke French, and he read *Positif* and knew that we were on his side. In Rome, I remember one year going to one of those dazzling parties that are easy to get invited to, the kind of thing you find in Fellini and Scola, and Sorrentino's *The Great Beauty*. Everyone was there: fashion designers, painters, philosophers, journalists, politicians. These parties were very free-spirited, completely improvised I think – nothing like French bourgeoisie planning their dinners three months in advance with little name tags. I was there to see *Roma* and publish an interview in *L'Express*. Some Italians asked me why that film? It didn't reflect Rome at all, they said. The next day, I took a taxi to the airport and ended up in a huge traffic jam – stormy skies, pouring rain, people abandoning their cars in the middle of the highway. It was completely Felliniesque! Imagination met reality. I subsequently met Fellini several times for various newspapers, and *Positif*. It was always extremely complicated because it was well known that he never said yes to anything. We showed up on Tuesday, the day of our appointment, and called to confirm. This nasal voice said, "Monsieur Fellini is not here. I am Carmen. He will be here tomorrow. He will certainly be able to see you tomorrow." It was him, of course, imitating the maid with a Spanish accent. The next day, we went to lunch at Cesarina's, one of his favourite bistros, where I just listened. He was wonderfully eloquent and funny. I saw him several times at Cinecittà, especially during the shooting of *And the Ship Sails On…* He was always drawing. He gave me one – very colourful, which I framed, depicting a young crown prince on a boat. He had this amazing free spirit, and yet was very simple, not at all pretentious.

Like Buñuel, he didn't like analysing or explaining his work.

No. But Buñuel really was the champion of avoiding interviews, with the exception of his extraordinary book, written with Jean-Claude Carrière, *My Last Breath*, which is very revealing. Fellini, on the other hand, could say a lot, but always in a roundabout way. It was like those appointments that always had to be delayed or rearranged. You would eventually get something out of him, but never if you asked him straight questions. His films were divisive. Take *Casanova*, for example – a gloomy, funereal, but still quite brilliant film. A lot of people didn't get what Fellini was doing to the myth of that character. He called Casanova a *stronzo* – an idiot. He couldn't stand him. That film was a commission, and Fellini bragged about having done almost nothing but commissions his whole life. That's an exaggeration, because he was also a screenwriter, the real brain behind *La Strada* and most of his films. I remember meeting to discuss another film, *Orchestra Rehearsal*, which I think is one of the best ever on totalitarianism. It's a metaphor for fascism, the will to power and control. He really admired Kubrick, even though they were very different. And Bergman too. They were kind of a trio of artists who greatly admired each other. What united them was a love of spectacle, imagination and childhood. This idea of childhood is so important. Many great creative minds, especially imaginative filmmakers like Tim Burton, Resnais and Fellini, have a childlike spirit about them. A child is fearless, doesn't overthink, and dives into the world because life hasn't yet taught them to be cautious, to avoid risks, to look before they leap. Initially, a child believes they can do anything, that everything is within reach. The great creators who impress me, the bold ones, who take risks, often have a sort of childlike nature to them.

Cassavetes, Scorsese, Malick

For the American filmmakers in Petite Planète cinématographique *you selected Cassavetes, Scorsese and Terrence Malick, who gave very few interviews.*

There was an embarrassment of riches when it came to Americans. I've met dozens of them, and recently published a collection of thirty interviews, dating from 1965 to 1970: *Une renaissance américaine*. For Petite planète, I chose Cassavetes, because he was one of the first to really shake up American cinema. He wasn't just some outsider – he was of crucial importance. The interview with Scorsese was the one I did with Michael Wilson, who has since become a leading expert on him. We met just after *Mean Streets*, when he wasn't on many people's radars. Today, it's impossible to even speak to him directly, but back then we spent three hours with him. I could have just as easily chosen Altman, Coppola, Woody Allen or Cimino for the book.

As for Terrence Malick, in addition to the deep admiration I have for him, it's fascinating just how few interviews he ever gave. I had been invited to a festival in Los Angeles in 1974 and asked Warner Bros. who this man was, as I had just seen *Badlands*, which I thought was thrilling. They gave me his phone number – which would be unthinkable today, and I called him to request an interview. He asked, "What's your name?" "Michel Ciment." "Are you the one who wrote *Kazan by Kazan*? I'd really like to meet you."

He agreed to meet because he wanted to meet me. Talk about role reversal! He told me he had written all over his copy of my book and that he reread it regularly, because for him, Kazan was the ultimate cinematic reference point. When you watch *Badlands*, there are references to George Stevens' *Giant*, but especially to Kazan's *East of Eden*. The police who arrest Martin Sheen's character even say he looks like James Dean. Even though Kazan is more materialistic in his approach, and Malick is certainly a visual poet, what must have also fascinated Malick about Kazan's cinema – and what fascinated me when I saw *East of Eden* at the age of seventeen – is its lyrical portrait of nature, filmed in Cinemascope, a style that broke with more realistic American cinema of the late 1950s – that of newcomers from television, like Sidney Lumet and John Frankenheimer – and also the glamorous studio cinema of Minnelli. Malick gave me an interview, one of only three ever published in forty years! He did another with a friend of his, Beverly Walker, an American journalist who published a much shorter interview than mine in *Sight and Sound*. And later, just one other: a sidebar in *Le Monde* about *Days of Heaven*, with Yvonne Baby, who knew Malick personally, through her husband and his family.

Leonard Kastle

Among American filmmakers we haven't talked about yet, Leonard Kastle stands out for making a mark in film history with just one film.

I met Kastle on his return from Pesaro, where *The Honeymoon Killers* had been shown. It was in 1971, at the height of anti-American sentiment. Since May '68, with Maoism and the Vietnam War, everyone was lining up to paint the Americans as the ultimate evil. Poor Kastle – it really wasn't his fault. He made his film, *The Honeymoon Killers*, on a shoestring budget. It was based on the real-life story of a crazily malevolent couple. The man, kind of slick-looking, had an obese partner, and together they would answer personal ads from women looking for fiancés. He would bring along this woman who pretended she was his sister, which made the victims less wary. Then they would slash their throats and get off on all the blood, and make love in a frenzy. The film was in black and white, with music by Mahler. The cinematography was raw, gritty, almost documentary-style, combined with this romantic music, which was really very striking. The film was actually begun by a young Scorsese at the very beginning, who at the time had made only one film. Kastle, who lived with a television producer named Warren Steibel, was a musician, musicologist and conductor who composed operas and wrote the screenplay. As they had very little money, Steibel entrusted the script to Scorsese, who was just starting to make a name for himself, but within a week Steibel was upset that Scorsese wasn't sticking to the script and that Leonard's vision was being betrayed, at which point Scorsese backed away, saying, "Let Leonard do it himself." And so Leonard Kastle, who had zero filmmaking experience, ending up directing the film himself – and the result is extraordinary. They took the film to the leftist stronghold of Pesaro, to the Mostra Internazionale del Nuovo Cinema, which is similar to Directors' Fortnight or Critics' Week in Cannes. At the end of the screening, the journalists stood up, confused, not knowing what to think. This obviously wasn't a Hollywood film, but at the same time, it was American. At that moment, Marguerite Duras, who was there, took the microphone and said: "The film is a masterpiece! It's attack on American values. It's a film of pure revolution!" And suddenly, the fifty people who were about to leave the room rush back in and ask Kastle for interviews, convinced – thanks to the high priestess of the avant-garde that was Duras – of the quality of the film! That's how Duras saved *The Honeymoon Killers*.

So you met him when he came back from Pesaro?

I invited him to dinner, and he came with Warren Steibel. My wife had made black sausage and white sausage, with apples and potatoes. During the conversation, we mentioned that the black sausage was made from coagulated blood, and the man who had terrified the world fainted. In every cinema where the film was screened, people were sick because the murders were so gruesome. We had to lay him down on the bed and fan him to revive him. The mere thought of blood in the black sausage terrified him.

Robert Altman

Altman is another one of those great directors you knew for many years.

The first Altman film I saw – *M*A*S*H* – was at Cannes, and I admit I wasn't impressed. I love comedy, but this one didn't make me laugh much. I just didn't get it. At festivals you develop a passion for a filmmaker, and feel frustrated when their work isn't recognised. At Cannes in 1970, I had boundless admiration for John Boorman's *Leo the Last*, which struck me as extraordinarily audacious, and I still prefer it to *M*A*S*H*. Even though it won the best director award that year, it was a real disappointment that Boorman didn't win the Palme d'Or. To me, it was unquestionably superior to *M*A*S*H*, which did win the Palme, and which I may have been too tough on. But starting in 1971, Altman won me over in quick succession, first with *Brewster McCloud*, then the Western *McCabe & Mrs Miller* and *The Long Goodbye*, with Elliott Gould, a completely fresh take on 1940s detective stories. There followed *Thieves Like Us*, not so well known but a really wonderful, more traditional film about the Great Depression, and the wondrously free-form *California Split*, with George Segal and Elliott Gould as a pair of gamblers. It was absolutely dazzling. And then, at the apex: *Nashville*, an ensemble film with twenty-four characters, a blend of music, sex and politics, a fantastic snapshot of American society. Even though I had a lot of admiration for Scorsese, Coppola, Schatzberg and others, at that time I considered Altman the great innovator of American cinema who was completely reshaping its boundaries. He was like a virtuoso – very prolific, making two films a year, each in a different genre, with his ensemble of actors reminiscent of Bergman's troupe, especially Shelley Duvall, who was born to play Olive Oyl in his *Popeye*. She also starred in the extraordinary *3 Women* with Sissy Spacek. And I liked Altman a lot as a person. He was a kind of buccaneer. He looked like Porthos from *The Three Musketeers* or Blackbeard the pirate. He was robust, he was a drinker, he smoked joints. On the set of *Short Cuts*, which I reported from, he had this phenomenal ability to take a half-hour nap and then jump back into action. I also attended a screening of rushes with the entire team. He embodied what Benayoun called the "fertile chaos of Robert Altman."

His career was quite chaotic.

He could create things out of disorder, and had an extraordinary ability to bounce back. At a certain point he basically disappeared. He came to Europe in the 1980s and made some films for television based on plays, and things like *Streamers*, work that barely saw the light of day and was released in very few cinemas and in very few countries. Paradoxically, it was thanks to his scathing, brilliant takedown of Hollywood, *The Player*, in 1992, that started everything up again for him. He was once again embraced by the industry that he had made such fun of, and after *Short Cuts* stayed in the spotlight until *Gosford Park*, one of his last films, which he shot in England. An amazing career. What was also interesting is that the deep-seated resentment he held towards American society and what it was becoming stemmed from a profound love of the country. He was from Kansas, and had been a dog tattooist, a traveling salesman and a horse-riding instructor. At one point or another, he did every job under the sun. He travelled far and wide, worked in television, and even made a documentary about James Dean. And he had this unbelievable stroke of luck, being the thirty-second person to be offered the script for *M*A*S*H*. Everyone had passed on it, but it ended up making him a commercial and critical sensation. What I admire about Altman is this dialectic, this tension that drives him. On the one hand, you can tell he has a deep love of country music, detective stories and pop culture. At the same time, he saw through all the conventionality and wasn't afraid to poke fun at it. His knack for ironic detachment came from a deep understanding of American culture, from the heartland. He was also a cinephile and adored European films – Bergman, Fellini. He was a bit like John Huston, who was a big Altman fan.

Clint Eastwood

You've met Eastwood several times.

I've followed his career closely. I liked some of the films he acted in, like *The Beguiled*, which was directed by his mentor, Don Siegel. When he visited Paris in 1971, I had the chance to meet him and found him extremely likable. In the early days, Eastwood alternated between personal films like *Breezy*, *Bronco Billy* and *Honkytonk Man*, none of which, by the way, did well at the box-office but revealed a somewhat hidden side of the man. The series he did – the very popular *Dirty Harry* action films – regardless of the brilliance of Siegel and others, didn't sit well with me because I found the philosophy of taking the law into one's own hands questionable. They were anti-establishment, but I didn't like the whole "law of the jungle" bit.

A series that he later took over as director.

He has certainly matured. And one of Eastwood's later films, *Gran Torino*, about a dying man who lives next door to a Vietnamese family, in which he explores the limitations of his tough guy persona, struck a chord with me. The character opens himself up to a different culture, and ends up protecting his neighbours from a street gang. We've been witness to the evolution and development of a director who has become one of the great American filmmakers: *Bird, Mystic River, Unforgiven* and the extraordinary diptych of *Flags of Our Fathers* and *Letters from Iwo Jima*, which is a unique undertaking, one film from the American point of view, another from the Japanese. I remember in New York there was a party at Mary Lea Bandy's place. She was the director of the film department of the Museum of Modern Art. Eastwood had slipped away from a Warner Bros. party to be there. He preferred the company of friends and film lovers and writers and critics like me, and other filmmakers, to studio big shots.

Did he feel that it was in Europe, in particular France, where he had been recognised as an important filmmaker?

Unquestionably. He said it publicly, and showed a certain independence of spirit when receiving the Oscar for *Unforgiven*. In front of an audience of Americans, he first thanked French critics, saying that they were the ones who first noticed him. And he had a strong bond with Pierre Rissient, who really put him on the map with French critics. I did a long interview with Eastwood about *White Hunter, Black Heart*, which was inspired by Peter Viertel's book about the making of John Huston's *The African Queen*. He was extraordinary in the role of Huston. I knew Huston pretty well, and I could really hear his voice – the intonations, the sarcasm, the swagger – in Eastwood's performance. It's one of the best films about filmmaking that exists. Cinema seen from the inside. Eastwood is an extremely important filmmaker and, at the same time, relatively marginal. When you look at the generational turnover in American cinema, directors usually last fifteen or twenty years, then fade away. But Eastwood has been directing for almost forty-five years, just like Woody Allen, who started in 1969. Eastwood started in 1971. And they're still going strong today, full of energy. They have never fallen into a routine, and continue to make wonderful films. Apart from them, in the United States, there are Scorsese and Terrence Malick, who took such a long break – twenty years – so he likely has great physical and intellectual reserves. But very few others. That great generation of the 1970s is by now almost a Lost Generation.

Eastwood's political beliefs might have been a problem for French critics.

I can understand why the *Dirty Harry* films attracted so much attention, but what really disappointed me was when Eastwood publicly criticised Obama and put his weight behind Bush father and son. At the same time, what strikes me in America is that people tend to get labelled. No right-wing French filmmaker would ever make something like *The Grapes of Wrath* or *How Green Was My Valley*. John Ford, who directed those two films, was very conservative – but that didn't stop him from eventually becoming a staunch advocate for Native American rights. He knew them, he worked with them. He made socially significant films about farmers and coal miners. His cinema is more complex than it appears. In France, it's hard to imagine a reactionary filmmaker adapting a novel like *Germinal*. I remember meeting William Wellman in Paris because he liked a feature that *Positif* had published about him. He was going to vote for McGovern, the Democrat, even though he was decidedly right-wing and famously conservative, simply because he didn't like Nixon's face! The Democrat seemed much more likable to him. It would be unimaginable for someone in France to vote for a left-wing candidate when they have long-held right-wing opinions. That's what sets us apart from Americans, who are more individualistic than ideological.

Polanski, Bertolucci and questions of modernity

Among the many filmmakers you have come into contact with is Roman Polanski.

I met him very early on, for *Positif*, at the beginning of the 1960s. Then Roger Tailleur and I interviewed him about *Rosemary's Baby*. He was on rue des Beaux-Arts with Sharon Tate, whose leg was in plaster, and we talked a lot about the film. He asked us a question about *2001: A Space Odyssey*, which had just been released and which he really liked: "Which is the longer film, *Rosemary's Baby* or *2001*?" We both replied, "*2001*," probably because it's a slow-paced and contemplative film. But *Rosemary's Baby* is actually a few minutes longer! It just goes to show how subjective our perception of a film can be and how it has nothing to do with its actual running time.

Polanski's career is unique.

We've already talked about the durability of French filmmakers, which might be unique. France is a country where filmmakers who started in the 1950s are still working, which hasn't happened much elsewhere. Polanski is connected to French cinema, even though he made films in Poland, then England, the United States, and finally France. He's had a very long career, from his short films in the 1950s to *Venus in Fur* at Cannes in 2013. Polanski was initially misunderstood because he began making films during the period of New Wave and was considered a part of that movement, but it didn't take us long to realise he was a much more classical filmmaker. He spoke of being influenced by *Citizen Kane* and films like Carol Reed's *Odd Man Out* and Olivier's *Hamlet*, and was inspired by quality English cinema that, according to Truffaut, doesn't exist. This classicism became more pronounced in his work, especially when you compare *Chinatown* to other American films of the era by directors like Altman, Scorsese or Malick. But at the same time, Polanski brought a fresh personal touch to his genre filmmaking, which is why Kubrick admired him – and the feeling was mutual.

His films Cul-de-sac *or* Repulsion *are very distinctive.*

What's interesting is seeing the evolution of the great creators of new forms, the filmmakers who truly disrupt the language of cinema. Welles, for example, more or less settles down in his later work, like *The Immortal Story* or even *Chimes at Midnight*. You could say the same for Resnais, who after having run up against traditional forms in his early films, then embraces classicism. Eisenstein too. After *Battleship Potemkin* and *October*, *Ivan the Terrible* has a more linear narrative and a more classical editing style. When they were young, they were all about breaking with rules, but all these great filmmakers, without diminishing their talents – they continued to do excellent work – gravitated toward classicism. Maybe classicism, not academism, is a guarantee of longevity. So many so-called modern works have aged and lost their allure. I watched a film recently – Bertolucci's *Before the Revolution* – which I no longer consider one of his major films, except for the last half hour. I prefer *The Spider's Stratagem* or *The Conformist*, which have a more classical feel and have definitely stood the test of time. A film like *Partner* always felt like a dead end to me. Bertolucci turned his back on his roots by suppressing his Viscontian side because the new cinema of the moment was all about radical ruptures *à la* Godard. Roger Tailleur and I saw *Partner* in Venice in 1968 and expressed our disappointment to Bertolucci. He was upset because he thought he had finally made a "modern" film. It was the same when I told Glauber Rocha that I didn't like the films he made in Europe and that he should reconnect with his Brazilian roots, the complete abandonment of which, when he arrived here, gradually pushed him into cerebral, self-indulgent cinema. I very much believe in Cocteau's line: "Un artiste chante le mieux dans son arbre généalogique." ["An artist sings best in his family tree."] I believe in roots. The New Wave killed off anyone they didn't recognise as a forefather – something I scold them for, as there was a great deal to admire in Autant-Lara, Clouzot, Clément and René Clair – and found mentors in Bresson, Tati, Ophüls, Renoir and Becker.

Godard, on the other hand, never found that "classical" tranquillity.

When it comes to careers of that length, he's really an exception – someone who never wanted to reconstruct, having destroyed everything. He kept on deconstructing the form, following a narrow path, losing his audience along the way, as if he was stuck in an eternal state of adolescence. Welles, aged twenty-five, arrives in Hollywood and exclaims that making a film is like playing with a big train set. Godard, on the contrary – as any child would – insists on breaking and trampling the toy. I mentioned that many creative people, especially visionaries, have retained something of a childlike spirit, but Godard is more of an adolescent. Adolescence is an extremely challenging period in life, a time of self-discovery, when one no longer possesses the innocence of a child but hasn't yet attained the maturity of an adult. Adolescents are arrogant. They feel as if they're up against the whole world and think they're right about everything. Eventually they grow up and gain a deeper understanding of life. Godard is an eternal teenager. "I don't seek, I find," said Picasso. Godard has always remained in the "I seek" mode, even if it means not finding. After the Cubist revolution, in the 1920s, a period that has been nicknamed "Retour à l'ordre" ["Return to order"] – to mythology, to the figurative work that he helped deconstruct – Picasso, by creating a series of canvases, was able to return to a more classical form.

Foreigners of French cinema

There is a French tradition that welcomes and even adopts filmmakers from other countries.

What was great about the French film industry, and what hasn't been emphasised enough, is that in a very different way from Hollywood in the 1930s, it assimilated a tremendous amount of foreign talent. In Hollywood, everyone was arriving from Europe. Refugees flooded into studios. Zukor, the boss at Paramount, who was Hungarian by origin, tried to discourage his compatriots: "You're Hungarian, but that doesn't necessarily mean you have talent!" In France, it happened in a more anarchic, wild and unique way, but from the very beginning there have always been a large number of immigrant filmmakers. In the 1920s there were the White Russians from the Albatros film studio, and the following decade the Germans arrived. In my own lifetime I've seen many foreign filmmakers come to France, including Raúl Ruiz, Otar Iosseliani and Robert Kramer, a great American who I backed for Critics' Week. His films *The Edge*, *Milestones* and *Ice*, about a clandestine revolutionary cell, had an extraordinary formal rigor. After Buñuel, there were the French films of Scola and Ferreri. And then the Poles: Wajda, who came to shoot *Danton* in France, Zulawski's *That Most Important Thing: Love*, and especially Krzysztof Kieślowski. His *Decalogue*, shot in Poland, is one of the great masterpieces of film. He came here to make *The Double Life of Véronique*, which is half in Polish and half in French, and then the *Three Colours* trilogy, which was produced by Marin Karmitz. France has been a hub, not just a country that has influenced world cinema. Of course, we shouldn't get all jingoistic about it. As Billy Wilder said, "Confucius wrote very interesting things without seeing Paris." But it's certainly true that many filmmakers of all backgrounds have found France to be a congenial place to work. One of the most recent examples is Asghar Farhadi's film *The Past*, produced by Memento Films after the triumph of *A Separation*.

The French co-production financing system and distribution support encourages exchanges with foreign filmmakers.

It also fosters the cinephilia I mentioned within the film community, which means that at Cannes, for example, out of the twenty films in competition, if there are four French films, there are eight others that are French co-productions directed by foreign directors. Without French financing, Mike Leigh wouldn't have made *Secrets & Lies* and David Lynch wouldn't have made *Mulholland Drive*.

Raúl Ruiz

The prolific Raúl Ruiz is an eccentric French filmmaker.

I've known him since the early 1970s, and he became a close friend. He advised Salvador Allende about cinema, and after Allende's fall took refuge in France, where he alienated other Chilean expatriates because he made *Dialogues of Exiles*, which didn't sit well with that community. Ruiz was his own man, never one to follow the crowd, deeply resistant to any regimentation. What's striking about him is his relationship to Surrealism, and to authors like Borges. If my conversations with Mankiewicz impressed me because of his brilliance and well-structured arguments, Ruiz's stood out because of the abundance of quotations and the richness of his references. As a filmmaker, he was both materialistic and profoundly influenced by the church. He loved the apocryphal gospels, those stories where Christ kills a classmate, his mother Mary comes to see the schoolmistress, and Jesus resurrects the friend he had slain. Ruiz loved these texts, and told me about them long before they were published in the Pléiade.*

He was a philosopher.

He was like an expanded, more out-there version of Peter Greenaway, coupled with an irresistible sense of humour and a love of tricks and jokes. We often dined together, either at my place or his, whenever he wasn't shooting. He sometimes made six films a year, and ended up directing more

---

* A collection of classical French literature published by Éditions Gallimard.

than a hundred films. He was very loyal and dependable. He wouldn't forget you. I was actually indirectly responsible for one of his films. One time we arranged to meet at La Hune bookstore before lunch, but he mixed up the dates and showed up a week early. While he was browsing, he found a copy of Klossowski's *The Suspended Vocation* and decided there and then to adapt it. Like Buñuel, he'd had a thorough Catholic education.

This is one paradox of the Surrealists.

Yes, but Buñuel and Ruiz took it further than most. You can really feel the theological influence in their work, even if they were just subverting it and playing around.

Otar Iosseliani

You mentioned Iosseliani, the great Georgian filmmaker.

I really like him. He managed to make films in France, like *Favourites of the Moon* and *Hunting Butterflies,* that are still so thoroughly Georgian. I first met him in Tbilisi, where he showed me around. He's nostalgic for Georgia, which suffered under the Soviets and then under various more or less authoritarian regimes. The thing with Otar is that he's quite a drinker. I had a similar experience with Losey when we did our interview book. When we arrived in Tbilisi, the table was already set with prepared dishes and six bottles of wine for four people. Then came the aperitifs and liqueurs. I couldn't handle it! I obviously got teased for being a wimp: "You're not a real man if you don't drink." My only defence was to carry some strong cigars, as big as chair legs, and offer them to my hosts. I used them like you would garlic against a vampire. There was a look of horror when they saw these cigars that were too smelly and intense for them, and they quit trying to make me drink like them, since they couldn't handle my cigars. Georgians have this belief that their homeland is like Arcadia, a paradise on Earth, and they even think that the paradise described in the Bible is actually their country. We would go through Georgia on our way to Armenia and toast Georgian women as the most beautiful in the world. Then, in Armenia, they would ask, "Aren't our women more beautiful than the Georgians?" The eternal rivalry…

Could you define the Georgian spirit of Iosseliani's French films?

It's a kind of nonchalance, humour and playful mockery, blended with a celebration of life and an ode to laziness…

Nikos Papatakis

Among your favourite "French foreigners" is long-time expatriate Nikos Papatakis.

A fascinating character I knew well, and who made only five films. He was a man of absolute integrity who cherished solitude and lived quite a monastic life, but he would respond to invitations. If you asked to see him, he was very happy, but he would never pick up the phone himself. He almost shut himself off. He wrote captivating memoirs, but they stopped at the point where he became famous, so he left out what would have interested his readers the most. Born to a Greek father and an Ethiopian mother, he was mixed-race and very handsome. When he was married to Anouk Aimée, it was said they were the most beautiful couple in Paris. And they both aged sublimely. He fought in the Ethiopian war against Mussolini before taking refuge in the south of France during the Occupation, where he met Prévert and his group, including Trauner, the production designer. After the war, he returned to Paris and created La Rose Rouge, the famous cabaret in Saint-Germain-des-Prés, where Juliette Gréco and Piccoli hung out. He participated in the Algerian War on the side of the FLN, then went to New York, where he was involved in the production of Cassavetes' *Shadows*. His fascinating first film *Les Abysses* is based on the story of the Papin sisters, which was also the starting point of *The Maids*, the play by Jean Genet – who was a friend of his. Genet was known for treating his friends badly, and they had a complicated relationship. In his final film, *Walking a Tightrope*, Papatakis told the story of how Genet convinced his young Arab lover to become a tightrope walker, which ultimately killed him because of the risky stunts Genet asked him to perform. In Greece he directed *The Shepherds of Calamity* and part of *The Photo*, one of the most beautiful films ever made about the emotions of exile and the weaving together of dreams and fantasies. France has turned out these kinds of unique and unclassifiable films like no other country.

Serge Gainsbourg

Sticking with eccentrics, tell us about the famous, underrated Serge Gainsbourg.

Gainsbourg is unique. Everyone adored him as a singer, but when it came to the films he directed – like *Je t'aime moi non plus*, *Équateur*, *Charlotte for Ever*, with his daughter, and *Stan the Flasher*, with Claude Berri – the critics didn't give him much love. *Équateur* was especially badly received at Cannes, although at *Positif* we really liked his films, the last two in particular, and wanted to meet him to talk about *Charlotte for Ever*. Jean-Pierre Jeancolas and I went to see him on rue de Verneuil, just opposite Le Terrain Vague, which used to publish *Positif*. The bookstore was open and Éric Losfeld, the boss of Le Terrain Vague, who published the Surrealists, was still working there. We arrived at Gainsbourg's at 10am and were still there at 5pm, although we did take a lunch break, which we spent with him in an excellent nearby restaurant. That kind of welcome and extended time with someone happens once in a lifetime. He was genuinely moved by our interest. The two long interviews we published with him aren't even mentioned in the Gainsbourg biographies. His film work is so under the radar that no one bothered to research the film journals. Those conversations were absolutely riveting. Gainsbourg was incredibly candid. He never said the name "Doillon," the director Jane Birkin left him for. He just called him "the director." After our meal, he even escorted us to Losfeld's place and bought some Tristan Tzara books for us. Later, with Philippe Rouyer, I went back to talk about *Stan the Flasher*. Gainsbourg was an emotional person. He was hypersensitive, a trait you often find in artists who come off as aggressive, provocative and polemical. Beneath that exterior, he had real depth. He didn't make films like some writers do because they want to walk the red carpet at Cannes. It was genuine passion for cinema that drove him. If his films had struck a chord with the audience, he could have had a full-fledged career as a filmmaker. He didn't quite win everyone over, maybe because his films were too eccentric and unconventional.

Australian cinema in the eyes of the critics

You're a big fan of Rolf de Heer, a unique Australian filmmaker.

Rolf de Heer's *Bad Boy Bubby*, which was shown at Venice in 1993, tells the story of a character who has been cut off from the outside world by his mother since birth and is virtually imprisoned in a basement. At the age of seventeen or eighteen, he finds himself outside, meets several people, and begins his journey of self-discovery. It's a very singular film, with shades of Voltaire's *Candide*. De Heer continued to make amazing films for twenty or twenty-five years, including *The Quiet Room*, another intense story about a little girl who would rather hide behind mutism than deal with her parents' constant fighting. *Dance Me to My Song*, a portrait of a physically disabled woman with cerebral palsy, is a reflection on human communication, and *Ten Canoes* is a remarkable film about an Aboriginal tribe. De Heer never really managed to establish himself, and critics never fully embraced his uniqueness. Two of his best films, *The Tracker*, a sort of Western set in the Australian desert reminiscent of the revered Monte Hellman, and *Alexandra's Project*, about a husband confronted with a recording of his wife's revenge, were never released in France. It's the kind of Australian cinema that has never caught on in France with the critics, perhaps because people from down under are even more British than the British. Even someone like New Zealander Jane Campion, from her debut feature *Sweetie*, had people scratching their heads. It was attacked and defended, applauded and whistled at Cannes. And think of George Miller, whose filmmaking is a lot more mainstream and action-oriented, but whose *Mad Max* was still very divisive. Peter Weir too. Some of the films were appreciated, but I don't know why Australian cinema never found its footing in France, whereas Argentinian or Iranian cinema quickly resonated. Such are the mysteries of criticism.

The evolution of French cinema (1): Sustainability

I would like to discuss the evolution of French cinema over the past twenty years.

First of all, French cinema has just as much energy as it ever did – and I include here work done during the Occupation, when many significant films were produced and filmmakers like Becker, Clouzot and Bresson began their careers. In *Histoire(s) du cinéma*, Godard criticises French filmmakers for working during that time, and for not standing up to the Nazis or joining the Resistance. But when films are being made in 35mm and the country is under the control of an occupying army, it's hard to expect French filmmakers to have had the suicidal bravery to criticise the Germans in their films. Godard compared French cinema with Rossellini's work, like *Rome Open City*, but it's well known that Rossellini was a member of the Fascist party and made three propaganda films – *A Pilot Returns*, *The Man With a Cross* and *The White Ship* – during the Mussolini era. He filmed *Rome Open City* only after American troops had landed in Sicily, when it was safe, even beneficial, to talk about resistance. So it seems a bit unfair to bash French filmmakers who, all things considered, managed quite well under the Occupation. There is hardly any anti-Semitism in films from that era, unlike the French cinema from before the war. An exception might be Henri Decoin's *Strangers in the House*, where Mouloudji's character is a bit shady. He's portrayed as an Arab, so we can't be sure. But that's a rare case. There were no Anglophobic films either, even though England was an enemy of Pétain and Germany.

French cinema has never really experienced a downturn.

Which has led to something quite unique: the sustained careers of great auteurs in France. There is nowhere else in the world where so many filmmakers have continued to make work for fifty or sixty years. Resnais started back in 1946 and was still at it in 2014. Varda kicked off with *La Pointe Court* in 1955 and she's still going strong. Cavalier, at over eighty, is still very active. Marker, who only passed away recently, had been going since the early 1950s. And Godard, also in his eighties, keeps on going. He's Swiss, but obviously has played a big role in French cinema. It's amazing to me, because most big-name American directors retire early. Very few work past their seventies. Directors still alive from the 1960s New Waves that appeared alongside the French one – from Japan, Quebec, Switzerland, Brazil, Poland, the former Yugoslavs, the Hungarians and Swedes – are almost all no longer working. They don't have the same kind of support system we have in France: a genuinely film-loving culture that generates audiences, public authorities who pay attention, producers who – regardless of what some might say – are also interested in audiences. And then there's the loyal public. That's something really special. There's nothing quite like it.

The evolution of French cinema (2): Recent trends

Several generations coexist side by side in French cinema.

It's always been lively, including in the 1970s when filmmakers like Alain Corneau, Claude Miller and Bertrand Tavernier emerged post-New Wave. Several new names also appeared in the 1980s and 90s, and something quite unique to French cinema is the emergence of many female directors, as well as some highly talented female cinematographers like Agnès Godard, Caroline Champetier, Hélène Louvart and Jeanne Lapoirie.

First among them was Nuith Aviv.

Yes, the Israeli who notably collaborated with Agnès Varda at a time when the profession was still considered almost exclusively male. Women were confined to roles as actresses, editors or script supervisors. There finally came a moment when as many excellent debut films were being made by women as by men – which unfortunately is no longer the case today. We saw the emergence of talents like Noémie Lvovsky, Laetitia Masson, Diane Bertrand, Dominique Cabrera, Brigitte Roüan, Valeria Bruni Tedeschi, Pascale Ferran and others. Some of them were friends of Arnaud Desplechin and Cédric Kahn, two very important filmmakers. We should also mention Olivier Assayas, Jacques Audiard, Bruno Dumont and François Ozon. Dumont might be even more fêted abroad than in France. What also strikes me is that none of these filmmakers define themselves in relation to previous generations. They never constituted a "movement," but instead were individual talents who managed to establish themselves and sometimes achieve real commercial success. Moreover, the New Wave itself was an extremely diverse movement. What fundamental connection is there between Chabrol and Godard? Or even between Truffaut and Rohmer? They were also very different individuals – not to mention Varda, Cavalier, Resnais and Demy.

The evolution of French cinema (3): Critics

How would you describe the critics' attitudes towards French filmmakers?

The attitude of the press towards French cinema is swinging between constant praise for many directors and, at the same time, a general negative verdict, even though there's no real reason to bash French cinema as a whole. People say there are too many films. But perhaps it's because there are so many films that we see many good ones. How can we accurately predict the degree of a film's success? André Malraux, while creating the *avance sur recettes* system that has decisively contributed to auteur cinema since the early 1960s and allocated subsidies based on scripts, once said in the National Assembly: "Si on pouvait imaginer *Le Cuirassé Potemkine* en lisant le scénario, on serait Eisenstein." ["If you could imagine *Battleship Potemkin* just by reading the script, you'd be Eisenstein."] I had a rather heated discussion one day with Michel Reilhac, head of fiction at Arte, because they rejected a project by Alain Resnais, an opera by Kurt Weill called *The Tsar Has His Photograph Taken*. Resnais had already begun working with the actors and singers, and the performance was less than an hour. An exciting project, especially for a Franco-German channel, combining one of the greatest musicians of the twentieth century with one of its greatest filmmakers. Reilhac said something like, "We didn't back it because we couldn't see what it would become." I reminded him of that phrase: "If you had known what it would become, you'd be Alain Resnais."

The evolution of French cinema (4): Middle-ground films

There is a lot of controversy these days about the mediocrity of some big-budget French films, while certain interesting filmmakers struggle to get their projects off the ground. Financing, television and a certain inertia among investors are often blamed.

Television has been both a saviour and a kiss of death for cinema. Television doesn't have the same aims as cinema. When

Anatole Dauman produced Resnais' early films, he wasn't concerned about ratings. He knew he was producing films in a highly professional manner because Resnais surrounded himself with the best collaborators. Dauman knew that with an audience of a few hundred thousand viewers, he would make money. Sometimes he missed the mark, as was the case with *Muriel*. But he found success with *Hiroshima mon amour* and Bresson's *Mouchette,* both of which he also produced. When television channels start to say they will only co-finance a film if it can be shown in prime time, a kind of censorship sets in. It's not ideological, as in the old Soviet Union – where, actually, they made quite daring films, as long as they didn't directly threaten the regime. For television, what matters is quantity: how many viewers are watching. Cautious television has, in a way, led to homogenised cinema. Producer Vincent Maraval recently raised concerns about the exorbitant salaries of certain bankable actors, whose names can easily attract financing because they are said to guarantee box-office success. But, of course, that's not always the case, because there are films designed to appeal to everyone that flop and, conversely, some low-budget films that hit the million-admissions mark. I wasn't a big fan of *Declaration of War*, but it was still a big success in cinemas. So it gets complicated.

Cinema isn't reducible to formulas, because no one really knows anything. If we could predict what will work, it would all be quite straightforward. Cinema doesn't work that way – which is a good thing. It's because we can't come up with foolproof formulas for success that producers and filmmakers are willing to take risks. What's unfortunate is that some of the big players like Gaumont, Pathé and UGC, who also own cinemas and should, in theory, be able to release more challenging films, too often play it safe, and even though from time to time they do produce quality films, not enough opportunities are given to important filmmakers. This phenomenon is compounded by the influence of the media. Nowadays, the key to promoting a film isn't print media, it's television. The evening news reaches millions of viewers – many more than a newspaper review ever could. But most of the time, television – which is also fixated on ratings – only invites actors from commercially oriented films, the kind of cinema that has no artistic ambition. I'm not knocking them entirely, but there are popular films with certain aspirations and those without. The stars who pull in the ratings get a five-minute slot to talk about their film, while other high-quality films get nothing. All this makes it challenging for what director Pascale Ferran calls "middle-ground films" to survive. It's a nebulous concept. Think of it as the political equivalent of moderate socialism – neither fully conservative nor entirely progressive. Yet historically, these films have been the pride of French cinema, including three-quarters of all César nominations and films competing at Cannes.

Perhaps it's necessary to revisit this concept of "middle-ground" cinema.

They're films with budgets ranging from 4 to 6 million euros, as opposed to the mega-budget films of 20, 30 or 40 million euros, made – as we have discussed – by true French cinema auteurs spanning several generations. The New Wave films of Chabrol and Truffaut had adult storylines and featured well-known actors. They were written by professional scriptwriters and had substantial but not extravagant budgets. The word "middle" refers to the money being spent on films that are certainly not average in their artistry. They're the kind of films that face the toughest hurdles to get made. At the same time, it's the kind of cinema that historically has shaped French film and made its reputation. At the recent Oscars, the French committee picked *The Intouchables* over *Rust and Bone*, thinking that a comedy about racism would win over the Academy voters in Hollywood, even though that's not what they typically expect from French films. For them, French cinema is more like Truffaut's *Jules et Jim*, Tavernier's *Coup de torchon* and Laurent Cantet's *The Class*. Accessible auteur cinema.

THE SEVEN CARDINAL VIRTUES OF THE CRITIC

What you should not do

What advice would you give an aspiring critic?

First and foremost, the temptation to be avoided at all costs – and that can become a critic's vice – is to want a film to be something other than what its author set out to make. In other words, the critic is writing about a different film, the one he wanted to see or make. We should judge a work in relation to its intent, then assess whether or not it's successful. Given its scale, a modest project might be successful, but if it exceeds the filmmaker's resources, it might also be a failure. What should absolutely be avoided is discussing a film that exists nowhere but in the critic's mind. As Billy Wilder said, "You can't blame Johann Strauss for not having composed Beethoven's Seventh Symphony." Someone who writes a polka isn't composing *Twilight of the Gods*. This should be recognised from the start. In short, the critic must look at the film as it is, not as what he wants it to be, or claims it is.

I'm reminded of the work of Clément Rosset, author of *Le Réel et son double* and *Lettre sur les chimpanzés*. His thesis – which resonates with me – is that reality is more real than the ideas we form of it, that reality is resistant to interpretation, to being distorted by lies and misrepresentation. For Rosset, facing reality was the ultimate test, which seems to me an extremely important philosophical lesson – and applicable to film criticism.

You answered the question by first stating what not *to do.*

And now, in no particular order, are the seven qualities that a good film critic must have.

1. Information

First is information, which is to say that the critic must know as much as possible about the film and its director in order to be able to convey details to the reader. How does it fit into the filmmaker's *oeuvre*? Who is the screenwriter? What are his previous credits and what influence has he been able to exert? What was the role of the cinematographer, the production designer, the composer? And, of course, the choice of main actors: have they worked with the director before? What do they represent in the director's imagination? These are things that the critic may already have some knowledge of, and which can be augmented with the help of the Internet. A critic can pull this off because he has studied cinema and has accumulated knowledge for ten, twenty, thirty, forty or fifty years. He owes it to his readers – whether children, secretaries, doctors or lawyers – who have other things to do with their time than study the history of cinema. You might just as well ask a mailman or nurse for their opinion. They might have interesting things to say, but lack the foundational knowledge that, in principle, the critic has. It's regrettable to note the ignorance of some critics and the factual errors that punctuate their writing. I consider such things to be of paramount importance.

2. Analysis

The second quality required of the critic is analytic ability. He must not content himself with saying "I like it" or "I don't like it," or "It's great" or "I lost interest." We couldn't care less about such things, because all this does is let us know if the critic had fun or was bored. It tells us absolutely nothing about the film. A piece of criticism must *analyse* a film – which unfortunately doesn't always happen. This analysis, in my opinion, should not be constructed according to a single framework, which locks the work away in a straitjacket. This way of doing things actually isn't much of a problem these days, and after having prevailed for so long, in such a negative way, the phenomenon has given way to a total absence of analysis. There were, for example, critics who reduced everything to a psychoanalytical interpretation. I reproached the Marxists for dismissing psychoanalysis, just as I did the fanatics of psychoanalysis for dismissing historical, political or sociological factors. There isn't just one way of looking at things. At one time, students revered semiology, Lacan, Marxist-Leninism, because they thought that a single interpretive tool was enough to unlock everything and analyse all films the same way. But not every film should be approached the same way.

We don't talk about *Puzzle of a Downfall Child* the way we do about *Salvatore Giuliano*. For the former, psychoanalysis is certainly a useful tool, and for the latter, knowledge of Sicily, of Italian political life and the Mediterranean mindset is crucial. You can adapt the tools to the film before you. This doesn't mean that for *Puzzle of a Downfall Child* a psychoanalytical interpretation is the *only* one that counts, but it is certainly going to be useful. As for *Salvatore Giuliano*, a socio-economic analysis can be applied, but consider also comparing the story to that of Christ, surrounded by the twelve apostles – as represented by Pisciotta's mob, who accompanied Giuliano. With his mother shrieking over his corpse, the Pietà is replayed in a small Sicilian village. Giuliano died at the age of thirty-three – the same as Christ, eliminated by an occupying power and because of his betrayal by Pisciotta, a Judas figure. We can also see in *Salvatore Giuliano* a metaphor for the war in Algeria, with an occupying contingent arriving from France. Moreover, disdainful Italians spoke of southern Italy as "*Africa a casa*" – "Africa at home." When I saw *Giuliano* in 1962, it struck me quite clearly as a film about the Algerian war, which means that we can discuss it in an economic, mythological and political context all at the same time. Conceptual tools can help with the analysis of a film, but you should never have just one theory to hand. This is why I think that the more the critic knows about culture in general, the more he will be able to deliver up competent and grounded analysis. Cinema – and it does need to be said again and again – is a synthesis of all the arts. It's the *Gesamtkunstwerk*, as Wagner defined opera, twenty years before the birth of cinema.

The "total work of art"?

With Wagner's demise, cinema comes to life, merging dramatic storytelling, visual arts, music and performance. That's why a good critic should have a broad knowledge of the arts. The same goes for great filmmakers. This might be what many young directors lack. The titans of cinema – Fritz Lang, Welles, Eisenstein, Renoir, Kubrick, etc. – knew so much. Visconti, Fellini and Tarkovsky were as familiar with painting as they were with literature. I wish students at La Fémis [France's national film school] would pay regular visits to the Louvre, read as many books as possible, and watch lots of films at the Cinémathèque. And so my second recommendation concerns the theoretical tools and cultural foundations that facilitate analysis. Without them, once again, anyone's opinion is valid – spontaneous and unburdened by the correctives and presuppositions of the critic.

3. Style

Third, criticism is a literary activity. It's a form of writing, even a literary genre. There's a certain beauty to be found in essays about cinema, just as there is in those about literature and painting. One can delight in reading an essay if it's well written, even if it's a minor genre. For example, I consider

Baudelaire's writing on art to be magnificent, but *Les Fleurs du mal* is even more magnificent. Gide's literary reviews are beautiful, but *The Counterfeiters* is even more beautiful. Some people are more essayists than creators.

Without placing the critic on the same level as the artist, criticism is an act of creation. Hence, style becomes a third necessary quality for a good critic. Georges Sadoul and even Jean Mitry never really struck a chord with me, although I appreciated their writing. But when I read Bazin, Truffaut, Rohmer, Benayoun or Tailleur, it was their *style* that really affected me, that made me truly understand the films they were writing about. Here again, the critical essay must in some way recapitulate the qualities of the work under discussion. The great filmmakers are creators who know how to shoot, who understand the texture of images and sounds, and how to direct actors. It's through their style that they get you involved in understanding the film. Similarly, we critics try to convey our thoughts through literary expression and the aesthetic emotion of style.

Of course, no critic possesses all these qualities in equal measure. Some have great analytic skills but are lacking in style. Others seduce us with style, but in the end we realise that they aren't quite as profound as they appear to be.

4. Passion

The fourth quality is passion, enthusiasm, a certain fervour. We readers must sense it in a critic – someone who is driven by a desire to convince, to share, to transmit. Perhaps I'm talking about myself here. In 1963, when I saw all the different kinds of cinema emerging from France and Italy, when I saw a Buñuel film, I told myself that I absolutely had to dive in and say something about it all. It was an extraordinary moment in time, and I was part of it. I was burning to express myself about what I had seen. If not much had been happening, if it had been a moment of quiet, as it was for example in the world of painting, I probably wouldn't have had the energy I did. So: passion and conviction. I think the great critics I've mentioned were similarly inspired. A desire to communicate their enthusiasm was palpable.

5. Curiosity

In my view, a critic shouldn't stick to the narrow field they have marked out for themselves and are very familiar with. They shouldn't be afraid to explore in new directions.

Curiosity must be maintained. Without wanting to disrespect him, I don't think that Truffaut – who had the knowledge, analysis, style and passion – was genuinely curious. He had his preferences and passions, and chose French cinema, Hollywood cinema, and one handpicked filmmaker from each country: Rossellini in Italy, Munk in Poland, Dreyer in Scandinavia. But he never explored much beyond that. He walked out of a screening of *Pather Panchali*, Satyajit Ray's Indian masterpiece, after half an hour, saying it was of no interest. He never ventured beyond the parameters of a relatively limited film culture. He read American and French literature, but I never got the feeling that he knew much about Italian literature. Perhaps he lacked curiosity.

6. A Hierarchy of Judgement

The sixth quality is the recognition of hierarchy, which means being able to say, "This is one of the three or four best films of the year," and to be able to explain why. I think I can say why *Barry Lyndon*, *Salvatore Giuliano*, *Providence*, *Apocalypse Now*, *Stalker* or *Casanova* are superior to most films that appeared the same year. This is an approach that has been frowned upon by some, because for them hierarchy means inequality. It's "undemocratic." Who are you to claim that a Mozart symphony is worth more than someone banging on a tin can? What gives you the right to judge? But that's a false sense of equality, which leads people to declare, "Why not me? I have as much right to the Palme d'Or as you do!" Personally, I'm an Aristotelian. I think that for more than two thousand years, aestheticians, art critics, people who judge artists, have been continuously creating hierarchies. Vasari told us who, in his opinion, were the greatest painters of the Renaissance. Explaining why I find one film is more important than another allows me to refine my understanding of my own tastes, while also shedding light on the work I'm writing about. Simply put, Shakespeare is a greater playwright than Jean de Létraz. This isn't always appreciated today, because everyone has to be given a chance, everything is equal, everything is on the same level. We're told not to be so judgemental.

It's often said that the only true judgement is the test of time. We make mistakes by overestimating or underestimating.

Absolutely. Time will ultimately decide both whether something will endure and if the critical judgement passed on it is still relevant. If I particularly like certain critics, it's because when I reread what they wrote fifty years ago, I see that the films they praised still hold up. It's what every journal does. *Positif* never stops making judgements and assigning grades. It does so every single month. Why feature a certain film on the cover? Why have three or four interviews per issue instead of twenty? To begin with, we don't have room for twenty interviews, so choices have to be made. Life is a constant series of choices. Why does a particular person write for *Positif* and not elsewhere? Because someone else didn't make the cut. We can't publish everyone. Some people refuse to serve on juries because it's impossible to choose one film over another. But that feels insincere. We do it all the time. The issue then becomes how relevant are the choices we make. For a journal or a critic, that's a risk worth taking. We judge a journal or a critic on the entirety of their choices over time. Does *Positif*, sixty years old, hold up? Is an issue published seventeen years ago largely irrelevant? Or do I want to read the whole thing because I'm interested in every one of the films mentioned in it? And have those films themselves remained interesting, and are they still worth watching?

To get back to the antagonisms between *Cahiers* and *Positif*, I think that in more than sixty years, these two journals, between them, haven't missed a single important filmmaker. I challenge anyone to name a director in the history of cinema who wasn't noticed by at least one of us, if not both. Sometimes together, sometimes separately, we have identified every outstanding filmmaker, regardless of what the filmmakers themselves have to say. After all, film directors are extremely touchy and sensitive to criticism, including those who claim never to read what's written about them.

Should we believe them?

It's nonsense. I don't believe it for a second. Every filmmaker reads their reviews. Back in the day when Henri Verneuil was at the peak of his commercial and critical glory, when his films were all over popular media, when he could cast whichever star he wanted and his films were making millions at the box-office – why did he rage on television and get so worked up about *Cahiers du cinéma* and *Positif* disliking them? Because deep down, he knew – despite his tremendous successes – that twenty or thirty years after his death people all over the world would be talking more about Bresson or Buñuel, even though they had a fraction of his financial success. Verneuil could have said, taking his lead from that well-known American catchphrase, "After reading the reviews, I wept all the way to the bank." But that's not how it plays out. They go to the bank *and* want the critics on their side. They dream of both. I can understand why a director whose films get good reviews but are unsuccessful with the public might be bitter and resentful. He can't understand why no one wants to see his work. The truth is that apart from a handful of troubled characters, or those with psychological issues, real artists long for success. Maybe they get used to failure, and even cultivate it, because it means they can position themselves as losers, which allows them to generate a certain cult following. When he made *The Rules of the Game*, Jean Renoir never said that he wanted to make a film that audiences would jeer at. He was convinced he had found a magic formula – a comedy, a drama, a mix of genres, a devilish tragicomedy, which would be a hit. It's generally mediocre people who say they aren't looking to be successful and who do everything they can to ensure that things don't work out for them. Maybe when they've chased after success so many times and come up short, they make failure the engine of their aesthetic, thinking that at least they'll have the critics on their side. If they were suddenly successful, they would no longer be able to use failure as a crutch.

I think, fundamentally, that great artists are upset by commercial failure and a lack of public appreciation. But a lack of critical recognition is just as agonising. Voltaire, for example, considered the greatest playwright of his time, whose tragedies were enormous successes, had every critic on his side, along with a considerable audience. And yet who today ever stages his work? It's important to be humble. There is no guarantee that three hundred years from now, even with the support of *Cahiers* and *Positif*, the filmmakers we have championed for the past sixty years will remain the greatest filmmakers in history.

7. Insight

The seventh quality is what I would call "insight," a specific ability to "see." Max Friedländer writes about this in his book *On Art and Connoisseurship*: "The expert's weapon and possession are less photographs, books, or a dictionary of characteristics, than concepts of visual imagination, gained in pleasurable contemplation and retained by a vigorous visual memory... And one should not underestimate knowledge. He who knows most, sees most. One should not, however, on the other hand over-estimate knowledge. It is of no use to him who cannot see." An art critic with "insight" can determine the identity and value of a painter by observing a mere detail in the canvas. "This isn't a Bronzino, it's a Rosso Fiorentino." That's what [American art historian] Bernard Berenson used to do.

Aren't you just talking about expertise when it comes the history of art?

No. What I'm interested in is applying this idea to the discovery of new talent. The biggest problem for festival directors is debut films. A film student with a minimum knowledge of film culture could curate an outstanding festival selection by including fifteen big names. What's more difficult is to thread in among them three unknowns. When Pierre Rissient was in a darkened room watching an anonymous film, he immediately knew when there was something worth looking at, and that it was the work of someone he should keep an eye on. That's what I call "insight," for a film critic. It could also be the insight of an expert, like someone able to recognise a painter's unique style at a glance. But the most important thing is the discovery of talent, without having any technical details, without the slightest knowledge of the filmmaker's previous work. When I was a member of the selection committee, this was what made La Semaine de la critique [at Cannes] so exciting.

You've listed seven qualities that a good film critic should have. But having four or five of the seven isn't too bad, is it?

Of course. Perhaps the only person I've ever known who possessed all seven cardinal virtues is Roger Tailleur. I'm not saying he was the best critic ever, but he is, in any case, one of the great French critics of the post-war period, and I think he ticked all the boxes that I've been talking about. Just read his anthology which Louis Seguin and I edited, called *Viv(r)e le cinema* [*(Long) Live Cinema*]. A great title, don't you think?

QUEL SPECTATEUR ÊTES-VOUS?
DIDIER PÉRON, *LIBÉRATION*,
29 SEPTEMBER 2012

Your first image?

Errol Flynn in *The Sea Hawk*: momentum, exoticism, adventure, grace, imagination, panache. What attracted me at the age of eight to go see a film was not, of course, the name of the director – in this case the excellent Michael Curtiz – but the star and genre (a pirate film).

The film (or sequence) that traumatised you most as a child?

Cocteau's *Beauty and the Beast*.

The film your parents prevented you from seeing?

I don't recall any restrictions, except for the legal one related to minors.

A cherished scene, or one that haunts you?

Two children being pursued on a river at night by Robert Mitchum in *The Night of the Hunter*. It's the most beautiful expressionistic portrayal of fear in cinema, along with Fritz Lang's *M*. It seems that Stanley Cortez's contribution to Charles Laughton's masterpiece, his only film, far exceeded that of cinematographer.

What film would you remake?

Sleep, by Andy Warhol (a static shot looped for six hours). It's an easy choice, and the comparison could never make me look bad.

The film you have seen the most (on TV or in cinemas).

2001: A Space Odyssey. Incidentally, it was produced by MGM, a company I don't particularly care for. But spaceships are just too irresistible.

The soundtrack stuck in your head?

David Raksin's score for Otto Preminger's *Laura.* Never has film music better evoked the absence of a character.

Who or what makes you laugh?

Peter Sellers in Blake Edwards' *The Party*, and everything Buster Keaton did.

A film in which it would be good to live?

Lubitsch's *Trouble in Paradise*: erotic, astonishing, elegant, moving. That no work by Lubitsch, the king of sophisticated comedy, appears in the list of the hundred best films in the history of cinema according to a recent poll by the English magazine *Sight and Sound*, as voted for by 846 critics and historians, proves the contempt in which comedy is held by the arbiters of taste.

A dream that could be the start of a screenplay?

The arrival of a train at a station. A passenger disembarks. He heads towards the launch platform of a rocket and boards it, bound for the moon.

Your life becomes a biopic. Who plays you? And who is behind the camera?

Gian Maria Volonte, filmed by Francesco Rosi, a master of portraying, among other things, the world of media. Take a look at *The Mattei Affair.*

The ultimate filmmaker?

Alain Resnais.

Which cinematic psychopath do you feel closest to?

Uncle Charlie in Hitchcock's *Shadow of a Doubt*.

The actor or actress you wish you were?

James Mason – after wavering between him and Cary Grant. Paired with some of my favourite directors: Ophüls, Hitchcock, Minnelli, Ray. Unforgettable in *North by Northwest* and the finest spy film ever made, *5 Fingers*, directed by Mankiewicz. Cerebral, vulnerable, refined, and deeply moving.

The last film you saw? With whom? How was it?

Stéphane Brizé's *Quelques heures de printemps*, with my wife. Simplicity and rigor, somewhere between Flaubert and Pialat.

One thing you dislike most about films?

People talking in cinemas. And up on the screen, actors who don't know how to talk.

The cinema disappears. An epitaph?

The End.

Final image?

The mushroom cloud and Vera Lynn singing "We'll Meet Again" at the end of *Dr. Strangelove*. Kubrick's first ingenious use of the contrast between music and image, a hallmark of his cinema.

BIBLIOGRAPHY

Books – French editions

Erich von Stroheim, Anthologie du cinéma, 1967
Kazan par Kazan, Stock, 1973; Ramsay-Poche, 1985
Le Dossier Rosi, Stock, 1976; Ramsay-Poche, 1987
Le Livre de Losey, Stock, 1979; Ramsay-Poche, 1986
Kubrick, Calmann-Lévy, 1980; final edition 1999
Les Conquérants d'un nouveau monde, essais sur le cinéma américain, Gallimard 1981; Folio, 2015
Schatzberg, de la photo au cinéma, Le Chêne – Hachette, 1982
John Boorman, un visionnaire en son temps, Calmann-Lévy, 1985; Marest, 2019
Dictionnaire du cinéma (co-edited with Jean-Loup Passek, Claude Michel Cluny and Jean-Pierre Frouard), Larousse, 1986
Elia Kazan, une odyssée américaine, Calmann-Lévy, 1987
Passeport pour Hollywood, entretiens avec Wilder, Huston, Mankiewicz, Polanski, Forman, Wenders, Le Seuil, 1987; Carlotta, 2022
Theo Angelopoulos (with Hélène Tierchant) Edilig, 1989
Le Crime à l'écran, une histoire de l'Amérique, Découvertes Gallimard, 1992
Joseph Losey, L'Œil du maître, Institut Lumière-Actes Sud, 1994
La Critique de cinéma en France (co-edited with Jacques Zimmer), Ramsay, 1997
La Petite Encyclopédie du cinéma (co-edited with Jean-Claude Loiseau and Joël Magny), Editions du Regard – RMN, 1998
Fritz Lang, le meurtre et la loi, Découvertes Gallimard, 2003

Petite Planète cinématographique, 50 réalisateurs, 40 ans de cinéma, 30 pays, Stock, 2003
Kazan/Losey, édition définitive, Stock, 2009
Une renaissance américaine: de Woody Allen à Robert Zemeckis, entretiens avec 30 cinéastes, Nouveau Monde, 2014
Jane Campion par Jane Campion, Cahiers du cinéma, 2014; final edition 2022
Dardenne par Dardenne, entretiens, Bord de l'eau, 2017
L'Odyssée de 2001, Institut Lumière-Actes Sud, 2018
Une vie de cinéma, Gallimard, 2019
Andreï Konchalovsky, ni dissident, ni partisan, ni courtisan, Institut Lumière-Actes Sud, 2019
Go West, entretiens avec 25 réalisateurs américains, Magnani, 2024

Books – English editions

Kazan on Kazan, Secker and Warburg, 1973
Kubrick, Collins, 1983; Faber, 2001
Conversations with Losey, Methuen, 1985
John Boorman, Faber, 1986
Elia Kazan: An American Odyssey, Bloomsbury, 1988
Positif 50 Years: Selected Writings from the French Film Journal (edited with Laurence Kardish), MoMA, 2002
Film World, Berg, 2009
Jane Campion on Jane Campion, Abrams, 2023

Films

Portrait d'un homme parfait à 60%: Billy Wilder (with Annie Tresgot), 1980
Elia Kazan, outsider (with Annie Tresgot), 1981
All about Mankiewicz (with Luc Béraud), 1983
Chronique d'un film annoncé: Francesco Rosi (with Christine Lipinska), 1986
John Boorman, un portrait (with Philippe Pilard), 2009
Il était une fois… A Clockwork Orange (with Antoine de Gaudemar), 2010

INDEX

3-Iron (Ki-duk), 271
3 Women (Altman), 277
4 Months, 3 Weeks and 2 Days (Mungiu), 201
4:44 Last Day on Earth (Ferrara), 237
5 Fingers (Mankiewicz), 307
7 Women (Ford), 134
8½ (Fellini), 34, 200, 272
12 Years a Slave (McQueen), 204
400 Blows, The (Truffaut), 33, 191, 192, 233
1984 (Orwell), 245
2001: A Space Odyssey (Kubrick), 115, 123, 131, 162, 183, 192, 240, 281, 306

Abbass, Hiam, 186
Abensour, Miguel, 75
Abysses, Les (Papatakis), 34, 286
À cause, à cause d'une femme (Deville), 34
Accident (Losey), 106, 200, 205
Achard, Marcel, 4, 192
Actors Studio, 98, 113, 150, 153-54, 265
Acts of the Apostles (Rossellini), 211
Adam, Ken, 118, 127, 128
Adamov, Arthur, 194
À défaut de génie (Nourissier), 1
Adieu Philippine (Rozier), 34
Adler, Laure, 86
Adorable Liar (Deville), 196
Adorno, Theodor, 209
Advise and Consent (Preminger), 26
Aerograd (Dovzhenko), 11
African Queen, The (Huston), 279
Agel, Henri, 13, 68

Age of Illusions (Szabó), 265
Age of the Earth, The (Rocha), 47
Aghed, Jan, 40, 157
A.I. Artificial Intelligence (Spielberg), 125
Aimée, Anouk, 4, 127, 286
Ain't Misbehavin' (Ophuls), 88
Akerman, Chantal, 181, 205
Alain Resnais: liaisons secrètes, accords vagabonds (Leutrat/Liandrat-Guigues), 146
Albertazzi, Georgio, 147
Alekan, Henri, 107
Alexander Nevsky (Eisenstein), 20, 225
Alexandra's Project (de Heer), 288
Alexandre, Alexandre, 171
Ali Baba and the Forty Thieves (Becker), 35
All About Eve (Mankiewicz), 154
Allen, Woody, 217, 224, 242, 274, 279
Allende, Salvador, 284
All the President's Men (Pakula), 176
Almodóvar, Pedro, 47, 192, 218
Alonso, Lisandro, 205
Althusser, Louis, 18
Altman, Robert, 50, 71, 88, 130, 172, 183, 205, 224, 229, 235, 237, 274, 276-78, 281
Amarcord (Fellini), 272
America, America (Kazan), 98, 99, 100
Amiel, Vincent, 64
Amour, L' (Haneke), 182
Amour-Érotisme et Cinéma (Kyrou), 32

312 A Shared Cinema

Anderson, Lindsay, 27, 154, 231-32, 241, 266, 267
Anderson, Paul Thomas, 241
Andersson, Bibi, 110
Andersson, Roy, 237
And Life Goes On (Kiarostami), 185
Andrei Rublev (Tarkovsky), 162
And the Ship Sails On (Fellini), 272-73
Angelopoulos, Theo, 106, 138-39, 144, 175, 22-24, 226, 252
Angels of Sin (Bresson), 22, 262
Anglaise et le Duc, L' (Rohmer), 224
Animal Farm (Orwell), 245
Anna Karenina (Tolstoy), 244
Anouilh, Jean, 4, 146, 210
Antonio das Mortes (Rocha), 69
Antonioni, Michelangelo, xi, xii, 10, 30, 32-33, 40, 41, 61, 91, 106, 170, 198, 208, 217-18, 232, 241
Antunes, António Lobo, 233
Aparajito (Ray), 267
Apocalypse Now (Coppola), 123, 300
Aragon, Louis, 9, 62, 163, 191, 193
Aravindan, Govindan, 267
Arbre, le Maire et la Médiathèque, L' (Rohmer), 224
Arcand, Denys, 184
Archilochus, 228
Argent, L' (Bresson), 262
Arland, Marcel, 10
Arnold, Andrea, 231
Aron, Raymond, 246
Arrangement, The (Kazan), 100, 105
Arrival of a Train at La Ciotat (Lumière), 191
Artaud, Antonin, 35, 202
Arvanitis, Giorgos, 138
Ashes and Diamonds (Wajda), 265
Ashes of Time (Kar-wai), 48
Assayas, Olivier, 196, 290
Atalante, L' (Vigo), 210
Atlantic City (Malle), 179
Attenborough, Richard, 183
Aubriant, Michel, 79
Aubry, Martine, 244
Audé, Françoise, 53
Audiard, Jacques, 290
Audiberti, Jacques, 194
Audrey, Wilder, 151
Augé, Marc, 90
Aurenche, Jean, 196
Auriol, Jean-Georges, 34

Autant-Lara, Claude, 195-96, 199, 231, 282
Avanti! (Wilder), 130, 151
Avatar (Cameron), 219
Avery, Tex, 30, 250
Avildsen, John, 183
Aviv, Nuith 290
Avon, Sophie, 84
Avventura, L' (Antonioni), 61, 170-71, 183, 205
Aymé, Marcel, 6
Azéma, Sabine, 147
Azoury, Philippe, 214

Baby, Yvonne, 275
Bacalov, Luis, 50
Bacon, Francis, 41
Bad and the Beautiful, The (Minnelli), 26
Bad Boy Bubby (de Heer), 287
Badiou, Alain, 63, 91
Badlands (Malick), 233, 274-75
Baie des Anges, La (Demy) 29, 34
Bait, The (Tavernier), 185
Bald Soprano, The (Ionesco), 210
Balibar, Étienne, 18
Ballad of Narayama (Imamura), 269
Balland, André, 258
Balthus, 41
Bandits a Orgosolo (De Seta), 26
Bandy, Mary Lea, 279
Barbe, Jean-Marie, 252
Barber, C.L., 20
Barbera, Alberto, 164
Barbier, Denis, 124
Bardèche, Maurice, 13
Barnard, Clio, 231
Barnet, Boris, 162, 181, 227
Barrier (Skolimowski), 177
Barry Lyndon (Kubrick), 115, 118-21, 126-27, 188-89, 236-37, 300
Bartabas, 135
Bartas, Šarūnas 205
Barthes, Roland, 39, 189
Barton Fink (Coen), 192
Bastide, François-Régis, 78-79, 81, 83
Bataille, Christophe, 85
Battle of Algiers, The (Pontecorvo), 113
Battleship Potemkin (Eisenstein), 131, 220, 222, 225, 281, 291, 314
Baudelaire, Charles, 12, 19, 50-51, 299
Bauer, Alfred, 171

Baxter, John, 121
Baye, Nathalie, 252
Bazaine, Jean, 12
Bazin, André, ix, 82, 191, 250, 299
Beaumarchais, 16
Beauties of the Night (Clair), 197
Beau Serge, Le (Chabrol), 196, 198
Beauty and the Beast (Cocteau), 305
Becker, Jacques, 35, 52, 191, 240, 282, 288
Becker, Jean, 213
Beckett, Samuel, 194, 210, 222
Beethoven, Ludwig, 11, 296
Before the Revolution (Bertolucci), 282
Beggars, The (Jacquot), 230
Begley, Louis, 119
Beguiled, The (Siegel), 278
Beineix, Jean-Jacques, 88
Belle de jour (Buñuel), 58, 192
Bellocchio, Marco, xi, 198, 201, 252
Bellour, Raymond, x
Benayoun, Robert, xvii, 14, 17, 28, 29-30, 32, 37, 42, 52, 60, 65, 78-79, 99, 132, 135, 146, 164, 193, 222, 227, 250, 255, 263, 277, 299
Benegal, Shyam, 267
Ben-Hur (Wyler), 151
Bénichou, Paul, 7
Benjo, Caroline, 258
Benton, Robert, 183
Béraud, Luc, 150, 155
Berenson, Bernard, 303
Bergman, Ingmar, 10, 91, 106, 131, 183, 200, 208, 217-18, 229, 233, 235-36, 246, 274, 277-78
Bergson, Henri, 16, 91
Bernanos, Georges, 9
Berry, John, 154
Berlin, Isaiah, 228, 247
Bernstein, Henry, 4, 146
Berri, Claude, 207, 259, 287
Berthomieu, Pierre, 65, 66
Bertolucci, Bernardo, 201, 280, 282
Bertrand, Diana, 290
Besnehard, Dominique, 86
Besson, Luc, 226
Bessy, Maurice, 110, 138, 164, 185
Best Way to Walk, The (Miller), 230
Beuys, Joseph, 217
Beylie, Claude, 26, 55, 140
Beyond Rangoon (Boorman), 50, 135

Beyond the Aegean Sea (Kazan), 156
Bidlowsky, Michel, 85
Bierstadt, Albert, 72
Big Heat, The (Lang), 36, 132
Big Sleep, The (Hawks), 10
Billard, Pierre, 79
Bing, Wang, 270
Bingham, George Caleb, 72
Binoche, Juliette, 156
Bird (Eastwood), 279
Birkin, Jane, 287
Birth of a Nation, The (Griffith), 71
Birth of Love, The (Garrel), 119
Bissière, Roger, 41
Bitsch, Charles, 43
Bitter Victory (Ray), 27
Black Cat, White Cat (Eastwood), 168
Black God, White Devil (Rocha), 48, 272
Black Peter (Forman), 162
Blaes, Ronald, 207
Blain, Gérard, 47
Blake, William, 45
Blind Date (Losey), 106
Blondin, Antoine, 18
Blow-Up (Antonioni), 217
Bloy, Léon, 9
Blue Angel, The (von Sternberg), 197
Bluebeard (Chabrol), 33
Blue Is the Warmest Colour (Kechiche), 218
Blue Jasmine (Allen), 242
Blues in the Night (Litvak), 153
Bogarde, Dirk, 106, 108
Bogart, Humphrey, 90, 154, 323
Bogdan, Adriana, 119
Bohème, La (Puccini), 154
Bolognini, Mauro, 95
Bong, Joon-ho, 270
Bonnaire, Sandrine, 185
Bonnaud, Frédéric, 214
Bonnie and Clyde (Penn), 74
Book of Dreams, The (Fellini), 192
Boom! (Losey), 69, 106-107
Boorman, John, xi, xiii, 45, 50, 71, 95, 129, 131-35, 144, 146, 188, 190-92, 201, 231, 252-54, 277
Booth, Margaret, 132
Borde, Raymond, 37
Borges, Jorge Luis, 7, 116, 284
Boris Godunov (Mussorgsky), 112
Borowczyk, Walerian, 250
Bory, Louis, 78-79, 84, 215

314 A Shared Cinema

Borzage, Frank, 200
Borzeix, Jean-Marie, 85, 86
Bost, Pierre, 196
Bosustow, Stephen, 251
Bouc, Alain, 246
Boucherie, Mehdi, 111
Boullet, Jean, 13
Bourget, Jean-Loup, 64, 146
Boutang, Pierre-André, 103
Bouteiller, Pierre, 79
Boy with Green Hair, The (Losey), 109, 136, 233
Brady, Alice, 161
Brakhage, Stan, 202
Brando, Marlon, 97-98, 105, 154
Brasillach, Robert, 13, 16
Braucourt, Guy, 185
Brault, Michel, 150, 153
Brauner, Victor, 28
Breathless (Godard), 27, 33, 191, 197-98, 233, 268
Brecht, Bertolt, 8, 9, 127, 138
Breezy (Eastwood), 278
Bresson, Mylène, 82
Bresson, Robert, 10, 22, 41, 81-82, 128, 169, 171, 199, 224, 228-30, 234, 248, 262-63, 282, 288, 291, 302
Breton, André, 8, 18-19, 28, 38, 42, 57, 134, 190, 191, 202
Brezhnev, Leonid, 89, 112
Bridges, Alan, 178
Bringing Out the Dead (Scorsese), 130
Brion, Patrick, 130
Brizé, Stéphane, 307
Brochier, Jean-Jacques, 258
Brocka, Lino, 185, 272
Bronco Billy (Eastwood), 278
Bronson (Refn), 201
Brontë Sisters, The (Téchiné), 189, 196
Brook, Peter, 71, 222, 227
Brooks, Richard, 90, 158
Brothers Karamazov, The (Dostoyevsky), 75
Bruni, Carla, 244
Bruni Tedeschi, Valeria, 290
Brusati, Franco, 176
Buache, Freddy, 226
Buffalo Bill and the Indians (Altman), 172
Buñuel, Luis, xii, 21-22, 46-47, 191-92, 208, 217-18, 229, 234, 237, 242, 267, 269, 273, 283, 285, 299, 302
Burke, Edmund, 17
Burnan, Maurice, 32

Burstyn, Ellen, 153
Burton, Tim, 191, 192, 198, 220, 241, 274
Bush, George H. W., 280
Bush, George W., 280
Butor, Michel, 91
Bye Bye Monkey (Ferreri), 177

Cabale des dévots, La (Revel), 246
Cabrera, Dominique, 290
Caesar and Rosalie (Sautet), 191
Caillois, Roger, 7
Calamity Jane, 72
California Split (Altman), 277
Camerini, Mario, 51
Campion, Jane, xi, 2, 95, 135, 143, 145, 185, 229, 242, 288
Camus, Albert, 18, 20, 246
Canby, Vincent, 268
Candide (Voltaire), 288
Caniff, Milton, 250
Cantet, Laurent, 293
Capra, Frank, 51, 140, 142, 244
Carabiniers, Les (Godard), 33
Carax, Leos, xi
Carmen (Bizet), 96, 273
Carné, Marcel, 195, 220, 234
Carrère, Emmanuel, 135
Carrière, Jean-Claude, 42, 179, 273
Carroll, Lewis, 45
Casablanca (Curtiz), 90
Casanova, Giacomo, 272, 273, 300
Cassavetes, John, 179, 183, 229, 236, 274, 286
Castle of Otranto, The (Walpole), 189
Castro, Fidel, 138, 247
Cat Ballou (Silverstein), 132
Catch Us If You Can (Boorman), 132
Cavalier, Alain, 196, 235, 262, 289, 291
Ceausescu, Nicolae, 247
Célérier, Stéphane, 258
Céline, Louis-Ferdinand, 75
Ceremony, The (Oshima), 251
Certified Copy (Kiarostami), 49
Cervoni, Albert, 184, 193
Ceylan, Nuri Bilge, 2, 201, 253, 272
Ceysson, Bernard, 207
Chabrol, Claude, 33, 43, 69, 88, 177, 196, 198-99, 221-22, 230, 258, 290, 293
Chahine, Youssef, 180
Chairman Mao's New Clothes (Leys), 246
Chalais, François, 176

Challenge, The (Rosi), 94
Chambon, Simone, 75
Chambre des magiciennes, La (Miller), 230
Champetier, Caroline, 87, 290
Chandler, Raymond, 151
Chang-dong, Lee, 270
Chan-wook, Park, 270
Chapier, Henry, 193
Chaplin, Charles, 6, 10, 12, 34, 51, 86, 117, 129, 138, 162, 183, 202, 222
Chaplin, Geraldine, 86
Chardère, Bernard, 37, 40, 50, 263
Chardin, Jean Siméon, 221
Charensol, Georges, 78-79, 218
Charles, Dead or Alive (Tanner), 46, 57, 184, 199
Charlotte for Ever (Gainsbourg), 287
Chateaubriand, 226
Chatrian, Carlo, 164
Chekhov, Anton, 236
Chénetier, Marc, 75
Cheray, Jean-Louis, 13
Chéreau, Patrice, 112, 135, 185, 259
Chiarini, Luigi, 164
Child, The (Dardenne), 166
Chimes at Midnight (Welles), 281
Chinatown (Polanski), 281
Chion, Michel, xi
Chirouze, Magali, 253
Chodowiecki, Daniel, 189
Christ Stopped at Eboli (Rosi), 130
Chronicle of a Death Foretold (Rosi), 96
Chungking Express (Kar-wai), 48
Churchill, Winston, 16, 54
Chytilová, Věra, 162
Cieutat, Michel, 147, 182, 220
Ciliga, Ante, 163
Ciment, Evelyn, 152, 249
Ciment, Gilles, 9, 250
Ciment, Jeannine, 122, 249
Cimino, Michael, 210, 211, 274
Cioran, Emil, 10, 57
Citizen Kane (Welles), 74, 131, 212, 220, 233, 262, 281
City for Conquest (Litvak/Negulesco), 153
City Lights (Chaplin), 191
Clair, Jean, 206
Clair, René, 34, 79, 186, 195, 206, 282
Clarke, Warren, 150
Class, The (Cantet), 293
Claudel, Camille, 8

Clayburgh, Jill, 177
Cleitman, René, 156
Clément, René, 7, 35, 88, 90, 186, 195, 198-99, 240, 282, 296
Cléo from 5 to 7 (Varda), 34
Clift, Montgomery, 98, 122
Clockwork Orange, A (Kubrick), 115-16, 118, 121, 124, 126-28, 131, 150, 182, 188, 206, 237
Close, Glenn, 213
Closely Watched Trains (Menzel), 162
Closet Children (Jacquot), 230
Clouds of May (Ceylan), 272
Clouzot, Henri-Georges, 186, 195, 196-97, 200, 282, 288
Clowns, The (Fellini), 272
Cocteau, Jean, 82, 282, 305
Codelli, Lorenzo, 40, 58, 60, 255
Code Unknown (Haneke), 182
Coen Brothers, 44, 45, 130, 198, 220, 241
Coen, Joel, 253
Cœurs (Resnais), 145
Cohn, Bernard, 14, 26, 28, 39, 184
Cohn-Bendit, Daniel, 39
Cold Breath (McQueen), 202
Cole, Thomas, 72
Colorado Territory (Walsh), 10, 71
Columbus, Christopher, 29, 262
Comencini, Luigi, 198, 232
Commager, Henry Steele, 20
Comolli, Jean-Louis, 51
Confession, The (Costa-Gavras), 84
Conformist, The (Bertolucci), 282
Confucius, 283
Congreve, William, 232
Conjugal Bed, The (Ferreri), 34
Conrad, Joseph, 6, 134, 245
Constant, Benjamin, 6, 57
Cooper, Gary, 5
Copley, John Singleton, 72
Coppola, Francis, 74, 98, 114, 132, 136, 199, 201, 253, 259, 274, 277
Corbeau, Le (Clouzot), 197
Cornaille, Roger, 13
Corneau, Alain, 68, 88, 196, 290
Corneille, Pierre, 6
Cortez, Stanley, 306
Corti, José, 7
Costa-Gavras, 84, 113, 115
Coulais, Bruno, 87
Counterfeiters, The (Gide), 299
Coup de torchon (Tavernier), 231, 293

Cournot, Michel, 79
Courtenay, Tom, 106
Cowie, Peter, 122, 186
Crime of Monsieur Lange, The (Renoir), 223
Criminal, The (Losey), 106
Cronenberg, David, 45, 190, 241
Crook, The (Lelouch), 88
Crothers, Scatman, 121
Crowd, The (Vidor), 191
Cukor, George, 26, 151-52
Cul-de-sac (Polanski), 281
Culioli, Antoine, 75
Curiosités esthétiques, Les (Baudelaire), 12
Curtiz, Michael, 240, 305
Cutting Heads (Rocha), 47
Cybulski, Zbigniew, 265

da Vinci, Leonardo, 129, 226
Dadoun, Roger, 69
Dagen, Philippe, 207
Daisies (Chytilová), 162
Dames du Bois de Boulogne, Les (Bresson), 262
d'Amico, Suso Cecchi, 47, 179
Damisch, Hubert, 91
Damned, The (Visconti), 106, 108
Damour, Christophe, 147
Dance Me to My Song (de Heer), 288
Daneliya, Georgiy, 172
Daney, Serge, 59, 85-86, 199
Dangerous Method, A (Cronenberg), 190
Danton, Georges, 117
Danton (Wajda), 283
Dardenne Brothers, 166, 191
Darwin, Charles, 21
Dauman, Anatole, 140, 145, 156, 251, 292
Daumas, Jacques, 252
Daves, Delmer, 158
Davy Crockett, 72
Days of '36 (Angelopoulos), 138
Days of Heaven (Malick), xiii, 140, 275
de Baecque, Antoine, 59
de Balzac, Honoré, 5, 6, 51, 129, 189, 205, 218, 223, 225-26
de Baroncelli, Jean, 184, 185, 193, 215
de Gaudemar, Antoine, 150
de Gaulle, Charles, 9, 62, 234, 244
de Hadeln, Moritz, 185-86, 226
de Heer, Rolf, 288
de Létraz, Jean, 300
de Luze, Hervé, 87

de Maistre, Joseph, 17
de Marivaux, Pierre, 5, 135, 224
de Montaigne, Michel, 50, 57, 250
de Musset, Alfred, 224
de Nerval, Gérard, 144
de Rabaudy, Martine, 83
de Staël, Nicolas, 12
des Forêts, Louis-René, 230
du Boisrouvray, Albina, 251
Dean, James, 98, 275, 278, 324
Death in Venice (Visconti), 107-108
Decalogue (Kieślowski), 283
Declaration of War (Donzelli), 292
Decoin, Henri, 35, 289
Deep End (Skolimowski), 177
Defaye, Christian, 81
Degas, Edgar, 210
Delacroix, Eugène, 44, 206, 218, 222, 227, 235
Delahaye, Michel, 59, 184
Delarue, Maryse, 69, 70
De Laurentiis, Dino, 172
Deleau, Pierre-Henri, 138
Deleuze, Gilles, 14-17, 44, 72-73, 126
Delevoy, Robert, 174
Deliverance (Boorman), 50, 132-34
Delluc, Louis, 34, 91, 197, 232
Delon, Alain, 108, 165
Delorme, Stéphane, 59
Delvaux, André, 119
Demain sera un autre jour (Tuhkuner), 66
Demeure, Jacques, 32
DeMille, Cecil B., 5-6, 34, 140-42, 154, 161
Demy, Jacques, 29, 34, 248, 291
Denevi, Marco, 106
De Niro, Robert, 153
Denis, Claire, 230
De Palma, Brian, 253
Depardieu, Gérard, 82
Départ, Le (Skolimowski), 177
Deray, Jacques, 179
De Santis, Giuseppe, 224, 232
Désenchantée, La (Jacquot), 230
De Seta, Vittorio, 26, 95
De Sica, Vittorio, 191
Desnos, Robert, 35, 202
Desplat, Alexandre, 87
Desplechin, Arnaud, 146, 199, 253, 290
Dessin animé après Walt Disney, Le (Benayoun), 60
Destinées sentimentales, Les (Assayas), 196
Deville, Michel, 34, 196, 255, 262

Devils on the Doorstep (Wen), 181
Dialogues of Exiles (Ruiz), 284
Diamond, I.A.L., 151
Diamonds of the Night (Němec), 162
Diary of a Country Priest (Bresson), 262
DiCaprio, Leonardo, 238
Dickens, Charles, 6, 223
Dickinson, Emily, 19, 135
Diegues, Carlos, 89, 201, 316
Différence et Répétition (Deleuze), 17
Dillinger is Dead (Ferreri), 178
Dirty Dozen, The (Aldrich), 132
Dirty Harry (Siegel), 278, 280
Dirty Money (Arcand), 184
Discreet Charm of the Bourgeoisie, The (Buñuel), 217
Discrète, La (Vincent), 86
Disney, Walt, 6, 60
Dispatches (Herr), 123
Djordjević, Kosta, 167
Doillon, Jacques, 86, 287
Dolce vita, La (Fellini), 165, 200, 222, 272
Domarchi, Jean, 43
Domecq, Jean-Philippe, 42, 206, 247
Don Giovanni (Mozart), 113, 115
Doniol-Valcroze, Jacques, 196
Dósai, István, 265
Dostoyevsky, Fyodor, 6, 211, 244
Double Indemnity (Wilder), 142
Double Life of Véronique (Kieślowski), 283
Douchet, Jean, x, 59, 155, 196, 254
Douy, Max, 87
Dovzhenko, Alexander, 11, 34, 106, 225
Do You Remember Dolly Bell? (Kusturica), 167-68
Dragić, Nedeljko, 251
Dragonwyck (Mankiewicz), 155, 158
Dreyer, Carl, 8, 11, 34, 244, 248, 300
Drieu la Rochelle, 248
Drive (Refn), 201, 205, 284
Dr. Strangelove (Kubrick), 125-26, 307
Draughtsman's Contract, The (Greenaway), 130, 160, 258
Dubček, Alexander, 162
Duchamp, Marcel, 206, 209
Duchateau, Jacques, 85
Dulas, Germaine, 197, 232

Dulac, Sophie, 258
Dumas, Alexandre, 209
Dumont, Bruno, 199, 201, 229, 290
Dunaway, Faye, 137
Dupeyron, François, 230
Duras, Marguerite, 5, 91, 114, 131, 276
Duvall, Shelly, 128, 277
Dylan, Bob, 138

Eakins, Thomas, 72
Earth (Dovzhenko), 11, 47, 225, 237, 285
Eastman, Carole, 137
East of Eden (Kazan), 98-99, 104, 109, 275
Eastwood, Clint, 278-80
Easy Life, The (Risi), 34
Ebert, Roger, ix, 240, 254
Eccentricities of a Blonde-Haired Girl (Oliveira), 235
Eco, Umberto, 47, 180
Edge, The (Kramer), 184, 283
Edwards, Blake, 38, 306
Egoyan, Atom, 182, 253
Eisenstein, Sergei, 11, 13, 20, 34, 94, 117, 161-62, 225, 262, 266, 281, 291, 298
Eisner, Lotte, 36, 141
Él (Buñuel), 217
Elimination (Panh), 85
Eliot, T.S., 23, 254
Ellrodt, Robert, 23
Elsaesser, Thomas, 40
Éluard, Paul, 163
Emerald Forest, The (Boorman), 133-43
Emerson, Ralph Waldo, 72
Empire of Passion (Oshima), 176
Enfance nue, L' (Pialat), 264
Enfants du paradis, Les (Carné), 197, 258
En soixantaine (Frank), 248
Epstein, Jean, 34, 197
Équateur (Gainsbourg), 287
Ertel, Rachel, 75
Erval, François, 140
Escape to Victory (Huston), 46
Etaix, Pierre, 34
Eustache, Jean, 184
Eva (Losey), 106
Excalibur (Boorman), 50, 130, 133-35, 179
Exorcist II: The Heretic (Boorman), 133, 253
Eyes Wide Shut (Kubrick), 124, 126, 129, 212

Fabius, Laurent, 244
Face (Ming-liang), 215
Face in the Crowd, A (Kazan), 99
Fahrenheit 451 (Truffaut), 231
Fallen Angels (Kar-wai), 48
Falling Leaves (Iosseliani), 184
False Servant (Jacquot), 230
Family Diary (Zurlini), 34
Fanfan la Tulipe (Christian-Jaque), 197
Fanny and Alexander (Bergman), 217
Farber, Manny, ix, xiii
Farewell, My Queen (Jacquot), 230
Farhadi, Asghar, 216, 284
Fassbender, Michael, 204
Fassbinder, Rainer Werner, 138, 185
Fat City (Huston), 157
Faulkner, William, 75
Faure, Élie, 13, 60
Favourites of the Moon (Iosseliani), 285
Favre Le Bret, Robert, 108
Fear and Desire (Kubrick), 121
Fechner, Christian, 81
Feelings (Lvovsky), 185
Feingersh, Ed, 42
Fellini, Federico, 10, 34, 91, 170, 190-92, 198, 200, 205, 211, 217, 220, 234-35, 242, 272-74, 278, 298
Ferran, Pascale, 290, 292
Ferrara, Abel, 237
Ferreri, Marco, 34, 177, 178, 179, 283
Ferro, Marco, 39, 136
Feu follet, Le (Malle), 34, 215, 326
Feuillade, Louis, 5, 209
Fields, W.C., 17
Figures in a Landscape (Losey), 107
Fille Seule, Le (Jacquot), 230
Fincher, David, 242
Fiorentino, Rosso, 303
Firk, Michèle, 31, 151
First Teacher, The (Konchalovsky), 89, 176
Fists in the Pockets (Bellocchio), 233
Fitzgerald, F. Scott, 75
Five Easy Pieces (Rafelson), 137, 202
Flags of Our Fathers (Eastwood), 279
Flaubert, Gustave, 19, 61, 88, 189, 218, 236, 307
Fleurs du mal, Les (Baudelaire), 299
Flynn, Errol, 5, 305
Fofi, Goffredo, 35, 40, 94, 198, 255
Foolish Wives (von Stroheim), 17
Forbidden Games (Clément), 197
Ford, John, 12, 21, 26, 71, 132, 134, 140, 142, 160-61, 191, 201, 208, 211, 218, 223, 234, 236, 244-45, 280
Forman, Miloš, 110, 158, 162, 167, 201, 245
Forsyte Saga (Galsworthy), 156
For Your Eyes Only (Glen), 263
Four Nights of a Dreamer (Bresson), 169
Four Troublesome Heads (Méliès), 191
Fraisse, Philippe, 64-66
Frank, Bernard, 248
Franco, Jesús, xiv
Franco, Francisco, 8
Frankenheimer, John, 47, 48, 275
Franz Joseph, 142
Frears, Stephen, 45-46, 115, 213, 229, 231, 252
Fregonese, Hugo, 38
Frémaux, Thierry, 164, 184, 186, 253
Fresnay, Pierre, 4
Freud, Sigmund, 21, 127, 142, 190, 235, 244
Friday Night (Denis), 230
Friedländer, Max, 302
Friedrich, Caspar David, 135
Frodon, Michel, 59
Fromentin, Eugène, 12
Frost, Robert, 20
Full Metal Jacket (Kubrick), 46, 123, 124
Funny Games (Haneke), 182
Furtwängler, Leon, 11
Fury (Lang), 36, 142

Gaál, István, 265
Gabin, Jean, 5
Gainsbourg, Serge, 287
Gainsborough, Thomas, 189
Galsworthy, John, 156
Gance, Abel, 34, 117, 223
Garcia, Nicole, 252
García Márquez, Gabriel, 96
Garcin, Jérôme, 79
Garrel, Philippe, 88, 119, 184
Gates of the Night (Carné), 234
Gauguin, Paul, 207, 210
Gauteur, Claude, 26, 140
Gautier, Eric, 87, 189, 194
Gélinet, Patrice, 86
General Line, The (Eisenstein), 262

Generation, A (Wajda), 233
Genet, Jean, 286
Germinal (Zola), 280
Ghaffari, Farrokh, 86
Ghatak, Ritwik, 267, 271
Ghobadi, Bahman, 237
Giacometti, Alberto, 222
Giant (Stevens), 275
Gide, André, 34, 163, 239, 299, 322
Gillett, John, 266
Gilliam, Terry, 45, 191
Girard, René, xiii
Giraudoux, Jean, 4, 210
Giscard d'Estaing, Valéry, 242, 243
Gish, Lillian, 66
Gleaners and I, The (Varda), 235
Globus, Yoram, 227
Gloria (Cassavetes), 179
Gobetti, Paolo, 94
Go-Between, The (Losey), 107-108, 136, 165, 190
Godard, Jean-Luc, 5, 27, 30, 33, 34, 41, 44, 79, 91, 106, 131, 144, 183, 186, 195, 196, 199-200, 226-27, 231, 241, 248, 250, 262-63, 268, 282-83, 288-90
Godfather, The (Coppola), 74, 136
Godrèche, Judith, 230
Golan, Menachem, 227
Gold Rush, The (Chaplin), 239
Goldwyn, Samuel, 102, 152
Gombeaud, Adrien, 42
Gomes, Emilio Sales, 13
Gopalakrishnan, Adoor, 267
Gören, Serif, 271
Goretta, Claude, 176, 177
Gosford Park (Altman), 278
Goudet, Stéphane, 49, 263
Gould, Elliott, 277
Goya, Francisco, 144, 189, 222
Gozlan, Gérard, 31
Grandmaster, The (Kar-wai), 48
Grant, Cary, 307
Gran Torino (Eastwood), 279
Grande Bouffe, La (Ferreri), 170, 178
Grande Illusion, La (Renoir), 223, 258
Grands Cimetières sous la Lune, Les (Bernanos), 9
Grapes of Wrath, The (Ford), 71, 221-22, 280, 337
Graver, Gary, 150
Gray, James, 130, 241
Great Beauty, The (Sorrentino), 273
Great Dictator, The (Chaplin), 222

Great Gatsby, The (Luhrmann), 238
Gréco, Juliette, 286
Greed (von Stroheim), 17, 74, 132
Green, Julien, 4
Greenaway, Peter, 45, 46, 160, 231, 258, 284
Gregor, Ulrich, 36
Gresset, Michel, 70, 75
Grieve, Ann, 75
Griffith, D.W., 142
Grosjean, Jean, 10
Group Theater, 101, 104
Guénot, Jean, 75
Guérif, François, 2, 68
Guérin, Nicholas, 55
Guerra, Ruy, xii, 31, 201
Guerre est finie, La (Resnais), 145, 200
Guitry, Sacha, 36
Güney, Yilmaz, 104, 271
Guns, The (Guerra), 69, 272
Guy, Michel, 108

Hallelujah! (Vidor), 34
Halliday, Jon, 100
Hamlet (Olivier), 281
Hammett (Wenders), 259
Hamp (Wilson), 106
Hands Over the City (Rosi), 34, 94, 95, 96
Haneke, Michael, 182
Happy New Year (Lelouch), 88
Happy Together (Kar-wai), 48
Harel, Philippe, 213
Hasford, Gustav, 123
Hathaway, Henry, 240
Hawks, Howard, 26, 37, 71, 140, 142, 183, 191, 248
Hayden, Sterling, 251
Heart in Winter, A (Sautet), 268
Heaven's Gate (Cimino), 211
Heidegger, Martin, 83
Hell in the Pacific (Boorman), 132, 134
Hellman, Monte, 137, 160, 288
Hellwig, Klaus, 156, 157
Henochsberg, Alexandra, 258
Herpe, Noël, 42
Herr, Michael, 123
Herzberg, Laurence, 53
Herzog, Werner, 134-35, 138
Heymann, Danièle, 84, 260
Hireling, The (Bridges), 178
Hiroshima mon amour (Resnais), 94, 131, 145, 170, 192, 203, 233, 239, 292
Hirst, Damien, 217

Histoire de l'art, L' (Faure), 13
Hitchcock, Alfred, xi, 6, 12, 26, 37, 61, 65, 100, 121, 130, 183, 194, 218, 229, 231, 236, 241, 248, 307
Hitler, Adolf, 8, 19, 82, 127, 142, 222
Hoberman, Jim, x
Hoffmann, Stanley, 20
Hogarth, William, 189
Hollande, François, 243, 247
Holy Lola (Tavernier), 49
Honeymoon Killers (Kastle), 233, 275, 276
Honeysuckle Rose (Schatzberg), 137, 138
Honkytonk Man (Eastwood), 278
Hope and Glory (Boorman), 130, 134
Hopper, Edward, 12, 41, 72
Hornick, Neil, 122
Horse Soldiers, The (Ford), 21
Host, The (Joon-ho), 270
Hôtel du Nord (Carné), 220
Hou Hsiao-hsien, 268
How Green Was My Valley (Ford), 280
Hrabal, Bohumil, 162
Hugo, Victor, 38, 190, 205, 239
Huillet, Danièle, 203
Hu, King, 185, 268
Hume, David, 16
Hunger (McQueen), 202, 204, 233
Hunters, The (Angelopoulos), 175
Hunting Butterflies (Iosseliani), 285
Huppert, Isabelle, 86, 177
Huston, John, 12, 32, 37-38, 46, 114-15, 134, 154, 157-58, 211, 235, 251, 267, 278-79

I Am Twenty (Khutsiev), 180
Ibn Saud, 113
Ice (Kramer), 283
Identification Marks: None (Skolimowski), 177
I Don't Hear the Guitar Anymore (Garrel), 119
Il bidone (Fellini), 10, 272
Il Grido (Antonioni), 10
Illustrious Corpses (Rosi), 95-97
Il me semble désormais que Roger est en Italie (Vitoux), 33
Il posto (Olmi), 26, 34
Il Vitelloni (Fellini), 272
Image-mouvement, L' (Deleuze), 17
Image-temps, L' (Deleuze), 17

I magliari (Rosi), 94
Imamura, Shōhei, 268, 269
I'm Glad My Mother is Alive (Miller), 230
Immortal Story, The (Welles), 134, 281, 337
Ingres, Jean-Auguste-Dominique, 206, 218
In My Country (Boorman), 50, 135
Innocence Unprotected (Makavejev), 160
In Old Chicago (King), 72
In the Mood for Love (Kar-wai), 48
In the Name of the Italian People (Risi), 239
In the Realm of the Senses (Oshima), 176, 252
Intimacy (Chéreau), 185
Intimate Lighting (Passer), 162
Intouchables, The (Toledano/Nakache), 293
Ionesco, Eugène, 194, 210
Iosseliani, Otar, 163, 184, 201, 283, 285-86
Irons, Jeremy, 177
Istrati, Panait, 163
Ivaldi, Christian, 79
Ivan the Terrible (Eisenstein), 11, 225, 281
Ivory, James, 45, 229

Jacquot, Benoit, 196, 230
Jacob, Gilles, 138, 143, 164, 166, 174, 176, 184, 253, 265-66
James, Henry, 229, 230, 245
James, Jesse, 72
Jancsó, Miklós, 201, 223, 265
Jaubert, Maurice, 26
Jaworski, Philippe, 75
Jaws (Spielberg), 74
Jeancolas, Jean-Pierre, 146, 287
Jeanne Dielman (Akerman), 181, 205
Je me souviens (Perec), 5
Jennings, Humphrey, 231
Jenny (Carné), 234
Je t'aime, je t'aime (Resnais), 145
Je t'aime moi non plus (Gainsbourg), 287
Johnson, Diane, 123
Joli Mai, Le (Marker), 34
Jousse, Thierry, 254
Joyce, James, 23, 111, 137
Judge and the Assassin, The (Tavernier), 106
Judge Priest (Ford), 211
Judt, Tony, 246

Jules et Jim (Truffaut), 293
Julius Caesar (Shakespeare), 96, 117, 227
July Rain (Khutsiev), 180
Jung, Carl, 190

Kael, Pauline, ix, 123, 133, 219
Kafka, Franz, 28, 212
Kaganski, Serge, 61, 214
Kahn, Cédric, 290
Kahn, Jean-François, 259
Kaige, Chen, 268, 269-70
Kanal (Wajda), 223, 265
Kandinsky, Wassily, 44
Kaplan, Nelly, 184
Karmitz, Marin, 69, 258, 272, 283
Kar-wai, Wong, 48, 129, 268
Kast, Pierre, 196
Kastle, Leonard, 233, 275-76
Kaufman, Boris, 98
Katyn (Wajda), 46, 223
Kawalerowicz, Jerzy, 40, 172
Kazan, Chris, 100, 111
Kazan, Elia, xi, xiii, 26, 33, 71, 95, 97-106, 108-115, 119, 135, 140, 143, 150, 152-56, 190, 223, 233, 262, 274-75
Keaton, Buster, 10, 17, 51, 202, 306
Kechiche, Abdellatif, 199, 218
Kehr, Dave, 240
Kermode, Mark, x
Kerr, Deborah, 105
Kershner, Irvin, 47, 251
Kes (Loach), 184, 219, 220
Kessler, David, 86
Kézdi-Kovács, Zsolt, 265
Khrushchev, Nikita, 89
Khutsiev, Marlen, 180
Kiarostami, Abbas, 49, 181-82, 185, 204, 235, 237, 258
Kidman, Nicole, 229
Ki-duk, Kim, 271
Kieślowski, Krzysztof, 283
Killing, The (Kubrick), 121
Killer's Kiss (Kubrick), 121
Kinatay (Mendoza), 215
King, Henry, 72
King, Stephen, 126, 128
King and Country (Losey), 30, 106, 114
Kings of the Road (Wenders), 171, 203
Kinoshita, Keisuke, 267
Kipling, Rudyard, 134
Klee, Paul, 44
Klossowski, Pierre, 285
Klute (Pakula), 176
Knave of Hearts (Clément), 35, 198

Knife in the Water (Polanski), 233
Koestler, Arthur, 101, 163
Konchalovsky, Andrei, 86, 89, 175, 201
Kosslick, Dieter, 186
Kourilsky, Isabelle, 122
Kozintsev, Grigori, 227
Kramer, Robert, 86, 184, 283, 333
Král, Petr, xv, 40, 42, 146, 266
Kristóf, Klára, 265
Kubrick, Stanley, xi, xiii-iv, 27, 44, 46, 64-65, 95, 98, 115-34, 141, 143-46, 150, 155, 162, 183, 188-91, 206, 208, 212, 225-26, 229, 233-34, 236-37, 241, 247, 274, 281, 298, 307
Kurosawa, Akira, xi, 211, 267, 272
Kusturica, Emir, 139, 165, 167-68
Kyrou, Ado, 14, 22, 28-31, 35, 37-39, 42, 60, 99, 263

L'Herbier, Marcel, 209, 232
La Boétie, Étienne de, 250
La Fontaine, Jean de, 13, 23
La Tour, George de, 12
Labadie, Jean, 258
Labarthe, André, 27
Lacan, Jacques, 230, 297
Lacemaker, The (Goretta), 177
Laclotte, Michel, 12
Laffay, Albert, 14
Lagesse, Éric, 258
Lainé, Simone, 2, 252
Lalanne, Jean-Marc, 59, 65, 84, 214
Lang, Fritz, 5, 11, 31, 34-38, 86, 132, 142-43, 146, 155, 160-61, 183, 200, 211, 221, 236, 241, 298, 305-306
Langlois, Henri, 10, 13, 36, 82
Lapoirie, Jeanne, 290
Lasch, Christopher, 199
Last Metro, The (Truffaut), 82, 231
Last Tycoon, The (Kazan), 153
Lattuada, Alberto, 198, 232
Laubreaux, Alain, 82
Laughton, Charles, 233, 306
Laundromat, The (Soderbergh), 50
Laura (Preminger), 306
Lawrence, D.H., 7, 23-24
Le Besco, Isild, 230
Le Fanu, Mark, 40
Le Nain, 12
Lean, David, 231
Leconte, Patrice, 81, 86, 195-96, 256
Ledoyen, Virginia, 230
Lefort, Gérard, 214

Legend of Saint Julien the Hospitaller, The (Flaubert), 189
Legrand, Gérard, xv, 17, 28, 37, 42, 87, 242
Leherpeur, Xavier, 84
Leigh, Mike, 231, 252, 284
Leiris, Michel, 34
Lelouch, Claude, 88
Lenica, Jan, 251
Lenin, 180
Leone, Sergio, 252
Leopard, The (Visconti), 34, 108, 165, 181, 271
Leo the Last (Boorman), 50, 132-33, 253, 277
Letters from Iwo Jima (Eastwood), 279
Lettre sur les chimpanzés (Rosset), 296
Leutrat, Jean-Louis, 146
Levinson, Barry, 183
Lévy, Denis, 63
Lewis, Jerry, 17, 32, 135, 146
Leys, Simon, 246, 248
Lhomme, Pierre, 87
Liandrat-Guigues, Suzanne, 146
Liebermann, Rolf, 112
Life of Galileo (Brecht), 9
Life of Oharu, The (Mizoguchi), 267
Like a Turtle on its Back (Béraud), 155
Liliom (Lang), 160, 200
Liliom (Molnár), 200
Linder, Max, 5
Lion Has Seven Heads, The (Rocha), 47
Lioret, Philippe, 186
Litvak, Anatole, 153
Livi, Jean-Louis, 145
Loach, Ken, 45, 134, 184, 201, 219, 231, 325
Loden, Barbara, xii, 100, 105
Loewenstein, Karl, 20
Logique du sens (Deleuze), 17
Lola (Demy), 29, 233
Lola Montès (Ophüls), 10
Lolita (Kubrick), 188
London, Jack, 75
Long Goodbye, The (Altman), 50, 277
Loos, Adolf, 37
Lorrain, Claude, 12
Losey, Joseph, xii, 30, 68, 69-71, 91, 95, 103-104, 106-15, 127, 130, 136, 143, 190, 200, 285

Losfeld, Éric, 18, 38, 55, 131, 287
Los olvidados (Buñuel), 217, 235
Lost Spring (Mazars), 86
Loulou (Pialat), 191
Lourcelles, Jacques, 13
Louvart, Hélène, 290
Love Affair (Makavejev), 160-61
Love's Labour's Lost (Shakespeare), 227
Loves of a Blonde (Forman), 57, 162
Love Story (Hiller), 119
Lowry, Malcolm, 157
Lubitsch, Ernst, 34, 183, 306
Lucas, George, 125, 126
Lucky Luciano (Rosi), 95
Lueger, Karl, 142
Luhrmann, Baz, 238
Lumet, Sidney, 98, 275
Lumière, 55, 164, 191
Lvovsky, Noémie, 185, 290
Lye, Len, 251
Lynch, David, 190, 242, 284
Lynn, Vera, 307
Lyubimov, Yuri, 112

M (Lang), 36, 197, 306
Macbeth (Welles), 20
Machine in the Garden, The (Marx), xiii, 20
Mackendrick, Alexander, 231
Madame Bovary (Flaubert), 189
Mad Max (Miller), 288
Magic Eye, The (Hornick), 122
Magnificent Ambersons, The (Welles), 210
Mahler, Gustav, 108, 275, 322
Maids, The (Genet), 286
Mailer, Norman, 227
Maîtres d'autrefois, Les (Fromentin), 12
Makavejev, Dušan, 104, 160, 162, 167, 170, 201, 255, 259
Makhmalbaf, Mosen, 237
Malcolm, Derek, 182
Malick, Terrence, xiii, 20, 72, 140, 183, 190, 241, 274-75, 280-81
Mallarmé, Stéphane, 223
Malle, Louis, 34, 179, 196, 215
Mallet-Guy, Alexandre, 258
Malraux, André, 11, 91, 239, 291
Malraux, Florence, 11
Maltese Falcon, The (Huston), 10, 158
Mandelbaum, Jacques, 61
Man Escaped, A (Bresson), 10, 20, 262, 313

Manessier, Aldred, 41
Manet, Édouard, 152, 222
Mankiewicz, Joseph, 36, 61, 102, 128, 141, 150, 153-56, 158, 190, 220, 284, 307
Mankiewicz, Rosemary, 156
Mann, Anthony, 44, 211
Mann, Michael, 241
Mann, Thomas, 108
Man of Iron (Wajda), 179, 223
Man of Marble (Wajda), 179, 223
Man Who Killed Liberty Valance, The (Ford), 132
Man Who Loved Women, The (Truffaut), 231
Man With a Cross, The (Rossellini), 289
Man with a Movie Camera, The (Vertov), 183
Many Wars Ago (Rosi), 95, 224
Mao Zedong, 246, 247
Marais, Jean, 70, 82
Marat, Jean-Paul, 117
Maraval, Vincent, 292
Marco Polo, 267
Mardore, Michel, 79
Margolin, François, 197
Marienstras, Richard, 75
Marie pour mémoire (Garrel), 184
Marion, Denis, 141
Marker, Chris, 34, 52, 262, 289
Marna, Roberte, 7
Marnie (Hitchcock), 236
Married Woman, A (Godard), 30
Marseillaise, La (Renoir), 160, 223
Martin, Yves, 13
Martinand, Bernard, 13
Marvin, Lee, 132, 133
Marx, Karl, 15-16, 18, 21, 36, 39, 94, 118, 127, 142, 180, 244, 247, 255, 267, 272, 297
Marx, Leo, xiii, 20
Mary (Ferrara), 237
M*A*S*H (Altman), 183, 276-78
Mason, James, 307
Masson, Alain, 17, 64, 146, 182, 188
Masson, Alex, 238
Masson, Laetitia, 290
Mathiez, Albert, 118
Mattei Affair, The (Rosi), 95, 97, 165, 306
Maupassant, Guy de, 189
Mauriac, François, 9, 79, 83
Maurras, Charles, 62
Max and the Junkmen (Sautet), 268
Mayer, Louis B., 102, 129
Mayoux, Jean-Jacques, 23-24

Mazars, Alain, 86
McBride, Joseph, 157
McCarthy, Todd, 157, 240, 254
McCarthy, Joseph, 101-102, 106, 109-10, 154, 157, 161, 240, 254
McDowell, Malcolm, 107, 128, 150
McGilligan, Patrick, 157
McGovern, George, 280
McLaren, Norman, 250
McQueen, Steve, 201-202, 204
Mean Streets (Scorsese), 138, 274
Meisel, Edmund, 225
Méliès, George, 191
Mélo (Bernstein), 146
Melville, Herman, 20-21, 75, 144, 244
Memories of Murder (Joon-ho), 270
Mendoza, Brillante, 215
Mendès France, Pierre, 15, 20
Ménégoz, Margaret, 258
Menzel, Jiří, 162
Mépris, Le (Godard), 33, 200, 205
Mérigeau, Pascal, 55, 157, 184
Mérimée, Prosper, 189
Merleau-Ponty, Maurice, 91
Merry Christmas Mr. Lawrence (Oshima), 69
Mészáros, Márta, 172
Métamorphose des dieux, La (Malraux), 11
Metropolis (Lang), 36, 221
Michalek, Boleslaw, 266
Michelangelo, xii, 235
Michelson, Annette, 202
Midnight in Paris (Allen), 242
Midsummer Night's Dream, A (Shakespeare), 227
Milestones (Kramer), 283
Milhaud, Darius, 34
Miller, Claude, 196, 230, 252, 290
Miller, George, 288
Milošević, Slobodan, 213
Minghella, Anthony, 183
Minnelli, Vincente, 26, 51-52, 211, 275, 307
Minority Report (Spielberg), 230
Miracle Worker, The (Penn), 26
Misérables, Les (Hugo), 190
Missing Picture, The (Panh), 85
Mistons, Les (Truffaut), 27
Mitchell, Eddy, 30
Mitchum, Robert, 5, 305
Mitry, Jean, xv, 12, 208, 221, 299
Mitterrand, François, 23, 96, 242-44,
Mitterrand, Frédéric, 251

Miyazaki, Hayao, 251
Mizoguchi, Kenji, 211, 237, 267, 272
Mizrahi, Simon, 255-56
Molière, 6
Molnár, Ferenc, 200
Monet, Claude, 152, 210
Monicelli, Mario, 198, 222
Monk, The (Lewis) 189
Monroe, Marilyn, 42
Monteiro, João Cesar, 86
Monteverdi, Claudio, 210
Moonlighting (Skolimowski), 177
Morales du Grand Siècle (Benichou), 7
Morandi, Giorgio, 41
Moreau, Jeanne, 139
Moret, Henry, 55
Moretti, Nanni, 181
Morlay, Gaby, 4
Moskowitz, Gene, 184, 219
Mother (Joon-ho), 270
Mother and the Whore, The (Eustache), 170, 203
Mouchette (Bresson), 292
Mouloudji, Marcel, 289
Mounier, Emmanuel, 18
Mouth Agape, The (Pialat), 264
Mozart, Wolfgang Amadeus, 210, 227, 300
Mr. Klein (Losey), 108, 113, 115, 130, 170
Mud (Nichols), 216
Mulholland Drive (Lynch), 205, 284
Müller, Marco, 164
Mungiu, Cristian, 201, 251
Munk, Andrzej 40, 265, 300
Munk, Eugene Braun, 108
Murakami, Haruki, 217
Murat, Pierre, 84
Muray, Philippe, 17, 170
Muriel (Resnais), 34, 145, 200, 292
Murnau, F.W., xiv, 11, 34, 36, 51, 74, 191, 202
Musician Killer (Jacquot), 230
Mussolini, Benito, 8, 51, 286, 289
My Favourite Season (Téchiné), 196
My Last Breath (Buñuel), 273
Mystic River (Eastwood), 279

Nabokov, Vladimir, 45, 124
Nadeau, Maurice, 23, 140
Name of the Rose, The (Eco),180
Napoleon (Gance), 117, 223
Narboni, Jean, 51, 59, 184
Naremore, James, 147

Narus, Mikio, 211, 267, 272
Nashville (Altman), 50, 277
Nazarin (Buñuel), 22, 267
Nelson, Willy, 137-38
Němec, Jan, 162
Neuhoff, Éric, 84
Newman, Paul, 98
Nichols, Mike, 183, 201, 216
Nicholson, Jack, 128
Nietzsche, Friedrich, 16, 57
Night and Fog (Resnais), 145
Night of the Hunter, The (Laughton), 233, 305
Nights of Cabiria (Fellini), 10, 272
Nimier, Roger, 18
Niogret, Hubert, 43, 60
Noguez, Dominique, 91
Noiret, Philippe, 195
North by Northwest (Hitchcock), 307
No Trifling with Love (de Musset), 224
Nourissier, François, 1
Nouvel, Jean, 112
Novarezzio, Claude, 5
Nozière, Violette, 177
Nuridsany, Michel, 26

O Lucky Man! (Anderson), 267
Oasis (Chang-dong), 270
Obama, Barack, 280
Objective, Burma! (Walsh), 222
October (Eisenstein), 86, 185, 225, 281
Odd Man Out (Reed), 281
Ökten, Zeki, 271
Old Boy (Chan-wook), 270
Oliveira, Manoel de, 235
Olivier, Laurence, 86, 196, 214, 281, 290, 330
Olmi, Ermanno, 26, 34, 95, 176
On Art and Connoisseurship (Friedländer), 302
One Flew Over the Cuckoo's Nest (Forman), 162
One Night... A Train (Delvaux), 119
On the Waterfront (Kazan), 97, 98, 103-104, 109, 150, 153-54
Ophélia (Chabrol), 33
Ophuls, Marcel, 88, 115
Ophüls, Max, 165, 282, 307
Orchestra Rehearsal (Fellini), 272, 274
Ordet (Dreyer), 8
Oriano, Michel, 70, 75
Orwell, George, 101, 163, 245-46
Oshima, 52, 138, 176, 201, 251, 268-69

Ossessione (Visconti), 233
Otchakovsky-Laurens, Paul, 55
Other Side of the Wind, The (Welles), 111, 150, 210, 212
Othon (Straub/Huillet), 203
Oulman, Alain, 120
Our Daily Bread (Vidor), 140
Ozon, François, 185, 199, 290
Ozu, Yasujirō, 181, 211

Pabst, G.W., 34, 234
Pacino, Al, 136
Padre Padrone (Taviani Brothers), 176
Padri e Padroni (Fofi), 198
Painlevé, Jean, 263
Paisan (Rossellini), 11
Pakula, Alan. J., 176
Panahi, Jafar, 237
Panh, Rithy, 85
Panic in Needle Park (Schatzberg), 136-38
Panofsky, Erwin, 209
Papatakis, Nikos, 34, 286
Paranaguá, Paulo Antônio, 40
Paris n'existe pas (Benayoun), 42
Parrish, Robert, 146
Partner (Bertolucci), 282
Party, The (Edwards), 306
Pascal, Blaise, 211
Pascin, Jules, 79
Pasolini, Pier Paolo, 33, 95
Passek, Jean-Loup, 90
Passer, Ivan, 162
Passion of Joan of Arc, The (Dreyer), 183, 220
Pas sur la bouche (Resnais), 145
Past, The (Farhadi), 284
Pather Panchali (Ray), 233, 267, 300
Paths of Glory (Kubrick), 27, 106, 126, 188
Path to War, The (Frankenheimer), 47
Patino, Bruno, 86
Paulhan, Jean, 10, 18
Pauvert, Jean-Jacques, 18, 38, 60, 246
Pavese, Cesare, 153
Pavlović, Živojin, 167
Payne, Alexander, 130
Peake, Mervyn, 45
Peleato, Floreal, 58
Pelechian, Artavazd, 163
Penn, Arthur, 26, 98, 153
Perec, Georges, 5
Pérez, Michel, 85
Péron, Didier, 5, 214, 305

Peroni, Pierre, 5
Perrault, Pierre, 201
Perros, Georges, 10
Pétain, Philippe, 16, 289
Pétillon, Pierre-Yves, 75
Petit, Laurence, 258
Petit Théâtre, Le (Renoir), 35
Phantom of Liberty, The (Buñuel), 217, 235
Philipe, Gérard, 5, 79, 198
Phillips, Gene D., 125
Philippe, Claude-Jean, 85, 140
Philomena (Frears), 213
Phobia (Huston), 46
Photo, The (Papatakis), 286
Pialat, Maurice, 16, 106, 129, 191, 259, 262-65, 307
Piano, The (Campion), 135
Picasso, Pablo, 203, 206, 283
Piccoli, Michel, 286
Piero della Francesca, 50-51
Pierre and Djemila (Blain), 47
Pierrot le fou (Godard), 200
Pig Across Paris (Autant-Lara), 197, 231
Pilot Returns, A (Rossellini), 289
Pingaud, Bernard, 242
Pinter, Harold, 109, 190
Pintilie, Lucian, 88, 201, 251-52, 258, 328
Pirate, The (Minnelli), 51
Pitiot, Pierre, 86
Pixar, 251
Place, Jean-Michel, 55
Platform (Zhang-ke), 270
Player, The (Altman), 278
Pleasure of the Text (Barthes), 39
Plutarch, 109
Pocket Money (Rosenberg), 173
Poetry (Chang-dong), 270
Poggioli, Renato, 51
Point Blank (Boorman), 50, 132, 134
Pointe Court, La (Varda), 289
Poirier, Léon, 223
Poiroux, Claude-Éric, 253
Poivre d'Arvor, Olivier, 86
Polac, Michel, 78
Polanski, Roman, 87, 115, 125, 127, 138, 145, 158, 190-91, 201, 235, 259, 265, 280-81
Pollack, Sydney, 124, 129
Pollock, Jackson, 41
Polonsky, Abraham, 140, 154
Pol Pot, 246-47
Poor Cow (Loach), 184
Popeye (Altman), 277
Porcile, François, 26

Portrait of a Lady, The (Campion) 229
Portrait of a Lady, The (James), 229
Porumboiu, Corneliu, 251
Pourquoi des philosophes? (Revel), 246
Poussin, Nicolas, 12
Powell, Michael, 45, 191, 229, 231, 259
Prairie Home Companion, A (Altman), 235
Preminger, Otto, 26, 31, 37, 142, 155, 199, 203, 211, 306
Presle, Micheline, 86, 192, 329
Prévert, Jacques, 13, 286
Princess Marie, 230
Princess of Montpensier, The (Tavernier), 229
Private Life of Sherlock Holmes, The (Wilder), 151
Proferes, Nicholas, 111
Proust, Marcel, 110, 203, 244
Providence (Resnais), 145, 300
Psycho (Hitchcock), xi, 61
Puccini, Giacomo, 210
Pudovkin, Vsevolod, 11, 34, 225
Puiu, Cristi, 251
Pusher (Refn), 201
Puzzle of a Downfall Child (Schatzberg), 136-38, 233, 297

Quai des Orfèvres (Clouzot), 197
Queen and Country (Losey), 134
Queen Victoria, 232
Quelques heures de printemps (Brizé), 307
Que Viva Mexico! (Eisenstein), 225
Quiet Room, The (de Heer), 288

Rabelais, François, 51
Racine, Jean, 6, 110
Rafelson, Bob, 137, 234, 255
Raksin, David, 306
Rampling, Charlotte, 202
Ramsay, Lynne, 231
Rancière, Jacques, 90
Raphael, Frederic, 124, 126
Rappeneau, Jean-Paul, 196
Rashomon (Kurosawa), 267
Ray, Satyajit, 266-68, 300
Ray, Nicolas, 27, 110, 307
Reagan, Ronald, 99
Rebatet, Lucien, 82
Rebel, The (Camus), 18
Reconstitution (Angelopoulos), 138

Red Desert (Antonioni), 30, 170
Red Detachment of Women, The (Jin), 44
Reed, Carol, 231, 281
Réel et son double, Le (Rosset), 296
Reenactment, The (Pintilie), 251
Refn, Nicolas Winding, 201
Reilhac, Michel, 291
Reisz, Karel, 27, 201, 231-32
Religieuse, La (Rivette), 82
Renoir, Jean, 35, 106, 129, 131, 157, 160-61, 191, 199, 210, 223, 229, 267, 282, 298, 302
Repulsion (Polanski), 281
Reservoir Dogs (Tarantino), 165, 233
Resnais, Alain, 12, 32, 34, 75, 87-88, 91, 115, 130-31, 145-47, 192, 200, 234-45, 239, 250, 262, 274, 281, 289, 291, 307
Resnais, arpenteur de l'imaginaire (Benayoun), 146
Return from the USSR (Gide), 163
Reunion (Schatzberg), 137
Revel, Jean-François, 246, 248
Rey, Jean-Michel, 258
Reynaud, Bérénice, xiv
Reynolds, Joshua, 154
Richard-Willm, Pierre, 4
Richier, Germaine, 12
Rimbaud, Arthur, x, 210
Rio Bravo (Hawks), 71
Riou, Alain, 84
Risi, Dino, 34, 198, 232, 239
Rissient, Pierre, x, 36, 38, 114, 136, 143, 184, 254-55, 279, 303
Riva, Emmanuelle, 147
River, The (Renoir), 267
Rivette, Jacques, 13, 31, 43, 65, 82, 186, 196, 226
Roads to the South (Losey), 115
Robbe-Grillet, Alain, 91
Roberts, Jean-Marc, 109
Robespierre, Maximilien, 17, 117
Rocha, Glauber, xii, 46, 47-48, 104, 160, 201, 262, 282
Rodin, August, 205
Rodrigues, Amália, 121
Rohmer, Eric, 18, 27, 40, 42-43, 56, 78, 88, 196, 220, 224, 270, 290, 299
Rolling Stones, The, 138
Roma (Cuarón), 273
Rome Open City (Rossellini), 191, 234, 289
Romer, Jean-Claude, 13

Rondi, Gian Luigi, 174
Roosevelt, Franklin, 71, 104
Ropars-Wuillemier, Marie-Claire, 69
Rosemary's Baby (Polanski), 280, 281
Rosenberg, Pierre, 12, 75
Rosière de Pessac, La (Eustache), 184
Rosset, Clément, 90, 296
Rosetta (Dardenne), 166
Rosi, Francesco, xi, 2, 26, 34, 50, 94-97, 106, 108, 113, 115, 119, 130, 134-35, 144, 150, 189, 198, 223-24, 252, 306
Rossellini, Roberto, 11, 106, 185, 211, 234, 289, 300
Roüan, Brigitte, 86, 290
Rouault, Georges, 79
Rouleau, Éric, 23
Rousseau, Jean-Jacques, 81
Rouyer, Philippe, x, 182, 287
Rousselot, Philippe, 87
Rozier, Jacques, 34, 201
Rubens, Peter Paul, 206, 222, 227-28
Ruiz, Raúl, 283-85
Rules of the Game, The (Renoir), 20, 35, 51, 65, 302
Russian Thinkers (Berlin), 228
Rust and Bone (Audiard), 293

Sabunsu, Bachar, 86
Sadoul, Georges, xv, 13, 16, 32, 164, 299
Saint, Eva Marie, 97, 104, 251
Saint-Jean, Michel, 258
Saint-John Perse, 254
Saint-Simon, Henri de, 79
Salamandre, La (Tanner), 46, 199
Salazar, António de Oliveira, 8
Saltzman, Harry, 176
Salvatore Giuliano (Rosi), 26, 34, 84, 94, 113, 297, 298, 300
Sandra (Visconti), 170
Sang-soo, Hong, 270
Sansho the Bailiff (Mizoguchi) 267
Santayana, George, 222
Sarkozy, Nicolas, 243, 244
Sarraute, Nathalie, 91
Sarris, Andrew, 22, 35, 136, 175, 254
Sartre, Jean-Paul, 8, 18, 19, 163, 234, 246
Saturday Night, Sunday Morning (Reisz), 233
Satyricon (Fellini), 170, 272
Saulnier, Jacques, 87

Saura, Carlos, 47
Sautet, Claude, 47, 120, 146, 191, 196, 251, 255, 262, 264, 267-68
Sawdust and Tinsel (Bergman), 57
Scarecrow (Schatzberg), 22, 136-38, 178, 267
Scarlet Empress, The (von Sternberg), 57
Scenes from a Marriage (Bergman), 217
Schatzberg, Jerry, 22, 95, 136, 137-38, 141, 178-79, 252, 272, 277
Schickel, Richard, 118
Schindler's List (Spielberg), 126
Schlöndorff, Volker, 180, 252
Schnitzer, Jean, 162
Schroeder, Barbet, 184
Schulberg, Budd, 102-103
Sciascia, Leonardo, 94, 174, 327
Scola, Ettore, 273, 283
Scorsese, Martin, 98, 130, 132-33, 136, 138, 168, 199, 242, 253, 255, 274-75, 276-7, 280-81, 335
Scott, Helen, 268
Scotta, Carole, 258
Scotto, Vincent, 8
Sea Hawk, The (Curtiz), 5, 305
Seberg, Jean, 27
Secret Ceremony (Losey), 69, 106-107, 190
Secret Defense (Rivette), 185
Secrets & Lies (Leigh), 284
Secret Sunshine (Chang-dong), 270
Seduction of Joe Tynan, The (Schatzberg), 137
Segal, George, 251, 277
Seguin, Louis, 29, 31, 35, 37, 99, 193, 303
Séguret, Olivier, 214
Selfish Giant, The (Barnard), 231
Sellers, Peter, 128, 306
Sen, Mrinal, 267
Senior, Julian, 120
Sentimental Education, A (Flaubert), 189
Separation, A (Farhadi), 216, 284
Servant, The (Losey), 106, 112, 114, 127, 190, 200
Seton, Marie, 13, 266
sex, lies and videotape (Soderbergh), 144, 165, 233
Seydoux, Nicolas, 264
Seyrig, Delphine, 147, 181, 205
Shadow of a Doubt (Hitchcock), 307

Shadows (Cassavetes), 125, 286
Shakespeare, William, 20, 45, 51, 75, 206, 222, 227, 234, 236, 300
Shame (McQueen), 204
Shaw, Bernard, 219
Shaw, Robert, 107
Sheen, Martin, 275
Shepherds of Calamity, The (Papatakis), 286
Sheridan, Richard B., 232
She Wore a Yellow Ribbon (Ford), 10
Shining, The (Kubrick), 46, 115, 121-23, 126, 128, 175
Shooting, The (Hellman), 137
Shoot the Piano Player (Truffaut), 231
Short Cuts (Altman), 130, 277-78
Short-Timers, The (Hasford), 123
Shostakovich, Dmitri, 225
Shout, The (Skolimowski), 177
Sicilian, The (Cimino), 210
Siclier, Jacques, 27
Siècle débordé, Un (Frank), 248
Siegel, Don, 109, 278
Silence, The (Bergman), 200
Simon, Claude, 91
Sineux, Michel, 6, 249
Singer, Isaac Bashevis, 75
Sirk on Sirk (Halliday), 100
Sjöström, Victor, 34
Skolimowski, Jerzy, 177-78, 201, 255, 265
Sleep (Warhol), 202, 306
Sleuth (Mankiewicz) 61, 128, 155-56
Soboul, Albert, 118
Socrates, 15
Soderbergh, Steven, 165, 241, 257
Sokorov, Alexander, 181
Solaris (Tarkovsky), 162
Solinas, Franco, 113, 115
Sollers, Philippe, 64-65, 207
Solzhenitsyn, Aleksandr, 112
Some Like It Hot (Wilder), 151
Songs from the Second Floor (Andersson), 237
Sontag, Susan, 199
Sorrentino, Paulo, 273
Sorrow and the Pity, The (Ophuls), 115
Soulages, Pierre, 228
Soutine, Chaïm, 79
Soutter, Michel, 176, 201
Spacek, Sissy, 277
Spartacus (Kubrick), 44, 126
Spider's Stratagem, The (Bertolucci), 282

Spielberg, Steven, 125-27, 129, 165, 217, 230
Splendor in the Grass (Kazan), 26, 98
Spoiled Children (Tavernier), 49
Spring, Summer, Fall, Winter... and Spring (Ki-duk), 271
Stalin, 9, 19, 101-102, 127, 154, 163
Stalker (Tarkovsky), 300
Stan the Flasher (Gainsbourg), 287
Starobinski, Jean, 188
Stavisky (Resnais), 145-46
Steamboat Round the Bend (Ford), 211
Steaming (Losey), 115
Steibel, Warren, 276
Steiger, Rod, 95, 97
Stein, Peter, 181
Steinbeck, John, 102
Stendhal, 51, 223, 225-26
Stevens, George, 175, 275
Stevens Jr., George, 175
Stevenson, Robert Louis, 116, 134
Stiller, Mauritz, 34
Still Life (Zhang-ke), 269, 270
St. Marie, Anne, 137
Story of Dr. Wassell, The (DeMille), 5
Strada, La (Fellini), 10, 272, 274
Strange Case of Angelica, The (de Oliveira), 235
Strangers in the House (Decoin), 289
Straub, Jean-Marie, 5, 44, 203
Strauss, Johann, 296
Stravinsky, Igor, 153, 203
Streamers (Altman), 277
Streep, Meryl, 235
Street Smart (Schatzberg), 137
Stroheim, Erich von, 10, 17, 34, 74, 131-32, 140-41, 143, 202
Sturges, Preston, 158, 181
Style du Général, Le (Revel), 246
Sud (Green), 4
Suitor (Etaix), 34
Sunrise (Murnau), 51, 65, 74, 183, 197
Sunset Boulevard (Wilder), 140-41, 156
Suspended Step of the Stork, The (Angelopoulos), 139
Suspended Vocation, The (Ruiz), 285
Suu Kyi, Aung San, 135
Sweet Hereafter, The (Egoyan), 182
Sweetie (Campion), 135, 144, 229, 288

Sweet Movie (Makavejev), 170
Sweet Revenge (Schatzberg), 137
Swift, Jonathan, 45
Swinton, Tilda, 231
Sympathy for Mr. Vengeance (Chan-wook), 270
Szabó, István, 181, 265

Tabori, George, 106
Tagore, Rabindranath, 266
Tailleur, Roger, xii, xiii, xv, xvii, 13, 29, 32-33, 35, 38, 65, 78, 97, 99, 132, 161, 193, 208, 250, 264, 280, 282, 299, 303
Take 100: The Future of Film, 100 New Directors (Bailey), 166
Tamer of Wild Horses (Dragic), 191
Taming of the Shrew, The (Shakespeare), 227
Tanner, Alain, 46, 176, 184, 199, 200-201, 215, 336
Tarantino, Quentin, 130, 166, 199, 226, 241, 253
Tarkovsky, Andrei, 162, 191, 192, 201, 262, 298
Tarr, Béla, 205
Tassone, Aldo, 197
Taste of Cherry, A (Kiarostami), 182
Tatarak (Wajda), 46
Tate, Sharon, 280
Tati, Jacques, 199, 282
Tavernier, Bertrand, xiv, 13, 38, 47, 49, 106-107, 118, 185, 196, 223, 229, 252-55, 290, 293
Taviani Brothers, 86, 176
Taylor, Elizabeth, 66
Téchiné, André, 189, 196
Teige, Karel, 266
Teixeira, Novais, 184
Tell Them Willie Boy Is Here (Polonsky), 140
Ten Canoes (de Heer), 288
Terayama, Shuji, 172
Terre em transe (Rocha), 47-48, 69
ter Steege, Johanna, 119
Tessé, Jean-Philippe, 59
Tessier, Max, 14, 55, 185
Tesson, Charles, 59, 164, 214
Tex Avery (Brion), 130
Thackeray, William Makepeace, 189
That Most Important Thing: Love (Zulawski), 251, 283
That Obscure Object of Desire (Buñuel), 235

Theorem (Pasolini), 63
Thérèse (Cavelier), 196
Thévenon, Patrick, 108
They Live By Night (Ray), 233
Thirard, Paul-Louis, 29, 31-32, 60, 193
Third Part of the Night, The (Zulawski), 251
This Sporting Life (Anderson), 233
Thomas, François, 130
Thoreau, Henry David, 72
Three Brothers (Rosi), 106
Three Colours Trilogy (Kieślowski), 283
Three Musketeers, The (Dumas), 90, 277
Thuillier, Jacques, 12
Thulin, Ingrid, 147
Tierchant, Hélène, 139
Tiger's Tail, The (Boorman), 50
Time of the Gypsies, The (Kusturica), 168
Time Without Pity (Losey), 68, 106-107, 114
Tintin (Spielberg), 230
Titian, 206, 228
Tolstoy, Leo, 6, 206, 211, 223, 244
Tonight or Never (Deville), 196
Top of the Lake (Campion), 143, 242
Totò, 255
Toubiana, Serge, 40, 59, 88, 198, 265
Touch of Sin, A (Zhang-ke), 269, 270
Touch of Zen, A (Hu), 268
Tourneur, Jacques, 37
Toyen, 28
Tracker, The (de Heer), 288
Tracy, Spencer, 36
Trafic (Tati), 63
Trauner, Alexandre, 286
Travelling Players, The (Angelopoulos), 138, 175
Treasure Island (Stevenson), 116
Tree Grows in Brooklyn, A (Kazan), 97, 109
Tree of Wooden Clogs, The (Olmi), 176
Tresgot, Annie, 31, 150-51, 153
Trial, The (Welles), 28-29
Trial of Joan of Arc, The (Dreyer), 171
Trip to the Moon, A (Méliès), 191
Trnka, Jiří, 250
Trouble in Paradise (Lubitsch), 306
Trout, The (Losey), 115
Truce, The (Rosi), 50, 96
Truffaut, François, 18, 26-27, 31, 33, 40, 43, 47, 51, 56, 65,

78, 81-84, 100, 121, 130, 173, 191, 193-96, 199, 217-18, 231, 236, 264, 267-68, 281, 290, 293, 299, 300
Trumbo, Dalton, 154
Tsai Ming-liang, 215, 268
Tsar Has His Photograph Taken, The (Weill), 291
Tuhkuner, Taïna, 66
Twain, Mark, xiii, 110
Twin Peaks (Lynch), 242
Two Weeks in Another Town (Minnelli), 26
Tzara, Tristan, 287

Ugetsu (Mizoguchi), 267
Ullmann Liv, 175
Ulmer, Edgar, 38
Ulysses' Gaze (Angelopoulos), 139
Una storia simplice (Sciascia), 174
Underground (Kusturica), 139, 167-68, 203
Under the Sun of Satan (Pialat), 264
Under the Volcano (Huston), 157
Unforgiven (Eastwood), 279
Unknown Masterpiece, The (Balzac), 129
Unmarried Woman, An (Mazursky), 177
Uomini contro (Rosi), 106
Uzal, Marcos, xi

van Gogh, Vincent, 170, 207, 210, 264
Vacances de Monsieur Hulot, Les (Tati), 10
Val, Philippe, 248
Valéry, Paul, 244
Valhalla Rising (Refn), 201
Vallée Fantôme, La (Tanner), 199
Valley of the Dolls (Robson), 161
Vaneck, Pierre, 4
Vanity Fair (Thackeray), 189
Varda, Agnès, xii, 34, 235, 289, 291
Vasari, Giorgio, 61, 300
Vathek (Beckford), 189
Vauvenargues, 60
Vécés étaient fermés de l'intérieur, Les (Leconte), 81
Velázquez, Diego, 221, 228
Venus in Fur (Polanski), 235, 281
Verdi, Giuseppe, 210
Verdun: Visions of History (Poirier), 223
Vérité sur Bébé Donge, La (Decoin), 35
Vernac, Denise, 141

Verne, Jules, 209
Verneuil, Henri, 301
Vertigo (Hitchcock), 21, 63, 236
Vertov, Dziga, 44, 162
Vial, Régine, 258
Vian, Boris, 32
Vico, Giambattista, 96
Vidor, King, 34, 140, 183
Viertel, Peter, 279
Vigo, Jean, 13, 50, 91, 210
Vilar, Jean, 33
Vincent and Theo (Altman), 50
Vincent, Christian, 86
Vincent, François, Paul and the Others (Sautet), 120, 267
Vinneuil, François, 82, 83
Visconti, Luchino, 34, 40, 47, 107-108, 170, 179, 198, 211, 222, 232, 282, 298
Visitors, The (Kazan), 105, 110, 150
Vitoux, Frédéric, 33, 38, 42, 248
Viva Zapata! (Kazan), 101
Viviani, Christian, 147, 220
Viv(r)e le cinema (Seguin), 303
von Sternberg, Josef, 11, 34, 35, 57, 128, 142, 183, 228
von Stroheim, Erich, 10, 140, 141
von Trier, Lars, 192, 205, 218
von Trotta, Margarethe, 47, 175, 180
Voix du Silence, Les (Malraux), 11
Volonté, Gian Maria, 95, 174, 306
Voltaire, 68, 81, 288, 302
Vonier, Fabienne, 258
Voyage to Italy (Rossellini), 234

Wagner, Richard, 210, 298
Waintrop, Edouard, 164
Waiting for Godot (Beckett), 210
Wajda, Andrzej, 40, 46, 179, 223, 265-66, 283
Wakhevitch, Georges, 176
Walesa, Lech, 223
Walker, Alexander, 125, 130
Walker, Beverly, 275
Walking a Tightrope (Papatakis), 286
Walkover (Skolimowski), 177
Walk with Love and Death, A (Huston), 251
Wall, The (Güney), 272
Walsh, Raoul, 71, 142, 183, 211, 245
Wanda, xii, 100, 111
Warhol, Andy, 26, 202, 204, 306
War Horse (Spielberg), 230
Warner, Jack, 102
Wartime Lies (Begley), 119

Water Drops on Burning Rocks (Ozon), 185
Weber, Max, 21
Wedding March, The (von Stroheim), 10, 197
Weill, Kurt, 291
Weir, Peter, 288
Welcome (Lioret), 186
Welles, Orson, xiv, 20, 28, 38, 98, 103-104, 111, 134, 138, 140, 150, 210, 212, 218, 262, 281, 282, 298
Wellman, William, 52, 280
Wen, Jiang, 181
Wenders, Wim, 40, 144, 158, 171, 253, 259
We Need to Talk about Kevin (Ramsay), 231
West, The (Mungiu), 201
We Won't Grow Old Together (Pialat), 264
When Father Was Away on Business (Kusturica), 165, 167
Where is the Friend's House? (Kiarostami), 185
Whistler, James McNeill, 72
White Hunter, Black Heart (Eastwood), 279
White Material (Denis), 230
White Ribbon (Haneke), 182
White Ship, The (Rossellini), 289
Why Did Bodhi-Dharma Go East? (Yong-kyun), 181
Wilder, Billy, 49, 102, 130, 141-43, 150-58, 199, 264, 283, 296
Wild River (Kazan), 98
Williams, Bernard, 150
Williams, Tennessee, 106
Wilson, John, 106
Wilson, Michael, 17, 43, 274
Wings of the Dove, The (Jacquot), 196, 230
Winock, Michel, 61, 242
Wise Blood (Huston), 157
Woman Next Door, The (Truffaut), 231
Woolf, Virginia, 23
Workers Leaving the Lumière Factory (Lumière), 191
World, The (Zhang-ke), 270
World of Apu (Ray), 266-67
Wyler, William, 151-52
Wu, Xiao, 269, 270

Yaguello, Marina, 75
Yang, Edward, 268
Yared, Gabriel, 87
Yeltsin, Boris, 89
Yimou, Zhang, 268, 270
Yol (Güney), 271
Yong-kyun, Bae, 181
You Ain't Seen Nothin' Yet (Resnais), 75, 146
Young Mr. Lincoln (Ford), 161
You Only Live Once (Lang), 36, 221

Z (Costa-Gavras), 84
Zanuck, Darryl, 101, 161
Zanussi, Krzysztof, 86, 89
Zardoz (Boorman), 133
Zhang-ke, Jia, 269-70
Zimmer, Hans, 50
Zimmer, Jacques, 214
Zinnemann, Fred, 244
Žižek, Slavoj, 90
Zoffany, Johan, 189
Zola, Emile, 223
Zukor, Adolph, 57, 208, 283
Żuławski, Andrzej, 251, 283
Zurlini, Valerio, 34, 95
Zvyagintsev, Andrey, 201

www.ingramcontent.com/pod-product-compliance
Lightning Source LLC
Chambersburg PA
CBHW070126080526
44586CB00015B/1581